Council Housing and Culture

Planning, History and the Environment Series
Series editor Professor Anthony Sutcliffe

Council Housing and Culture

The History of a Social Experiment

Alison Ravetz

363.5850941
R25c

First published 2001 by Routledge,
11 New Fetter Lane,
London EC4P 4EE

Simultaneously published in the USA and Canada
by Routledge
29 West 35th Street, New York, NY 10001

Routledge is an imprint of the Taylor & Francis Group

A © 2001 Alison Ravetz

Typeset in Sabon and Frutiger by NP Design & Print
Printed and bound in Great Britain by Biddles Ltd, Guildford and Kings Lynn

This book was commissioned and edited by Alexandrine Press, Oxford

British Library Cataloguing in Publication Data
A catalogue record for this book is available from the British Library

Library of Congress Cataloging in Publication Data
A catalog record for this book has been requested

ISBN 0–415–23945–1 (hb)   0–415–23946–X (pb)

Contents

Acknowledgements

Thanks are due to the Nuffield Foundation who supported the early stages of research for this book through a Social Science Research Fellowship held by the author 1989–90.

Kind permission to reproduce illustrations has been given as follows:

The Architects' Journal: pages 68 and 148

Broadwater Farm Youth Association: page 222

Collection of Dr Richard Turkington: pages 140 and 143

Collection of Wilf Dyson: page 168

Watling Community Association: pages 140 and 143

(*The Watling Resident* is housed at The Local Studies & Archive Centre, London Borough of Barnet).

To Joe

Chapter One

Introduction

'. . . one of the greatest revolutions this country has now seen is in progress.'

Housing, 24 May 1920

'Council housing is facing extinction . . . By the year 2000, council housing may have become a historical relic.'

The Eclipse of Council Housing, Ian Cole and Robert Furbey, 1994

If its lengthy antecedents are included, council housing just bridged three centuries as it passed the year 2000. For a number of years its end had been anticipated and at the time of writing is a more real prospect than ever before. If it does end, however, it will be in a certain sense only: that of ownership. The bulk of the buildings remain, and will remain for many years to come, providing homes for people as well as a sizeable part of Britain's townscapes and built environment.

Most British people with any awareness of social affairs attach some meaning – and mostly a negative one – to the term council housing; but only those who were adult through a significant part of the twentieth century could have some realistic understanding of its *raison d'être* and purpose. Even then, it is more likely that their knowledge relates to its history after 1945 than to its inception and early years between the wars. Why should it be of interest to resurrect this old history, if those who had some experience of it feel that they understand it, and its perhaps imminent demise makes it irrelevant to those who did not? Not the least reason is, of course, the cause of historical accuracy. A collective knowledge of events is accumulated as they unfold, and where social affairs are concerned, this is inevitably within a partisan framework. In the process much gets forgotten or foreshortened, and the memories of what was experienced harden into an orthodoxy. There comes a point when this body of accumulated knowledge needs reassessment for new generations, who inherit a jumbled assortment of assumptions, value judgements and disjointed material remains not easily related to one another. It is here that, with distance of time, a more balanced overview can begin to be constructed.

The roots of council housing are found in two places: one is the evolution of urban governance during and after the industrial revolution, when the gradually recognized problems of poverty and public health generated systems of control by central and local government. Upper-class feelings and beliefs about poverty set the framework in which council housing could begin to be a possibility, and reactions against urban slums eventually gave rise, through model industrial villages and the garden city movement, to its early physical form. This has been a very productive area of scholarship for forty or more years and it forms, so to speak, the bedrock of our subject. The other area is less obvious as well as far less researched, and there is probably much further work to be done on it. This is the association in the later nineteenth century of utopian socialism and communitarianism with the land question and nascent town planning, and the linking of these to the idea of state-provided working-class housing. More light was thrown once it was established that council housing had a serious architectural pedigree, which was traced out in a small number of studies of particular periods and schools of aesthetics. Very broadly, the first part of this book reviews these twin sources, tracing their imprint on the decisions and dilemmas that surrounded the beginnings of state responsibility for working-class housing, and seeing how they shaped the legislative and financial structures set up for council housing at its inception in 1919.

These mixed beginnings conditioned much of the operation of council housing in its active years from the 1920s to the 1970s. The original utopianism could coast only for so long, and by 1939 it was already seriously compromised; but the establishment of the Welfare State in 1945, followed by the 'technological revolution' of the 1960s, revived it, albeit in new forms. The vital half century when council housing was established and operated to its fullest extent is the subject of the second part of this book. It was a period when the nuclear family home became pre-eminently important for all classes, as the seat of personal and marital fulfilment and the focus of consumption; and for many, a council tenancy provided the first opportunity to attain to this. At its peak around 1975 council housing supplied nearly a third of the nation's housing stock and (since it was primarily for families with children) the homes of something more than a third of the population. Not long after that time, steps were taken to stop it growing, and eventually to shrink it, as its always latent problems combined with wider social and economic change, to the point where its early idealism was completely forgotten and it was viewed more in the light of dystopia than utopia.

What is available as evidence for this crucial half century? The sequence runs something as follows. For a generation from the 1930s, the main interest was in council housing as a brave new social experiment, the bestowal of 'ideal' homes and estates on society's poor and uncouth. A series of carefully researched studies (at the time called urban sociology, but today more likely to be called ethnography) examined the changes in working-class life resulting from the translation from the old, so-called slums to this new world. This school of research tapered off in the 1960s, when council tenants were no longer considered poor but, rather, members of a newly affluent working class. The few later studies of this kind, therefore, concentrated on a new concern, the problem estate. Another body of information came from government reports such as the series on estate management of the Central Housing Advisory Committee and – less valuable because of their restricted focus – a series of postwar technical studies of tenant reactions to the design of their homes and estates.

The academic field of housing studies that emerged in the later 1960s was mainly concerned with fast developing housing policy and its implications for the social structure. The bulk of its publications were strongly in favour of council housing in principle and vociferous for its expansion, but at the same time critical of its mode of operation. The implicit contradiction between these two positions went unrecognized, and consequently the possibility that the failings of council housing might owe as much to its intrinsic qualities as to party political positions was not considered. Nor, for the most part, was the architectural dimension of council housing and its implications for the inhabitants, although this did become a specialized field of architectural research. Other commonly neglected areas were housing management and the contributions of tenants and their families to the development of estates. There was in fact abundant evidence for the last, in the form of tenant organization records, estate histories and reminiscences, but they were too fragmentary to attract serious scholarly attention. At the same time the fact that council housing was almost always looked at in isolation from other parts of the housing system and housing stock conferred a bias where its failings were easily exaggerated or misinterpreted, in ignorance of corresponding evidence for other tenures and types of housing.

The study of council housing has so often been presented as the history of housing policy that its broader contributions to twentieth-century material culture and working-class life have not received as much attention as they deserve. While history is concerned to interpret and re-interpret the evidence, always mindful of the filters through which it is transmitted, the study of social policy advances with the creation of new policy, taking for its historical foundation a broad consensus as to 'the way things were', without seeking to revise that consensus. For the social scientist, old records and accounts lose their interest once their relevance to current policy making is exhausted; but for the historian, seeing the past through ever shifting perspectives, they remain of value. It is true that the council housing does indeed provide a case study of an important social policy, but it is one stretching over several generations and so asking for its own historical analysis. A major state intervention in the market, it was eventually incorporated into the Welfare State, where it took its place alongside the national systems of health, insurance and education. Like these, it co-existed with the market, although in a very different balance since, unlike them, it never became a nearly universal service, but for most purposes remained exclusive to the working class. The way it was structured, in particular its direct provision and management by local government, set the British housing system apart from the rest of the capitalist world. In its closest European neighbours, state subsidy was normally channelled through independent housing agencies so that tenants were not, as here, direct clients of the local state. This distinctive power relationship of the British system infused its whole operation and among other things helps to explain why its ending, or fundamental transformation, after 1980 could not be done without raising serious questions of ideology and allegiance.

British council housing, therefore, was a social experiment whose story affords an opportunity to anatomize a major policy failure, or alleged failure. While smaller-scale policies costing correspondingly less may be held publicly to account when they are deemed to fail, much more ambitious ones operating over large timescales are not accorded an inquest on wasted resources, or calling to account of the persons or bodies responsible. The original and daring goals of council housing were quickly lost to sight after its two most 'utopian' phases, in the 1920s and following 1945, so that it moved forward with a mounting public sense of failure, but without any counter-balancing indices of success. Indeed, no firm criteria of success or failure were ever established. The small-scale successes of council housing, as innumerable tenants' accounts confirm, were in the personal and domestic spheres, and nothing like as spectacular as its public failures could sometimes be – as in the episode of high-rise estates, for instance. But a close look at the evidence raises the interesting possibility that what were seen as failures were not so much failures in performance as, rather, a failure to realize ideals and intentions that were in the last resort unrealizable.

While much about state housing in Britain was driven by opportunity – notably events around 1914 – it could not have had the driving force and support that it did if it had not embodied a core belief of society: complete trust in the power of 'ideal' environments to bring about not only material but social reform. The grounds for this were in the degrading effects of the urban slums, although the earliest slum clearances were done with public health objectives and carried no regular obligation to rehouse the people displaced. It was philanthropic industrial magnates in the second half of the nineteenth century who demonstrated the feasibility of their own model villages for sober and well conducted industrial populations; but although their houses and estates became patterns for early council housing, even they did not imply a policy for housing the masses. For such a thing to arise required the fusion of two deeply rooted elements of British culture: a white-hot, outraged anger at the impacts of poverty on the lives of people, that was expressed in religious evangelism and the many different kinds of socialism; and the rich varieties of utopianism expressed in communitarian experiments, co-operatives and certain aesthetic movements. Rooted in all this complexity stood the phenomenon of the English garden city movement, which had utopian inspirations but also borrowed freely from the industrialists' model villages and, in pursuit of its objectives, endorsed state intervention in housing and planning. The eventual, and most recognized, outcome was British Town and Country Planning, with its state-funded new towns, after 1945. But a somewhat earlier and less recognized outcome was the system of council housing that was strongly motivated and coloured by the evangelism and idealism from which it had sprung.

This heredity was of crucial importance for various reasons. It encouraged and reinforced the habitually passive status of council tenants by preventing them having direct influence or control over their housing. There was always an official presence in their lives – most immediately, the estate managers; but beyond and in many ways controlling these, a host of others acting in official and professional capacities. Of a deeper significance was the fact that the concept and material embodiment of council housing did not spring from working-class culture. Although working-class leadership, with scarcely an exception, supported and campaigned for it, it did not in fact arise from working-class experience or experiment, but came from a radical intelligentsia in the years around 1900. The grounds for its appeal, both individually and collectively, to most working people are sufficiently obvious. Many of the technical and design features it incorporated were already enjoyed by the higher classes (and were soon to be translated into a new market for comparatively humble owner occupiers), which made it a natural aspiration for the working-class people and their advocates. The social idealism of its originators was beyond question, and at this time state intervention was being invoked in working-class interests – in particular against exploitative landlords. From here, it was no big step to acceptance of the state itself as landlord. No alternative vision for housing was advanced by the organized working class. Any dissent or resistance, therefore, was individual or, in rare cases of collective resistance to slum clearance (as in Manchester's Hulme in the 1930s), took the form of protest against rather than campaigning for any set of proposals. Prospective tenants were easily wooed by the promise of higher technical standards, particularly of plumbing and sanitation, which enticed them even into high-rise flats, where disillusionment subsequently and often quickly set in. And during all this time there was, for some, an alternative, individualistic way of housing themselves, through home ownership – often of houses not unlike those being condemned as slums, or newer houses that could quite often be inferior to those being built by councils.

The whole operation was a culture transfer amounting to a cultural colonization: a vision forged by one section of society for application to another, to whom it might be more, or less, acceptable and appropriate. The tenure and design, together, were instruments of social reform; but this did not carry any new social programme over and above that implicit in the original inspiration. It asked nothing more of tenants than to live in the houses and to participate in estate life in ways approved by the middle-class reformers. At the same time, institutionalization had it own momentum, which culminated in locations, scales and types of estate (most notably high-rise flats) devised for every conceivable practical, technical and political reason except the willing anticipation and assent of the future inhabitants.[1] It was a situation that precluded any spontaneous estate evolution, and in the last resort it was untenable, so leading to a series of crises that demanded the drastic remedies discussed in the third and last part of this book.

Council housing was a significant part of twentieth-century working-class history that was arguably more significant for many lives than employment and trade unionism which have mainly monopolized attention. It was particularly crucial for the history of working-class women, in their domestic role, and so by extension to children, although aside from oral history and tenants' own publications there is little sustained narrative of this. References to the catalytic part played by mothers and grandmothers on estates, however, are too frequent to be overlooked, especially in the most recent period.

The question how council housing should be judged, in respect of its contributions to working-class life and culture, is one on which there has been a strange reticence, at least in latter years. At the time of writing, the school of empirical research, coupled to polemic in favour of council housing, has been superseded by pragmatic analysis of the effects of rapidly changing policy, and for the time being judgement on the achievements of council housing is apparently suspended. Earlier critiques came from a number of seemingly mutually incompatible positions, the commonest of which (still in currency today) was to see council housing as an achievement of working-class struggle and a victory over the state. Another view, supported by the detailed politics of around 1914–18, was that it was a strategy of the state to deflect social revolution; while yet another saw it, in Marxist terms, as a crude device to 'reproduce labour' for the industrial system. All seem to overlook what was probably the single most compelling conscious motive of housing reformers, that it was counted on to lift people out of poverty.

At this juncture a historical approach is useful, for it allows these several propositions to be transcended rather than contradicted. In practice, council housing had to deal with a divided tenant population that corresponded better to the Victorian notion of layered and plural working classes than to the twentieth-century concept of a single, unified 'working class'. This then permits council housing to be seen as concessionary or diversionary, enabling or disabling, for different groups in different phases of history. It can be credited with lifting many from degrading poverty, household drudgery and disease, while politically and culturally its effects were less enabling. In catering for, it also accentuated, the defensiveness and passivity that were hallmarks of working-class culture, while only in the most perfunctory way providing substitutes for the neighbourhood networks and self-help strategies it disrupted. A long-term, and of course unintended, consequence was the virtual ghettoization of some estates, where poverty was reinforced by single-class schooling and health care, with an almost complete deprivation of the classic twentieth-century pursuit of shopping and consumption of goods.

This is the legacy forming the subject matter of the last and admittedly least historical part of this book, which seeks to capture the flavour and direction of changes still only just in train. After the strenuous efforts of the 1980s to dismantle council housing by privatization, policy focused on attempts to involve tenants of the residue in its regeneration. Here at last there could be seen some practical outcome of the often hidden, overlooked and apparently irrelevant communitarian strand that had contributed to the origins of council housing a century earlier. Through the heydays of 1920-1970 it seemed to survive only in such things as squatting and co-operatives, which only tangentially touched council housing. Although it might have been expected from past history to be important, co-operative housing of one kind or another never became more than a tiny fraction of British housing in general, and still less of council housing. Perhaps more important than is usually credited was the emergence of various 'community' professionals who developed new spheres and standards of professionalism, in community development, architecture, technical and planning aid, where they worked not so much *on* as *with* client populations. They were, so to speak, latterday counterparts of the 'enlightened elite' who had inspired council housing in the first place; but there was a crucial difference in that they sought to encourage people to define and serve their own needs.

There were in this potentially enormous implications for a new 'urban governance', based on a politics largely outside the conventional framework of political parties and programmes. To ask tenants and their families to take collective responsibility for their estates not only went counter to the prevailing trends of an individualistic, anti-collectivist society, but would ask a lot of any population, let alone one that was by definition deprived and kept in a state of dependency. It was a deeply revolutionary proposal, therefore, and how far it would lead to lasting change – in the provision and management of housing, the relationship of people to their environments, or people to the state – is still too early to predict with any confidence at the start of the twenty-first century. At this distance of time, however, it may be both possible and legitimate to recapture some of the early idealism that inspired council housing, with the spirit of enquiry of those studies executed when it was still a brave social experiment. The story of its daily operation and eventual crises is not, perhaps, a comfortable one for those who prefer to see the past in terms of rights and wrongs; who adhere to the simple polarities of 'Left' and 'Right' in politics and prefer a simple vision of a unitary working class; or who look for purity in utopian agendas and programmes of reform. It is, rather, a story of ambivalence, ambiguity, frustration and contradiction, where nothing had quite the results intended and everything is open to qualification. There is however no doubt of the importance of the story for twentieth-century lives and environments, and so of its continuing consequence to the present century.

NOTE

1. Dunleavy (1981).

Chapter Two

A Domestic Revolution: Poverty, Respectability and Housing Reform

'Some Paradox of our natures leads us, when once we have made our fellow men the objects of our enlightened interest, to go on to make them the objects of our pity, then of our wisdom, ultimately of our coercion . . .'
Lionel Trilling, quoted on frontispiece of Gertrude Himmelfarb,
Poverty and Compassion, 1991

Domestic Revolutions and the State

The era of mass provision of council housing, which began in 1919 and lasted to around 1980, has left a large legacy, not only in bricks and mortar (or steel and concrete) but in certain social outcomes, the implications and problems of which are still becoming manifest. Certain dualities lie at the heart of the subject and it is necessary to come to terms with them to form a true understanding of it. These are that something that is so disparaged could have had its roots in genuine social idealism; how a highly visible state policy using large-scale public resources could be applied to something so intimate and personal as the family home; how its first 'garden-city' form and Arcadian iconography could be an explicit reaction to the industrial system, and to world war; and how the cosy new domestic environments created could be part of formal town planning. The pattern for the last arose, not from those people intended to benefit, but from a host of housing reformers and professionals who assumed that it was what the beneficiaries needed, and ought to want. It then became an instrument of 'social engineering', with a coercive as well as an idealistic side, dictating where and how the masses should live in order to bring about desired improvements in their lives.

In what sense could British council housing be described as revolutionary?

It had been preceded by several earlier domestic revolutions or, more strictly, evolutions that had taken place over centuries, with many regional time lags and variations. An early milestone was the division of the medieval or earlier house or 'hall', with its common hearth and undivided space, into separate functional areas or rooms that could be made exclusive to particular household members by the addition of internal walls, lobbies and passages, to serve emerging social distinctions between lords and followers, women and men, parents and children, indoor and outdoor servants. Another important evolutionary step was the removal from the home of primary production for the market. As home-based production was displaced by the factory system, the industrial worker's home became, in effect, a dormitory for the brief hours not spent in mill, mine or factory. Over the same period it became possible for the merchant's or industrialist's home to be removed from his place of business in town centres, as these became increasingly polluted and socially undesirable. The resulting wave of suburbanization among leaders of commerce and industry is placed in the early decades of industrialization, around 1790–1830,[1] and it was followed by ever widening suburban expansion serving the rising classes of 'clerks' – white collar workers and their families, and others who were not tied to factory hours. This suburban growth was not yet strongly associated with home ownership, although this increased during the century, even amongst the better-off working classes, for the overwhelming majority of all classes rented their homes from landlords. Victorian and Edwardian suburbanization was related to the availability of transport: railways, omnibuses and, later, electric trams. It was not, of course, until the 1930s that the rise of mass car ownership started to liberate the home from its close tie to public transport.

The suburb was more than a place: it was a culture in which the dominant influence was the home, physically and conceptually isolated from other urban activity and the public sphere. It served new patterns of marriage where housework and care of children were not counted as 'work'. Selected by occupation and financial means, it was natural that the newly suburbanized should feel like pioneers, participants in a new and better way of life. They could feel superior to those they had left behind, as well as resenting and looking down on any new waves of suburbanites who eventually caught up with them. Those who could then played the game of leapfrog. This ability of the privileged to be one step ahead of the masses established the centripetal form of urban growth, and with it the most crucial and enduring aspect of the housing system: that at any given time the most up-to-date, spacious and best dwellings were appropriated by the more privileged members of society, leaving others to occupy either what they left behind, or purpose-built, inferior housing stock.

The greatest wave of Victorian suburbanization took place in the last 30 or 40 years of the century, when it catered for the fast expanding middle and superior working classes in the then newly introduced 'bye-law' housing. The bye-laws, which have come down to us in the form of present-day building regulations, were the first 'revolution' (as opposed to evolution) in housing standards brought about by the state. They arose from concern that the insanitary conditions and public health hazards of older housing should not be perpetuated in new development, and they governed such things as street widths, the distance between buildings, details of construction, drainage, windows and size of rooms. Many towns had developed their own sets of bye-laws earlier in the century and continued to use these, while London observed its own Metropolitan Code, derived from the great London Building Act of 1774, which caused it to lag behind the rest of the country until special measures were taken in the 1890s. But to meet the requirements of the Public Health Act of 1875, a national code was issued by the Local Government Board and circulated to all urban sanitary authorities – a useful reminder that this particular domestic 'revolution' was rooted in public health rather than housing, and that it had an in-built bias to urban rather than rural affairs.

The bye-laws were not restricted to any one house type, quality or social class, and there continued to be many local variations. They applied to any grade of new housing for which there was a market. Typically, in England, this meant terraced housing, which was built in huge quantities from around 1870 to 1914 – so much so that it still comprises roughly a quarter of the total housing stock. What are usually referred to as bye-law houses, however, are the smaller and lower-class varieties which, for all their benefits to health, came under general attack for their grimly utilitarian nature, their endless dreary streets, and their alleged (although in fact seldom total) lack of architectural refinements. Of more social importance than these, however, was the fact that the higher standards imposed priced such housing beyond the reach of the poorest classes,[2] unless with some sort of subsidy. The problem was given endless consideration, and it was generally concluded that it would be resolved by the operation of 'filtering': that is, as the more fortunate gradually decanted themselves into new and better housing, those beneath them could move up the scale by taking over their vacated homes. The theory was to be crucial for the inauguration of council housing, and to the extent that it corresponded to some real patterns of mobility it could not easily be contradicted.

The design and appurtenances of houses built under the bye-laws reflected an evolution that went back a century or more.[3] Many of the details were expressions of status and had symbolic meanings: notably the crucial distinction of fronts and backs, where the rear of the house, hidden from public view, contained the sanitary offices and other service areas, with little thought for the convenience of houseworkers or family recreation, while the front was for public display, so far as this was consistent with privacy. Though the Victorian house derived in many respects from the aristocratic town mansion, it developed some distinctive features of its own. Most important of these was its downstairs front parlour, the chief marker of a family's social and cultural position. Where money allowed, a buffer zone from the street was provided by a front garden which, however small, was surrounded by a hedge or railings. Domestic seclusion was also supported by the progressive banning or exclusion from the streets of time-honoured trades, pastimes, customs and displays that had once engaged all social classes but now lingered only in poorer and more disreputable districts.

This was the domestic setting of several generations of Victorians and Edwardians. Like the first suburban settlers before them, they were inventive in developing their own cultural patterns, where status and respectability were paramount,[4] with wives playing a crucial role. With or without living-in servants and often taking in lodgers to make ends meet, the emblems of success of wives and mothers were spotless houses and well turned-out children. Narrow suburban horizons were habitually disparaged and mocked by the intellectual classes, for whom the very term 'suburban' was almost one of abuse,[5] and their pattern of lengthy visits to country houses of friends or long leases of picturesque cottages (so conveniently available at this time) must have contributed to the success of the garden city movement that was instrumental to council housing.

The particular 'domestic revolution' that is the subject of this book was not, then, the first one to be brought about by policy, for that distinction must go to the bye-laws. Many of the earliest, hand-picked and 'respectable' council tenants must in fact have been born and brought up in bye-law houses, for only somewhat later were batches of tenants taken from the pre-bye-law slums. For different sorts of tenant, therefore, access to council housing could present a different experience. For some, a new council house was a transitional step from a sanitary and relatively well-built but increasingly old fashioned house to one with modern design and technology: the essence of the change was for them mainly technical. For others the leap was much greater, for it was not only a technical but a big cultural leap.

Before it was possible for the state to take responsibility for working-class housing, a number of sacrosanct tenets had to be overthrown or strongly modified. One was the right of public authorities to intervene in what had always been the field of private enterprise, and another concerned the relationship between central and local government: how far municipal authorities could properly act without state sanction, and how far the state could or should coerce them. A still deeper issue was the responsibility of the state, or any other part of society, towards the poor, which was linked to questions about the causes of poverty and how far the poor should be helped, and how far any help would simply pauperize them further.

Society, Poverty and the Poor

Although it may at first seem remote from council housing, Victorian and Edwardian attitudes towards poverty explain a great deal about its origins and even its present-day problems and dilemmas. The full title of the 1918 report which marked the formal start of twentieth-century council housing ran as follows: 'Report of the Committee appointed by the President of the Local Government Board and the Secretary for Scotland to consider questions of building construction in connection with the provision of dwellings for the working classes in England and Wales, and Scotland' – more commonly referred to as the Tudor Walters Report, after the Committee's chairman. While it has become habitual to use the term 'working class', our Victorian forebears would have referred, more precisely, to the working or labouring *classes*. Alternatively, they would use a different, blanket term, 'the poor', which for them embraced large sections of all the lower classes, whether working or not, since it merely described a financial status. These distinctions, however irrelevant they may seem to us now, do in fact have a strong bearing on the slow beginnings of council housing.

The industrialization and urbanization of Britain threw up new categories of workers in manufacturing, transport and other industries, for the most part heaped together in fast-growing urban centres that posed a challenge to old systems of behaviour, beliefs and values. Among other things it demanded a shift of attitude towards their social inferiors by members of the higher classes, who had previously encountered them mainly as domestic servants, estate workers, apprentices, tradespeople and so on, with whom some sort of face-to-face relationship was possible. They were confronted, now, by new and alarming concentrations of uncouth strangers, who might seem not so much exploited as dangerously independent. Early nineteenth-century towns and cities had no systems of local government and local services to cope with the growth. Existing structures were obsolete and often corrupt: town councils were typically small, self-perpetuating oligarchies, and many vital local functions were in the hands of parish vestries or semi-independent boards of commissioners. Even after important reforms in the 1830s, the electorate was confined to the small minority who were property owners or ratepayers, and the great majority of men, as well as all women, were excluded from full citizenship.

The only formal social security apparatus was the Poor Law, which from 1834 was administered by elected Boards of Guardians. This 'New Poor Law' continued to reflect the assumptions and needs of a predominantly rural society, rather than a mushrooming urban-industrial one.[6] Its main purpose was not to deter or eradicate poverty which, as a status ordained by the Almighty, was not regarded as dishonourable, but rather to prevent anyone benefiting unfairly from 'outdoor relief', a supplement given to those in excessive poverty living in their own homes. If this was denied to the workshy and shiftless, it was reasoned, they would be forced to enter reformed and enlarged 'union' workhouses shared between parishes, in which living conditions were purposely harsher than any they could obtain by staying outside. Under this principle of 'less eligibility', the new workhouses set out to stigmatize their 'paupers', splitting up their families and setting them apart by demeaning dress and restrictions over their movements.

In the event, the New Poor Law never achieved all its objectives, and the new regulations were unevenly and sometimes leniently applied. The ending of outdoor relief, in particular, was successfully resisted in many areas both by the poor and their Guardians. But the workhouse system left an indelible mark on working-class consciousness and on all policies for working-class welfare. It operated as a deterrent, so that many who qualified were put off from seeking help, and it reinforced the idea that poverty itself was a crime. It is suggested that the horror of the workhouse was responsible for a 'widespread working-class indifference' to political reform[7] – the self-reliance inculcated by the system was dearly bought, in withdrawal from, rather than engagement with, the state.

Other than the Poor Law, the remedies for poverty could only lie in private philanthropy, and the fact that the Poor Law had itself grown from roots in the Church of England reflected the fact that almsgiving had always been a Christian duty. In rural situations the first dispensers were expected to be the parson and squire, their wives and daughters taking a leading role, though in deeds rather than money. Thus they visited the village poor almost as a matter of course (the heroine who caught a mortal disease from infected cottagers was almost a cliche of the Victorian novel) and no household management book lacked a recipe for 'nourishing soup for the poor'. Genteel ladies had the advantage over men of automatic access to the homes of the poor and to intimate scenes of birth, illness and dying – a role that they kept well into the era of council housing. Meanwhile a rising urban aristocracy of wealthy manufacturers and merchants, many of them new and enthusiastic suburbans, were engaging with the new problems of industrial poverty. Many were Nonconformists, notably Quakers and Unitarians, who were excluded from local government until 1835, but their 'evangelical conscience' was shared by outstanding Anglicans such as those in the Clapham Sect that grew up round William Wilberforce from the 1780s onwards. Themselves living in family-centred and supposedly idyllic circumstances, they expressed a sense of responsibility for the towns where their fortunes were made by establishing institutions to foster science and self-improvement, and by taking an active interest in the physical and moral state of the poor.

This set the mould of Victorian and Edwardian philanthropy, at the heart of which was an unquestioned assumption of the moral superiority of the upper classes and their inalienable right to supervise the lives of the poor, who were expected, at best, to be docile if ignorant, but at worst to be 'vicious'. As the classes became increasingly separated in space, the poor seemed more and more 'another nation', the areas they inhabited a fascinating but alarming *terra incognita* where charity assumed the nature of a 'mission' – thus the founder of the Salvation Army gave the title *In Darkest England* to his proselytizing book of 1890. To the higher classes the moral and physical conditions of poverty seemed inextricably mixed, and a shrewd observer of Victorian philanthropy maintained that its practitioners were 'more alarmed by the degeneration of the poor than moved by compassion for their unhappy state.'[8]

There was persistent tension, however, between philanthropy and another unshakeable Victorian principle, that of self-help. For many years there was a deep conviction that every man should support himself and his own, on the comfortable assumption that work was available for all who were really willing to do it. It had to be admitted that there were special periods of 'distress' arising from dips in trade or personal crises, which justified a temporary relaxation of the principle, and this led to the well known distinction between the 'deserving' and the 'undeserving' poor, which legitimized charity to those suffering special or temporary hardships outside their own control. These included the sick, the aged, widows, orphans and cripples, as well as genuinely repentant sinners such as reformed prostitutes. In practice, the line between the deserving and the undeserving was impossible to hold with any consistency. At the same time, the situation was further confused by the impulsiveness of the givers, as well as the overlaps of a plethora of competing charities which, not surprisingly, was exploited by the unscrupulous and sharp-witted.

In time, the effects of all such charitable efforts came under scrutiny. In one quarter, indiscriminate giving was held to weaken the will and morals of the poor and was blamed for increasing poverty rather than eliminating it. In another, an emerging social science offered a new idea: that there could be underlying economic or other causes of poverty that no individual, recipient or donor, could rectify. In this view poverty was caused not so much by the moral degeneracy of the 'undeserving' as by such things as low wages, fluctuations in trade, or hopelessly unhealthy environments – and it was the slowly dawning realization of the last that gave rise to housing reform, as we shall see in the following chapter. After the middle of the century efforts were made to increase the efficiency of charity. Charitable bodies began to cooperate and merge; districts were divided up and distribution systematized – an approach that climaxed on a national scale with the foundation in 1869 of the Charity Organization Society (COS) (which continued in the next century as the Family Welfare Association).

The COS confined its efforts strictly to those of the 'deserving' poor who were either not eligible for poor relief, or for whom such relief would clearly be degrading. Its emphasis was on helping such people to help themselves, so that they would eventually become independent of charity altogether. Allowances were arranged by district caseworkers, who provided continuous personal supervision. Some of them were paid stipends and the COS provided training, as well as producing surveys and reports and, in 1903, a 'School of Sociology' which was eventually absorbed into the London School of Economics. It could be said that the main achievement of the COS was not that it ever reached its goal of a systematic and fair structure of poor relief, which was in the last resort impossible, but that it provided a learning experience for a generation or more of its workers, among them some key people who became forerunners or initiators of state welfare, such as Charles Booth, the author of the great social survey of London, Samuel and Henrietta Barnett, the founders of Toynbee Hall, and Beatrice Webb, with her husband Sidney, a Fabian Society member and co-founder of the London School of Economics. In applying its 'scientific' approach to charitable relief, the COS eventually supplied proof as to whether or not the problems of poverty could be solved by individual effort, and the verdict of experience was that they could not.

Another assault on poverty came from the 'settlement' movement, initiated by the Barnetts with their foundation of Toynbee Hall in Whitechapel in 1884. Settlements, as the term implies, were an attempt on the part of the educated and privileged to live among the poor, 'to plant in a centre of vice, squalor and misery, a little oasis of education, refinement and sympathy'.[9] Toynbee Hall was modelled on the Oxbridge college, with living accommodation for young graduate men who took up residence for varying periods of time. They were expected to influence local life by becoming councillors, Poor Law Guardians and leaders in local affairs, and to create and run educational and recreational activities for the local people, and one of the lasting legacies of the movement is the Whitechapel Art Gallery and Library. The Hall called to many men with a social conscience and, over time, its luminaries included William Beveridge (the architect of the Welfare State and former COS worker), the social philosopher R.H. Tawney, Albert Mansbridge (one of the founders of the Workers' Educational Association), and the later Prime Minister, Clement Attlee, who was its secretary in 1910. Though Samuel Barnett was an Anglican vicar (of St Jude's in Whitechapel), the Hall was non-sectarian and sometimes gave support to political movements and strikes; but although it worked for an active democracy it was not interested in socialism or the class struggle. Rather, it depended on personal relationships to bridge the gap between rich and poor. Henrietta Barnett, who made the Hall her vocation, started numerous activities, including mothers' meetings, guilds for servants and working girls, convalescent homes and a gymnasium. Above all there were her 'at homes' for local people that had both a social and a cultural intent.

Other universities and some schools were quick to take up the example of Toynbee Hall. The settlement pattern had a particular appeal to upper- and middle-class women for, disenfranchized and both legally and economically subordinated to fathers or husbands, it presented an honourable way to penetrate the world beyond the home. Hitherto, women had little chance of formal public service. There was no statutory bar to their being Poor Law Guardians provided they met other conditions, but it was not until the 1890s that they began to come forward in any numbers; and aside from a brief period around 1870 they were barred from standing in municipal elections until 1882. One avenue for them was the religious community such as the quasi-monastic, High Anglican 'sisterhood' or the low church deaconesses. These, with various Nonconformist counterparts, proliferated in the late 1800s, devoting themselves to neighbourhood work and founding hospitals, orphanages and Houses of Mercy for reformed prostitutes. In many ways this was an extension of their traditional family role, as the title 'sister' implies. Others were quick to grasp the secular advantages of settlements, which sanctioned their living and working together as single women. The Women's University Settlement, founded in 1887, was followed by many others, foundations of schools and colleges, or simply of individuals with particular missions, socialist, pacifist or spiritual. These settlements differed from the more formal ones of men: not only were their premises less grand, as might be expected given women's lesser wealth, but they laid less emphasis on buildings and more on the services offered.[10]   Typically, they used old, converted buildings as bases for girls' clubs, mothers' circles, evening classes, holiday schemes, and so on. They quite often supported co-operative and trade union activities and provided training for their own workers, growing numbers of whom were salaried.

Cumulatively, women's charitable work made a major contribution to the emergence of the caring professions and the shaping of social policy, although there were those who deplored this 'feminization' of public affairs, a price of which was the disparaging image that attached to social work, including housing management.[11]   There were also some uncomfortable paradoxes involved, such as the fact that those who made a vocation of upholding the ideal of the family to their clients were walking demonstrations of women's ability to survive outside the family. They were also young, middle-class women with little if any experience of housework and budgeting, who presumed to tell poor, hard-pressed wives and mothers how to manage their homes.

It is difficult for present-day people to feel much sympathy with the underlying assumptions of Victorian philanthropy.   If not complete indifference to suffering, it seems to reveal either a heartless rationalization of social inequality (calling to mind the phrase 'cold as charity'), or else high-minded interventions ('do-gooding') in the lives of presumed social inferiors. Also involved was a good deal of concealed self-interest, ranging from the titillated horror of ladies who treated 'slumming' as a pastime, to a considerable professional advantage. The dedicated East End socialist George Lansbury viewed Toynbee Hall with some cynicism, as an ideal springboard for men who hoped to carve out careers in politics and the professions;[12] and that ever sharp observer, Beatrice Webb, committed to her diary thoughts about COS work and rent collecting in East London: 'One thing is clear in my mind, it is distinctly advantageous to us to go amongst the poor. We can get from them an experience of life which is novel and interesting: the study of their lives and surroundings gives us the facts wherewith we can attempt to solve the social problems; contact with them develops on the whole our finer qualities . . . Perhaps the worst result for us is that our philanthropy is sometimes the cause of pharisaical self-congratulation'. She added, however, that any genuine philanthropist she had ever known was 'far too perplexed at the very "mixed result" (even if he can recognize any permanent result) of his work, to feel much pride over it.'[13]

But latter-day contempt for Victorian philanthropy is apt to miss much of its essence. This lay in the immensity of the gulf between rich and poor, in supreme upper-class confidence in its mission to civilize, whether in slums or far-flung imperial colonies, and in addition some appreciable degrees of real concern, compassion and piety. The settlement movement was perhaps one of the fullest examples of the latter and it provided an inspiration to some who continued to opt to live and work amongst the poor in the period between the wars. They included, for instance, the Catholic priest Basil Jellicoe, whose mission was in the slums of Somers Town in North London, and Alfred Salter, a doctor, lifelong pacifist, borough and LCC councillor, and later MP, who with his wife Ada devoted their lives to their neighbours in Bermondsey. Starting in the 1920s with the vision of turning this slum area into a 'garden village', they presided over massive slum clearances in the borough before 1939, reluctantly conceding that it should be redeveloped with blocks of flats. They also introduced many health and cultural services in this desperately and deprived part of London's East End.[14]

Changing Attitudes: the 1880s

The 1880s saw significant changes in the class landscape and the way that social problems were perceived. Citizenship was widening: though still related to property values, the suffrage was extended to lodgers and recipients of outdoor relief, though not as yet to women. A unionized artisan elite became more established, its unions recognized and its security boosted by co-operative and building societies. The white collar classes were expanding into many new services and occupations, and the main body of the working classes, served by the 'new unionism' of the unskilled, was developing a settled, 'respectable and self-respecting' urban culture that was apolitical but fundamentally conservative and with a vigour of its own. Various of the middle classes were either beset with fears of a new-found working-class militancy (there was an outbreak of rioting in London's West End in 1885) or concerned for those of the poor who were decent and hardworking but victims of economic and housing problems beyond their control.

Social science now made a significant contribution, through its systematic analysis of problems of poverty. A Social Science Association had been debating questions of policy for some 30 years, but a qualitative step forward was taken by Charles Booth (1840–1916), member of a Liverpool Unitarian merchant family and coincidentally related by marriage to Beatrice Webb, who worked as one of his assistants before her own marriage. Booth began his huge and painstaking study of the London poor in the later 1880s, and published *The Life and Labour of the People of London* between 1891 and 1903. Initially he began it to challenge a socialist claim that a quarter of London's population lived in extreme poverty. To his surprise, his investigations revealed that in some boroughs the proportion was in fact closer to a third. He confirmed and elaborated the conventional wisdom of a social hierarchy, in which he distinguished eight different layers. The bottom two consisted of the 'abject' and semi-criminal poor, who to all intents had no social usefulness at all. In ascending order above these were the very poor with only casual earnings; the poor with intermittent or small but regular earnings; those with regular 'standard' earnings; higher-class labour; and the lower and upper middle classes. The only levels that could safely be allowed to intermix with any mutual benefit were the three uppermost ones. Below these, it was desirable to keep the different levels strictly apart, as any one of them was prone to contamination by the layer immediately below it.

As for the two bottom layers, like most other theorists and reformers of his time, Booth supposed that the only thing to be done was to break them up, ideally by dispatching them to 'colonies' either overseas or at home. Among other things, this would have the merit of releasing the space they occupied for others. The two bodies that did not scruple to concern themselves with such social outcasts were the Salvation and Church Armies, founded in 1878 and 1882 respectively, and their missions to this 'submerged tenth' did not endear them to other reforming bodies. The Salvation Army's founder, General William Booth (no relation to Charles), proposed a range of such colonies as the 'way out' of 'darkest England' for these abandoned masses.

Another survey that both reflected and helped shape a new understanding of poverty was Seebohm Rowntree's study of working-class York in the late 1890s, published as *Poverty* in 1901. This broke new ground by distinguishing primary from secondary poverty. Primary poverty was found to apply to some 15 per cent of the working-class population, who simply could not earn enough to sustain life; but a further 28 per cent were in secondary poverty, where a regular if joyless existence could be maintained provided there was no interruption to income, no unforeseen misfortune, and above all no spending on drink or other recreations – all of which were big assumptions. Another and more descriptive contribution to poverty studies was made by the Women's Group of the Fabian Society, which sponsored Marjorie Spring Rice's study of lives of poor working-class wives which appeared in 1913.

One outcome of these surveys was that many who had previously put their trust in 'charity organization' and cultural initiatives like settlements now looked more favourably on state intervention. For instance Samuel Barnett, who always on principle refused alms even to the most pitiful of beggars lest he should corrupt them, was brought to the conclusion that the experiment of persuading or coercing the poor to pull themselves up by their own efforts had failed. This was inevitable, as the causes of their distress were systemic and societal, rather than individual. In the view of Alfred Marshall, the influential Professor of Political Economy at Cambridge, 'extreme poverty ought to be regarded, not indeed as a crime, but as a thing so detrimental to the State that it should not be endured.'[15] Seeing people as victims of circumstance rather than morally defective made it more acceptable to those of a variety of political persuasions to look to state protection against unemployment and old age, those unforeseen or unavoidable calamities that could push the vulnerable over the edge.

A turning point was the 1909 Royal Commission on the Poor Law from which time responsibility for one category of person after another was shifted from philanthropy to the state. It was not that the end of charity was seriously contemplated – on the contrary, there continued to be a lot of agonized discussion about who did or did not 'deserve' it; but rather, it was that in future it was to take the form of personal service rather than physical relief.[16]

Notes

1. Davidoff & Hall.
2. Cullingworth (1966), p. 16.
3. Muthesius.
4. Thompson, F.M.L.
5. Carey.
6. Thompson, F.M.L.
7. Thompson, F.M.L, p. 359.
8. Simey, p. 52.
9. Simey, p. 131.
10. Vicinus.
11. Simey.
12. Meacham (1977).
13. Webb, p. 85.
14. Brockway.
15. Mowat, p. 124 (with reference to the Royal Commission on the Aged Poor, 1895).
16. Simey.

Chapter Three

Housing for the Poor

'Are the tenants to be picked, all doubtful and inconvenient persons excluded, or are the former inhabitants to be housed so long as they are decently respectable?'

Beatrice Webb, *Diary* Vol.1, 1885

Slums and their Elimination

Like other problems of poverty, the housing of its poor arose haphazardly and without foresight in industrial society. The housing of the rural poor had often been unhealthy, but at least it did not occur in the same massive concentrations as urban housing, which had degrees of pollution, overcrowding, infestation, disease and lack of water and sanitation hardly credible to anyone reared in the later twentieth century.[1] The period of explosive growth in cities with heavy industries was from the 1800s to the 1830s. A serious outbreak of cholera in 1832 alarmed those with a social conscience, but for the most part there was 'a pervasive apathy about the whole subject of sanitary improvement, which seemed to be of relatively minor importance when set beside the contemporary achievements of industry and commerce'.[2] It was, therefore, an uphill struggle for reformers although they produced investigations and reports in abundance, including the five reports of Edwin Chadwick, Secretary to the Poor Law Commission, in the 1840s. Positive action would have been still further delayed but for a second serious cholera epidemic in 1848. In that year the first Public Health Act was passed, setting up a Central Board of Health and local boards with some authority over sewerage, water supply, pollution from offensive trades, and other matters. Over the middle decades of the century, measures to order and improve the urban environment were taken in many towns, under both local acts and Acts of Parliament. The latter included the earliest to relate to working-class housing but were for the most part to do with the removal of 'nuisances'. Gradually town councils took control of water and gas supplies, laid drains and sewers, paved and lit miles of city centre streets. Later, this energy was applied to other undertakings such as electricity supply. Birmingham in the mayoralty of Joseph Chamberlain in the 1870s was the outstanding example of such municipal enterprise, or what was labelled 'gas and water socialism'.

The Public Health Act of 1872 divided the whole country into urban and rural sanitary districts, under a Local Government Board that succeeded the Poor Law Board. From this time the worst of the epidemic diseases began to abate, although the continuation of the worst wards created that stark contrast between riches and poverty – the grand city and its shameful depths – that was so characteristic of Victorian society. Most towns and cities had their notorious slums, and those of Glasgow, Newcastle, London and some other places remained bywords well into the twentieth century. As we have seen, the main state intervention in housing was the bye-laws, which did not reach down to the poorest, many of whom lived without homes of their own. Other than the street, the shelter available to them was the common lodging house, where beds could be rented by the night, or even in shifts by day. Such housing as they could afford to rent consisted of buildings that might have stood since medieval times, newer stock shoddily built for the quickest return, or once better-class family houses now let off by the room, or even subdivision of room. A particular blight of many towns was the cellar dwelling: dark, damp and subject to flooding. Both ancient buildings and purpose-built but inferior housing were likely to be crammed together in airless, undrained and unlit courts and yards, deficient in privy accommodation and water supply. They were also likely to be badly overcrowded: accounts of two or even more households sharing a single room are not hard to find. At the same time, such dwellings often stood on land that could command a very high price for commercial expansion, or was at risk of appropriation for new thoroughfares or new railway lines and stations, for which many thousands lost their homes without compensation. Slum areas, therefore, simultaneously suffered from the meanest of uses and the highest prospective demand and market value.

But what, in fact, was a slum? Then as later, the answer was not straightforward, for the meaning of the term was a shifting one. At first, it did not have a sinister connotation but simply referred to quiet back alleys, while areas known to be criminal were called 'rookeries'. But from the middle of the century, a 'slum' began to be seen as an area of congested, polluted and disease-ridden housing, with every kind of criminality and depravity. It was, however, unclear how far this was due to the buildings, and how far to the people: which was cause and which effect. Shoddy buildings and lack of water made it impossible for the inhabitants to lead clean and decent lives. At the same time, there was no house, however good to begin with, that could not degenerate into a slum with enough overcrowding and misuse. It was in the interest of many to believe that slums were in fact the creation of 'slum people' who chose to behave in a depraved way – a race apart, with their own territory and customs. Even to such a dedicated socialist as John Burns it occurred that 'it is not always the pigsty, it is sometimes the pig, that is to blame'.[3] The conventional wisdom that slum dwellers created slums, still current a century later, could be used to justify their clearance and the dispersal of their populations, when this was expedient for whatever reason. It took a considerable act of faith to hold that it was both possible and worthwhile to bestow decent houses on people from the slums.

Such doubts and fatalism partly explain the slow pace of state intervention in working-class housing. The first legislative measures were introduced in 1851 by Lord Shaftesbury, the great factory reformer, to address the scandal of common lodging houses. These gave local authorities powers to regulate and even provide lodging houses; but the degree to which they exercised the latter power was negligible. It was 17 years before the next piece of legislation, the first of a series of housing acts dealing with slum property, which formed an enduring part of environmental health policy down to the present day. The Act of 1868, introduced by an independent Liberal MP, William Torrens, permitted local councils to put closing orders on houses that were 'unfit to live in', and to require owners to demolish or repair insanitary houses, with default powers to do this themselves and charge the owners. The Cross Act of 1875, introduced by a Conservative Home Secretary, gave powers to declare whole areas 'insanitary' and to prepare reconstruction schemes for them. This Act, which applied to towns of 20,000 population and above, laid the foundations of all later slum clearance procedure: the 'designation' of an area, compulsory purchase of the property standing on it, and compensation of the owners. Schemes could be proposed by one Medical Officer of Health, two Justices of the Peace, or twelve ratepayers, and perhaps it says much for the level of concern amongst the last that so few areas were actually tackled at this time.

There are three things of importance to note: firstly, that intervention in housing was only thought to be justified on the grounds of danger to public health, and this was where its administration remained until the establishment of a Ministry of Housing and Local Government in 1951. Secondly, the main reason for inaction or long postponed action was the protection of property. Not only was the owner's right to do as he wished with his own property held sacrosanct, but if for public health reasons this right was infringed, the owner had to be handsomely compensated. He received full market value for the site, without taking into account that the buildings on it were insanitary or even 'unfit to live in', until the Act was amended in 1879 to address this point. In addition he was paid a 'solatium' or extra allowance of 10 per cent, to compensate for the enforced nature of the sale. This meant that clearance of 'insanitary' areas cost town councils more than they were prepared to pay, especially when as time went on they were progressively dominated by small businessmen with a keen eye on the rates.

Lastly, when the question was raised whether local authorities should themselves build homes for the working classes – and it had been Torrens's original intention to give them this power – there was entrenched opposition to such an invasion of the sphere of private enterprise and profit.

Conventional attitudes towards charitable relief could be invoked here, for subsidizing people's housing would surely pauperize and corrupt them, like any other charitable handout. Leading reformers, including Lord Shaftesbury and most of those in the Charity Organization Society, were strictly opposed to state-aided municipal housing on these grounds. There were, however, circumstances and places where it eventually became difficult to tolerate inaction. Some of the worst conditions were found in Scottish cities, and Edinburgh, Dundee and Glasgow carried out improvement measures between the 1860s and 1880s, under private or public acts. In London, where some of the oldest and most notorious slums were situated, the Metropolitan Board of Works, by 1882, carried out schemes on fourteen sites, involving the displacement of nearly 23,000 people. The cost was great, for at first it was obliged to rehouse all those displaced on the same site. Even when this obligation was relaxed to rehousing half the numbers on any site, the costs of clearance far exceeded the price that a normal housing developer was prepared to pay for the land.

In practice, the challenge could only be taken up, and then not without difficulty, by the new philanthropic housing trusts. The inspiration for these went back to a reform movement of the 1840s, when two societies, the Metropolitan Association for the Improvement of the Dwellings of the Industrious Classes and the Society for Improving the Condition of the Labouring Classes, were set up, with royal and aristocratic patronage respectively. The Association set out to be a commercial enterprise while the Society was a charity, but the aim of both was to demonstrate that it was possible to build healthy homes for working-class people that brought a reasonable return on investment. Both built lodging houses and family tenements, although their preference was to build high standard and self-contained family accommodation, even at the cost of higher rents and lower returns or dividends. Many of their buildings remain, the Association's Streatham Street Flats of 1849, near Covent Garden, having stood the test of time particularly well.

While the two societies set out to demonstrate the practicality of healthy tenements even on expensive metropolitan sites, the charitable or 'philanthropy and five per cent' housing trusts that followed on their example in the 1860s did not in fact find this easy, even with the benefit of access to cheap loans from 1866. The Peabody Trust and Waterlow Improved Industrial Dwellings Company, founded in the early 1860s, responded to the challenge in different ways. The latter stuck firmly to self-contained flats, building considerable numbers in central and East London down to the 1890s; but the Peabody trustees dropped their standards to tenements that were 'associated' – that is, with shared WCs and sinks – in order to cater for people lower down the social scale while still trying to make the 4 or 5 per cent return that could be ploughed back into further building. Even with lowered standards it was not always possible to achieve this, as the dozens of new companies and trusts of the 1870s–1880s also discovered. Some of them followed the Peabody example and built to less than ideal standards, while others built self-contained dwellings, including cottages, that were intended for more affluent workers. Many of these trusts actively continued to build until 1914 and some, like the Sutton Trust, had their most active period after 1918; but in general their salience declined after 1900, while that of municipal housing rose. In London, one of the reasons for this was that they were unable to meet the rising standards demanded by the newly created London County Council.[4]

The Growth of State Intervention

Local government housing powers were now increasing. Investigations into the effects of the Cross Act, which was amended in 1879 and 1882 to make it easier and cheaper for authorities to apply, found that very few had used it at all, and then in very small schemes. There was a new climate of concern with a sense, almost, of rising panic in the 1880s. A new legal obligation on all railway companies to run cheap, early morning trains for workmen, imposed by an Act of 1883, now made it possible for more people to move away from crowded urban centres; but there was a growing problem of overcrowding in London which, it was gradually conceded, was partly due to the operation of the Cross Act itself. Housing was also being lost to expanding commercial areas, and a downstream shift in the labour market was causing acute overcrowding in the East End. Under such pressures, the poorest were clearly unable to fend for themselves, but even the thrifty, sober and respectable working man was helpless in the face of absolute shortage, and therefore at risk of that social contamination by the lower classes that Booth had warned about.

The 'moral panic' found voice in a short tract of 1883 by a Congregationalist minister, Andrew Mearns, which claimed to be an investigation into the godless and immoral condition of London's 'abject poor'. Sparing the reader little in its physical descriptions of '. . . courts reeking with poisonous and malodorous gases . . . rotten staircases, dark and filthy passages, swarming with vermin, intolerable stench, accretions of filth', and vividly hinting at the incest resulting from desperate overcrowding, Mearns was sure that 'this terrible flood of sin and misery is gaining upon us.'[5] Yet in spite of the apparent inefficacy of decades of philanthropy and his own stated conviction that 'the State must secure for the poorest . . . the right to live in something better than fever dens',[6] he rather surprisingly concluded the remedy was yet more missions and house-to-house visiting by the bountiful.

It was in such circumstances that a Royal Commission on the Housing of the Working Classes was proposed by the Conservative leader, Lord Salisbury, who had been active in housing issues 30 years before. Witnesses to the Commission repeatedly affirmed that overcrowding was now seriously affecting the 'deserving' and respectable classes – so, incidentally, making it harder to support the theory that slums were creations of those who lived in them – and they stressed the prevalence of one-room homes and the threat these posed to sexual morality. While remaining noncommittal about municipal housing and strongly in favour of working-class home ownership, the Commission did recommend that local authorities should have powers to buy land and build housing, aided by cheap government loans and cheap public transport. The Housing Act that followed in 1885 is not now regarded as a particularly important one: on the face of it, it simply codified the three main planks of legislation up to this point, the Shaftesbury, Torrens and Cross Acts. But to some at the time, the fact that it extended the definition of lodging houses to permanent family dwellings seemed 'nothing less than an invitation to socialism'.[7] Salisbury himself did not give his approval to municipal housing, but the Act appeared to condone it, and London County Council and also Liverpool City Council used the Act to build their first working-class tenements.

The range of theoretical approaches to working-class housing that was now possible stretched across the political spectrum. The right-wing Conservative 'sanitary' approach of the Cross Acts was to restrict the role of the state to public health and the removal of nuisances. The Liberal view of Joseph Chamberlain was that private landlords should be tightly regulated by local authorities, with penalties for houses that were insanitary or unfit to live in. There was a broad agreement, which in the long term proved to be right, that the future for the respectable working classes lay in home ownership. That the state itself should take responsibility for building working-class housing was for long a minority view, and the general feeling was that the agents of any reformed housing should be the charitable trusts. Eventually, it was Conservative rather than Liberal opinion that conceded the necessity for direct state intervention in housing. The COS, which as early as 1873 had set up a Dwellings Committee to discuss remedies, agreed that private charity could not cope with the magnitude of the problem. Failing redevelopment by the housing trusts, it recommended that the London authority should itself build on sites it had cleansed of slums. It was the Conservative opposition that in 1912 and 1913 introduced bills to give Treasury funds for slum clearance in urban areas and new housing in rural areas.

Meanwhile the faction of 'radical centralizers' wanting more state intervention, who included the Barnetts, the Webbs and the newly established London County Council, had helped precipitate the Housing of the Working Classes Act of 1890, a consolidating Act that was the foundation of all housing law for nearly a century. It sharpened the housing powers of local authorities by making slum clearance somewhat less discretionary, and 'Part III' of the Act enhanced their powers to build and manage their own housing. These were still discretionary, but it was an inducement that they were now allowed to keep any housing they built for a period of 10 years, and in 1900 they were permitted to buy land for housing outside their own boundaries – a concession of much importance to the LCC.

The Views of the Poor

It has been remarked that in all the voluminous evidence given to the 1884 Royal Commission, 'the inhabitants of the slums were not given a chance to tell their own story',[8] and that the poor were in fact never consulted about the kind of help that would be most useful to them.[9]   Undoubtedly, reformers believed themselves to be sufficiently familiar with the lives of the poor to know what they wanted, but their reforms in effect imposed their own views, standards and priorities.   Such certainty became a justification for state intervention, for in the words of an influential public figure, 'a man ought not to be allowed to live in a bad home'.[10]   There is disappointingly little evidence of formal working-class involvement in the struggle for housing reform until the late nineteenth century – something that should be borne in mind in view of a claim frequently made that council housing was 'a major concession to working-class interests by a reluctant state.'[11]   Leftwing activists were often disillusioned by working-class apathy towards housing and even the radical Workmen's National Housing Council, founded in 1898, which headed a number of London groups working for housing reform, felt that 'whoever else takes the housing question seriously, the mass of those most affected by it – the working people – have not done so.'[12]   There are obvious reasons why housing had to wait virtually to last in the great series of working-class struggles that included the Corn Laws, the Charter, the New Poor Law, and the fight for trade unions.   Quite apart from the unsettling question of how far the poor really wanted better housing – and even the Marxist inclined Socialist Democratic Federation found that 'the slum dweller in nine cases out of ten loves his slum'[13] – housing was regarded as the realm of women and children, and therefore of little political or economic importance.   Moreover its driving force of respectability divided rather than united the working classes, reflecting as it did, not class as usually defined, but something more subtle: the place of a person or family in the social hierarchy, as determined by the quality of their domestic life and culture.

Working-class/middle-class distinctions have come to mean so much less since 1945 that the crucial importance of 'respectability' to Victorians and Edwardians is difficult for people of today to grasp.   It needs to be rescued from our own misconceptions, for it is neither a retrospective present-day invention nor a spurious and hypocritical construction of its own time.[14]   On the contrary, it was endlessly articulated by working-class people, including the very poor battling against their own circumstances, and it still has a powerful hold on some of our oldest citizens today.   Linked very largely to place of residence and quality of homes, 'respectability' was essentially a measure of distinction.   Oneself, home and near neighbourhood were almost invariably described as 'respectable', while the opposite – the 'rough' – was a term attached to others at a distance, even when that distance was no more than a street or part of a street.   It may well have been that the function of the concept of 'respectability' was to confer some sort of security during periods of rapid and unsettling social change: a bulwark for those who stood most to lose in an involuntary social mixing that could easily suck them down into circumstances beyond their control.

The importance of respectability goes far to explain the great antagonism towards the Poor Law reform of 1834.   Being thrown on the mercy of 'the

House' (workhouse) was almost the worst fate that could befall, and even having to claim outdoor relief came to be 'equated with loss of respectability'.[15] The precise content or meaning of respectability was not fixed, but had countless variations in different social groupings, times and locations; but its most essential and enduring ingredients were temperance or even total abstention from alcohol, cleanliness, and an orderly domestic life that depended, amongst other things, on the regular payment of rent.   The condition of the home played a crucial part in establishing a family's level of respectability, both as judged by itself and by others.   The universally recognized signifiers were spotlessly clean windows and doorsteps whitened by scrubbing; lace window curtains (fore-runners of present-day nylon 'nets') which could be draped to reveal an aspidistra in a parlour window.   If the house boasted a parlour, it held the family treasures and symbols of culture, most importantly the piano, and it was set aside for music practice, school homework and serious business, as well as festivals and family ceremonies, and formal hospitality.

Obviously not all, even of the 'respectable', could aspire to all this.   Many lived in houses without parlours and – depending on place and time – many had to make their family homes in part only of a house, even a single room. In such circumstances, water, slops and fuel had to be carried through the house, perhaps up and down several flights of stairs, whilst a perpetual war on vermin needed to be waged.   But this did not necessarily negate a family's respectability, and those who managed well in such circumstances were given credit by the charitable workers whose recommendation might be needed for access to aid of various kinds.   It was the wives who were crucial in setting their families' level of respectability, and with it their social standing and self-respect.   It was their tireless work and efforts that could distinguish them from the 'abject' social dregs who in the words of Charles Booth 'don't study their homes'.[16]   When it was functioning normally, one of the ways the housing system assisted respectability was the freedom of movement made possible by weekly tenancies (as opposed to the yearly or longer tenancies of the higher classes).   Many commented on the mobility this allowed: people could trade up or down the housing scale as their circumstances changed, and it was common practice to move within the same street simply to get accommodation that was in a better state of repair or decoration, often for the same rent.   Tenants were evidently sharp observers of the housing stock around them and to some extent were able to manipulate it by lobbying landlords or agents.

Another way of controlling one's housing circumstances was through home ownership, which became an increasing aspiration for many people as the century wore on.   By 1914, it is conventionally estimated at 10 per cent overall, but in some districts it could be double this amount.   The early building societies which enabled people to buy their homes by instalment payments are frequently quoted as a classic example of working-class self-help.   In their early form as 'terminating' societies, they pooled the contributions of a group of members, building and allotting houses as they were able, and winding up their affairs when the needs of the group were met. This was in contrast to the 'permanent' societies which became, in effect, lending and borrowing banks. Building societies undoubtedly brought home ownership within the reach of more people, although their great expansion waited until the period between the wars; but they certainly did not make it available to the poor nor even all who included themselves in the respectable classes. Respectability did not, at this time, depend on whether one owned or rented one's home, but rather on standards of domestic life.

Another route to ownership was that offered by various forms of collective or co-operative ownership. Co-operative societies became involved in the provision of housing from the 1880s, but their dwellings were of a conventional kind and their relations with their tenants differed little from those of any landlord.[17] Co-partnership, which arose around the turn of the century, was a way for working people to become responsible for their own housing. Members of a co-partnership society paid a share, perhaps in instalments, and ultimately became joint owners of their estate. This form of tenure was prominent in the development of Bournville model village, described below, and it became particularly significant for the growth of garden cities and suburbs, where it proved an ideal vehicle for their particular design and community ideology. By 1914, there were upwards of a dozen co-partnership societies catering, overall, for some 35,000 people; but their ideological colouring, with the sizeable financial stake they required of members, meant that this particular tenure was biased towards the upwardly aspiring working or even middle classes, rather than the poor.

In general, the way the housing system was constituted served to fragment rather than unite the lower classes. Finding and maintaining a home and using it to establish a particular social position were all, by definition, individual and therefore divisive actions. The only thing that might perhaps contradict this were the tenant protest movements and rent strikes that were apparently endemic in landlord-owned housing, which early in the nineteenth century was subject to 'frequent communal rent riots'.[18] A new wave of unrest was set off by the 1867 Electoral Reform Act which, in its efforts to extend the franchise, ended the system of rate compounding by which landlords paid lower rates for batches of houses. Tenants who were now for the first time made responsible for paying their own rates should of course have had their rents reduced, but landlords often failed to do so. The compounding system was soon reinstated but tenant unrest continued in many parts of the country, most particularly in Glasgow and London's East End. The scores of tenant defence leagues that arose were, however, largely composed of a respectable elite, including yearly as well as weekly tenants, which dissociated itself from the poor in slums. The latter had their own peculiar ways of getting back at landlords, whether through vandalizing the property, doing 'moonlight flits', or simply not paying the rent. These were scattered and individual strategies that in total amounted to a sort of guerilla warfare.[19]

The question is how far the rent strikes were in any way a concerted movement with, for instance, municipal housing as one of its aims. Some of the tenant leagues did call for municipal housing and there were some political groups, like the Manhood Suffrage League (whose weekly *House and Home* circulated in Working Men's Clubs) that saw rent strikes as an instrument of mass radicalization; but it appears that the tenant movements remained scattered and evanescent – they never, for example, had a national federation. This did not mean that they were without a discernible influence on government policy, although it does perhaps help to explain why more socially aware working people could so readily accept the ideals and models for reformed housing that were put before them by the enlightened middle classes.

Octavia Hill: a Conservative Radical Approach

There remains to consider one unique contribution to housing reform, in the work of Octavia Hill, whose combination of an ultra conservative philosophy with close and sensitive insights were offered by no one else. She had a lasting influence on housing practice, if not on mainstream policy, by pioneering – rather in spite of herself – a method of housing management which was later adopted into council housing practices and became the foundation of a new profession of housing management.

Hill was the grand-daughter of the public health pioneer and housing reformer, Dr Southwood Smith (one of the three founders of the Metropolitan Association mentioned above). She was the daughter of a father involved in Owenite communities and of a mother who practised the progressive Pestalozzi system of education. From her early teens she supported herself, as well as helping to pay off old family debts, but lacking the protection of either father or husband (although her grandfather was a pillar of support to the family) she was limited to the small number of occupations then open to women. At first she pursued the ladylike one of painting on glass, which she learned from John Ruskin and applied in a ladies' work co-operative that also gave training to slum children. Later, with her sisters, she ran a small private school. She at last found her true vocation through Ruskin, who spent some of his large inherited fortune on a block of slum property, locally known as 'Little Hell', for her to manage. Eventually Hill built up a large portfolio of London houses owned by the Ecclesiastical Commissioners and others, including her own friends and associates. She gathered a large team of women helpers, voluntary and salaried, many of whom were later to have distinguished professional careers in housing. One of her lady helpers was Kate Potter, who on her marriage passed her 'patch' onto her young sister Beatrice, later the wife of Sidney Webb.

Hill was a pioneer in a number of respects. She catered, if not for the completely abject, for those she described as 'destructive' and criminal: above Booth's two lowest levels but below any that the COS would have considered 'deserving'. Her 'system', although she was always at pains to deny that she had one, was to get to know and understand such people in their present homes: 'You cannot deal with the people and their houses separately . . . the

inhabitants and their surroundings must be improved together.'[20]   A fervent
believer in self-help, she encouraged them to improve themselves by paying
more of their income on rent and taking two rooms rather than one.   Girls
were paid to clean the common passages and unemployed men to do small
repairs.   Classes, bands, drill, May Day celebrations and country excursions
were organized.   Trees and flowers were planted.   A personal relationship with
tenants was crucial to fostering a sense of community responsibility, and this
was something that in Hill's opinion could never be offered by any large
housing company or philanthropic trust: 'Individuals cannot do what the
companies can do, and the companies cannot do what individuals can do.'[21]

In many respects her housing work paralleled that of settlements, and some
of her lady managers did in fact choose to become neighbours of their clients
(on which Beatrice Webb committed some withering comments to her diary).
By today's standards, the approach was undeniably patronizing.   Hill, to
whom her tenants were 'my dear poor', admitted to the Royal Commission
that her style of management was 'a tremendous despotism, but it is exercised
with a view of bringing out the powers of the people, and treating them as
responsible for themselves within certain limits.'[22]   She did, however,
experiment with ideas and practices that waited another 80 years to be
rediscovered: namely her use of rehabilitation or improvement of the housing
stock, as more appropriate for the really poor than demolition and rebuilding;
the need to involve them in any improvements for these to be successful, and
her appreciation of the delicate relationship between people and their homes.
While her incentives to tenants were intended to 'nerve them' to self-help and
decency,[23] she also respected their personal autonomy.   Such a blend of
authority and empathy was clearly too personal and too subtle to be
replicated on a more general and bureaucratic scale.

Hill's social contribution did not end with housing.   She was also a pioneer
in rescuing and preserving open spaces for the people, an issue of rising
importance in London in the 1870s and 1880s, when disused cemeteries and
similar spaces were very much at risk from building development.   Open space
for city dwellers was a concern of some of the housing trusts, who provided
gardens and allotments for their tenants, and it was a key issue in the
campaign to save Hampstead Heath – one outcome of which, as we shall see,
was the creation of Hampstead Garden Suburb by Henrietta Barnett.   Hill
became a member of the Commons Preservation Society in 1875 and 20 years
later was one of the small group that founded the National Trust.

Her influence in the housing movement was pervasive, and one that would
be hard to overestimate.   She endlessly gave evidence on housing matters to
government and other bodies, and late in life was one of the judges of the
Letchworth Cheap Cottages Exhibition described below.   Her career not only
spanned a long period of years but the great shift of attitudes, from the era of
benevolence and charity reform to the altogether different climate of state
intervention, and its linking to the garden city at the turn of the century.

Two who concurred in this connection between the poor and their wider
environments were Patrick Geddes and his wife, who pioneered the

improvement of some of the tenements in Edinburgh's old town, which they combined with the creation of gardens and open spaces. A biologist by training, Geddes applied his own brand of social science which he applied to the evolution and planning of towns, so making a major contribution to the emerging profession of town planning. In spite of his pioneering projects, however, he made clear in his Cities in Evolution of 1915 that he believed that very nearly all existing housing, including that of the higher classes and recent bye-law stock, belonged to an outmoded, 'paleotechnic' era of development: if not actually slum, it was 'semi' or 'super' slum. He saw the way forward, therefore, as the newly built town extension or suburb planned on garden city principles, and in this he was expressing what had become the conventional 'progressive' wisdom of the day.

Precursors of Council Housing: Tenements

By the time municipalities began to build working-class housing, the two patterns they could follow were the model tenements and model villages. Tenements took precedence, and not only in time but for the same practical reasons that had applied to the housing trusts, that they accommodated at least as many people as had previously lived on a cleared site, and they enabled workers to live within walking distance of their employment. The first two purpose-built blocks were in fact built by a Birkenhead Dock Company for its own men in 1845. So although those taking an interest in housing repeated endlessly that tenements did not make suitable homes for English families, they were the inevitable first choice for local authorities.

Certain technical constraints helped to determine their design. Load-bearing walls and the absence of lifts meant an effective height limit of five to six storeys, the two topmost ones often forming a two-storey apartment under a mansard roof. The infamous Window Tax, repealed in 1851, lasted just long enough to affect tenement design, for blocks with internal staircases were classed as a single dwelling with many windows and taxed accordingly, but those with balcony access escaped this burden. Larger tenement estates normally included a common bath house and laundry, often under the roof, and children's playgrounds, which were sometimes located on flat roofs. Gas lighting and cleaning of corridors were included in the rent. The notoriously strict tenant supervision was helped by the hollow layout of estates, whose cliff-like buildings lined the perimeter, with few entrances that could be closely observed.

It was the exception rather than the rule for English tenement estates to incorporate shops at street level. Where shops were present, they had street frontages and this, perhaps unintentionally, helped to integrate the estates into their surroundings. So, in a more subtle way, did some of the architect-designed blocks of the pioneer housing societies, which were not all that different in form from urban terraced houses of the gentry. Thus to a contemporary it seemed that a block built by the Metropolitan Association in St Pancras, 'if covered in plaster . . . would resemble a nobleman's dwelling.'[24]

The more general case, however, was that tenements were easily recognized for what they were: 'improved dwellings for the poor' that, as such, attracted stigma.

Socially, the model tenements fell into the dilemma of all new and reformed housing, that it entailed rents too high for the really poor. The Peabody Trust, as we have seen, tried to overcome this with its 'associated' dwellings', but when the East End Dwellings Company, launched from Samuel Barnett's St Jude's, tried to cater for 'the poorest class of self-supporting labourers' they were defeated by the LCC's prohibition of single-room apartments.[25] Tenements, therefore, did not so much replace the slums as substitute new populations for their original ones, and it is clear what was the answer to the question Beatrice Webb asked in her time as a rent collector: 'Are the tenants to be picked, all doubtful and inconvenient persons excluded, or are the former inhabitants to be housed so long as they are decently respectable?'[26] The St Pancras estate mentioned above numbered amongst its residents clerks, doctors, artists, people living on private means, and some even with living-in servants, as well as members of the 'aristocracy of labour', and for a time the estate had a library and reading room. This state of affairs could, of course, be justified by the 'filtering' that was expected to result.

The management of tenements also reflected their bias towards the more respectable working classes. Rent had to be paid a week in advance and there were prohibitions against lodgers and home-based trades, which ruled out a staple support of many poor women, the taking in of laundry. Tenements were so managed as to enforce certain domestic standards: we are told, for instance, that in a block built by an aunt of Viginia Woolf, lace curtains and potted geraniums were required.[27] In an essay on tenements that she contributed to Charles Booth's great survey, Octavia Hill concluded that they suited decent families who 'kept themselves to themselves': 'It is a life of law, regular, a little monotonous, and not developing any great individuality, but consistent with happy home-life, and it promises to be the life of the respectable London working-man.' For the 'destructive' however, tenements became 'a sort of pandemonium' and in their case small houses were always preferable.[28]

The paradox of tenements, and one passed on to council flats later, was that the people for whom they were suitable were precisely those who were likely to move away once houses and transport became available. If they could afford the relatively high tenement rents they were likely to afford the extra costs of suburban living. At the turn of the century, on the LCC's Boundary Street estate mentioned below, 10 per cent of tenants were both willing and able to leave. The outcome was that the poorer tenants did eventually take their place, which doubtless contributed to their bad reputation. They were perhaps unfairly criticized for unhealthiness and the strict management that might not have been entirely disagreeable to their original inhabitants. But although it was often overlooked, even the most utilitarian tenements provided several successive generations with a leap forward in their living conditions.[29]

In Scotland the case was different, for here as in most parts of Europe tenements were the indigenous tradition (and one that began to be revived towards the end of the twentieth century). All classes had lived in the cliff-like tenements of medieval Edinburgh, until the creation of the new Georgian town enabled the higher classes to decant themselves. As late as 1860, tenement living was given an accolade by a committee of skilled working men, to whom the Englishman's separate family house seemed 'a very selfish idea'.[30] In Glasgow there was a surge of tenement building for all classes in the later 1800s and, with the street level shops that they frequently had, they made up a major part of the city's fabric. Tenements here had imposing common stairwells, often colourfully tiled, which gave access to apartments of a range of sizes, some even grand enough to have had servants' accommodation. It was normal practice to provide box beds in all rooms, even the kitchen, and a 'single end' or one-room apartment was often tucked in between larger dwellings. To meet the huge influx of poor Irish, once grand tenement blocks were subdivided and extensions built on their 'backlands' or areas designed for drying greens. In an effort to keep down overcrowding, 'ticketing' was begun under a local Police Act in 1866: metal tickets were attached to buildings, showing the permitted number of residents, and midnight searches were made. Extensive slum clearance began at this time but, as in London, redevelopment was put in the hands of trusts, the city itself building only lodging houses until the 1880s. Higher standards for new tenements were brought in by an Act of 1892, which set limits to the number of apartments per stair and required internal water supply and WCs.

In spite of the notoriety of the slums, it was not until the interwar period, when Scottish authorities built suburban estates for their more affluent tenants, that tenements became specially identified with the lower working classes. Their use by a wide range of classes and their general acceptance before that time helps to explain Clydeside's momentous rent strikes of 1915 which made a lasting impact on the whole housing system, for these were as much a middle- as a working-class movement.

Precursors of Council Housing: Model Villages

The other model for council housing, the model village, should be distinguished from housing put up by many employers for their workers on the docks, railways, and so on, for utilitarian reasons. There was a long tradition of the creation of housing schemes for new industries, many of them in deeply rural areas – a tradition so strong, in fact, that it has been credited with contributing as much as 10 per cent of the Victorian housing stock overall.[31] As well as being much more comprehensive, the model villages were expressions of their founders' social and political ideals. They were not necessarily exclusive to their own employees, and many things besides homes were provided, for they set out to be microcosms of what in their founders' view was an ideal society. By convention, the series of model villages is taken to begin with New Lanark, built around a cotton spinning mill about 1785 by the father-in-law of Robert Owen. After marrying his master's daughter, Owen then used it for some years as the testbed for his own social theories; but in so far as its ideology derived from the Enlightenment and the French Revolution rather than Victorian evangelism, New Lanark belongs as much to the tradition of utopian communities as that of philanthropic capitalism. Its workers' housing consisted of one-room apartments in tenements that were perhaps its least innovative feature. Its great mills, co-operative store, nursery for pauper children, schools and grand community centre or 'New Institution for the Formation of Character' were the most outstanding things in this village embodying Owen's atheist faith in the perfectibility of human nature. Meeting setbacks, he soon turned his energy towards alternative communities and co-operation, as will be seen in the next chapter.

A series of Victorian model villages began in earnest in the 1850s, when Bromborough Village on the Wirral was begun for Price's Patent Candle Company, and others in the West Yorkshire textile region began with Saltaire. The first was credited with being the first garden village, whereas Saltaire was more like a small, high-density town. It intentionally lacked public houses and other noxious parts of real urban environments, but had an abundance of cultural amenities bestowed by the benevolent but all-powerful mill owner, Titus Salt. As in all model villages the main emphasis was on the houses, which here were built in a range of sizes for different ranks of workers, though all had their own water and gas supply and back yard with WC. A network of interlinked families built further settlements in the region, notably Akroydon in Halifax where several streets of houses in the 'Gothic' style were set round an impressive public green square. Its artisan residents were helped by its founder, the owner of the city's immense carpet factory, to buy their homes through special arrangements with the Halifax Permanent Building Society.

A generation later there was a fresh burst of model village building and there was even a shortlived Society for Promoting Industrial Villages whose chairman, in 1884, published *Industrial Villages: a remedy for crowded towns and deserted fields*. The Society's visions included well-built cottages with gardens, a 'green belt' with farms and allotments, playgrounds and sports fields, schools, co-operative stores and, if possible, libraries, art galleries and coffee houses – but not, again, any public houses. This tradition of model villages lasted well into the twentieth century. The Linotype estate at Broadheath and Vickers' Vickerstown at Barrow in Furness were started around 1900. Woodlands model mining village near Doncaster was designed in 1907 by the winner (Percy Houfton) of the Letchworth housing competition, to be mentioned again later. Sir James Reckitt, producer of 'Reckitts Blue' for whitening laundry and other indispensable household items, founded his Garden Village in Hull the following year. Between the wars, among others, the Bata shoe company built its East Tilbury estate, Bowaters' built Kemsley in Kent, Wedgewood Barlaston Hall, and the Crittall metal windows company the 'village' of Silver End in Essex.

Without any doubt the two seminal model villages were the late nineteenth-century foundations of the Lever soap and Cadbury cocoa magnates: Port Sunlight and Bournville respectively, with Rowntree's New Earswick following close behind. William Lever, the maker of Sunlight Soap and founder of what eventually became Unilever, bought the land for Port Sunlight in the Wirral in 1887 and created the village over the next 30 years. Dominated by its monumental works and embodying the 'Spirit of Soap', the village enjoyed the extremely low housing density of 5–8 houses per acre. But as at Saltaire, the houses themselves had small back yards, while the abundant open space was given to allotments and public parks. The open-plan, turfed front gardens – later copied in North American suburban development – were adopted here to prevent the early tenants converting individual front gardens into chicken runs.

The village of Bournville was begun by George Cadbury and his brother with the building of a factory and sixteen houses for key workers in 1879. The village proper was not started for another 16 years and in 1900 a Village Trust was founded, supposedly to guard against too much control by Cadbury. His first intention was to offer the houses for sale, with a 50 per cent deposit and 15-year repayment period. They were not built for the poor, therefore, but for 'a superior class of quiet and respectable tenant',[32] not necessarily Cadbury employees, who in fact constituted less than half. But as early purchasers bought houses only for speculation, Cadbury later decided to lease them. Much of the development was done by housing societies operating under the then new Industrial and Provident Societies Act of 1893, and the first was Bournville Tenants, a workers' housing co-operative founded in 1906.

Bournville looks more modern than Port Sunlight, largely because of the importance given to the private domestic garden. Its overall housing densities were in fact slightly higher and there were other respects, such as its external WCs, in which it may not have been so trend-setting as the other village. It also had generous public open spaces, including works recreation grounds, a village green and allotments, but the main emphasis was on domestic gardens. Taking up three-quarters of the house plot, the long back garden was designed both for recreation and production. It was planted by the Company, who undertook to prune its fruit trees for the first 3 years. Tenants had access to advice, lectures and competitions, and Cadbury did detailed calculations of the value to families, in money as well as health, of the produce they could grow. The houses were semi-detached or in short terraces, set in leafy streets, and so much thought was given to appearance that even how the estate would be seen by passengers in passing trains was taken into account.

New Earswick, the creation in 1904 of another Quaker cocoa magnate, Joseph Rowntree, owed much to Bournville. Here also houses had front and back gardens, and there were leafy streets, a school, shops, community centre and sites for churches. In a deliberate break with paternalism, New Earswick was developed and managed by a trust and there was a village council that perhaps had a wider remit than its counterpart at Bournville. Rowntree had intended that tenants should eventually buy their homes, and he hoped to create a balanced community. An attempt at really low rent accommodation was unsuccessful but tenancies were allocated on a proportionate basis to certain categories: sons and daughters of existing tenants to provide continuity; teachers, doctors and other professionals of obvious value to the community; and people in genuine housing need. Some of Octavia Hill's trainees were used as housing managers.

All three villages made a significant impact on housing policy and also town planning, and the hope of all their founders that they would set a trend was largely realized. They were constantly visited and were hosts to new ideas, in particular that of the garden city. Lever helped to establish the profession and academic discipline of town planning and endowed its first university chair at Liverpool. Cadbury and Rowntree, with his son Seebohm Rowntree, were leaders of housing research and theory through the first third of the twentieth century, and Bournville Village Trust's publication, *When We Build Again*, was one of the seminal texts of postwar reconstruction in the 1940s. But it was Seebohm Rowntree who played the most crucial role in the opening years of the century, both as personal adviser to Lloyd George, the Director of Welfare in his Ministry of Munitions, and member of his 1917 Reconstruction Committee. Rowntree's vision was for municipalities to own or lease land, or themselves develop belts of new villages. More than either Port Sunlight or Bournville, which devolved into individual ownership at a fairly early stage, New Earswick remained a testing ground for new ideas in housing, and the Rowntree Foundation in time became the leading funder and initiator of British housing and social research.

At the heart of the model village was the cult of family and home, within a heavily paternalistic environment. All Bournville tenants were presented with Mrs Cadbury's *Rules of Health*, and advised not to use double beds, sleep with their mouths open, or leave tealeaves to stew in the pot. Next to the home and garden, there was emphasis on the benefits of beauty in landscape, fine art and adult education. Bournville had its Ruskin Hall, and Port Sunlight its art gallery closing the vista of its formal central park, and dedicated to the memory of Lady Lever. The other essential element of the model village was a concept of 'community', closely tied to the idea of the village. This in turn rested on an invocation of history that, however spurious, was a goad to action. Its physical expression was an imitation of the medieval: houses with exposed timber frames, tile-hung walls and diamond-paned casements. The villages imitated or even reconstructed historical buildings. The little shelter in the middle of Bournville village green was a copy of the Dunster buttercross, and Rowntree's gift to his village was a 'folk hall'. The 'village green' was a ubiquitous motif and revived rural customs a staple of community life – May Day, in particular, which was one of the chief concerns of the Bournville village council.

The villages were known worldwide as exemplars of good housing and planning practice. But what they were chiefly admired for was their appearance and design, while other aspects were relatively ignored, including innovations in industrial management. At the Rowntree works, for instance, women social workers were introduced in 1891, the eight-hour day in 1896, and a workers' pension scheme in 1905, with work councils, the five-day week and profit sharing following after the Great War. For the most part the model villages were admired as the single harmonious communities their founders wanted them to be, with no essential difference between employers' and employees' interests. The price paid was, of course, the acceptance of paternalism and elimination of deviance and militancy. We are told that when Lever toured his village it was, among other things, to confirm that any worker off sick had placed his boots in the window, as proof that he really was indoors and not truanting to the big city. For those who could tolerate this degree of control, the model village offered an unprecedented quality of environment and culture, and there is evidence that this was appreciated by many: 'The warmth and genuineness of operative responses to paternalistic overtures cannot be doubted.'[33] Those unable to do so, however, took themselves off to the sooty but free air of the chaotic urban environment for, as a trade unionist wrote to Lever in 1919, 'No man of an independent turn of mind can breathe for long the atmosphere of Port Sunlight. The profit-sharing system not only enslaves and degrades the workers, it tends to make them servile.'[34]

Steps towards Council Housing: Direct Building by Local Authorities

The model village was more compelling than the tenement as a pattern for council housing for various reasons. It lacked the unsavoury image of tenements, and it accorded with the suburban aspirations of the upwardly mobile, so appealing to those who were most idealistic about reforming working-class life. But at first tenements were the only realistic choice for central sites, because of their higher densities. In the new LCC, where a 'Progressive' alliance (of Liberals, Fabians and the Social Democratic Federation) took control in 1898, a Housing of the Working Classes Branch attracted a group of progressive young architects who designed two outstanding tenement schemes. The first, at Boundary Street in Poplar, was built 1893–1900 on the site of the notorious Old Nichol slum which had contained some 5700 people, nearly half of them in single rooms at densities close to three persons per room, and with a death rate more than twice that of London as a whole. It was replaced by upwards of a thousand tenements, the majority with two or three rooms, and all but a few with their own scullery and WC. Still striking about the estate is a certain architectural grandeur and urbanity. It contained shops, pre-existing schools and churches, a new laundry building and tree-lined 'boulevards' radiating from a central park with bandstand and promenades.

The second scheme, built at Millbank on a site released by demolition of a prison of that name between 1897 and 1903, was even more notable architecturally because of its picturesque 'arts and crafts' design. Smaller and

A tenement block on the Boundary Street estate built by the newly established London County Council, under the Housing of the Working Classes Act 1890. The site, known as The Nichol and the setting of Arthur Morrison's novel *A Child of the Jago* (1907), was a notorious slum 'represented' in 1889. A master plan for the new estate was approved in 1893. Of more than 1000 tenements, over half were self-contained with their own scullery and WC. Others shared these facilities or had their own WCs on common landings. The estate was envisaged as 'a picturesque urban village' and boasted its own laundry, shops and central park with parades and bandstand.

denser than Boundary Street, it also had a central garden and tree-lined streets. The cost of these estates, which were built without any subsidy other than that involved in the site acquisition, entailed rents that automatically excluded the really poor. A higher class of people moved in, therefore, and the larger apartments were let to middle rather than working-class families, including policemen, clergy and teachers. Even then, both voluntary removals and evictions for non-payment of rent were high.

The LCC continued actively to build tenements until 1914, although not always to such high architectural standards. On the Tabard estate in Southwark, building continued with little break through and beyond the Great War; but after 1918 'cottage' estates easily outnumbered tenements. The LCC had begun such estates as soon as it was permitted to build on land beyond its boundaries, and a series of large suburban estates was begun with Totterdown Fields in Tooting. They had high site densities and at first stuck to rigid street plans, but their houses had features of arts and crafts design and high standards, including front and back gardens, upstairs bathrooms and internal WCs – with the inevitable corollary of high rents. Those estates built shortly before the outbreak of war, Norbury and Old Oak in Hammersmith, although with lowered dwelling standards, began to show the influence of the garden city in their more picturesque road layouts.

The most revolutionary thing about these municipal cottage estates was their turning inside out, so to speak, of the time-honoured class geography of the city. The working classes had always been tied to the centre where their jobs were located, while only the more privileged could radiate outwards. These new estates, however, exploited the way that public transport enabled a section of working people to live in suburbs, or even beyond the edge of the city. Outside London, in so far as they built at all, other municipalities built tenements rather than cottages, though only on a small scale. Liverpool built its first working-class tenements as early as 1869, under the Shaftesbury Act, but its next scheme was the grand Victoria Buildings of 1885, which had an internal landscaped playground and street frontage shops. Sheffield and Leeds were among cities that built small, central schemes around the turn of the century. Others like Birmingham and Manchester adopted a compromise between tenements and cottages, in two- and three-storey apartment blocks. No other authorities at this time had London's incentive for suburban cottage estates, but Sheffield bought land at Wincobank for the 'Flowers' estate in 1900 and the competition for its design was won by Percy Houfton of Woodlands model mining village, mentioned above, who was later replaced by the second competition winner, the architect of Bournville.

In the years leading up to the First World War, a number of cities were becoming impatient to build cottage estates, but the policy instruments and finance were as yet lacking. Before they could materialize in any number, a new impetus was needed: some burst of ideological energy, to ensure that cottages rather than tenements became the standard working-class housing of the new century. The burst, when it came, was from four sources: the embryonic Liberal welfare state of the early 1900s and in particular its preparedness, as part of its Land Campaign, to introduce a programme of state housing in rural areas; the almost automatic application of the newly available garden city design ideology to such housing; and the curious transference of this to the new housing forced on the state by the exigency of an all-out war.

NOTES

1. Ashworth; Cherry (1972).
2. Ashworth, p. 65.
3. Brown, Kenneth, p. 114.
4. Tarn (1973).
5. Mearns, p. 2.
6. Mearns, p. 15.
7. Himmelfarb, p. 66.
8. Wohl, p. 242.
9. Simey.
10. Mowat, p. 124.
11. Cole and Furbey, p. 50.
12. Wohl, p. 320.
13. Wohl, p. 319.
14. Himmelfarb.
15. Thompson, F.M.L., p. 353.
16. Booth, Charles (1903), p. 164.
17. Birchall.
18. Englander, p. xvii.
19. Englander.
20. Hill, Octavia, pp. 102–103.
21. Royal Commission (1884–85), para 8939.
22. Royal Commission (1884–85), para 8967.
23. Royal Commission (1884–85), para 9170ff; Hill, Octavia, p. 186.
24. Denford, p. 32.
25. Tarn (1973), p. 100.
26. Webb, p. 134.
27. Darley.
28. Booth, Charles (1902), III, pp. 31–32.
29. White, Jerry.
30. Horsey, p. 21
31. Joyce.
32. Durman & Harrison, p. 3.
33. Joyce, p. 149.
34. Creese, p. 103.

Chapter Four

The Utopian Roots of Council Housing

'The choice is no longer between Utopia and the pleasant ordered world that our fathers knew. The choice is between Utopia and Hell' (William Beveridge).

W.H.G. Armytage, *Heavens Below*, 1961

Utopianism and Communities

The two men who firmly put council housing in the mould of the garden city were Ebenezer Howard (1850–1928) and Raymond Unwin (1863–1940). Although he was the originator of the garden city idea and movement, Howard's influence was more on town planning than housing. Unwin was the master planner of the first garden city at Letchworth in Hertfordshire, and also of Rowntree's New Earswick, Henrietta Barnett's Hampstead Garden Suburb, and some of the wartime state settlements. He was strongly influenced by the Arts & Crafts movement, a blend of aesthetics and social theory, to be described below. The cultural background of both men was radical, and though they were undoubtedly impressed by the model villages their own contributions came more from a tradition of utopianism and communitarianism than from upper-class benevolence and reform. One of the qualities of utopianism is that through its intensity of feeling, it is able to retain its hold over people's imaginations in the face of glaring practical failures or, more insidiously, fatal compromises. This proved to be part of its legacy to council housing, whose protagonists often seemed blind to the degree of compromise and loss of idealism that were required of them.

Besides changes in ideas about poverty and the relative responsibilities of individual and state, the decade of the 1880s brought a ferment of ideas in religion, spiritual experience, concepts of community, land reform, and visions of society. In the words of the social visionary, Edward Carpenter, 'the

Socialist and Anarchist propaganda, the huge trade union growth, the Theosophical movement, the new currents in the Theatrical and Artistic world, the torrent even of Change in the Religious world, promised much.'[1] Today's clearly marked boundaries between the secular, religious and artistic worlds did not then apply: the term 'socialism', for instance, was given to a wide range of social initiatives and programmes that appealed, variously, to conservatives and progressives, religious believers and sceptics. Thus Toynbee Hall's founders called their book of 1888 *Practicable Socialism*,[2] and Charles Booth, whose survey was both criticized and praised as socialist, did not scruple to own a debt to Owenism and Chartism.[3] F.D. Maurice, the charismatic figurehead of the Christian Socialists, one of many Unitarians active in social affairs (though he later joined the Church of England), inspired many in different fields of endeavour. An illustration of the numerous personal and ideological links and overlaps is provided by Octavia Hill, with her Unitarian grandfather and Owenite father, herself strongly influenced by Christian Socialism. She taught at Maurice's Working Men's College and was linked to the new currents in aesthetics not only through her patron, Ruskin, but through acquaintance with William Morris and C.R. Ashbee. She was also on familiar terms with the Barnetts, although disagreeing with many of their tenets.

The roots of Howard's and Unwin's radicalism lay in utopian socialism and communitarianism, which made it democratic rather than paternalistic, anarchist rather than authoritarian; and its anarchism was strongly related to spirituality and self-realization. A spiritual strand was of course strong in all evangelistic social reform, but there were now new influences coming in from the American Transcendentalism of Ralph Waldo Emerson and Henry Thoreau (whose account of his sojourn by Lake Walden was published in 1854) and from Eastern mysticism as distilled by the Theosophical Society. Co-founded by Helena Blavatsky in 1875, this sought to distil the 'Universal Divine Principle' of all the world religions, whose teaching was also 'socialism of the noblest and highest type.'[4] Theosophy did not directly lead to new communities, although many communitarians were Theosophists and Anthroposophy, which seceded from it in 1913, gave rise to the Camphill Villages, the largest and most stable network of new communities after 1950.

Both secular and spiritual movements led to the foundation of new, small and self-sufficient communities established as alternatives to centralized industrial society. Their emphasis was on individual as well as social regeneration, expressed in all aspects of life including food, dress, livelihood, gender relations and, of course, homes and settlements. The early seedbed of utopian (as distinct from 'scientific' or Marxist) socialism was the peculiar phenomenon of 'Owenism' which arose from the long career of Robert Owen. In his brief time at New Lanark, the huge profits from cotton manufacture that paid for his experiment appear to have given him an indelible belief that there was a vast, untapped economic surplus, waiting only to be put to use by an enlightened leader. Generalizing from his model settlement, he put forward 'Mr Owen's Plan', a proposal for purpose-built colonies for paupers. When this failed to get the backing of the British government, he set out for America where be bought himself another proving ground, the former colony of a religious sect at New Harmony. Here his next social experiment could proceed unhampered by the burden of pauperism or the factory system; but the re-founded community soon became a financial disaster, which resulted amongst other things in the enforced disposal of New Lanark.

On his return to Britain, however, Owen found himself the prophet and leader of an unwieldy social movement. Though no friend of democracy, and in spite of atheistic and heretical views (for instance on marriage) that might be expected to alienate all 'respectable' people, Owen seems to have reappeared at a crucial moment in working-class evolution, when a new class consciousness was emerging. Owenism or Owenite socialism first found expression through a wide and loose co-operative movement that as well as the trading of goods involved self-improvement through education and science, production, and labour and produce exchanges. None of these were to be regarded as ends in themselves but only as they would lead to a new social framework of Owenite 'villages of co-operation'.

There was a great burst in the formation of co-operative societies in the 1820s and later a similar growth of trade unions or 'guilds', again with a wider remit than the term now implies, for through them a whole new society was to be created and Owen's 'Grand National Moral Union of the Useful and Productive Classes of the United Kingdom' was to have land colonies and its own parliament. Undaunted by the government's attempt to break it, Owen proceeded to create further 'universal' unions based on industry, knowledge and 'rational religion'. One of the outcomes was the 'Halls of Science and Home Colonisation Society' of 1840, and Owen himself became governor of one of its handful of communities, at Queenswood in Hampshire, which had emblazoned on its Harmony Hall the letters 'C M', to mark the commencement of the millennium. (The over-grand hall proved to be financially crippling and the community came to an end 6 years later.)

While his interventions in the projects he inspired were almost invariably disastrous, the charismatic Mr Owen never quite lost his following, presumably because he embodied things of fundamental importance to radicals and activists of the time. They included a belief in the power of moral example to effect social change, and in an essential community of interest between classes – hence the possibility of peaceful rather than violent social revolution. Important for its eventual bearing on housing was his fixed faith in the ideal community as the building block of a new society. As he confessed, 'the mission of my life appears to be to prepare the population of the world to understand the vast importance of the second creation of humanity . . . by creating entirely new surroundings', so that eventually, 'a new human nature would appear to arise from the new surroundings.'[5] In this respect Owen was at one with the later founders of model villages; but what distinguishes his career is its progression from colonies for paupers and social misfits to the ideal community of self-selected members who, in the nature of things, would be amongst the most educated and enlightened of society.

Something of the same juxtaposition of material improvement and abstract idealism would reappear in council housing when it used the form of the garden city to remedy problems of poverty.

Chartism was the other secular movement concerned with new communities, having as its ultimate aim the re-settlement of the working population on the land. Under the leadership of Feargus O'Connor, and at a time when Chartism's political force was already waning, five villages were founded, with 2–4 acre plots whose settlers were chosen by lot. Almost immediately, the villages ran into legal and financial difficulties, and they were closed down by Parliament in 1851. The practical outcomes of Owenite and other communities, with others not mentioned here, were small. They generally lasted no more than a year or two and were constantly plagued by threats of bankruptcy, internal quarrels, members' inexperience (whether of organization or getting a living from the land) and by hugely over-ambitious plans stemming from the charismatic style of their leadership. Their lasting influence was, however, in the realm of ideas. While clearly they did not come remotely near creating a new society, they helped to expand the limits of the existing one.

Land Reform

Implicit in the Chartist and other communities was the idea of a Golden Age, when the land had belonged to all people in common. The belief that it had been taken by theft by the Norman invaders after 1066 can be traced through various medieval peasant movements, the writings of Sir Thomas More (the coiner of the term 'utopia') and the Puritan revolution. It took new strength in the industrial revolution, through the idealization of a rural past, as seen in the hugely popular writings of Oliver Goldsmith and Robert Burns, and again in the polemics of William Cobbett, 'the Poor Man's Friend', who straddled extreme conservatism and utopianism. In the early 1800s Cobbett extolled 'the Cottage Economy of Old England' with its roast beef and abundant home brew, and at the opposite end of the century, and of the political spectrum, the same populist intensity is found in Robert Blatchford's *Merrie England* (1895), which similarly inveighed against the factory system and industrial economy. Blatchford's socialist weekly, *The Clarion*, reached huge numbers of homes, both of the working and rising middle classes, its jingoistic appeals to 'the nation' feeding on a yearning for recognition of the common people, and assurance that their long oppression could be brought to a peaceful end. Indeed, this nostalgia for an imagined rural past continued to be powerful through the twentieth century, where it is met again, for instance, in J.B. Priestley's *English Journey* (1934) and became much of the stuff of Second World War official propaganda. Overall, its importance for British culture, and specifically for the design and marketing of homes and estates, can hardly be overestimated: it provided the iconography of the model villages and speculative suburbs, and in due course of council housing also.

Blatchford called for the nationalization of land, as well as the means of production, which he saw as the prerequisite of 'practical' or back-to-the-land socialism. The question of land, its cost and ownership, was playing an increasingly important part in Liberal politics. J.S. Mill and others founded the Land Tenure Reform Association in the 1870s. It included the eminent naturalist Alfred Russell Wallace, who wanted to extinguish private land ownership and called for the nationalization of both land and houses. In 1881, Wallace founded the Land Nationalisation Society, to further a programme that involved labour colonies for the unemployed.

Liberal thinking about land absorbed the doctrine of the 'single land tax' expounded by the American Henry George in his *Progress and Poverty* of 1879, which acquired a large following in Britain. The proposal, which clearly owed much to George's observation of the immense profits made from speculation in the abundant wilderness territories of America, was for a levy on the unearned 'increment' or rise in price of land that resulted from development and urbanization. Such a tax, he argued, would render all other taxes unnecessary, so making it possible to eradicate poverty. It was a seductively simple idea, with obvious appeal to any who wanted to re-shape society without recourse to revolution, particularly those who wanted to shape a new society by means of ideal settlements that could be planted on land that was somehow immune from market forces.

It was the Liberal view that rises in land values went untaxed, while those who had created the value – both capital and labour – were disproportionately taxed through urban property taxes or rates, which were rising steeply at this time, partly because of the growth of local authority services. A tax on the increase in value or 'betterment' of land when it changed hands might partially or wholly replace rates, which could in itself be sufficient to dispose of the housing problem, by bringing down the cost of new building. Land reform was taken up by the London Liberals in the early 1890s, and a land valuation tax became increasingly accepted as part of the Party's programme, with broad support from the trade unions and co-operative societies. Lloyd George's 'People's Budget' of 1909 imposed a 20 per cent tax on profits of the sale of land (the 'unearned increment') and a tiny tax on the value of undeveloped land, while the 1909 Housing and Town Planning Act imposed a levy of 50 per cent on any rises in value attributable to local authority planning schemes. These at first had little practical effect on housing, but the report done by Seebohm Rowntree for Lloyd George's Land Enquiry Committee was the prelude to a Housing Act of 1914, the purpose of which was to enable better-off agricultural workers to escape the tyranny of tied cottages and live on smallholdings with garden-city style houses.

Utopian Communities of the Late Nineteenth Century

There was a burst of community building towards the end of the nineteenth century, channelling the energies of land reform, co-operation, pursuit of the simple life, and social or spiritual self-realization. One of the formative influences was the aesthetic-cum-social critique of industrial society that had sprung from the architect Augustus Pugin the Younger (1812–52), a designer and decorator of churches in the gothic revival style and a propagandist for the principle of 'Gothic'. For him, this went far beyond mere style, for he argued that its essence of functionality and integrity of design made it socially relevant. This was demonstrated in his *Contrasts* of 1836, which juxtaposed views of the unpolluted and beautiful pre-industrial city and the squalid, polluted and corrupt industrial city with architecture in the classical or 'pagan' style. Pugin maintained, as Ruskin and Morris would later do, that the medieval craftsman, as member of a guild, lived a life infinitely superior to that of his latter-day descendant, the factory hand, who had been stripped of all autonomy and pride in his work. The Battle of the Styles – a fight to the death, as it were, of Gothic and Classical – occupied the history of architecture through much of the nineteenth century, and it has to be understood as a battle of social and moral, as much as aesthetic, import.

Following this, the torch for Gothic was taken up by John Ruskin, although he personally was hostile to Pugin, among other things because of his Catholicism. Ruskin's chapter on 'The Nature of Gothic', in his *Stones of Venice* of 1851–53, which came to have almost canonic status, linked aesthetic theory and social action. It was used as the manifesto of Maurice's Working Men's College, and was similarly adopted by William Morris as the credo of his design company. This Ruskinian 'socialism' however was as ambiguous as Owenism had been. Ruskin himself never owned it: he was self-avowedly anti-democratic, an aesthete and elitist, whose mission was to reverse the evils of industrial society and to bring all that was best of art, science and past civilizations to working people. In the utopian tradition, he undertook at his own expense many idealistic social experiments, over and above the purchase of slum property for Octavia Hill to manage. With his endless flow of inspirational writings and 'addresses' to working people, these made him into a figurehead and catalyst for working-class self-improvement – besides the renowned Ruskin College at Oxford, the working person's university which was to educate many eminent politicians and legislators, Ruskin's work gave rise to countless 'Ruskin Halls' and other eponymous projects.

One of his experiments was the St George's Guild, founded in 1871 and intended to expand into a quasi-religious network of agricultural and craft villages on improved or reclaimed land that was worked without the aid of the machinery that he abhorred. Each village was to contribute a tithe to a national fund for more land purchase, and to finance such things as a lending library of literary classics for members. Only one guild settlement, at Totley near Sheffield, lasted any length of time, and this was supported by other projects in Sheffield, a city Ruskin admired because of its craft metalworking tradition. A tiny St George's museum was established in the district of Walkley, later to become the city's Ruskin museum, library and gallery. The founder poured objects of art and science into the collection and provided photographic prints to enable working people to savour the heights of European culture in their own homes.

One of Totley's close observers was Edward Carpenter (1845–1929) who lived at Millthorpe and inspired the nearby colony of Norton Hall. Once curate to F.D. Maurice, Carpenter was also a disciple of Walt Whitman, and in the early 1880s he discovered the sacred Indian *Bhagavat Gita*, which influenced his own *Towards Democracy* of 1883. He and the Norton Hall colony (one of whose founders was the originator of Mapleton vegetarian foods) sold produce and sandals in Sheffield market. Like Owen and Ruskin before him, Carpenter's influence was difficult to define and strongly individual, but pervasive. His main emphasis was on the simple life, with a mystical attachment to nature and a mission to challenge conventional views of masculinity and femininity; but he also came within the ambit of socialism and anarchism through an affiliation to the Tolstoyan Fellowship of the New Life, founded in 1883, which among other things invited the Russian anarchist, Prince Kropotkin, to speak in Sheffield on his gospel of mutual aid and co-operation.

There was now an active interchange of English and Russians, many of whom sought asylum in Britain, and a growing connection between Count Tolstoy and English anarchist communities. A Tolstoyan, J.C. Kenworthy, with the social mystic J. Bruce Wallace, founded the Brotherhood Church in 1891 and the Brotherhood Trust 3 years later. The Trust was a co-operative producer and trading venture whose profits were to be used for land purchase, with the ultimate aim of replacing capitalist society by a co-operative commonwealth. Through its organ *The New Order*, it actively promoted new communities, and five Tolstoyan ones were founded, the longest surviving of which was Whiteway in Gloucestershire, whose members were building its community hall in 1925.[6] Bruce Wallace eventually went to live in Letchworth Garden City, where he attracted a lively group of Tolstoyans and others, who looked on this new venture as a promising social experiment. The Trust eventually merged with the London Co-operative Society in 1920, while the Church remained both Christian and Marxist, one of its contributions to history being to host the Fifth Congress of the Russian Social Democratic Party which was attended by Lenin, Stalin and Gorki.

The common factors of the utopian communities were their commitment, in varying degrees, to common ownership, their mingling of manual and intellectual work where printing, publishing and schooling were often important, and some inclination towards self-sufficiency. Almost all were rurally based, the only exceptions being two examples of 'industrial communism' in Leeds and Blackburn, which tried to capitalize on the growth industries of the time, bicycles and electrical repairs.[7] Overall, their major, if diffuse, contribution was to pioneer what the later twentieth century would call an 'alternative' lifestyle: non-acquisitive, pacifist, vegetarian, unconventional in dress and other behaviour. They inclined, if not towards feminism, then to new roles for women, with demonstrations of partnerships outside marriage, whether 'free union' or homosexual.

In the domestic sphere, communities naturally lent themselves to communal living arrangements, although they still usually treated domestic work as a female responsibility. Some were interested in labour saving and divisions of labour, but co-operative housekeeping – the sharing of conventional domestic arrangements, if not their outright abolition – followed a rather different path. Co-operative housekeeping was practised in American Owenite and other communities, where in the Owenite tradition, it depended on specially designed buildings or settlements, which set it rather apart from the practical opportunism of other communitarians. Towards the end of the century it was taken up, on one hand, by scientific reformers of the home and its domestic arrangements, and on another by feminists, of whom Charlotte Perkins Gilman was the most outstanding. Her ideas, which were to abolish housework rather than reform it, naturally appealed to those many members of the middle classes who had long been worried about the paucity or inadequacy of servants, as well as to socialists like Blatchford and 'scientific' social reformers like H.G.Wells, whose *Modern Utopia* of 1905 proposed 'kitchenless' houses. It was Wells who pressured Ebenezer Howard to bring co-operative housekeeping into his Garden City, and its benefits for single working women were seen at Hampstead Garden Suburb. Its momentum was sustained in the years leading up to the first World War, when the Fabian Women's Group founded a committee 'to reorganize domestic work' and Alice Melvin, the instigator of several housing schemes in London, headed a Society for the Promotion of Co-operative Housekeeping and Household Service.[8] It lasted long enough to prompt a small reference in that foundation document of council housing, the Tudor Walters Report; but by now it was quite far from utopian communities as a force to change society.

Few in number, for the most part small and shortlived, overwhelmed with practical difficulties and internal dissension, the Victorian and Edwardian communities were in no position to have much influence on policy-making. They were not absorbed into the mainstream ideologies and politics of the Labour movement and Marx and Engels, who scorned the Chartist experiments, continually criticized utopian socialism as a diversion from the class struggle. The founders of the Fabian Society, for their own but not dissimilar reasons, turned their backs on communitarianism by seceding from the Fellowship of the New Life soon after its formation. Fabian doctrine pinned its hopes on the development of an expert elite using a scientific approach to social reform within a strongly centralized state. Nor were the utopian communities of any interest to the emerging Labour Party, which in these years put its main effort into trade unionism. They did, rather surprisingly, find support in the pacifist George Lansbury, an idol of the working classes, whose radical 'Poplarism' was not supported by his Party although he became its Leader in 1931. Lansbury had earlier worked with an American manufacturer-philanthropist, Joseph Fels, on schemes to settle the unemployed on smallholdings, and he embodied that fusion of religion with socialism that is so strong in the utopian tradition.

The party that was naturally in sympathy with the communitarians was the Independent Labour Party, whose foundation in 1893 predated that of the Labour Party by some years. Though remaining small and restricted to certain localities, the ILP supplied much of the Labour movement's strong emotional appeal. To a large extent the heir of Christian Socialism, it was also influenced by the Labour Church, the foundation in 1891 of a former Unitarian minister who wanted to encourage a more working-class oriented socialism, on the principle that 'the Labour Movement is a religious movement.'[9] In the next few years so many churches and chapels affiliated to it that it was 'difficult at times to distinguish between their activities and those of the ILP, and between the political and the religious, for they were closely connected.'[10] With its endorsement of spiritual renewal and of evolutionary rather than revolutionary change, the ILP attracted many who would later become prominent, like the first Labour Prime Minister, J. Ramsay MacDonald, who had also passed through the Fellowship of the New Life.

The Realization of Utopia: Bellamy and Howard

The shifting boundaries of communitarianism, its strong emotional appeal and (for its protagonists) its apparently limitless potential could without difficulty be attached to the concern with land, the degradation of cities, and suggestions of building colonies for their poor. The extent to which a section of established and enlightened society was, so to speak, panting for a programme to put into operation is seen in the reception of the American Edward Bellamy's utopian story, *Looking Backward*, which made its British debut by instalments in the journal *Brotherhood* in 1889. It almost instantly gave rise to a nationwide network of Nationalist Clubs and the Labour Nationalisation Society was founded in 1892 to promote Bellamy's proposed 'national socialism', with a rapid growth of members that anticipated Howard's garden-city movement 10 years later. It influenced such people as Count Tolstoy and Madame Blavatsky and, in British intellectual circles, H.G. Wells and G.B. Shaw – though not, however, William Morris, whose anarchist utopia, *News from Nowhere*, was written by way of a riposte.

Bellamy's tale of a traveller to the future outlined a revolutionary social system, termed 'nationalism' rather than socialism, which had arisen from a spontaneous and peaceful revolt against monopolistic capitalism. It was organized on almost military lines by a centralized state run by enlightened and incorruptible bureaucrats, with a centrally planned economy that provided cradle-to-grave security for all its citizens. All, including women and children, were set to work in a national army of labour, and paid equally. From ages 25 to 45 they were allowed to choose their own occupations, and at 45 they began their retirement. The new society was 'a paradise for womankind' as it had no housework or domestic cooking. Families took their meals in private dining rooms in palatial public buildings – it may be noted that ladies were still required to withdraw after dinner, leaving the men to port and cigars.

One of those who came under the spell of the book was Ebenezer Howard, who helped arrange its English publication, although on his second reading he had reservations about its basic totalitarianism. Although it has become almost customary to portray Howard as the epitome of 'ordinary' man whose simple common sense allows him to triumph where others with more pretensions fail, he was in fact neither ordinary nor conventional, but rather, a product of the utopian and communitarian tradition, while spiritualism was a dominant force in his life. As a very young man he had gone to America, where he tried his hand at homesteading and failed. He stayed a while longer in Chicago, where he joined the following of Cora Richmond, a clairvoyant, 'prophet' and minister of the Spiritual Church. On his return to London in the 1870s, he became involved in the Zetetical Society (whose members at the time included G.B. Shaw and Sidney Webb) which sought 'to make spiritualism a new religion of liberation and science, as well as a force for social reform.'[11]

While in America, Howard could not fail to be impressed by the opportunities for community building in a country that as yet lacked frontiers and was 'almost embarrassingly rich in utopian ideas and utopian ventures.'[12] It was widely held there that the conditions of life in utopian communities were superior to those of normal urban or rural existence, for work was shared, there was more equality of men and women, less insecurity, and high levels of comfort, as well as intellectual stimulation. His American experience was perhaps crucial for the young Howard's confidence in his own ability to contribute to the current of ideas; for he was of lower middle-class origins, lacking university education and maintaining a foothold in the professions as a Hansard stenographer – albeit this had the benefit of exposing him to endless parliamentary debates. He was by bent a practical man and an aspiring inventor who, looking around, saw overcrowded towns and depopulating countryside equally in need of social, economic and moral renewal. He was convinced that this could best be brought about through individual and co-operative effort, without recourse to central government or party politics, given the fundamental requirement of land.

In 1893 Howard publicly launched an idea that had been in his mind for some time and which he had written up the previous year in a MS entitled 'Commonsense Socialism'. The occasion was a meeting called in support of a failing communitarian venture in Mexico, for which J. Bruce Wallace of the Brotherhood Trust had been seeking English recruits, and the outcome was a resolution to start a home colony with collective ownership of land. An abortive attempt to buy a suitable estate in Essex followed, while Howard spent several more years refining his ideas, which he eventually put into book form and published privately. *Tomorrow: a Peaceful Path to Real Reform*, appeared in 1898, to be re-issued with some revisions in 1902, under the new title of *Garden Cities of Tomorrow*.

The Garden City: Visionary and Real

This change in title might suggest a switch in emphasis, from the 'peaceful path' with its political inferences, to the physical product or settlement. The principle of peaceful revolution did however remain of crucial importance. In relation to political ideologies, Howard placed himself firmly between individualism and socialism – of either state or municipal variety. He saw some merit in both kinds, but thought them too polarized or too blind to certain aspects of human nature and societies to be sufficient. In contrast, his own proposals would, like the utopian communities, bring about a new social order through force of example, without disturbing vested interests; and this was because they would utilize the most important of all resources: human skill, labour, energy and industry.

In spite of its apparent practicality, Howard's book is infused with millenarianism. The quotations heading each chapter are drawn from Ruskin, Tolstoy and Goethe, among others. The new order, it claims, will bring about 'a new sense of freedom and joy'.[13] Liberated from the bad influences of existing cities, the new garden citizens will behave in an enlightened manner – as seen, for instance, in their response to a dishonest trader who 'if he charges prices which are too high, if he misrepresents the quality of his goods, if he does not treat his employees with proper consideration in regard to hours of labour, wages, or other matters, he will run a great risk of losing the good-will of his customers, and the people of the town will have a method of expressing their sentiments regarding him which will be extremely powerful; they will simply invite a new competitor to enter the field.'[14] To the end of his life, when the movement he had inspired was channelled into state-sponsored new towns, Howard stuck to his belief that further independent foundations such as he proposed would bring about radical social change through example and persuasion.

Howard evidently had limited experience of provincial cities, although as a child he had lived in a number of country towns, and his work was largely concerned with the reform and ultimate replacement of the metropolis, which he believed crippled its inhabitants physically and spiritually. This was a time of serious economic depression and depopulation in the countryside which, no less than the big city, needed renewal. His goal, therefore, was the creation of an entirely new society expressed in a new type of 'town-country' settlement, a 'Garden City' set in a rural estate, which would combine the best of existing metropolitan and rural life, while avoiding the negative aspects of both. How he evaluated the good and bad qualities of each is seen in his famous diagram of the 'Three Magnets' where 'town' and 'country' alike are unfavourably compared with 'town-country', which avoids all their defects. The idea makes no reference to the many other types and scales of settlement, such as small market towns or villages, and in this respect it was literally ideal, in that it depended on a proposition abstracted from reality rather than checked in detail against it.

As with many others, the key to peaceful revolution was in Howard's view the ownership of land, although he demurred from Henry George's forthright condemnation of landlords who, he thought, should not be expropriated since most people shared their values and would behave similarly if they could. What was needed was an alternative and better system that would draw people away from the bad old ways by force of example alone, and this is what the Garden City would provide. The first and essential step, therefore, was the purchase of all the land that would ever be needed, and this was possible because the eventual and optimum population size of 32,000 was already settled. This would require a thousand acres of urban area and five thousand of rural estate. The site could be purchased at farmland prices and held in trust for the community, yielding a fixed 4 per cent return for investors. As the garden city grew and values rose, there could not be any speculation in land but the rising rents and rates could be used to finance public works, as well as old age pensions and other benefits for its citizens. Though not very expansive on this point, Howard evidently anticipated that the population would be a social cross-section, including some from the slums who 'have always lived in the obscurity of a London court.'[15] His own next door neighbours in Letchworth were in fact a family from the slums of Hoxton.[16]

The garden city and its rural estate would be symbiotic. Farmers would find a ready market in the city, whose waste products would fertilize their land, so giving a high degree of local self-sufficiency. Besides providing produce, beauty and recreation, the countryside would accommodate such things as homes for the deaf and blind, orphans and convalescents, while the city would be serviced by the most up-to-date technology, including an electricity supply.

Once the new city reached its projected size, further growth would be accommodated in a 'Social City', consisting of a network of garden cities short distances apart. The original foundation would now become one of a ring of satellites around 'Central City', an entirely new settlement some three miles away across a green belt. Howard changed his ideas about this Central City: at first it was to arise under the strategic direction of the state, but later he suggested that it would evolve naturally. Little is said about it, other than that its population would rise to a ceiling of 58,000. As it became established, the superior attractions of the Social City would draw people from London, which would steadily depopulate. Rents there would fall, but this would have to be compensated by a corresponding rise in rates, which in turn would cause more people to leave. Eventually, the worst slum property would cease to have any market value at all and its owners, bowing to the inevitable, would simply let it go, thus making 'some restitution for the great injustice which they have so long committed.'[17] The way would then be clear for the reconstruction of the entire existing metropolis – an anticipation that, as the outcome of a small, independent experiment in community building, might be regarded as the ultimate demonstration of Howard's essential utopianism.

The government and administration of the garden city would owe nothing directly to the state, and since its trustees would automatically have the considerable powers of landowner, its administration could be arranged in the most ideal way. The council of management (open to both men and women) would be formed from the elected chairpersons and executive heads of the twenty-seven municipal departments, grouped under Public Control, Social Purposes and Engineering, but municipal activities would be comparatively restricted, as many undertakings would be carried out by other tiers, described as semi-municipal, pro-municipal, and co-operative or individualistic. Many undertakings, including house building, would be done by non-profit agencies, and many local decisions made by 'local option' or referendum – for instance, whether or not public houses should be allowed. As always with Howard, the emphasis is on tolerance, flexibility and maximum choice: no one should be prevented from doing anything provided that it was in a general sense for the public good.

The most serious defect in the programme, as it turned out, was that it did not specify the particular role of the trustees. In so far as Howard considered the matter at all, he assumed that they would have the good of the enterprise so much at heart that they would voluntarily resign their powers to the citizen body as soon as this was appropriate – and certainly once the development was completed, when their role would be finished. In the event, no Trust, as such, was created, but a joint stock company of the conventional kind, which was deaf to any appeal for transfer of power from itself to community. The directors of the first garden city, in fact, behaved as any company directors in making the interests of shareholders their first priority.

Once the book was published things moved forward amazingly quickly. A Garden City Association was founded in 1899 by a mixture of utopians and others, including members of the Brotherhood Trust and Land Nationalisation Society. Within a year there were over 300 members, among whom were LCC councillors and industrialists. A company, Pioneer Garden City Ltd, with Howard as director, was registered in 1902 and the following year a site in Hertfordshire was bought at Letchworth, where some 400 people already lived. Construction of the town, at first called simply Garden City, began at once, and Howard moved from London to take up residence there in 1906.

From the start he was sensitive to charges of utopianism, and he stressed the need for 'vigilance against intrusion by cranks and scoundrels'.[18] His determination to give respectability and credibility to the movement showed in his choice for the Association's chair of Ralph Neville, a distinguished barrister and former Liberal MP. Neville, who was a great believer in tenant co-ownership, of which there would be a large amount in Letchworth, introduced Howard to Cadbury and Lever, who agreed to join the Board. Thomas Adams as Secretary (later town manager) organized the first Garden City conference at Bournville in 1901, followed by another at Port Sunlight a year later. The two conferences firmly placed Howard's programme in the tradition of the model industrial village, with low-density cottage housing for its workers – indeed, at the first conference he declared that he saw his scheme as 'but a step beyond Bournville'.[19] The strategy evidently worked: G.B. Shaw, for instance, who with other Fabians had mocked Howard as just another utopian fantasist was won over by the realism of this conference.

Yet for all this rapid start and translation to respectability, Letchworth Garden City was slow to develop and only did so with many compromises. Howard had either overlooked or been grossly over-optimistic about the difficulty of raising the purchase money from investors, and he had not reckoned with the huge costs of roads, drainage and other infrastructure, which exceeded the cost of the land itself. It also took far longer than he had allowed to persuade industrialists to locate their businesses here. In 1906 the town's fortunes were boosted by the arrival of Dent the publishers and W.H. Smith the booksellers, and over the following years twenty-five factories were established. Letchworth attracted *avant garde* firms producing things that appealed to progressive intellectuals: Spirella corsets, Jaeger woollens, an arts-and-crafts weavery, a sandal maker from Carpenter's Millthorpe. It eventually proved to be an ideal location for light engineering, including automobile manufacture, and in the First World War an armaments factory was located there, inviting retribution in the form of a Zeppelin raid.

Because of the difficulty of attracting industrialists, the board of directors almost immediately abandoned Howard's radical proposal of leases with regular and frequent revaluations of rent, to capture any betterment for the town. These were changed to conventional leases at fixed rents, 99 years for residential and 999 years for commercial use. The one principle retained, however, was that the company kept the freehold, even though this was at the cost of Lever's resignation in 1904. As might be expected, the Board was more concerned with the town's economy than with the revival of the rural estate, although Adams tried to develop this through smallholdings and farms, with a research centre and plots for self-builders, in the spirit of Howard's intentions. Other than a co-operative society which sublet the land for a dozen cottages and ten acres of fruit, nothing came of this, and in the end Letchworth resembled other towns in having a surrounding countryside (formalized as 'green belt' after 1947) that was a commercially farmed frame for the town – in the words of one outspoken resident, it was 'an anaesthetised space defining the edge of the urban area.'[20]

In practice, then, the 'Garden City' was converted into a somewhat idealistic but at bottom conventional product of capitalist industry and development, 'a good place in which to live, even for the poor' but 'not a machine for real reform.'[21] Many of its earliest citizens were attracted out of ideological commitment, which gave it a special character that has lingered down to the present. It is difficult to know what Howard really thought about this actual garden city, as compared to the one of his vision. At the Bournville conference, where a variety of possible development agents had been canvassed, he had stoutly declared that 'he did not care who carried out his Garden City scheme.'[22] Undoubtedly his first preference would have been for co-operative development, but aside from the co-ownership housing societies the co-operative movement played disappointingly little part, the CWS even declining to take the option of opening a store in Letchworth. One of those most sympathetic to Howard's ideals was C.B. Purdom, who came as a young man in 1904 to work at Letchworth and was later invited to be Howard's biographer. In his book on the movement, Purdom gave Howard space to address the question, 'how far have the original garden city ideals been realised?' Howard answered, only to a small degree, and this largely because of 'the sordid task of raising money.'[23] Yet he never lost his faith in the power of example, to which end, in 1919, he arbitrarily put in a bid for land for his second garden city at Welwyn, also in Hertfordshire, although this happened to wreck the delicate negotiations of Purdom and others who were trying to coax the government to channel its postwar housing programme into a chain of workers' garden cities.

Howard moved to his second Garden City at Welwyn in 1921 and lived there until his death 7 years later. Loaded with honours, he devoted much of his last years to leading what had now become an international movement. But though deferring to and humouring him, the Letchworth directors had been careful to exclude him from any real managerial responsibility. They gave him a public relations role and paid him a small stipend, but kept him firmly away from potential investors. It remains an open question how far this was the consequence of Howard's incompetence as a town manager, and how far the result of his still radical and worryingly independent leanings.

NOTES

1. Carpenter, p. 245, quoted Buder, p. 34.
2. Barnett & Barnett.
3. Booth, Charles (1903).
4. Blavatsky, p. 79.
5. Hardy, pp. 23-24.
6. Hardy.
7. Hardy.
8. Dyhouse; Pearson.
9. Pelling, p. 135.
10. Pelling, p. 135.
11. Buder, p. 12.
12. Kumar, p. 137.
13. Howard, p. 151.
14. Howard, pp. 98–99.
15. Howard, p. 122.
16. Beevers.
17. Howard, p. 156.
18. Buder, p. 80.
19. Harrison, p. 6.
20. Steeley, p. 15.
21. Steeley, p. 16.
22. Harrison, p. 4.
23. Purdom, p. 291.

Chapter Five

The Artistic Inspiration of Council Housing

'What appears to us as the image of one section of society is actually fabricated by a quite different class.'
Daniel Miller, *Material Culture and Mass Consumption*, 1987

Arts and Crafts and the Garden City

The struggles to establish the first Garden City showed how much compromise was needed to put the idea into practice. It was 1913 before Letchworth paid a meagre 1 per cent dividend to investors, and another 10 years before the intended 5 per cent was paid. It took some 70 years to realize Howard's dream of surpluses which, as welfare was now a function of the state, were applied to sport and other amenities, including a museum of Letchworth history. A Trust of loyalists had meanwhile fought off a takeover by a property company, and when this was succeeded by a Heritage Foundation, Letchworth was at last – in 1995 – able to have resident trustees.

As a more realistic blueprint for social change than any of the communitarian experiments, the garden-city proposal was almost bound to be annexed into central policy-making. It never, of course, replaced London, whose capacity for renewal and growth had been underestimated by Howard, but its direct descendants were a series of state-sponsored new towns of the 1940s to 1970s. Its less well known legatee, however, was state-sponsored council housing, and here the contribution of the firm of Parker and Unwin, the master planners of Letchworth, was crucial. Howard, who could not have foreseen their appointment when he was writing his book, had only done a sketch plan of his ideal city. It lacked technical specifications, particularly in regard to its houses, but its circular form with a magnificent 'crystal palace' encircling the centre and public park came directly from utopian tradition.[1] When it came to the drafting of a plan for the actual city, a number of applications were invited from the more progressive practices of the day. The choice of Parker and Unwin was in many ways an obvious one, for they were emerging as leading authorities on reformed house design, particularly as applied to smaller and cheaper houses. Unwin had met Seebohm Rowntree at the Bournville Conference of 1901 and was invited by him to design New Earswick. Like Howard, the two partners (who were also brothers-in-law) spanned many of the strands of nineteenth-century utopianism, spiritual movements and social reform. Raymond Unwin (1863–1940) grew up in Oxford, where he met both Ruskin and William Morris. An engineer by training, he at first worked for a Derbyshire coal and iron company whose owner was also a poet and social visionary and he was a frequent visitor to Edward Carpenter's Millthorpe. As well as being active in Morris's Socialist League, Unwin belonged to the Fellowship of the New Life and the Labour Church, opening his Letchworth home to their meetings, and he was a trade union and ILP supporter. His eventual career, however, lay in promulgating town planning and developing public policy, while Barry Parker (1867–1947), who had trained under an arts-and-crafts architect-designer in London, remained in the role of architect and did more, at ground level, to translate their ideas into council housing. Both partners aspired to Edward Carpenter's 'simple life' with its unconventional standards of diet and dress. Unwin designed his family's clothing and household textiles, and wore the approved arts-and-crafts gear himself.

The distinctive ingredient that the Parker-Unwin practice brought to Letchworth and grafted onto Howard's vision, was the arts-and-crafts critique of industrial society which derived from the 'Gothic' school of aesthetics, as well as the social criticism of such as Cobbett, Carlyle and Blatchford. Its most immediate influence was the writer, poet and designer, William Morris (1834–96). Although he founded no communities, Morris expressed in his tales and verse, and above all in his *News from Nowhere* of 1890, a utopian vision of a future society that was strongly coloured by his admiration for an idealized, pre-industrial past. Morris spent the greater part of his working life amongst the Pre-Raphaelite Brotherhood and on his own prolific writings and design work, and it was not until the age of fifty that he became active in political movements. At first he subscribed to Liberalism; then, disillusioned, he moved steadily towards Marxism, first through Hyndman's Social Democratic Federation, and later through his own Socialist League. He built on Ruskin's message, but extended it almost to the point of reversing it; for while Ruskin believed social redemption would have to come through the re-creation of true art, for Morris, art was the expression rather than the determinant of society. Believing with Marx that the pre-ordained agent of revolution was the industrial working class, he held that this class must be educated before it could bring about a society where labour became dignified and its products beautiful.

Morris's main sphere of influence was the home, where his design work ran foul of the awkward fact that his ideal furnishings, carefully designed and crafted, were in effect accessible only to those with money. The same contradiction would always bedevil attempts to make design suitable for a democratic society, as was seen in the Art Workers' Guild (to which he was elected in 1888), or, between the wars, the Modern Movement in architecture and the Bauhaus school of design. Not only were craft products invariably more expensive than mass-produced ones, but most working people perversely preferred the latter, as symbols of status and wealth, whereas hand-produced objects reminded them of the poverty they were trying to escape. A further incongruity was the proposition that the people had to be educated into good taste before they were fit to spearhead social change. This had strongly authoritarian implications, for only after they had been taught how to live could they be trusted to make choices for themselves. There were some uncomfortable ambivalences here that were reminiscent of a confession made by Unwin in his early socialist years, that 'I walk about and alternately loathe the people and long to be one with them.'[2]

It was a principle with Morris that everything to do with the home, not only the building but all its contents, should be harmoniously designed according to his dictum of having 'nothing in your houses but that you do not know to be useful, or believe to be beautiful.'[3] In practice, this meant the rejection of the then fashionable and over-elaborate domestic style of furnishing, in favour of a quasi-medieval simplicity. This was seen in the various products of the Morris school of design: purpose-built, often bulky and virtually 'built-in' pieces of furniture such as dressers, settles and bookcases; the use of unadorned materials like exposed wood and brick; and uncluttered, open-plan interiors – everything, in fact, that was the antithesis of conventional, late-Victorian taste, and which appealed to the progressive intelligentsia of the day. The influence of such design is not yet exhausted, for it is seen in the vogue for stripped pine and Morris revival wallpapers and textiles.

Morris put his ideas into operation in his own home, the 'Red House' of 1860, designed by his friend and lifelong disciple, Philip Webb. Despite being and looking consciously 'medieval in spirit', this building is claimed as a prototype of functional, modern architecture, where the interior dictates an asymmetrical exterior. In the later years of the century there followed a series of large, individually designed houses in a new, informal 'Domestic Revival' style for wealthy clients, usually in rural settings, by such masters as C.A.F. Voysey, Edwin Lutyens and Reginald Blomfield (the last two of whom later reverted to classicism). Several of the architects concerned were involved with garden-city settlements, notably Lutyens, who was responsible for the church and chapel that dominated the centre of Hampstead Garden Suburb.

These domestic revival mansions had an incalculable influence on later and more humble housing for middle-class suburbans, not least on the ubiquitous speculative 'semi' of the 1930s. A crucial stage in this transition was provided by Richard Norman Shaw, a critic of Morris rather than an admirer (on the grounds that he catered for the rich), who was one of those who developed a hybrid style, part English, part Continental, which went by the name of 'Queen Anne'. In 1877 he was commissioned to design a complete new suburb at Bedford Park, the venture of a radical developer, which was intended to bring the business and artistic classes into neighbourly proximity. Both socially and architecturally, the estate proved remarkably successful, gaining wide publicity – among other things, it appeared as 'Saffron Park' in G.K. Chesterton's *The Man Who Was Thursday* (1908). Its main contribution to housing design was an innovative house plan that eliminated the basement, the normal working quarters of servants in larger urban houses, and brought the ground floor into a direct relationship with the back garden. Such houses, set on long, winding, tree-planted streets, were easily absorbed into the model village tradition, particularly at Bournville, the main part of which was designed by a youthful arts-and-crafts architect, W.A. Harvey.

Shaw took into his office a succession of rising young architects who later became distinguished arts-and-crafts designers. One was the mystic W.R. Lethaby, who worked for the LCC's Technical Education Board chaired by Sidney Webb, where he set up the Central School of Arts and Crafts, catering for men and women of all ages and conditions. Another assistant was C.R. Ashbee, a friend of Carpenter who in his student years had lived and taught at Toynbee Hall, where his 'Ruskin class' developed into a co-operative Guild of Handicrafts. He later led the Guild from the East End to Chipping Camden, where it briefly flourished, revitalizing the village with new cottages and a school, before failing as a business venture in 1907, although the Guild remained in being to 1919. Unlike Ruskin and Morris, Ashbee saw value in machine production in certain circumstances, and in his book of 1917, *Where the Great City Stands*, he went beyond the usual arts-and-crafts boundaries by advocating town planning to reform the 'purposeless' industrial city. His ideal city was self-governing and owned its own land and industries – to which end he advocated municipal housing.

The Special Contributions of Parker and Unwin

This, then, was the ideological background of the Parker-Unwin partnership. In the 1890s, while carrying out a series of commissions for middle-class homes, they had developed ideas for ideal working-class housing, including an 'urban quadrangle' of co-operative housing. They were joint authors of *The Art of Building a Home* (1901), a collection of essays, sketches and photographs, which expressed the Morrisonian belief that functionality should coincide with beauty. In 1902, Unwin's *Cottage Plans and Common Sense* was published as a Fabian pamphlet and contribution to the campaign against the slums, which in effect translated the Parker-Unwin design philosophy into a worker's cottage arranged 'as if no custom in connection with such buildings had ever grown up.'[4] They agreed with the principle that a functional interior should determine the exterior and insisted that living rooms should face the sun, as they so often failed to do in bye-law housing. This meant that the facades might be unconventional, lacking symmetry and perhaps with kitchen or even larder windows facing the street. The back projection common in so much bye-law housing was abolished in order to admit more sunlight and air, and this gave rise to a double-fronted plan.

Internal space was to be maximized – something they claimed was more important for smaller houses than larger ones – and this led to the elimination of entrance halls, passages, and the symbolic but (as Unwin believed) non-functional parlour. There was to be a single living room, as large as possible and ideally two storeys high, with stairs rising directly to an open gallery, and a huge ingle-nook chimney recess. (Such two-storey living spaces were revived by le Corbusier in the 1920s, when they seemed daringly modern.) This redesigned living room could then be an 'almost enchanted space where family members might experience a constant lift of spirits';[5] and its uncarpeted floor and Quakerly simplicity of furnishings would, for Unwin, leave 'time to think and money with which to educate our children to think also.'[6] Behind the rationale of economy and functionality, there were of course both social and design aspirations that were deeply romantic, and these were expressed in stylistic features such as the plunging roof lines, gables and casement windows, and tree-lined, winding streets.

The first opportunity to put these ideas into practice on a settlement scale was at New Earswick, a virgin site on the edge of York. His houses and those of Parker, who added many more built as council houses with government subsidy after 1919, were in short terraces, culs de sac or bays set back from the road. The plan reserved sites for shops and public buildings, one of which was a 'Folk Hall' looking something like a medieval tithe barn. On winning the commission to design Letchworth, the partners set up office and also homes there. While New Earswick was never intended to be other than a 'village', the master plan for Letchworth was clearly premised on the assumption that it would have a civic centre, on the axis of a long, straight 'boulevard' with main roads radiating from it. The plan has been described as a sensitive attempt to apply Howard's ideal conception to the features of this particular site. As it was, there was no capital with which to develop a town centre. A shopping parade was developed by private enterprise, but the centre itself remained undeveloped, in spite of Unwin's call for a 'Letchworth 1914' project to commemorate the first 10 years. Marked out 'temporarily' by a line of poplars, its plots were sporadically filled by municipal and educational buildings over many years. On the same axis and north of the railway, Unwin's plan for a further civic space was effectively sabotaged when the company directors chose to site the Cheap Cottages Exhibition there, and after this was cleared away the site was dominated by 'Castle Corset', the Spirella factory. As a result the town had a permanent divide between north and south of the tracks: industrial areas with workers' housing and middle-class residential areas. At the same time Howard's hoped-for girdle of dispersed, clean industries powered with electricity never materialized but instead factories were clustered in the conventional way. Letchworth, then, was not so much an integrated city as 'a patchwork of small planned sites without a broad control.'[7]

The partnership's main contribution to the town was in housing. As well as private commissions, they designed schemes for the co-partnership societies that did much of the development, again making extensive use of the cul de sac and 'greens' between the houses. It was their fixed principle to uphold standards even in the cheapest cottages – Unwin had once threatened to resign his engineering post over the issue of bathrooms in miners' houses – and it went sorely against the grain to cut corners to make rents low enough for the lowest paid workers. This brought them into conflict with the Company over their Cheap Cottages Exhibition, sponsored by *Country Gentleman* and *Spectator* magazines in 1905, although they had already produced cottages for less than the £150 set as the ceiling price in the competition. But they did not advocate the lower standards entailed, they were fearful that the very considerable public interest aroused by the exhibition would make people think of the Garden City as a place for cheap weekend retreats or second homes for middle-class Londoners.

Disenchanted with the directors on this and other counts, and leaving Parker in Letchworth, Unwin left for Henrietta Barnett's Hampstead Garden Suburb, where he was more free to create what 'an industrial town should be'.[8] For many years, Barnett had been taking deprived East Enders to Hampstead Heath for recreation or recuperation, and she was now working with others to safeguard the ground known as the heath extension from the speculative development that was likely to follow the opening of Golders Green tube station. Her idea was a settlement where homes for working people at the end of a twopenny tube fare from London would be subsidized by larger houses for the wealthy. Like other model village builders, she counted on ideal cottages, with their all-important gardens, to 'develop a sense of home life and an interest in nature', as 'the best security against the temptation of drink and gambling.'[9] In the event, the more affluent settlers had to be reassured that their working-class neighbours would not be too close, and the civilizing elements of tennis courts and bowling greens, which became such a regular feature of council estates after 1919, were for the poorer rather than the wealthier residents. It was the poor, in other words, who were given and to a degree held responsible for those patterns of living that reformers considered to be ideal.

As well as a range of classes, the Suburb was intended to accommodate deprived groups like widows, spinsters and the blind. This provided an opening, at last, to provide the quasi-collegiate residential quadrangle that Parker and Unwin had long wanted to build, its central space inspiring 'the spirit of co-operation' and leading to 'further association'.[10] Two quadrangles were built in the Suburb, neither for ordinary families: The Orchard, a scheme of flats for the elderly, and cloistered Waterlow Court, a scheme of fifty flats for genteel, professional, spinsters. The preferred layouts for the smaller family houses were as at New Earswick and Letchworth in culs de sac or round open greens. There was a strong economic argument for this because they permitted more houses per length of made-up road. At Hampstead, also, the cul de sac was the best way of utilizing a narrow shelf of land; and since, unlike Letchworth or New Earswick, this was a district governed by bye-laws, a private Act of Parliament had to be obtained to waive the usual road and footpath widths.

Though it was called a suburb, the ground plan of the settlement had the same odd juxtaposition as at Letchworth of residential informality and formal urbanity, with wide roads radiating from a central square. However Unwin's master plan was soon overlaid by other influences, particularly that of Edwin Lutyens who was appointed consulting architect shortly after Unwin's arrival. Lutyens, who was later to be the designer of imperial New Delhi, changed the intended centre to a massive Anglican church (a new St Jude's), a chapel, girls' school and institute which faced each other across an open and rather lifeless space. This was at odds with Unwin's picturesque vision of a 'perfect arts-and-crafts village'[11] largely modelled on the precepts of the Viennese architect-planner, Camillo Sitte, whom he had lately come to admire. The romantic, medievalizing quality he had intended survived only in the tall 'gateway' blocks of shops and flats at the Finchley Road entrance to the Suburb and the turreted 'great wall' that separated the houses of the wealthy from the Heath.

All the Parker-Unwin settlements had low overall densities of houses. At Letchworth, the range was from four to the acre in more expensive quarters to 8–12 on the working-class estates. These were far lower than Howard had indicated in his book and the precedents were, of course, Port Sunlight and Bournville with their philosophy of open space, enjoyment of nature, and gardening as necessary antidotes for the disease and immorality of urban life. In his pamphlet of 1912, *Nothing Gained by Overcrowding*, Unwin definitively established twelve-to-the-acre as the most economic standard to build to, demonstrating that better value for money was obtained by building houses with large gardens around open green spaces at ten or twelve to the acre, than the thirty or more that the speculative developer would normally attempt, because of the lengths of road frontage and road intersections that were eliminated. In reality, given the same price for land, the low-density houses were inevitably more expensive, and the logic only worked for cheap, greenfield sites; for in Parker's own words, 'Except where land is really expensive it will always be found that the length of road per house in a development has far more bearing on the finance of that development than has the cost of land per acre.'[12] As living outside built-up areas was taken to be the ideal, the logic was not questioned, and this had incalculable effects for early council housing which, it was accepted, should follow the rule of twelve to the acre, or eight in rural areas. It also adopted the Parker-Unwin layouts, which became a cliche of estate design in the interwar years, with the addition of large circles or 'circuses' with wide, radiating roads that were evidently derived from the masterplans of the garden-city settlements.

The Culture of Letchworth

A new and 'planted' settlement does not follow the normal pattern of evolutionary development. Unlike towns in history that grew up around some industry or service, a town that owes its origins to an ideological programme has to search for an economic *raison d'être*. The model industrial villages escaped this problem by being founded round an already established industry;

and so, perhaps, did Hampstead Garden Suburb, through its proximity and underground link to London; but the development of Letchworth was compromised by the need to find investment and industry. One outcome was that the poor, the unemployed or casually employed had no place there. The Cheap Cottages exhibition was an attempt to attract the whole social cross-section, and a hundred of the 121 cottages constructed for it remained in permanent use. At the time, however, the press unkindly remarked that they were more likely to become tasteful second homes for townspeople than genuine labourers' cottages[13] – so confirming Parker's and Unwin's worst misgivings. The town had no room for its own building workers, who had to find lodgings outside – in any case, so it was reported, they found nothing to interest them there: even the Skittles Inn, though used for union meetings, was depressingly 'dry'.

The upper working class was catered for by the largest developers of Letchworth, the co-partnership societies, which were able to build with cheap government loans under the 1893 Industrial and Provident Societies Act. As well as affordable homes, these societies provided educational opportunities for their members, and the Co-Partnership Tenants' Housing Council published a monthly magazine and organized classes and festivals. Among the middle classes, those who prided themselves on being cultured were critical of the working-class tenants who showed no sense of 'community', or found their sanitized surroundings boring. The Parker-Unwin design tenets were those of a middle-class intelligentsia who, one suspects, were not averse to a little discomfort for the sake of aesthetic principle. It is not difficult, for a period long before whole-house central heating, to imagine the discomforts of an open-plan living area from which stairs rose directly to the bedrooms. The 'respectable' working classes were in general unhappy with Unwin's attempts to eliminate the parlour, which had such symbolic importance for them[14] and some of the Letchworth residents were affronted by such 'simple life' details as plank doors with latches, which merely reminded them of poultry sheds. It appears that their notions of social progress were different from those bent on elevating their domestic standards.

Some sort of cultural consensus, however, seems to have resulted in a *Merrie England* culture of the kind already in place at Bedford Park and Bournville, with folk dancing, May Day ceremonies, medieval plays and 'that quintessentially high-minded middle-class pursuit, the masque'.[15] Letchworth became a 'kind of mecca' for 'cranks',[16] many of them commuters from London, who came to enjoy a climate sympathetic to their own pet causes, whether vegetarianism and health food, dress reform (typically smocks and sandals), or temperance, which was repeatedly confirmed by local referenda. Also prominent were Esperanto, which engaged Howard in his later years, theosophy, Christian Socialism, pacifism and probably, for the time, a fair degree of sexual equality. The garden citizen was easily spotted by his 'far-and-near spectacles, knickerbockers, and of course sandals . . . Over his fireplace – which is a hole in the wall lined with brick – is . . . a large photo of Madame Blavatsky, some charming old furniture, several Persian rugs,

&c.'[17]   The Company's directors had scant sympathy with such 'cranks', who gave the place a regrettable public image.

One of Letchworth's innovations was the implementation of two co-operative housekeeping schemes. Homesgarth, which was announced in 1906 and opened partially complete 5 years later, had a quadrangle of thiry-two apartments for professionals on 'meagre' incomes. The apartments had minimal cooking facilities and meals were expected to be taken in a central kitchen-dining block. Howard, after the failure of his second marriage, moved into it, leaving only to migrate to Welwyn Garden City. The communal facilities were soon progressively restricted and the apartments converted into conventional, self-contained flats. A second development, Meadow Way Green, was opened in 1916 and extended after the war. It was a scheme of cottages for single business women, with communal dining room and kitchen, and co-operative housekeeping arrangements where each tenant was responsible for housekeeping for a fortnight at a time. Later opened to men, it always had a long waiting list, and its founders, the Misses Pym and Dewe, contributed much to the cultural life of Letchworth into the Second World War period.

Disillusion seems to have set in early amongst some of the more idealistic Letchworth citizens. A union to watch over residents' interests was founded in 1905, and the board of trustees was suspected of sacking *The Letchworth Citizen*'s editor, an ILP-er, for campaigning for a minimum wage in the town's industries. Tenants on rent strike in 1915 who appealed to Howard for help found that he refused to intervene. Meanwhile some of the founder residents were leaving, or they later defected to Welwyn Garden City – among them the two, C.B. Purdom and Frederick Osborn, who would do the most to channel the garden-city idea into a programme for state-sponsored new towns.

It appears, then, that while the first garden city had lasting traces of its utopian roots, it was turned by compromise into something far closer to the model industrial village. The utopian community was in essence a spontaneous and autonomous creation, with seeds of a classless society; but the paternalistic model village imposed a supposedly ideal environment, a 'benefit' conferred by one class on another, with no fundamental change in the social structure. There were, however, some overlaps between the two, which help to elucidate the garden-city experiment and consequently its derivative, council housing. One such overlap is in the area of personalities and their motivation – for utopian communities, as shows clearly in the careers of Robert Owen and others, were not devoid of authoritarian leaders, and at the same time the model village movement attracted idealists. The ground common to both approaches was a sense of outrage at existing social conditions, with the energy to set about reform. Both, therefore, attracted religiously or morally inspired people. The critical difference was whether they saw reform as coming best from above, or through opting for a life of personal transformation.

Another critical though subtle difference was in attitudes towards the built environment, and the value vested in it. In either case the environment created was the physical embodiment of a set of beliefs, although in the utopian community this was often compromised by lack of resources and having to make do with whatever property was available. But while for the model village a healthy and ideal environment was the purpose of the exercise, for the utopian community the environment was not so much an end in itself as the expression of a new social order, where experiment in areas such as co-operation and gender relations could take place. It was easy, however, to take environmental for social change, rather than merely a mechanism of change. This is what seems to have happened in the case of Parker and Unwin, whose houses and low-density layouts became increasingly objects in themselves, an 'iconography' whose signature was 'winding streets with white gabled cottages and red roofs . . . a visual shorthand for a low-density and open form of housing development.'[18] In effect this reified the environment, making it synonymous with social change. Amongst other things it resulted in enhancing the professional role of the designer, while reducing the importance of non-material aspects, such as relationships between people.

This had not, of course, been in Howard's intentions, although it must be said that a proposition to change society through a new kind of city placed him in the camp of the philanthropists rather than the communitarians. He himself, as we have seen, was not a little ambivalent on this score, but to the end he kept his trust in the power of individual initiative to set fundamental social change in train. At the time, it was perhaps difficult to discern the blurring of the two approaches, or to appreciate the potential hazards this would involve. Widespread admiration for the Garden City and the enthusiasm of many of the early residents could be seen as confirmation of its social achievements and, as we shall see, it was assumed there would be a similar success when its design principles were applied to council housing. Here also, physical improvement was equated with social or cultural change, and only after some years did it become clear that to make design paramount opened the fatally widening gap between the 'ideal' environment and the lifestyles and values of those who inhabited it.

This is not, of course, to say, that the innovations of the Garden City did not in themselves change attitudes. Its reformed houses and layouts set standards for all later housing policy, below which no reformers were willing to go. This success did, however, mean that the Octavia Hill approach of gradualistic improvement of existing environments, concentrating on the intimate relationship between people and their homes, had no realistic chance of being absorbed into mainstream policy. Even to William Morris, whose anarchism might be supposed to make him think differently, it was outrageous that Hill 'actually allows herself to say that after all it is not so bad as one might think for a whole family to live in one room.'[19] This led him and generations of housing reformers after him to the conclusion that even tenements or flats were preferable to slums and overcrowding.

NOTES

1. 'Ward and Centre of Garden City' plan, Howard, p. 53.
2. Day, p. 161.
3. Morris, William, p. 108.
4. Unwin (1902), p. 2.
5. Meacham (1994), p. 86.
6. Unwin (1901) p. 23.
7. Jackson, Frank, p. 71.
8. Day, p. 176.
9. Meacham (1994), p. 97.
10. Beevers, p. 110.
11. Davey, p. 175.
12. Joseph Rowntree Village Trust, p. 19.
13. Miller.
14. Swenarton (1981).
15. Meacham (1994), p. 95.
16. Parliamentary Debates (1962), col. 315.
17. Swenarton (1989), p. 152.
18. Buder, pp. 102, 95.
19. Darley, p. 232.

Chapter Six

Garden City to Council Estate

'The significance of council housing for the social structure of Britain has been a topic of some controversy, with a disagreement between those who see it as being achieved by working-class pressure from below, and those who see it as being imposed from above in order to control and contain working-class threats to the established order of society.'

M.J. Daunton, *A Property-Owning Democracy?* 1987

Utopia Ltd.

The implementation of the Garden City at Letchworth made two significant contributions to policy: the concept of a planned, balanced and self-contained town, which influenced the development of town planning and eventually led to the series of state-funded new towns after 1945; and its small house types which provided the link between the model village and council housing from 1919. Lying somewhere between the two was the concept of the 'estate', which became an indispensable element of the new council housing. It is significant that 'estate' – both the word and the concept – appears in the December 1920 issue of the official journal *Housing*, which was circulated free to local authorities when they were beginning to implement the 1919 Housing Act.

The question how council housing might have developed without the precedent of the garden city is an interesting one. Sutcliffe suggests that there might have been more co-partnership housing, as many reformers wanted, or that co-operative societies, trade unions and public utility companies could have been involved in the provision of working-class housing, as in many European countries.[1] The co-partnership societies that played such a big role in the development of Bournville, Letchworth and Hampstead Garden Suburb, also played a vital part in the dissemination of garden-city style suburbs, which became popular with private house builders. The first Housing and Town Planning Act of 1909 gave councils powers to assist such

Dr and Mrs Salter's garden village estate, Bermondsey (London Docklands). Dr Alfred Salter, elected MP in 1922, and his wife Ada, in 1909 London's first woman councillor and later mayor of Bermondsey, devoted their lives to making its notorious slums beautiful and healthy. Their plans for a Bermondsey garden village with tree-lined streets could not get under way until the first Labour government and its Wheatley Housing Act of 1924, and the estate proper was held up till 1928. After 1930 the Salters reluctantly conceded the necessity of building council flats but the early garden village cottages, pictured here, were remembered and imitated by the Cherry Gardens Action Group in 1988, when it wrested control of riverside land from the London Docklands Development Corporation and designed its own ideal houses with the London Borough of Southwark.

societies, but in their measures for rural housing the Liberals envisaged housing development being done by public utility societies.

After the first World War, however, housing societies and trusts were not active developers, although they were recognized in successive housing acts and given access to preferential loans and other assistance. Part of the explanation must be that only a minority of them had ever built cottage estates, which were now the favoured mode of development; nor could they operate on the scale that now appeared to be necessary. But it was also the case that local authorities no longer required or encouraged their contributions, for with (at first) more than generous subsidies, strengthened powers of compulsory purchase of land, and general acceptance that they would be able to own their estates in perpetuity, authorities had every reason to assume that they were all but exclusively responsible for the provision of working-class housing .

There were also deeper underlying reasons for the role they now took in working-class housing, which were to do with the rise of town planning in the opening years of the century, when much publicity was given to the planned 'town extensions' of those European cities where sites of demolished ramparts were available for municipal development. More autonomous than their British counterparts, such cities were able to control the planned development of these areas. Germany, in particular, was regarded as outstanding – a lesson taken to heart when public opinion was shocked at the poor physical condition of Boer War recruits, which was blamed on unhealthy housing and environments, at a time when Germany was Britain's greatest military rival. An influential figure who tirelessly upheld the 'German example' was the Manchester industrialist and benefactor, T.C. Horsfall, an admirer of the Barnetts, William Morris and the Christian Socialists, who argued that Britain should imitate Germany by adopting municipal land purchase, cheap transport and preferential borrowing rates for working-class housing. This was taken further by J.S. Nettlefold of Birmingham, the first British city to set up a town planning committee, which sent a delegation to study German town extensions. Nettlefold, a brother-in-law and business partner of Joseph Chamberlain, was the coiner of the term 'town planning'. He was also the author of a resolution passed unanimously at the annual conference of the Garden City Association in 1907, that 'town planning may be described as the application of the Garden City idea to existing cities and their suburbs – the application of business principles to the solution of the Housing problem.'[2] The conference called for a new town planning Act to bring existing towns 'as near as possible to the Garden City ideal',[3] which would involve both municipal land ownership and their siting within an agricultural belt.

The Association itself was now moving towards advocacy of town planning in general, rather than a programme for more garden cities. It augmented its name to Garden City and Town Planning Association, and by 1913 its executive had dropped the creation of new garden cities from its agenda, so in effect pinning its hopes on planned suburbs. The National Housing Reform Council and the Association of Metropolitan Corporations, chaired by

Nettlefold, were vigorously lobbying for a town planning act. Nettlefold also took the chair of a new housing committee set up in Birmingham in 1901, and the city dominated by the Cadbury family with their outstanding village of Bournville became the first local authority to pass a resolution in favour of town planning and municipal land purchase.

Meanwhile Raymond Unwin was campaigning in all quarters for both planning and working-class housing, his influence bringing over the three environmental professions of architecture, civil engineering and surveying, and playing a leading role in the foundation of a professional Institute of Town Planning in 1914. At first, the majority of its members were architects, and Thomas Adams became its first president. Of all the many bodies, national and local, campaigning for municipal housing at this time, the great majority were happy to accept its association with town extensions, low-density suburbs, and town planning. Only the Workmen's National Housing Council (WNHC), founded in 1898 by Fred Knee, a Fabian and Social Democratic Federation member, regarded town planning as diversionary from the real housing problem, which should be addressed by more vigorous use of Part III of the 1890 Housing Act. However the President of the Local Government Board, John Burns, went along with majority progressive opinion and seemed happy to be the first to bracket housing with town planning in his Act of 1909. Burns, a self-educated engineer who had first entered Parliament as a Labour independent candidate, was an admirer of the model villages (especially Bournville), as well as Letchworth and Hampstead Garden Suburb. He made no distinction between the utopian, socialist and model village traditions and seemed happy to invoke Ruskin, Morris, and even Sir Christopher Wren in support of his new legislation, extolling the benefits of open space and low housing densities for the health and wellbeing of the working classes.

So without any perceived incongruity (unless by the WNHC), Burns's Housing and Town Planning Act coupled the 40-year-old corpus of housing law, rooted in public health, with the most up-to-date planning instruments available at the time. In practice, this meant permissive powers for local authorities to control new areas of development, with so much emphasis on roads that it was widely assumed that town planning was very much the province of the municipal engineer.[4] History has judged the Act to be weak and ineffective on both its heads, but its housing provisions had some potentially important clauses. These included the obligation on local authorities to adopt Part III of the 1890 Act (that is, to build council estates), and revoking their obligation to sell them after 10 years. For the first time, therefore, councils were legitimized as permanent landlords to the working classes. The only further ingredient that waited until 1919 to be added was a regular subsidy from central government.

The planning measures of the Act, on the other hand, were entirely discretionary. Both urban and rural districts could buy land through compulsory purchase, lay it out and service it, but they were still obliged to pay its full market value, with the additional 10 per cent 'solatium'. In view of this, and a lack of the necessary administrative structures, it is not surprising that only a handful of authorities got to the point of submitting schemes. Five of the thirteen English schemes submitted came from Birmingham, and only two received formal approval. They followed the garden-city precedent in having low housing densities, open green spaces, and sites for public buildings. Their considerable emphasis on reserving land for arterial road links from the new, planned settlements to pre-existing cities or conurbations implied that they would no longer so much replace these as merely fit more conveniently into them.

The Impact of War

Possibly the stalemate in the inception of a subsidy for housing would have lasted longer but for the advent of war in 1914. This immediately caused large movements of population, not only for military but for industrial purposes. It was imperative for munitions and other industrial workers to be moved around the country, and they needed accommodation wherever they were sent. Wages rose as the economy was geared to war production, and the social system was disrupted. There were to be some significant working-class gains – for instance, soldiers' wives got cash payments they had never received before – but the class structure did not so much disintegrate as, in the words of one historian, become 'compressed'.[5]

Other than war purposes, virtually no new building, maintenance or repairs were carried out; building costs doubled in the 4 years of war, and the labour force was dispersed. Inflation and general shortages meant that rents began to rise, both from profiteering and from landlords' attempts to recover their own rising costs. In time of war, rent strikes were a far more serious matter than in peace: not only did they disrupt the housing system but they could be symptoms of a wider civil unrest. The situation was particularly serious in Scotland, where rents had already been pushed up by the House Letting and Renting Act of 1911, and there was an emotive issue of serving men's wives or widows, who were put at risk of eviction if they were unable to pay raised rents. On 'Red Clydeside', already under suspicion for being opposed to the war, the government was nervous that a link might be made with shipyard strikers, and so lead to a general strike. Rent strikers here included in their number members of the respectable working classes, and there was evidence that their organization 'rested largely in the hands of local labour groups'.[6] In fact, the detailed history of tenant protest from long before this time makes the government's fears seem unwarranted: the strikes were more likely to be merely 'the culmination of the pre-war struggle between landlord and tenant';[7] but the participants seem to have traded on government fears and used the situation to press for council housing. Their posters carried such messages as: 'Defence of the realm: government must protect our homes from Germans and landlords, or the People will protect themselves'; and, 'Our husbands, sons and brothers are fighting the Prussians of Germany. We are fighting the Prussians of Partick. Only alternative Municipal Housing.'[8]

Two outcomes of this situation moulded British housing for good: the 1915 Rent Act, and state housing for war workers. The former, which was introduced by a Conservative member but received all-party support, had the full title of Increase of Rent and Mortgage Interest (War Restrictions) Act. Its eventual effect, though neither foreseen nor intended, was to shift the entire balance of the British housing system. Applying to 'small dwelling-houses', its purpose was to hold all rents and mortgage interest payments to the level of August 1914. This was coupled to security of tenure for tenants as long as they remained in a tenancy – a measure that, in the long term, froze the private rented sector into immobility; for if people moved from their fixed-rent accommodation it could only be to property that had been vacated and was therefore decontrolled and likely to have higher rents.

The measure was on the face of it an outrageous interference in property owners' time-honoured rights to do as they liked with their own: so much so, in fact, that an explanation seems required. In general, landlords were at this juncture at a low point, having suffered from an overall surplus of property in the years leading up to war, and they were now victims of inflation, as were their tenants. But while it is arguable that some landlords, at least, had a case for putting up rents, tenants were still suffering from the after-effects of the end of the rate compounding mentioned in chapter 3 above. Even so, the market might yet have revived, for the present crisis could simply have been another of the regular downturns of the 'building cycle', rather than a terminal stage. On this reasoning, the 1915 Act ensured that a temporary slump became a lasting crisis. According to one historian, it showed that the government had lost its faith in market forces to meet the crisis needs of wartime,[9] but it was not yet keen to build estates for war workers, although this was shortly to be forced upon it, for fear of raising people's expectations and setting a precedent. Hence the Act may have been 'a step towards avoiding any real onslaught on housing conditions by encouraging people to stay put',[10] at the same time affording some valuable thinking space.

Another historical argument might perhaps be grafted onto this: that landlords were in general a small and isolated section of the capitalist class. The majority were small owners (often, in fact, widows and daughters), and far from wealthy themselves. They could, therefore, be sacrificed by a government anxious to avoid social unrest and to appease the populace.[11] The measure was in any case a temporary one, to last for the duration of war plus six months, 'and no longer': in which respect it was comparable to other measures such as the commandeering of factories, that were justified by the national emergency. In the event, when rent control was reviewed in 1918 it was found that the 35 per cent rise justified by higher costs and overdue repairs was out of the question, and it was extended for a further year from early 1919, with still more houses brought within control

The second major impact of the war was to prompt direct state provision of housing for war workers. There was a recognized need to compensate such people for the confiscation of their right to strike and other freedoms when they were directed to work in different places. The 1914 Housing Act and

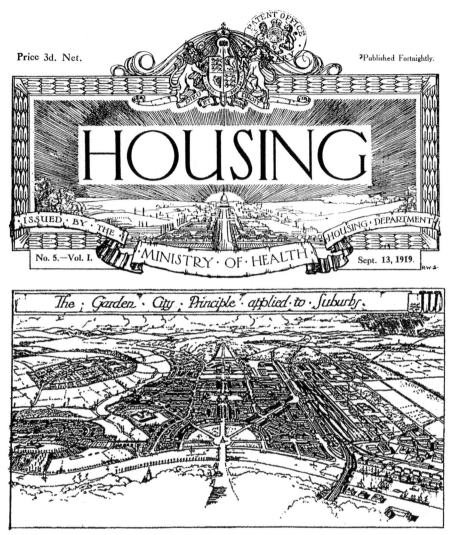

Above: Header of Ministry of Health journal *Housing*. The journal was published from July 1919 to June 1921, at first fortnightly and then monthly from 1 March 1921. It was free to local authorities, for whom it was primarily intended, but was also on sale price 3d. at bookstalls.
Below: 'The Garden City Principle applied to Suburbs. Unwin's version of an ideal town, illustrating his Warburton lecture of 1912' which shows a similar planning ideal (Frank Jackson, *Sir Raymond Unwin*, 1985) – but this is a ubiquitous motif in early town planning journals and other planning literature of this period.

another of 1915 expedited the provision of housing for Admiralty workers in the Rosyth Dockyard, and other government employees. The presence of Seebohm Rowntree as Director of Welfare in the Ministry of Munitions, where Raymond Unwin also served, ensured that the garden-city influence would make itself felt in any schemes built under these Acts. Indeed, it is almost as if the rural idyll embodied in the garden-city idea was all the more compelling because of its contrast with the machine of war. Well Hall estate at Eltham, built by the Office of Works in 1915 for workers in the Royal Arsenal at Woolwich, was designed with a great variety of picturesque cottages along romantically winding streets that evoked countless English villages. The architect, Frank Baines, was of the Arts & Crafts school and once apprentice to Ashbee. The estate contained around 1300 cottages and some flats, at an overall density of twelve to the acre.

For some years, the Admiralty had been relocating torpedo factories in Scotland, and it recognized the need to provide housing for workers from the south, who would be shocked at the low standards of Scottish housing, and particularly the tenements. Garden-city type schemes, though alien to its history, were not entirely new to Scotland at this time. A number of private companies had already built 'garden suburbs', and Unwin had drawn plans for a co-ownership suburb in Glasgow. Howard himself visited Greenock, whose Commissioner wanted to redevelop it as a garden city. The Treasury, however, balked at what it considered the extravagance of Well Hall, which had proved extremely expensive, and they pressed now for temporary hutments. But the necessary timber was in short supply, while the infrastructure of roads and drains would have been as costly as for permanent dwellings. With pressure from the War Office, therefore, the Treasury agreed to fund thirty-eight estates 'on Garden City lines'. Four were built by local authorities, and others by various firms with the aid of grants, including, for instance, Barrow, built by Vickers, and Dorman Long's Dormanstown near Redcar. The Ministry of Munitions built thirteen schemes on its own account, including two townships at Gretna for workers on high explosives. Together, these catered for 13,500 people in houses, temporary timber bungalows and hostels designed to be convertible to houses at a later date, with shops, schools, churches, meeting halls, hospital, laundry and cinema. Stylistically, the houses were simpler than at Well Hall but, although plain, they had some handsome 'Queen Anne' and Georgian features, and the centre of the township had a dignified central avenue. The architect was Unwin, assisted by colleagues from Hampstead Garden Suburb, and it was Unwin who drew up the master plans for Rosyth and several other estates.

Homes Fit for Heroes: the 1919 Act

The crisis of war, therefore, set a pattern of direct state intervention in working-class housing, even though at the time this was seen as temporary. Events moved towards a general acceptance of its indefinite continuation. In 1917, a Royal Commission on the Housing of the Industrial Population of Scotland, which had been appointed 5 years earlier, published its report. Though the appallingly low standards, shortages and overcrowding it described clearly pre-dated any wartime emergency, they would have to be addressed in any postwar reconstruction. After reviewing the extent to which existing housing and town planning powers had been used by Scottish authorities up to now, the report concluded that 'the disorganisation flowing from the war makes an immediate revival of uncontrolled commercial enterprise on an adequate scale impossible. There is, in our view, only one alternative: the state itself, through the local authorities, is alone in a position to assume responsibility.'[12]

The main players in the final chapter of the struggle for council housing were the Ministry of Reconstruction, the local authorities under the jurisdiction of the Local Government Board, the Treasury, and the War Cabinet and its successor, the coalition government led by Lloyd George. The Liberals had always been opposed to municipal housing for their emphasis had always been on land reform with a land tax, with housing societies and co-operatives to do development, while both Treasury and local authorities were wary of the cost of any programme to themselves. Many of the latter were in fact mindful of their housing needs and straining to start building to meet them, but they were still thinking mainly in terms of the 1890 Act, and looking to exceptional government action to deal with the immediate emergency. The Local Government Board, having consulted leading housing and planning organizations, was convinced that private enterprise would not be able to deal with this and it set about circulating all authorities to find out what their needs were, intimating that some sort of temporary subsidy would be forthcoming. An alarmed Treasury then intervened to hold back the circular.

The Ministry of Reconstruction represented everything that was most progressive for its time, as was seen in its application of garden-city design to the munitions estates. It was headed by Dr Christopher Addison, a close associate of Lloyd George and previously his Minister of Munitions. Its housing panel, set up in 1917 with Seebohm Rowntree and Beatrice Webb amongst its members, recommended that the government should make good the wartime deficiency of dwellings in the first year of peace, and then for a further 5 years supply the nation's annual needs through a local authority programme, with a state subsidy and strong central control. To the Ministry, housing might have seemed the last necessary push of the war effort.[13] For the idealistic Addison, it was crucial for social reconstruction, as well as for a resumed public health crusade, and to that end he campaigned for a Ministry of Health that would embrace housing and break the old tie of this to the Local Government Board. He himself became the first Minister of Health, having already introduced a second Housing and Town Planning Act in 1919.

Meanwhile the Tudor Walters Committee appointed by the Local Government Board 2 years earlier had presented its report. Sir John Tudor Walters who chaired it was a Liberal MP who had played a prominent part in the debate on the 1915 Rent Act, and other members were Frank Baines (who, however, resigned his place before the report was published) and Raymond Unwin, whose ideas the report clearly reflects. Applying to Wales and Scotland as well as England, it became, so to speak, the 'Bible' of the new council housing.

All these developments must be seen in the context of a real fear of social revolution.[14] However unjustified this might seem with hindsight, it should be remembered that the rent strikes prompting the 1915 Act were still fresh in people's minds. In July 1916, an Inquiry into Industrial Unrest had reported to the government that the eight areas it had studied were all disaffected, and that housing problems were a major factor in seven of them. In May of the following year, strikes among engineering workers raised the stakes still further. Provision of better housing was now seen as necessary to placate the workforce, and in July 1917 the Cabinet overruled the Treasury and authorized the Local Government Board to send out its delayed circular. The Treasury still held back, seeking a formula for subsidy that would cost it less. At last it appeared to strike a compromise where costs would be divided 75:25 in favour of local authorities, with the proviso that where their costs rose above the proceeds of a penny rate, the Exchequer could increase its contribution.

In the last months of the war, fears of civil disturbance increased. There was a police strike in the summer of 1918, a London Underground strike, and threats of electricity and coal strikes, while the Cabinet was warned of the possibility of a general strike. In Glasgow, a strike for a forty-hour week was described by the Secretary of State for Scotland as a 'Bolshevist rising'. Demobilization raised still further concerns. Around the time of the Armistice there were mutinies in garrisons on both sides of the Channel, which had to be pacified by increases in service pay, and in July 1919 there was a boycot of peace celebrations. The Cabinet were seriously alarmed by the possible

Official inspection of a prefabricated estate under construction in Liverpool (probably Larkhill) by the Minister of Health (Dr Christopher Addison) in 1920.

consequences of several million highly trained and disaffected servicemen and conscripted industrial workers being let loose when, for the first time in history, rioters would be 'better trained than the troops'.[15]

It was in this climate, with who now knows what mixture of rhetoric and sincerity, that Lloyd George on the day after the Armistice was signed made his historic promise of 'habitations fit for the heroes who have won the war' – in common parlance, 'homes for heroes'. It fell to Dr Addison to make this a reality, and for those who might still have lingering worries about cost, the Parliamentary Secretary to the Local Government Board assured the Cabinet (who now received fortnightly Home Office reports on the activities of revolutionary organizations in Britain) that subsidized housing would indeed be an insurance against revolution. Even Lloyd George was now won over to the idea and argued that such houses would be worth the price, however high. The Act was speeded on its way through Parliament by all parties, and a number of MPs asserted that people would be reassured from just seeing the houses go up – they wouldn't even need to experience living in them.

The revolutionary feature of the Act's housing provisions was that they obliged all authorities to survey their districts, estimate their housing needs, and build to meet them, using the recommended standards and the subsidies available. There were dual aims here, which were not entirely compatible with one another. The new houses were both to remedy the housing shortage and to set pioneering standards. The quality of the house was of equal importance to meeting the shortage; for in order to 'provide visible proof of the irrelevance of revolution'[16] it needed to be superior to anything previously built for working-class occupation, both internally and externally. The two aims were, as always, to be reconciled by 'filtering'. It was accepted that the tenants of the new houses would be drawn from the artisan elite, in time honoured fashion, but this addition to the housing stock would benefit everyone by releasing older accommodation.   Addison passionately believed that this limited programme of garden-city houses would benefit the slum dwellers, and later, betrayed and embittered at the premature termination of his Act, he chose for the title of a book he published, *The Betrayal of the Slums*.

It was understood that the programme of housing under the Act was strictly temporary, an emergency measure to meet postwar conditions, although a reasonable allowance of time, up to March 1927, was given for things to return to normal. It was not therefore envisaged, at least officially, that the new council landlords would replace private ones, only that they would fill a gap until private development resumed. A further Housing (Additional Powers) Act passed at the end of 1919 in fact offered a lump sum to private builders, to build houses at specified rents, although Addison's intended limitation of these to working-class tenants was dropped at the committee stage. For the time being, however, private building was limited by rising costs and shortages, and it was to be the best part of 10 years before the full recovery of the housebuilding industry. When it did recover, times were changed: in particular, new means of financing purchase through building society mortgages, coupled to an expansion of the white collar classes, meant that it was now more attractive to build homes for owner occupiers than for landlords to rent.

In spite of all the concessions given, there was still in 1918 considerable nervousness about the willingness or ability of local authorities to act with the necessary urgency. They were again circulated by the Local Government Board with details of the subsidy proposed, and asked to submit schemes at standard densities of twelve houses to the acre (eight in rural areas) that could be completed within twelve months of being given approval. On the division of costs, Addison was won over to the argument that authorities would not be willing to pay more than the product of a penny rate, and after much demur the Treasury agreed to pay the balance, on condition that there would be a review in 1927, by which time it was judged that building costs would have returned to normal.

Where the rents of the new council houses were concerned, the situation was hopelessly confused by the divided aims of the policy. The Ministry ruling was that by 1927 rents should bring an economic return on two-thirds of the actual building costs, but meanwhile they were to achieve the impossible feat of corresponding to local working-class rents, with allowance made for the superior quality of the houses, as well as being such that the intended tenants could afford. In practice, they came out at two to three times higher than prevailing (frozen) rents of pre-1914 housing, while rates, which tenants often did not distinguish from rent, were also higher. Once the immediate postwar boom ended, wages fell, so reinforcing the situation where council rents were beyond the reach 'of any but the most affluent heroes'.[17] In a spirit worthy of Octavia Hill, however, the journal *Housing* commented that 'they will realise that a thing worth having is worth paying for.'[18]

The Failure of the Addison Act and the Building Guilds

With the implementation of his Act, there began to unfold a personal tragedy for Addison. There was a range of estimates of how many new houses were needed, all revolving around half a million, when the existing housing stock was around eight million. The Housing Advisory Panel had predicted a need for 300,000 new dwellings in the first year of peace, to make up for the lost war years, and then a steady 75,000 annually. This was based on the information obtained by circulating local authorities, although it was unclear whether they were reporting the actual shortage or only what they thought would be desirable. Addison's own target was 200,000 a year for 3 years, as the essential minimum if some inroads were to be made into the slums. At the same time, astonishingly little thought was given as to how the building industry would be able suddenly to get back into production on such a scale. In the event, there were endless problems and delays. Demobilized men refused to come back, preferring easier kinds of work, and the shortage of labour continued while at the same time the main builders' union, the National Federation of Building Trades Operatives (NFBTO), tried to gain concessions for its members, in particular opposing any 'dilution' by unskilled workers. Contractors, for their part, preferred to undertake repair work or to build anything other than houses, because of the controls and uncertainties that hedged these round; and indeed councils themselves might give preference to other kinds of development that would bring in higher rate income. To Addison's dismay, not a single house was completed by the end of 1919, while building costs were spiralling upward. He felt deeply betrayed by the building workers, asking 'Can one class, one trade, permanently stand in the path of the community, and in its own class-interest bar the way to progress, prosperity, and resettlement?' He added that 'the State which will submit to such action is saddling itself with a sectional tyranny.'[19]

Whether or not it was fair, it was the builders who took most of the blame for the slow progress of the housing programme. To try to compensate, Addison resorted to several strategies: the use of prefabrication, to cut out skilled trades; a lowering of standards, which among other things involved skimping on garden paths and fences, the purchase of below-standard houses from private builders, and the introduction of a new type 'C' house intermediate between the 'B' parlour and 'A' non-parlour house. He hoped to raise more capital through 5-year Local Housing Bonds, sold in £5 bundles and yielding 6 per cent. It seemed appropriate that 'the particular classes which will most benefit by the whole housing scheme should put their own money into it';[20] but the bonds were successful in only a few places and did not raise the hoped-for sums.

The desperate efforts to get the housing programme moving explains one of its odder episodes, the use of building guilds. Guild socialism was a late flowering of utopian socialism and the two people associated with its rise were A.J. Penty, a one-time Fabian, theosophist and assistant draughtsman at Hampstead Garden Suburb, who took as his text Ruskin's 'Nature of Gothic', and S.G. Hobson, Fabian, ILP-er and member of the Labour Church in Letchworth. A Guilds Restoration League was founded in 1906, with the aim of linking Arts & Crafts and the trade unions, and a National League was set up in 1915, though with political rather than artistic aims. The rise of building guilds owed much to a Christian Socialist employer who with another guild socialist, G.D.H. Cole, promoted a Builders' Parliament, which was taken up in the Whitley Industrial Councils in 1918. Later, in the 1930s, when C.B. Purdom and Patrick Geddes were involved, the movement became European, while Penty himself moved steadily towards Fascism.

Building was the ideal industry for the application of guild socialism, because it was so labour intensive; and the Addison housing programme seemed to offer the ideal opportunity, because of its promise of large and continuing contracts. The first local guild was formed early in 1920 in Manchester, where Hobson managed to get the sympathy of both the NFBTO, the City Council and the Ministry of Health. Addison was won over by Unwin to the idea of using building guilds. More remarkably, owing to the obvious inability of private contractors to deliver, they briefly got the support of Sir Alfred Mond, the millionaire founder of ICI and Addison's successor as Minister of Health. Addison guaranteed the guilds twenty contracts on their preferred 'cost plus' terms, which worked out at £40 per house plus 6 per cent of actual costs. Eventually there were about 150 guilds in existence, which altogether produced about ten times as many houses, the bulk of them in East London

The building guild was imbued with Christian Socialist and arts-and-crafts ideals. It was intended to belong to all its workers, architects, white collar workers and operatives alike, and the guildsman was guaranteed to be paid for life regardless of fluctuations in the trade. There were no shareholders, and profits were ploughed back into the service. The ultimate purpose was to revive 'the true craft spirit of the Middle Ages'.[21] The guilds did prove cheaper than private contractors and the quality of their work was agreed to be good. There was a waiting list of men wanting to join and, in marked contrast to usual conditions in building, guildsmen took great pride in their work. Their downfall, therefore, was not caused by their own defects but simply because when building costs began to fall, private contractors were interested in bidding for work again, and the guilds were undermined by Mond's insistence that they should compete on exactly the same basis as private contractors.

By now, the cross-party consensus for council housing was rapidly breaking down. As fears of revolution subsided, right-wing support for a large housing programme was no longer forthcoming. Lloyd George was now bent on developing the centre ground in politics with Conservative support, and he found it expedient to sacrifice Addison, who was pilloried for the supposed failure of his housing policy, publicly humiliated in Parliament and forced to resign his ministry. His housing programme was summarily halted in July 1921, only days before the formation of a National Building Guild, and it proved fatal for the guild movement. The new Minister of Health refused to honour Addison's undertakings, and consequently the guilds lost the backing of the Co-operative Wholesale Society as guarantor. Although the NFBTO was willing to step in, its constituent unions were not, and the guilds went from crisis to crisis. The Manchester one failed in 1922, having received sixteen of a promised twenty contracts, but the London Guild managed to survive to 1924.

Deeply embittered by the whole experience, Addison later joined the Labour Party where he continued his housing crusade. In all, his two Acts were responsible for the building of nearly 214,000 houses: 170,000 by local councils, 39,186 by private enterprise and 4,545 by public utility societies. They were still under construction in 1923, but the context and the underlying philosophy of his measures were never to be repeated, although in the words of his memorialist, it was Addison more than any other who 'transformed the housing of the working classes from a capitalist enterprise into a social service.'[22]

The Later Years of the Garden City Movement

Where did this sequence of events leave Ebenezer Howard and his movement? The answer is germane to the course of council housing. Howard himself had no time for the dilution of his programme by so-called garden suburbs, whether of private enterprise or local authorities, and he appears to have shown no interest in the general application of council housing. He was, however, prepared to go along with any endeavour that seemed to lead in the general direction of his own unwavering ideal of independent new settlements. He had no sympathy with the war, when he upheld his own pacifist principles and helped Frederick Osborn to evade conscription. At a time when the Garden City and all it stood for seemed to be in eclipse, he was greatly heartened by a small pamphlet, The Garden City after the War, written by Purdom on his discharge from the army in 1917. It proposed that, to meet the coming housing shortage, fifty or more new towns each with 50,000 population should be created. Purdom, Osborn, Howard and a Letchworth publisher formed the 'New Townsmen' group, whose New Towns after the War was published in 1918. Shortly afterwards, they were able to capture control of the Garden City and Town Planning Association. It is to be noted that they talked now of 'towns', rather than the symbolically loaded term 'city'. Explicitly repudiating utopianism, they looked to public ownership, rather than self-government. 'The garden city [they declared] is not in the line of Utopian communities. It is not a scheme for the localised trial of revolutionary self-contained economic systems . . . Remaining part of the commercial system, the garden city collects together and organises, in a scientific manner, the most up-to-date methods of production, taking into account not only the conditions of competitive industry, but the well-being of all concerned.'[23]

This, then, was one direction taken by the garden city movement, and its concessions to conventional values could not have been plainer. The New Townsmen were not successful in their lobbying of Addison to locate the new state-subsidized housing in 'new industrial centres' – that is, planned garden-city settlements. Addison was of the view that the housing emergency was too grave to be held up by any further legislation, and declined to include town planning in his housing Bill. It did appear in his Act, however, although in a much subordinate role to housing, and taking only half as much space as it had in the Burns Act of 1909. Some further reference to garden cities was eventually provided in the 'Additional Powers' housing Act at the end of 1919, which enabled local authorities to acquire land 'for the development of garden cities or for the purpose of town-planning schemes.'[24]

The New Townsmen had more success with the Labour Party which, largely through the advocacy of Herbert Morrison (who as a conscientious objector had spent his war service working in a Letchworth market garden), endorsed the '100 New Towns' programme. Morrison led a Labour controlled LCC from 1934, and the London green belt began to be created from around that time. Meanwhile, as Chief Adviser to Greater London's Regional Planning Committee, Unwin had come to assent to new and economically independent towns (as opposed to mere satellites), and the Marley Committee had been appointed to examine the experience to date of garden cities and satellite towns. During these years, the Depression and its effects on the stricken areas – the shipyards and mining regions particularly – had an incalculable effect on policy. The Barlow Commission set up in 1937 to consider 'the distribution of the industrial population', reported in 1940, its report reflecting the degree to which it was influenced by the garden-city lobby, which was remarkably active and effective through these years. There was a growing acceptance of a centralized planning system, and events culminated in the passage of the New Towns Act the year after Labour came to power in 1945.

Howard, meanwhile, had fired his parting shot by buying the land for Welwyn Garden City – an impulsive action that nearly alienated Purdom and Osborn. This second garden city strove to avoid some of the mistakes of Letchworth. It was originally intended that all the residents should be shareholders and that there would be a place for 'civic directors' on its governing board. But the early years were difficult, and once more principles were sacrificed to attract investors. Like Letchworth, the town was developed in accordance with company law, and again Howard's hope of regular rent revisions – this time every 80 years – had to be abandoned in favour of conventional leases that brought in more working capital. But the freehold of the land was again preserved, and the company undertook more of its own development, including sand, gravel and brick production as well as construction, than had been the case at Letchworth. It also owned the electricity undertaking, public transport, and a central department store. The town plan, with an impressive centre in neo-Georgian style, made it seem more unified and urban than Letchworth had ever been.

As in the first Garden City, the working classes here were in something of a minority. Among the earliest settlers were a Quaker group who had followed Howard from Letchworth to form a co-operative farm and dairy, which lasted for about 10 years, and who were also the instigators of another co-operative or 'associative' housing quadrangle of kitchenless flats in 1922. The connection with food reform was maintained in the 'Welgar' shredded wheat factory, owned by an American company. In general, Welwyn lacked the cultural eccentricity of Letchworth, from which it was separated by the great divide of the first World War. It developed into a quiet residential town that was marketed as a 'railway suburb'. By 1928, however, financial collapse was threatening, in spite of personal help from the directors and an application for a government loan under the second Housing Act of 1919. Purdom was forced to leave, and subsequently the articles of association were abandoned, to make the town more appealing to investors. The civic director posts, never in any case effective, were abolished. The shareholders were given full equity and the citizens excluded from any interest in the company or its profits. Osborn soon followed Purdom, both reaffirmed in the belief that the only way forward for the garden-city idea was through state-sponsored new towns.

Having reached a population of only 13,500 by 1938 (with a target of 50,000), Welwyn was absorbed into the first wave of new towns after 1946. This effectively ended its independent existence as a garden city, leaving

Letchworth to stand alone as the truest embodiment of Howard's experiment. The state-sponsored new towns then became the main vehicle of the garden-city ideal. This was accepted as such by the GCTPA, as by historians of planning ever since, to the extent that its legacy to council housing is all but overlooked. The 'Mark One' new towns, which began with Stevenage in 1946, were designed to cater not only for the decentralization of London (in a ring round the home counties) but for dispersal of industrial populations in South Wales, the Durham coalfield and the Clyde-Forth corridor. Although various agencies, including some local authorities and the Co-operative Permanent Building Society, had shown an interest, it was very clear that the programme was to be strictly under government funding and control, each town having its own appointed development corporation which retained the freehold. The programme was conscious of how far it improved on the interwar council estates. The new towns were intended to attract middle-class as well as higher working-class populations, and also the retired, and they would have a variety of tenures. They were to be self-contained, with a full range of urban and cultural amenities. In the event, they attracted very little private housing until the mid-1970s, and had no council housing. Their rents were inevitably high, as they had to support continuous new development and (as in the early years of council housing) there was no pre-existing stock for rent 'pooling'. The outcome was a restricted though relatively affluent social composition and, with inevitable delays in provision of public amenities, a concentration on private domestic lives to the exclusion of an urbane culture.

The first generation of new towns showed their garden-city inspiration in their comparatively low densities and population targets, though both were higher than garden-city limits; in their commemoration of Howard in various road and place names; and – not least – in the cultural elitism of the Chairman of the New Towns Committee, Sir John (later Lord) Reith, who anticipated a concert hall, art gallery and two cinemas (for high- and low-brows respectively) in each new town. Reith, however, went out of his way to repudiate any connection with the garden city movement, and in fact the only government report to acknowledge it remained unpublished. 'It is as if the [New Towns] Committee did not want to cite any non-government literature relating to the new town in case it was contaminated by Howard's ideas.'[25] In the later generations of new towns, population targets were raised from an initial 50,000, to a quarter or even half a million, and by this time, in the 1970s, they were no longer intended to be freestanding settlements but rather 'regional growth points' which absorbed large pre-existing populations.

In housing and planning standards and design, the new towns were trail-blazers, attracting the best and most innovative designers and practitioners and, with much government attention and funding, using the most advanced practices of community development. With the benefit of such attention and plentiful funding, they were in every respect more privileged than council estates which, in the nature of things, had to accommodate populations who did not have the opportunity to move to new towns. The common ground between the two was that both looked to a reformed built environment to bring about social progress; but in the case of the estates this was coupled to a long tradition of dealing with poverty and the slums that, for most practical purposes, the new towns were free to ignore.

NOTES

1. Sutcliffe (1981).
2. Sutcliffe (1981), p. 78.
3. Buder, pp. 102–103.
4. Cherry (1974).
5. Winter, p. 5.
6. Orbach, p. 13.
7. Englander, p. 208
8. Horsey, p. 10.
9. Orbach.
10. Orbach, p. 23.
11. Daunton.
12. Royal Commission (1917), para. 2237.
13. Swenarton (1981).
14. Wilding; Swenarton (1981).
15. Swenarton (1981), p. 78.
16. Swenarton (1981), p. 87.
17. Swenarton (1981), p. 83.
18. *Housing*, I, 23 (24 May 1920), p. 301.
19. *Housing*, II, 34 (25 October 1920), p. 102.
20. Swenarton (1981), p. 120.
21. Swenarton (1989), p. 183.
22. Shock, p. 7.
23. Beevers, p. 154.
24. Housing (Additional Powers) Act, title.
25. Thomas, p. 9.

Chapter Seven

The Utopian Legacy

'And yet, these places were built to offer the poor a better life.'
Jeremy Seabrook, *Landscapes of Poverty*, 1985

Utopianism runs into the Sand

The second part of this book is concerned with how council housing operated in practice, given the strange mixture of the utopian and the expedient in its origins. How far did it achieve its primary purposes, the elimination of poverty and the improvement of working-class living patterns and culture, and what sorts of settlement did it create? From the beginning there was no suggestion that such a long expected and costly social experiment should be monitored or assessed in any formal way. The premature ending of Addison's programme would have pre-empted this at the time, but it is unlikely that the idea would have occurred to anyone. Those responsible for policy were always confident of the outcomes, although in the nature of things these could only begin to appear after long periods of time and social change.

By 1919, some authorities were eager to build and some had plans prepared that could, in default of any better means, be carried out under Part III of the 1890 Housing Act still in force. Typically, these plans included 'parlour' and 'non-parlour' houses for 'ordinary' and slum clearance tenants respectively, and provision for private enterprise houses on estates was common. It appears that councils were inundated with applications as soon as they had any houses to let. While most tried or intended to give priority to their ex-service 'heroes', this conflicted with the need to ensure that the rent was paid. In the event a large proportion of tenants was middle- rather than working-class, especially in Scotland where no stigma attached to renting from councils.[1] A proportion of tenancies was quite often set aside for council employees[2] and in Liverpool tenants of parlour houses included master mariners, civil servants, bank managers and architects.[3] Here and elsewhere, some tenants had maids or even living-in servants.

The Addison houses, as we have seen, were intended to set precedents in design and create a new layer in the housing stock, to permit 'filtering up'. Even in the limited time the Act was in force it did apparently facilitate localized movement, as on the Becontree estate where in the early years dissatisfied tenants found it possible to move back to vacant accommodation in East London. Had the Act been allowed to run its course into the period of lower building costs, its aims might have begun to be fulfilled; but it would, presumably, have taken many years for filtering to have had a significant effect on the housing system as a whole, and meanwhile it would have been overtaken by circumstances, which included a sharp rise in the marriage rate after 1919, which led to an unforeseen rise in demand for homes.

The prevalent view only a few years after the termination of the Act was that the need for higher-rent housing was now satisfied, while the market for cheaper home ownership was also saturated.[4] Yet the housing shortage was worse now than it had been at the end of the war. Newly formed households were unable to set up homes of their own, and a revision of rent restriction in 1923, which deregulated private rents when dwellings were vacated, effectively locked the poorest into their slums. Once ended, the Act was swiftly consigned to history. It was held to have been financially ruinous and to have over-idealistic standards that could only be afforded by those not deserving of public subsidy. The parliamentary debate on housing resumed when the new Minister of Health, Neville Chamberlain, introduced his own Housing Act in 1923, and there was a feeling of setting out anew. The only tribute paid to Addison was from David Kirkwood, a Scottish Labour MP, to whom he was 'a great and noble man' who had changed the face of British housing forever: but his high ideals meant, of course, that 'he had to go'.[5] Chamberlain's measures were really a continuation of Addison's 'filtering' policy, which had included another Housing Act ('Additional Powers') that subsidized private developers. Claiming that private housebuilding was now reviving independently of subsidy, Chamberlain targeted a more strictly controlled and temporary grant on such developers, to encourage them to cater lower down the social scale than before. They were offered the choice of a lump sum per house or a 20-year grant of £6 a year, although it appears that the selection of purchasers and tenants was left to depend on the size and quality of the houses, if not indeed on chance. Local authorities, and also housing societies, qualified for the same grants, but only if they could convince the Ministry that private enterprise was unable to provide what was needed.

'Filtering up', then, was still the prevailing doctrine. As Minister of Health, Addison had appointed Chamberlain to chair the Slum Areas (later Unhealthy Areas) Committee, and its second and final report of 1921 attached the ending of the slums to town and country planning, garden cities, and the decentralization of industry. But Addison himself was soon rendered powerless, and the Conservative Chamberlain did not have the same idealism. His Act did begin to address the problem of the slums, but provided only half of the costs of any clearance, which was not enough to encourage authorities to embark on large schemes, especially now that they were grappling with their new responsibilities as housing developers and managers.

For those on the Left, Chamberlain's policy only reinforced the belief that the state alone should provide housing for the working classes, and the challenge was taken up by a new Minister of Health under the first, shortlived Labour government. John Wheatley was one of the 'Red Clydesiders', once a child coalminer, former ILP member and Glasgow city councillor. His strategy was two-pronged. To avoid the pitfall that had trapped Addison he won over the building industry with guarantees of large and continuing programmes of construction; and he transformed the Chamberlain subsidy by giving priority to local authorities, at the same time increasing the size and duration of grant. Any losses over and above the combined subsidy from central and local government were to be borne by rents, although at the same time these were to be based on private (controlled) rents in the district. Paradoxically, this meant that Wheatley treated tenants rather less well than Chamberlain, whose Act made councils rather than tenants stand any losses.[6] Another point of interest is Wheatley's complete absence of reference to the building guilds now winding up – from his centralist, Marxist standpoint he would not, of course, have wished to support guild socialism. Instead, he favoured direct labour organizations of local authorities, first developed under the LCC Progressives in the 1890s. These had increased in number and by 1924 were responsible for nearly 10 per cent of councils' housing contracts. Both Conservative and Labour remained well disposed towards them, until private contractors became interested in undertaking such work. At this point, in the 1950s, Conservative governments began so to control and limit them that they were mainly confined to repairs and maintenance rather than new building.

Because the Wheatley Act passed through the Commons simply as a financial measure – a change in subsidy to 'rebalance' Chamberlain's which remained in force – it was not hotly debated like its predecessors. The one issue that did generate strong feeling was Wheatley's decision, in spite of pressure especially from the Liberals, not to raise the standards of the council house above those set by Chamberlain. But his general policy was little opposed and was actively continued by the Conservative government that almost immediately came to power. Perhaps the fact that building costs had so recently been sky-high, and that private enterprise was already encouraged by the Chamberlain Act, helps to explain this cross-party consensus. In reality, the choices available were not so much between one or other ideological polarity (though later generations have preferred to see it this way) as between a number of difficult options and schools of thought, where leftwing socialism and even residual New Liberal and utopian beliefs still played a part.

Over half a million dwellings were built with Wheatley's subsidy – more than twice those built with Addison's, and the largest number under any of the inter-war housing Acts. Unlike the Addison houses, which were equal in urban and rural areas, the balance was now strongly towards the former. By the mid-1930s there was growing hope that Britain would be able to solve all its housing problems by the end of the decade.[7] Building costs had fallen sharply, private house building for rent had returned to pre-1914 levels, and there were signs that the absolute housing shortage would soon be ended. In such a context, however, the continuance of the slums could only seem more scandalous. The typical working-class accommodation, now and for a generation to come, was the pre-1914, landlord-owned stock under rent control. Originally a stop-gap measure, this was progressively extended throughout the inter-war period. In 1920, in consideration of the need for repairs and other extra costs, a 40 per cent increase on the 1914 rent was allowed; but at the same time, because of the growing housing shortage, more houses were brought under control. In 1923, 'decontrol by movement' was introduced, when control was lifted on a change of tenancy. Ten years later, the system of control was further refined and only the middle band of houses was treated in this manner. The more expensive ones were exempted from control altogether, and the least expensive were now fully and permanently controlled.

These various measures had a number of mixed motives: on the Right, the placation of people in housing need and a desire for the revival of private landlords; and on the Left, a wish to protect the working classes and tolerance of control to keep the older houses viable until such time as they were wholly replaced by council housing. There is an impressive array of evidence to show that housing was not a bad investment for many landlords over this period[8] while both Right and Left seem to have ignored the spread of working- and lower middle-class owner occupation in this pre-1914 stock. The complete physical elimination of the slums was finally addressed by Arthur Greenwood, Minister of Health in the second Labour government of 1929–31. His Housing Act of 1930, intended to complement rather than replace Wheatley's, gave a differently structured subsidy that was related to the number of people rehoused rather than each new dwelling supplied. There was also an extra allowance for sites that were unusually costly to develop, or where development had to take the form of blocks of flats. Even with a smaller compulsory contribution from local authorities, the measure nevertheless yielded a subsidy half as large again as Wheatley's. At the same time authorities were urged to reconsider their rent policies and to differentiate between those families able to afford an economic rent, and therefore not deserving subsidy, and those unable to afford even a subsidized rent who could now at last be catered for.

One way in which they were, was by returning to the practice of the philanthropic trusts and building blocks of flats on cleared sites. Although the term was not yet in use, this was, in effect, used to bring about the 'comprehensive redevelopment' of obsolete urban centres, often in combination with major road improvements. Liverpool's 'Central Redevelopment Area', with St Andrew's Gardens and other imposing flatted estates, was the outstanding example; but Manchester did the same on a smaller scale, and in Leeds the estate of Quarry Hill Flats (with others never built) was conceived as part of a re-planned city centre. Greenwood's slum clearance legislation was intended as part of a comprehensive package of town and country planning, which was to have an Act of its own, independent of housing. His legislation was overtaken by the coming to power of a National government with a narrower vision. The weaker Act that resulted was not used by many local authorities and is generally judged ineffective. It did, however, for the first time cover all land, rural or urban, developed or undeveloped, and under it some three-quarters of English land (less in Wales and Scotland) was brought under planning control. At the same time steps were taken towards a London green belt and the decentralization of industry.

Idealistic hopes for council housing at this time were defeated by the economic crisis that brought the National government to power. In 1933 it at last terminated the Wheatley subsidy and at the same time launched a 'crusade to eliminate the slums'. Local authorities were charged to 'clear their slums' within 5 years, after which there was to be another 5-year programme to eliminate overcrowding. The ending of the Wheatley subsidy for general housing needs (as distinct from rehousing for slum clearance) represented, to those on the Left, a return to Victorian sanitary policy and the betrayal of a sacred principle. To the economist Marion Bowley, doyenne of informed leftwing opinion, it was tantamount to the state relinquishing working-class housing completely, for 'practical responsibility for dealing with any but the very worst housing conditions had been abandoned.'[9] This was, however, to overlook another important measure (an Act of 1936) that allowed all previous subsidies and the rents based on them to be pooled. This meant in effect that the entire stock of council-owned property (with the exception of that built under Addison, which stayed under direct control of the Ministry) could in theory be made available to people from the slums, as and when its former tenants vacated it.

Out of nearly four million dwellings built between 1919 and 1939 (equivalent to roughly half the whole housing stock of England and Wales in 1921), over a million were built by local authorities, and nearly one-seventh of the remainder had received some subsidy from the state. But the inherent contradictions of state-supported housing were unresolved, while it was contributing its own layers of privilege to those already endemic in the general housing system. The tests for qualification for rent remission were, for those affected, indistinguishable from the detested 'means test' for the dole, and the new financial regime meant that different rents, or even no rent at all, could be charged for identical houses. Giving priority to slum clearance had the effect of privileging those who happened to live in 'declared' areas, while passing over others who might be in equal or greater need; and the high levels of demand entailed discriminatory selection policies, which will be traced out in the following chapter. Had the programme to deal with overcrowding had time to become effective, doubtless it would have added further social and moral confusions.

In such respects it is interesting to contrast the private landlord sector. Landlords never made any claims to serve social equity, and they catered for a wider range of social classes than council housing, although admittedly without much evident efficiency. Particularly with its return to a 'sanitary' approach, castigated though this was by the Left, council housing at least tried to address social equity. Its great failing was that, as it became the increasingly monopolistic provider of working-class rented housing, no government was able or willing to provide or fund it generously enough to meet the needs of all who needed or wanted homes at moderate rents. Marion Bowley blamed local authorities for the inadequacy of their building programmes. She also drew attention to the crucial point that those same high design standards that had been both inspiration and justification of council housing were a major contributor to high rent levels, and its consequent failure to reach many of those whose interests it was supposed to serve.

The Continuing Threads of Utopianism: the Dwelling

Both dwellings and estates were instruments for achieving council housing's twin aims, of remedying the housing problem and reforming the working classes culturally; but after the Addison-Tudor Walters era the principal emphasis was on the dwelling, the collective environment of the estate taking second place. In the early stages of the programme the emphasis was naturally on the type, cost and quality of the houses, while after 1945 the idea of the estate as an expression of a better society was channelled into the new towns. The development of policy for the houses rested on a number of assumptions, explicit and implicit, about what they could be expected to achieve and how far their standards could be lowered or changed without endangering this.

A quiet revolution in housing standards was taking place at this time, quite independently of council housing.[10] Between the wars there emerged the 'ordinary' twentieth-century family house, typically built for owner occupation, which incorporated new cooking and sanitary arrangements. It was specific to neither middle nor working classes, although it was designed on the premise that living-in domestic servants would be lacking, and like council housing (although not so obviously) it had its roots in the Garden City. The council house, on the other hand, was little influenced by private housing through this period. If anything it declined from the early utopian levels set by Raymond Unwin and the Tudor Walters report, under pressure of political and financial realities.

Before and during the 1914–18 war the detailed design of any housing that local authorities might build was the concern of the Local Government Board (LGB), who were thinking of poorer rather than more affluent tenants, and so were inclined to discard even such 'luxuries' as the parlour and a separate bathroom for the bath (otherwise placed in the scullery). Some found these recommendations archaic, and in particular a Women's Housing Sub-committee appointed by the Ministry of Reconstruction was deeply critical of the idea of dropping parlours and bathrooms, as well as many finer points of detail. They had toured model villages and garden-city projects and gone to some trouble to canvass working-class housewives' opinions throughout the country. However the LGB took huge offence at what it chose to consider their ignorant criticisms and in the end only their more general and less pointed comments were published.[11]

Addison also thought the LGB backward-looking, and once he became its president he brought in the housing 'radicals' who had worked with him in Munitions and Reconstruction, making Unwin one of its two new chief architects. They became largely responsible for the 1919 Manual of examples and recommendations (the first of a long series of such manuals) which was circulated to local authorities for guidance in their new housing programmes. Its content was based on the Tudor Walters Report and hence its ideas for the most part reflected Unwin's. The Tudor Walters Committee was just as subject as the LGB to considerations of 'Economy and Despatch';[12] but with true arts-&-crafts cum garden-city idealism, it staked its hopes on these being compatible with good design. In fact, more than compatible, essential: for lowered standards could only in the end be a false economy. 'Whereas in the past it had appeared that the lowering of housing standards was the only route to economy, the Tudor Walters Report suggested that these savings could be achieved by expertise in design.'[13] Various technical innovations were also anticipated at this time, such as smoke abatement, communal central heating (said to be underway in Salford and Manchester) and passenger lifts for tenements, all mentioned in the Ministry's journal *Housing*.

However, its ambivalence on a good many points suggests that the Tudor Walters Committee was more affected by economic constraints than it admitted. Of its three proposed basic house types, each with a parlour and non-parlour version, the simplest had the bath in the scullery, as the LGB had suggested. In this, and also the middle type which had a ground-floor bathroom, the WC was placed in a lobby outside the scullery. Only in the highest type were both bathroom and separate WC placed on the first floor, the normal arrangement for the new owner-occupied house. The Report gave a range of recommended room sizes, which were in fact lower than those in the LGB Manual. The non-parlour houses, although conforming to Unwin's personal preference for a single living room, could be welcomed or criticized (depending on political stance) as 'economy' types.

With all these changes, the irreducible core of the Tudor Walters recommendations was a self-contained, two-storey family 'cottage' set in generous front and back gardens, having its own front door, water supply, cooking and sanitary arrangements. The norm would be three bedrooms (which satisfied concerns for sexual propriety, as well as convenience) but exceptionally, two- or four-bedroom houses might be built – the last particularly useful if the household included a lodger. Densities of twelve to the acre in urban and eight in rural areas meant an abundance of green space, although this was of limited use, for children were always forbidden to play on it – in some places the forbidden open plots at road intersections were called 'the council' by estate children. But the cash benefit to tenants of the crops they could grow in their back gardens was the subject of detailed calculations, and it appears that many tenants took pride in their vegetable plots, as well as good shows of flowers in their front gardens – all the more creditable as gardening was not common to all working-class urban traditions. It was recognized that the level of cultivation was crucial to the character of estates – they were a 'rough-and-ready index of the character of a neighbourhood.'[14]

Soaring building costs and the desperate need to get houses up as quickly as possible meant that the ideal Tudor Walters designs were in use for barely a year. The shallow, wide-fronted house plan favoured by Unwin (not recommended by Tudor Walters but meanwhile approved by the Ministry of Health) was proscribed. An overall reduction in floor areas effectively converted Tudor Walters minima into maxima – incidentally causing one of the new regional housing commissioners to resign in protest – and other targets were garden paving and fences. Addison's successor at the Ministry of Health, not sharing his garden-city ideals, imposed still more drastic changes. The number of recommended house types was reduced and the non-parlour, two-bedroom house, previously thought undesirable except for a small minority was brought into favour. A new 'intermediate' house type was introduced with a cooking range in the scullery, which was now big enough to eat in, freeing the living room to do service as a parlour. (Although this looked like a retrograde step at the time, it was in fact an anticipation of the post-1945 house.) Under the new design regime, rows of terraced houses were made longer, and semi-detached houses discouraged. Roof lines were simplified, and any departures from simple rectangular forms frowned upon. The cottage flat, built in large numbers by speculative builders before 1914 and also on the Well Hall estate (see Chapter 6), had been disparaged in the Tudor Walters Report. It was now used on a large scale by local authorities. Built four in a block that resembled a pair of semi-detached houses, it was a way of bringing rents within reach of more people.

Such economies proved to the satisfaction of some that the government was no longer 'led astray by visionaries'[15] but was prepared to house the maximum numbers at minimum cost. The essential core still remained – perhaps most importantly the low density – and by the time the Commons debated Chamberlain's Act the municipal 'cottage' was so well established that it was queried by only one MP. The main focus of interest was still the parlour, and the Act's author was defensive about charges of depriving the working man of this mark of social status. It could be left to local councils, he insisted, to decide whether or not to fit such a room into the reduced house plan: a parlour of 10 ft 6 in by 9 ft 4 in, 'big enough to court in', could be got even into the most minimal home. This provoked uproar, particularly from David Kirkwood: 'Do you think I was to sit calmly in my seat and listen to my class being insulted in that fashion? Let me tell you that the working class know how to court and the individual who spoke does not.'[16]

Parlour houses continued to be built under the Wheatley Act but, as we have seen, its author disappointed his supporters when he declined to reverse Chamberlain's cuts. The trend in house size continued downwards and if a parlour was provided, a Manual of 1927 suggested that it need be 'little more . . . than a recess opening from the living-room.'[17]. Standards reached their lowest around 1936, when 'it was not without difficulty that the fundamental principles of Tudor Walters were maintained in the face of pressure for the "minimum standard house".'[18] But there was never total abandonment of the core principles and, with losses, there were occasional surprising advances, like the stipulation of the Chamberlain Act that all houses built with subsidy should have a fixed bath 'in a bathroom'. In spite of all their shortcomings, the newly built houses with their large gardens and many up-to-date features seemed positively palatial to their first tenants.[19] Particularly appreciated by those used to sharing accommodation was possession of their own front door and their own bathroom – or even just a bath.

Contrary to the impression sometimes conveyed in housing literature, it was never part of British policy to 'build down', or provide inferior types of dwelling for the poorest, although the possibility was sometimes discussed. The Dutch policy of providing special accommodation for 'difficult' tenants was mentioned with some admiration by the Central Housing Advisory Committee of the Ministry of Health (CHAC) in 1938, but it was thought unsuitable for Britain as it would lead to social ghettos.[20] To cope with extreme poverty in the Depression some councils doubled two families into a single house, but the LCC's experiment of a purposely inferior 'hygienic flat' at 'Tenement Town' (Oak Estate in Lewisham), where bathrooms were shared between three housholds, was apparently unique. By 1955, a few authorities had considered 'the possibility of building special houses of tougher construction and without some of the amenities of a normal house', where people could be taught home-making skills by the National Institute of Houseworkers; but such houses would not qualify for subsidy. At the same time, the usefulness of a stock of 'intermediate' or halfway housing was conceded because it did not demand of a poor tenant 'a standard of living so far in advance of his existing one as to make him despair of attaining it.'[21] For this, CHAC looked to the pool of older houses, many of which eventually came into municipal ownership, as did disused military camps, many of which were squatted and later licensed to the squatters. In general, the accommodation allotted to those excluded from the housing system was the workhouse or its legacy, the 'Part III' hostel, which will be mentioned again in the last part of this book.

What has led many to believe that councils deliberately built inferior dwellings for the poorest is, of course, the succession of different subsidies that gave rise to distinctive types and qualities of housing, and the inevitable matching of these to different types and qualities of tenant. On many large estates the results of this were 'clearly visible on the ground'.[22] The situation was seen at its most institutionalized in Glasgow, where people were graded according to their eligibility for 'Ordinary' (1919 and 1923 Acts), 'Intermediate' (1924 Act), and 'Rehousing' (1930 and 1935 Acts) property – the last category intended for the roughest people from the slums kept under close supervision. The hierarchy of dwellings brought social consequences, as will later appear. But low as standards were allowed to fall, it was a descent from something that had started as 'ideal'. Nor did lower standards inevitably follow from particular subsidies. In Liverpool, for instance, standards that had reached the lowest permissible levels around 1926 were actually raised in the later 1930s; and in Leeds a militant Christian Socialist Chair of Housing, Charles Jenkinson, defiantly built suburban estates of unimpeachable 'garden city' appearance and quality for people from the city's worst slums.

The design evolution of flats was different from the house or cottage, for here trends were upwards rather than downwards after 1930. Although the Tudor Walters Report had strongly discouraged their use, flats continued of necessity to be built in London, for the same reasons as before 1914. But most large cities avoided multi-storey dwellings until pressured by the clearance and overcrowding programmes of 1933–39. Even then, it required a new infusion of idealism to overcome the inherited prejudice against what were still seen as outmoded tenements. This, when it came, was from Continental example, notably the blocks of flats built or influenced by masters of the Bauhaus school of design which flourished in the Weimar Republic from 1919 to 1933. Confronted by the need to rehouse their vast slum populations, pragmatic British local councillors and their chief officers went on official tours to view new estates in various European cities. What made the greatest impression, although they were in fact little more than a pastiche of true Bauhaus principles, were the gigantic estates of workers' flats built by the shortlived socialist regime of Vienna, some of them later used as military centres of resistance to the Nazis. The standards of their individual apartments were quite low in comparison to Britain, but the provision of such amenities as creches, landscaped gardens and, above all, abundant window boxes left indelible memories with British observers.

This helped to establish the modern flat as an acceptable family home. An early pioneering estate was Ossulston near Euston, planned in 1925 to have a combination of private and public dwellings, with basement car parking, heights up to nine storeys, passenger lifts, district heating and other innovations. Most of these were dropped for reasons of economy; but with its interior courtyards, outward facing shops and colourful street market the estate fitted well into its surroundings and had a stylishness reminiscent of the LCC's turn-of-the-century Millbank. New and improved standards for flats were introduced by the LCC and a number of other large cities from 1930. Heights were still limited to five or six storeys because lifts were thought too expensive for working-class tenants, and the usual access was by external balconies, although flats in Manchester and Leeds had internal stairs and small private balconies. Room sizes were enlarged, bringing flats closer to houses; a bathroom replaced the bath in the scullery; and electric lighting became universal.[23] Flats were designed in a range of sizes to correspond to the actual variety of households, and there was more emphasis on estate amenities as a necessary compensation for high-density living. Playgrounds and common laundries had been present in many nineteenth-century tenements, but on flatted estates of this period provision often included a tenants' hall for use on both public and private occasions.

All this showed the possibility of good modern homes in blocks of flats, but in spite of their 'modern' appearance they were not all that different in structure and form from the old tenement blocks. The great exception was the massive Quarry Hill Flats estate in central Leeds whose plan was explicitly modelled on Vienna's Karl Marx Hof but which was constructed in a French prefabricated system. It also incorporated the French 'Garchey' waste disposal system and it was the first council estate to install passenger lifts to almost all its dwellings. There was an ambitious plan for estate amenities which included a lavish community centre with theatre, tennis courts and bowling greens, a kindergarten, and mortuary. Most of these were either not provided or never completed, but there was a very successful estate laundry and ironing room which lasted for the lifetime of the estate.

Utopianism in the Post-1945 Council House

Britain emerged from the Second World War with an even greater housing need than in 1918, for not only had building and maintenance been suspended for the duration of war, but a sizeable proportion of the stock had been destroyed or put out of action, particularly in old industrial and docklands districts. People's standards and expectations were higher than 20 years before (thanks in no small measure to council housing between the wars) and another legacy of war was a sense of common purpose, even if this was to a degree the product of propaganda. The concept of 'the people' had to some extent edged aside class divisions, and delivery was expected on the promise of a 'brave new world' that had sustained the country through six hard years. 'The new Britain must be Planned', declared a leading Modernist, Maxwell Fry, in a special edition of the weekly *Picture Post*; and his piece was illustrated with views of Quarry Hill Flats and a model of the proposed new Coventry city centre. The following article, '*Plan the Home*', by the progressive housing specialist Elizabeth Denby, was illustrated with one of Liverpool's central estates of flats and '*The Little House – a cottage for city workers at Welwyn Garden City*'.[24]

The course of housing policy in the early postwar years uncannily echoed that of the 1920s, when a fleeting idealism was followed by compromise and consensus. As half a century before, progressive young architects were eager to work for the LCC on its expanding housing programme. Labour's minister in charge of housing was the fiery ex-miner and trade unionist Aneurin Bevan; but to the disappointment of the town and country planning lobby housing was not incorporated with the new – and as it turned out shortlived – Ministry of Town and Country Planning, but remained a division of the Ministry of Health. It was while engaged on the monumental task of creating the National Health Service, therefore, that Bevan also had to deal with the revival of council housing; but his scant time for this was partly compensated by his compelling vision which saw it as permanent and universal, its new estates like 'modern villages' where all classes would live in harmony. In his 1949 Housing Act, therefore, he removed the historic stipulation that it should be exclusively for working-class use. Although this had no immediate practical impact – for in the acute shortage tenancies were bound to be given to those in greatest need – it had symbolic and potentially portentous implications for the more distant future.

Bevan had a unique window of opportunity to put his ideals into practice, for the continuation of materials rationing and building licenses, with cheap public sector borrowing, gave state housing programmes several years start over private ones. Rent control was still in force, holding private rents to 1939 levels, and it was Labour's expectation that private landlordism would quietly wither away, its remaining stock eventually being taken into municipal ownership. Owner occupation was intended to suffer a similar attrition, although it would be tolerated as a fringe tenure, 'an extension and expression of the personality of the owner'.[25] Ultimately the Labour government intended four-fifths of new housing to be built by local authorities.

Only the difficulties of postwar reconstruction, therefore, stood in the way of a re-inspired public housing sector, and its design standards were set by the Dudley Committee appointed by the Ministry of Health in 1942. Their report of 1944, with supplementary material from the town planning ministry, reiterated the fundamental Tudor Walters principles: that good design was essential and should be done (as was by no means always the case to date) by good architects. Estates should not simply be unobtrusive but contribute 'positively to the beauties of the town and countryside',[26] and they should also have the full range of social amenities. The rigid and monotonous 12-to-the-acre density should be relaxed, and dwellings should include the reformed flat and also maisonettes, which the Committee clearly knew little about although it was well disposed towards them. In the light of pre-war experience, authorities were again urged to co-opt women onto their housing committees.

The majority of dwellings were still expected to be three-bedroom family houses, with generously increased floor areas, an extra downstairs WC for larger households, and an improved interior layout tailored to the actual living patterns of families. The parlour was now recommended only for rural houses and, apparently without argument, the single living-room house became standard. The scullery also disappeared, replaced by a generous sized working or dining kitchen where cooking was done on gas or electric cookers, rather than a coal range or open fire. Houses should be linked by outbuildings, which would not only enhance their appearance and provide storage space, but cater for 'those activities which it is the object of the new educational programme to bring about, e.g., individual hobbies, odd jobs, and active rather than passive forms of recreation.'[27] While not all these recommendations were immediately put into practice – the coal range, for instance, survived for a number of years in coal mining areas – they were, again through a series of official manuals, incorporated into local authority practice.

Thus the standards of early postwar council houses were set high. Another innovation was a subsidy for hostels, flatlets and bungalows for old people who, apart from some forward-looking authorities in the 1930s, had not been catered for in council housing and had only charitable trusts or derivatives of the workhouse to look to if they were unable to live alone. The new and generous old age pension, Bevan argued, would enable them to live in such places with as much independence and dignity as the middle classes who lived out their days in residential hotels. He had to do battle with his Chancellor to hold down council rents, and also stuck stubbornly to the quality of his houses, arguing that 'while we shall be judged for a year or two by the *number* of houses we build . . . we shall be judged in ten years' time by the *type* of houses we build.'[28] But the numbers achieved were disappointing, for although the target set by the previous government was reached by 1948, it had been a serious underestimate of need. The required 300,000 units a year were not achieved until 1953, when it fell to a Conservative minister of housing, Harold Macmillan, to celebrate the symbolic 300,000th house of the year – even then, two-thirds of the total were supplied by private developers. The price paid for this speeding up of the housing programme was his 'People's House', which sacrificed all the space and other gains of the Dudley Report.

The next official attempt to raise housing standards – and as it turned out the last – was embodied in the 1961 Parker Morris Report, *Homes for Today and Tomorrow*, whose proposed standards were made mandatory for local authorities and housing associations between 1969 and 1981. Whereas the Dudley house was in direct line of descent from the Tudor Walters 'cottage', updated by new construction techniques and more rational internal planning, the Parker Morris dwelling was a fresh interpretation of Modernist principles which were now reaching a wider audience in Britain, especially as the works of the architect-visionary Le Corbusier became more widely known. The Report dispensed entirely with ground plans and elevations, and its prescriptions applied equally to houses and flats. Internal arrangement was to be governed to fit actual patterns of living in a fast changing and technological society, and external appearance or 'style' was therefore irrelevant. In an early demonstration scheme of Parker Morris recommendations the box-shaped, partly timber framed dwelling had external walls of brick and glass, and internal planning that was 'not about rooms so much as 'the activities that people want to pursue in their homes.'[29] All parts of the dwelling were to be used throughout the day, unlike the conventional arrangement where the bedrooms were used only at night, so that the whole house should be heated, although domestic central heating was still relatively undeveloped in Britain at this time. At this point the ideal dwelling finally abandoned all Tudor Walters prescriptiveness concerning which rooms should be used for cooking and eating.

Parker Morris recommended floor areas which brought sizes, even of flats, back to something near or better than the early Addison and Dudley houses; there was a much improved provision of power points for the many electrical appliancies people were now acquiring, and an external space allowance for one car per dwelling. The garden, though much smaller than in Tudor Walters layouts, was no longer looked on as a source of food for the family, but rather as an 'outdoor room' with an important leisure function. In a way now familiar, these high standards began to be compromised once the new standards became mandatory in the public sector, as an imposed 'yardstick' forced designers to squeeze them into an overall cost envelope. Floor areas intended as minima were treated as maxima and overall densities reduced. Even so, there was a flexibility that could be turned to advantage by good designers and it is generally held that the Parker Morris house was of a quality that was never surpassed. It was used on the remarkable Byker estate mentioned below, and by innumerable housing co-operatives and tenant design groups of the 1980s, who clothed it in a revived 'domestic vernacular' with pitched roofs and small windows reminiscent of the garden-city 'cottage'.

The Continuing Threads of Utopianism: the Estate as Settlement

Although the bulk of its report concerned the design and layout of houses, it is clear that what the Tudor Walters Committee had in mind was not a simple housing estate but a fully functioning settlement of garden-city comprehensiveness: 'It is generally agreed that to cover large areas with homes, all of one size, and likely to be occupied by one class of tenant, unrelieved by any other types of dwelling occupied by different classes of society, is most undesirable, even where the depressing effect of monotonous unbroken rows is avoided';[30] and it was anticipated that the new housing schemes would eventually contain playing fields, allotments, open spaces, shops, business premises, schools, churches, clubs and institutions, as well as larger and higher class houses. Together, these would provide a local economy and meet 'the social, educational and recreational needs of the prospective tenants.'[31] Most of these would have to be done through other agencies, but the housing scheme would provide 'suitable sites obtained at the original value of the land.'[32]

Any proposals had of course to meet concern for 'economy and despatch', but the Report was confident that these could be reconciled with good planning and design. It was important that housing should not be held up by waiting for town planning legislation, and in any case it did not need to be, for the basic prescriptions for road widths and housing layouts had long since been agreed. The Report recommended that the LGB should have power to exempt housing schemes from any bye-laws or restrictive regulations – Hampstead Garden Suburb, though not mentioned, was the obvious precedent. Good design if 'exercised with trained imagination' would be sufficient to maximize the qualities of a site, achieve the most ideal house design and layout, and provide 'coherent design, grouped round some central idea.'[33] Even if cheaper in the short run, badly designed or located schemes could only be a false economy, because they would result in unlettable houses. One of the assumptions of the argument was, of course, that future tenants would be in a position to exercise choice.

In the event, the desperate need to get some houses up, the inner workings of authorities dealing for the first time with housing and, one may surmise, the priority given to homes over estates in most minds, meant that something very far from these high-flown expectations emerged. The possibility of municipal garden cities was never realistic, although it had occurred to Howard, in spite of his opposition to municipal housing, and Unwin thought in terms of municipal satellite towns or suburbs. Sheffield's estate at Wincobank (page 39 above) was hailed in its time as 'a miniature garden city'.[34] The Ministry of Health supported the idea of municipal satellites in its 1919 Manual, and the August 1920 issue of *Housing* published an ideal estate centre plan, with institute, 'concert lawn', 'pavilion', and the inevitable tennis courts and bowling greens.

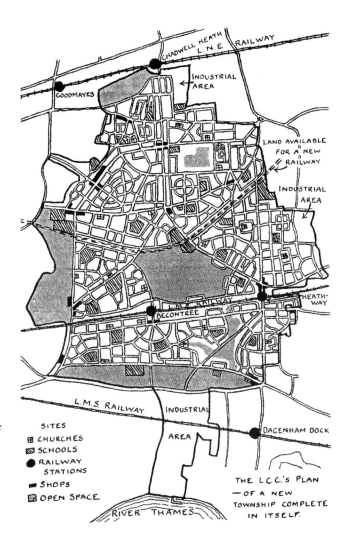

The LCC's 'Plan of a new township complete in itself.' The layout of the Becontree estate, begun under the Addison Housing and Town Planning Act, 1919.
(*Source*: Young, 1934)

A number of forward-looking authorities were thinking of garden-city type developments at this time.[35] Bristol and Grimsby (the latter persuaded by their regional housing commissioner) were planning garden suburbs, and Manchester commissioned a leading town planner, Patrick Abercrombie, to investigate the feasibility of such a development at Wythenshawe. The LCC's original intention for the 3000 acres of rural land that it compulsorily purchased at Becontree and Dagenham was 'a new township complete in itself', encircled by a ring road and incipient green belt, with a dignified civic centre and plots reserved for all conceivable urban needs.[36] Nor was it expected to be exclusive to workers as higher rents were to be charged to the professional families expected to live there. The LCC's Roehampton estate of 1920-27 was looked on as a garden city by its tenants, and the council also had a number of projected garden-city type schemes such as Grove Park in south-east London.[37] In practice, there was no administrative or other machinery to bring about such municipal garden cities or suburbs. At Becontree and Dagenham, houses had to be rushed up in advance even of roads and basic services, and the development of the estate was not helped by the fact that the land fell under the control of not one but three different authorities. By the time Dagenham achieved urban district status in 1926, over 6000 houses were already built and occupied.

The nearest approximations to municipal garden cities were Manchester's Wythenshawe and Liverpool's Speke. The former was mooted in 1919, but delayed amongst other things by strong opposition from the council's Conservative faction. The land beyond the city boundary was bought in 1926, when Barry Parker was appointed its chief planner, and building began in 1927. Two years later, the hall and park were gifted by the leading Liberals, Ernest and Shena Simon, the latter playing a large role in the estate's subsequent development. The site was technically a rural district of Cheshire, which the city did not manage to bring within its boundaries until a private Act of 1930, but the township was always intended to be a satellite of Manchester and Parker (who withdrew in 1941) made a virtue of providing 'sites suitable for all purses and all classes of society; we thus avoid the danger of creating a satellite town populated by one class made up of those bordering on or just above the poverty line.'[38] Wythenshawe was slow to develop: even its house building was held up by the district council's slow provision of mains services; but by 1939 it had a population of around 35,000, roughly a six-fold increase over 1921. The first shopping parade had appeared in 1932, and the first schools in 1934; but there was still no cinema and a huge deficiency of social facilities of all kinds gave it, in the view of Manchester's chief planner 'a somewhat anaemic social atmosphere' lacking a 'robust community life'.[39] Its greatest strength lay in its healthy rural surroundings and its contented 'socialisation'[40] so superior to the individualism of private enterprise. The houses were popular in spite of their high rents, and the early residents prided themselves on never having to come face to face with anyone from the slums.

Meanwhile garden-city ideology was channelled into the comprehensive Town and Country Planning Act of 1947, which put into effect much of the basic planning framework the movement had worked for: control of development, the dispersal of industries, building of new towns, and an increase in green belts, later followed by the establishment of national parks. Local authority satellite town development came a very poor second to the series of state new towns, which absorbed the cream of planning talent, idealism and resources. Wythenshawe was planned anew by the city architect in 1945, when a second 'parkway' was added to the ground-breaking, landscaped, dual carriageway of that name in Parker's plan. Densities were increased and houses laid out in the traditional pattern of culs-de-sac or 'closes'. A social cross-section was to be achieved by building pockets of low-density, high-amenity housing. The township had two segregated industrial areas and was surrounded by green belt. Its civic centre, on a different site from that proposed by Parker, was intended to have a hotel, two cinemas, a large public hall and a parish church. In the years that followed much effort was put by churches and community bodies into building up local identity and pride. The long deferred industrial growth came in the 1950s, and then largely in the form of light industry employing as many or more women than men. The civic centre was not even begun until 1960 and only officially opened in 1971; a theatre, hospital and market followed later. There was still a very strong desire for 'home rule', but Wythenshawe never won its independence, even with an eventual population of over 100,000.

Liverpool, meanwhile, had embarked on a policy to buy outlying sites for the redistribution of industry and population. Most of the resulting settlements began in the postwar period, but Speke, on the outskirts of the city, had been begun before 1939 as a self-contained 'community unit' encircled by a green belt, with houses for a social mix – some of them, even at this early date, supplied with garages. It was to be built without subsidy, with economic rents, and all development was to be strictly controlled, with 'regard to the formality of the lay-out'.[41] The Corporation had powers under a private Act to erect factories, eventually owning eleven out of a total of twenty-nine. When house building began in 1937, however, it was with 'overcrowding' subsidies. The city architect's revised town plan of 1947 showed a formal centre with community hall, parish church, open-air theatre, two cinemas, band arena and park (with bowling greens and tennis courts, as ever), but the reality was remote from this and Speke became known as a deprived council estate.

A satellite town at Burton Constable put forward for the city of Hull in 1945 had no practical means of implementation, and was eventually displaced by the massive peripheral estate of Bransholme. Kirkby, the largest of a series of 'overspill' estates for Merseyside and the nearest postwar approximation to Speke, grew from a rural area of 3000 people to a township of over 50,000 in the 10 years after 1952; but Liverpool's request to have it designated a new town was refused (it achieved independent Urban District status in 1958). Other would-be municipal new towns belong to the 1960s: they included Tyneside's Killingworth and the GLC's Thamesmead, built in the distinctive architecture of their time, with massive deck-access blocks. Thamesmead had a certain independent status but self-proclaimed 'new town' schemes like

Seacroft in Leeds and Belle Vale in Liverpoool were little more than housing estates writ large, with all the familiar problems of deprived populations marooned in expensive and technically faulty buildings, their special features amounting to little more than district shopping centres of varying fortunes.

From 1947, the development of ordinary council estates came under the jurisdiction of the Town and Country Planning Act. Here and there, the garden-city estate plan lingered on. It had been used in large estates of temporary 'prefabs' put up around the end of the war, and on a war workers' estate in Liverpool which had the same intended life of 10 years.[42] More permanently, it was used by the eminent planner, Sir William Holford, in the design of an ideal 'village' with green, school and shopping parade, to replace a former air force camp in Oxfordshire that had been squatted and licensed.[43] But there was now an entirely new philosophy for estate planning, in the 'neighbourhood unit', an American concept of the 1920s. It was recommended in an appendix to the Dudley Report by a study group of the new Town and Country Planning Ministry, which argued that in all towns of more than 50,000 people, neighbourhoods – which were equated with 'community' and 'social well-being' – had been 'mutilated' by urban growth and no longer functioned as communities. The remedy was to replace the obsolete neighbourhood with a rationally planned scheme that, as well as fitting into an overall town plan, would be 'a comprehensive entity in itself.'[44] Various optimum sizes for the unit were mooted, the consensus usually arriving at between 7,000 and 10,000, which was related, not very carefully, to school provision.

The reorganization of the whole urban environment into neighbourhood units was never, of course, achieved – for even mass slum clearance did not give opportunities on that scale; but they shaped the planning of the early new towns. The concept itself indicated the degree to which older urban neighbourhoods were seen as expendable, even though 'strong feeling for them still exists in some places.'[45] Urban development plans had as their organizing principle a concentric city with rings of increasing housing density towards the centre. This delivered densities that were much as before in the outer suburbs – that is, from eight to twelve houses per acre – but in inner areas they could rise to twenty-five or even thirty dwellings per acre. The Dudley Report was critical of the uniformity of Tudor Walters estates and stressed the need for a mixture of dwelling sizes and types, to fit a varied population and taking into account the needs of single people and the elderly in particular. Instead of the Tudor Walters formula with its stereotypical notions of homes and families, densities from now on were calculated in terms of 'bedspaces per hectare'. There were two points where, in practice, the new ideal broke down. Housing subsidy did not extend to housing for single people, and the social mix was of household types, not of tenure. Exclusively for council tenants, estates remained primarily working-class.

The new model for estate design was 'Radburn' planning, acknowledged in the Dudley Report and recommended in a 1949 Housing Manual, which became universal from the early 1950s onwards. The small unfinished settlement of Radburn in New Jersey had been one of a number of experimental settlements promoted by the Regional Planning Association of America in the years of the Great Depression and New Deal. They took their original inspiration from visits of members to Unwin and Parker, and to Hampstead Garden Suburb, which they particularly admired. Two points of English model villages and garden suburbs, in particular, were re-interpreted for the American context: the limited dividend or co-operative housing society, and the use of the cul de sac. Radburn, 'a town for the motor age', could be seen as the 'garden city plus motor car'. It had dual and quite separate circulation systems for cars and pedestrians. Houses were put in 'superblocks' that cars could penetrate only by means of culs-de-sac leading to back entrances of houses. Their other side, containing the main living areas, turned inwards to face, first their own private gardens, then a public green space where a network of footpaths gave safe access to all the necessary urban amenities. This layout, in a misunderstood and corrupted form, was re-imported to Britain where it was applied to council housing and new towns from the early 1950s onwards. The British version of Radburn made two changes that were crucial to its operation: houses were built in short rows or terraces rather than in pairs or detached, and garages were grouped in courts at some distance from and often out of sight of the houses. The last point, which arose partly from official reluctance to foresee the growth of car ownership amongst council tenants, and a similar clustering of children's play areas, was to prove one of the problem points of estates in the years to come.

'Radburn type', rather than authentic Radburn, planning then became the hallmark of the 1960s and 1970s. As used, it became a merely mechanical repetition of 'superblocks' stamped, as it were, over landscapes without reference to land form or local atmosphere. Patterns that looked logical on the drawing board were at ground level confusing and disorienting. Signs with arrows pointing to runs of 'odds' and 'evens' were provided, but this was a poor substitute for conventional streets and side streets. It was difficult to distinguish the backs from fronts of houses: in a conventional sense they had neither, and the ubiquitous footpaths effectively deprived them of all privacy. Visitors, and even residents themselves, had difficulty locating addresses. It hardly needs saying that there was little prospect of the full range of urban amenities needed to complete the logic of the plan and make an estate 'an entity in itself', as the Dudley Report would have had it.[46]

The same style of planning was also applied to the deck-access estate, where the maze of footpaths was replaced by a limited number of 'decks' giving access to scores of apartments above and below as well as on deck level. Here technological ingenuity was added to a design philosophy humane in origin but now dominating over mere human comfort and convenience. It might be thought something of a tribute to the power of utopian idealism that even in this situation the old nostalgic 'village' iconography lingered on – as, for instance, in the 1200-home deck-access Hunslet Grange estate in Leeds, designed in the 1960s as four 'villages' grouped round a large green open space, the first of them endowed with its own short row of shops and a pub.

Seeing off Utopia: the High-Rise Experiment

The ultimate episode of utopianism in British council housing was the brief boom in high-rise housing from 1958 to 1968. The occasion was the resumption of slum clearance announced by Macmillan in 1954. Just as 20 years before, this quickly usurped provision for general housing needs, whose subsidy was withdrawn in 1957. Over the next 20 years some 1.2 million pre-1914 dwellings were demolished in England and Wales (equivalent to roughly 7.5 per cent of the whole housing stock of 1961), incidentally probably doing more than 50 years of rent control to extinguish private landlordism.[47] The demolished areas had been the home territories of working-class people for upwards of 70 years, in many places for well over a century, and the finality of their removal can only raise the question, how much people stood to gain from such wholesale destruction of their habitat.

Many of the displaced were sent to outlying estates; but the cleared areas also needed redevelopment, and while some land was taken for roads, commercial or industrial uses, it was accepted that the principal use would be working-class housing, as before, but now exclusively in council ownership. Typically, the new estates were 'mixed rise' as recommended, but in this period there was an overwhelming proportion of high flats. The building of flats had picked up more or less where it had broken off in 1939. Estates then left unfinished were now completed, and others were built to plans passed before the war. Quarry Hill Flats had already shown the feasibility of carrying heights up to eight storeys, and they soon passed through this limit to eleven, then to around fifteen, and in exceptional cases to thirty or more storeys. Most of the technology needed to build so high was available before the war, but additional impetus was given by a special lifts subsidy in 1946, the advent of the tower crane, and progression of prefabrication into fully industrialized building systems. Large-scale contractors were anxious to get big housing contracts to try out these systems, which promised to eliminate much of the need for skilled labour and to offset extra costs by speedy completion. The National Building Agency was set up by central government in 1963 to urge local authorities to take up industrialized building systems.

High-rise flats peaked in the mid-1960s, when blocks over nine storeys high accounted for up to a quarter of all council housing approvals in some years, and considerably more than that in particular districts. The episode had its symbolic ending in 1968 with a disaster in a 22-storey tower block, Ronan Point in Newham, where a small gas explosion caused a corner of the building to collapse like a house of cards, with four fatalities. But the chapter was already drawing to a close by this time. The year before, the subsidy that was biased in favour of height had been withdrawn, and many in voluntary and charitable agencies were concerned about the social problems of high flats, particularly the difficulties of bringing up children in them. Now, even many architects 'stood appalled' at what their profession had apparently unleashed.[48]

Although ultimately flats above six storeys were never more than a tiny proportion of all local authority housing (by 1991 amounting to little more than 2 per cent), their distribution was uneven and their concentrations highly visible. In clearance areas, while each separate compulsory order site was quite small, placed side by side in rolling programmes they covered extensive tracts of inner cities. Virtually the whole of the large district of Hulme in central Manchester, for example, was cleared and redeveloped with high-rise in the 1960s, and in some inner London boroughs it formed half or more of the councils' stock. Glasgow's Hutchesontown-Gorbals by 1971 had 208 towers comprising nearly 21,000 homes. Birmingham, which had resisted high flats before 1939, created 463 high blocks, many of them in suburban locations, giving 'the largest concentrations of tower-block flats of any city in Western Europe.'[49] Densities increased to around fifty units or 200 persons per acre, and in exceptional cases went up to 350 – a bizarre contrast to the Tudor Walters formula of twelve family homes to the acre. Estate sizes increased correspondingly. In 1939 the Quarry Hill Flats estate with under a thousand units was famed as 'the largest in Europe'. This was not strictly true in fact, but it was easily surpassed by postwar high-rise estates, among which Southwark's Aylesbury estate with over 2,400 units was reputedly the largest single housing contract ever let.

There developed a range of building forms that included the slab, often containing two or more layers of maisonettes and sometimes raised on the stilts or *pilotis* recommended by Le Corbusier. There were tower blocks with a variety of ground plans, and eventually 'deck access' complexes of slabs linked at different levels by bridges, which could be served by a limited number of larger lifts placed at deck intersections. Slabs and towers were mixed with conventional two-storey houses with gardens, to realize the 'mixed rise' estate recommended in the Dudley Report. The architectural effect of varied building heights was also used to justify the placing of high blocks on peripheral estates, where there was no imperative land shortage.

From the view of economic efficiency, there was no convincing justification for high-rise housing. Its claim to deliver fast, cheap, high-quality buildings was not demonstrated at the time, and further passage of time, with many demolitions, only made it more hollow. Design faults, skimped workmanship and inadequate supervision were hugely magnified by the scale of contracts. High-rise dwellings so constructed were particularly prone to damp and mould, and the electric heating systems (inserted when gas was banned after the Ronan Point disaster) were often ineffective and hugely expensive to run. The later conversion of some blocks to different populations did not mitigate their earlier failings. Judged by the problems they set out to solve, high-rise public housing had to be deemed 'an innovation that failed.'[50] Any potential users were incapable of covering the cost of the experiment, and the only demand came from those with an interest in commissioning and supplying them. Never debated in Parliament, the episode clearly had a momentum of its own. The question must then arise how such a risky, expensive and (as it turned out) wasteful experiment could ever have been embarked upon?

The answers lie in the great range of vested interests there were in the programme.[51] The many different agents involved included both central and local government (each for its own reasons desperate to clear the slums); the main political parties, vying to demonstrate their ability to do the same; environmental health professionals zealous in their public health mission; town planners anxious to renew obsolete urban areas and protect the green belt from encroachment; and architects impatient to create 'Modern' architecture. At the same time there was comparatively little opposition. The media, which later made capital from horror stories of 'high-rise hells', was in the crucial period uncritically approving, and countless press reports, like official opening brochures, proclaimed each successive scheme in terms little short of millenarian. Those architect-planners of the old school who still voiced reservations were easily dismissed by their colleagues as nostalgic romantics hostile to 'the city' – though this was in the nature of an abstract concept of metropolitan life that had little to do with the daily lives of most urbanites. There was no mechanism by which prospective tenants could have mounted opposition, even had they been motivated to do so. Most were in any case desperate to escape bad housing conditions and ready to be seduced by the fittings and spaciousness of their new homes.

For a brief period, then, high-rise seemed to promise a quick and trouble-free way of fulfilling everyone's dreams. The central government subsidy was structured to increase with height, so that flats in 6-storey blocks got more than twice the subsidy on houses, and flats in 15-storey blocks nearly three times as much. Local authorities had little choice but to use this subsidy. Some, like Manchester, showed a certain reluctance towards building high but others, like land-locked Salford and inner London boroughs, had no choice if they wanted to hold on to their populations yet were unable to extend their boundaries. As in the mid-1930s, it was essential to have a new image to drive the programme forward, and this was supplied by the Modern Movement, now better understood and also better served by new technologies and organization of building than during its brief vogue in Britain at that time. Probably the most enduring contributions to the design of high flats, and to postwar building in general, came from the masters of the Bauhaus and their many demonstration projects; but the images most easily popularized – indeed plagiarized – were those of Le Corbusier's imagined 'vertical cities' for mass society. These were his 'Contemporary City for Three Million People' of 1922 and his 'Radiant City' of the 1930s, where all lived in '*unités*' or single buildings that were 'neighbourhoods' for 2,700 people, with the full range of services and amenities. His proposed plan for Paris would have eliminated all the irrational clutter of the streets, to replace it with massive skyscrapers set in abundant open space. These were ideas that were in the strictest sense ideal: plucked out of the air by the architect-visionary without reference to political or other constraints. For Le Corbusier and those who followed him, therefore, 'the building of housing in forms recognized to be unpopular but desirable in terms of elite aesthetics or technological sophistication seemed uncontroversial, a legitimate exercise of professional power.'[52] His powerful evangelism 'made high-rise a central image in modernist architecture', leaving its mark on 'virtually all contemporary architects.'[53] Such sublime assurance fitted the mood of the time, which still firmly believed in the enlightened professional using his expertise for the good of society, while carried away by the 'white hot technological revolution' promised by the first Labour government to come to power after 13 years. High flats brought both these things together, offering an apparent 'technological shortcut to social change'.[54]

It is interesting to compare this utopianism with the earlier, garden-city variety. Historically, the movements had common ground in Arts and Crafts, which were an important influence on the young Le Corbusier (whose *unités* were to contain workshops where residents could pursue their favourite crafts) as well as a springboard for modernist theory in general.[55] Both advanced their own ideal settlement as a practical alternative to social revolution. Both sought to combine nature and civilization (though by very different means) and both believed in the reform of society through material betterment, in particular better homes for the people. Each, therefore, was deeply humane. But Modernism beat out its own path by espousing 'the Machine' for a mass society. The love affair of architecture with mass production and high technology, which began with the Futurists around 1900, was refined into a social-cum-aesthetic philosophy whose espousal of large scale and centralization contrasted sharply with the garden-city preference for small scale and decentralization. The Garden City was embedded in English, if not British, tradition, harking back to mythic rural and communitarian visions. The Corbusian utopia, in contrast, 'had no history. It sprang full-grown from one man's imagination.'[56]

This was an inherently risky situation, where the application of abstract theory and its quite subtle aesthetics (owing more than was admitted to good materials and careful workmanship) could be used to promote certain building technologies and construction companies. The architecture was further distorted and corrupted by the economies, bureaucracy and politics of a large public programme, so that what in the end it delivered – forests of close-set towers in an unreformed urban environment – was precisely what Le Corbusier had warned against. Most dangerously of all, its application was widely separated from, and lost sight of, its real users, the inhabitants of the buildings. The RIBA chose to believe, somewhat against the evidence, that sociology had given high-rise housing the necessary stamp of approval.[57] In the event, examples of estates or buildings that satisfied both the Modern Movement aesthetic and social criteria are few. Two possible candidates were the 31-storey tower blocks of Erno Goldfinger in London, which after years of decay were eventually appreciated and hotly defended by some of their residents. The handsome white towers and slabs of the LCC's Alton West estate at Roehampton, built in rolling parkland, were fulsomely praised as a faithful realization of the Corbusian ideal – so missing the point that his towers were intended to replace and provide all the functions of an entire city, and not merely a suburban housing estate. Council housing was a tempting opportunity to implement the image without its real social purpose and content. The block designed for the Gorbals by the celebrated Sir Basil Spence (likened by him to 'a great ship in full sail on washdays'[58]) in its outward form imitated the Corbusian *unité* on stilts; but while asking for (and being refused) other uses than housing within it, he must have known that subsidy constraints would not permit this. Within a generation of its unveiling by the Queen, it was demolished as unviable.

A truer interpretation of the Modern was the redevelopment of Byker in Newcastle by a member of Team Ten, an English offshoot of the international modern architecture group, CIAM. Built to Parker Morris standards, it was clothed in a Swedish idiom with wood and bright colours, but expressed the essential humanity of Modernism because it was designed with thought as to how it would be used by its inhabitants. In general, architecture was judged by architects, and expounded to students, while still in pristine condition or as a model, when it was treated more as an art object than an environment to be lived in. This was only a short step to putting the interests of architecture before those of people. At Hunslet Grange in Leeds, a deck-access estate whose 1200 front doors were all painted white, the estate managers found that small children who had gone out to play were unable to find their own door again, and so requested that the doors be repainted in a range of different colours. The request was refused, on the grounds that it would destroy the 'architectural unity' of the buildings. Other times, designers of estates were apparently taken in by their own images: the very quickly

The vision for Hulme. Architects' drawing of one of the four Crescents of 'Hulme V', with (inset) their sketch of one of the Regency terraces of Bath from which they took their inspiration. To reinforce the message, the Crescents each bore a name from the canon of British architects: Robert Adam, John Nash, William Kent, Charles Barry. (*Source:* Wilson and Womersley, 1965)

notorious Hulme Crescents in Manchester, for instance, which were endowed with names from the canon of British architects, were modelled on and seriously likened to the classical crescents of eighteenth-century Bloomsbury and Bath.[59]

The pity of the situation was that, in the absence of any real understanding between themselves and architects, the other agents of high-rise were also so taken in by the architectural imagery. The practical realities of high-rise living became apparent to residents very quickly, although managers perhaps understandably ignored them as long as they could. Some of the most serious problems involved getting up and down in lifts that were programmed to stop only on every other floor and often failed, and the multiplicity of 'neighbours' who might never be encountered face to face. This was aggravated to an extreme level in deck-access buildings where a 'cross-over' arrangement of flats and maisonettes gave up to eight party-wall or floor-to-ceiling neighbours who were heard but not seen, in addition to the comings and goings of a wider public along decks running above living room and bedroom ceilings. The slotting together of apartments in these blocks also meant that front doors were often placed a floor above or below the dwellings to which they belonged. The decks themselves, open to wind and rain and seldom overlooked by windows, felt lonely and could be dangerous. Yet deck-access design, first put into practice at Sheffield's Park Hill estate in 1957, was allegedly the product of close study of traditional working-class life by Team Ten members, who sought to reproduce the safe and sociable streets of yore, without the danger and din of traffic.[60] Park Hill itself was perhaps the best example of its kind, if only because its sloping site enabled the decks to meet ground level at various points, but the spate of deck-access estates that followed throughout the country were not so happily placed.

In comparison, the modest garden-city derivatives looked like models of practicality, although as we shall later see this was no guarantee of their social success. It is however noteworthy that when high-rise and deck-access blocks were demolished, the replacement chosen by tenants themselves was always in the form of houses, occasionally with two- and three-storey flats mixed in, and always in a 'domestic vernacular' style with pitched roofs, relatively small windows, and gardens, that were oddly reminiscent of the Tudor Walters municipal 'cottage'.

NOTES

1. Bowley.
2. Baylis.
3. McKenna.
4. Simon, E.D; Bowley.
5. Parliamentary Debates (1923) col. 376.
6. Holmans.
7. Census (1935).
8. Holmans.
9. Bowley, p. 140.
10. Ravetz with Turkington.
11. Ravetz (1989).
12. Tudor Walters Committee, title page.
13. Swenarton (1981), p. 111.
14. PEP (1947), p. 65.

15. Swenarton (1981) p. 161.
16. Parliamentary Debates (1923), col. 372.
17. Burnett, p. 233.
18. Burnett, p. 245.
19. Rubinstein.
20. CHAC (1938).
21. CHAC (1955) p. 14.
22. Burnett, p. 247.
23. An exception was Kensal House, a classic of the Modern Movement by Maxwell Fry built as a show project for the Gas Light & Coke Company, which later came into council ownership
24. *Picture Post*, p. 21.
25. Ravetz (1995b) p. 160.
26. CHAC (1944) para. 55.
27. CHAC (1944) para. 55.
28. Foot, p. 82.
29. Ministry of Housing and Local Government (1961) para. 13.
30. Tudor Walters Committee, para. 53.
31. Tudor Walters Committee, para. 42.
32. Tudor Walters Committee, para. 53.
33. Tudor Walters Committee, para. 56.
34. Sheffield Handbook of Workmens Dwellings.
35. Swenarton (1981).
36. Young, T., p. 281.
37. Baylis.
38. Creese, p. 257.
39. Nicholas, p. 32.
40. Simon, A.P., p. 40.
41. City of Liverpool, p. 56.
42. Mitchell and Lupton.
43. *Municipal Journal*.
44. CHAC (1944) 'Site Planning and Layout', para. 16.
45. CHAC (1944) 'Site Planning and Layout', para. 13.
46. CHAC (1944) 'Site Planning and Layout', para. 16.
47. Holmans.
48. Cooney, p. 177.
49. Power (1987a), p. 52.
50. Cooney, p. 175.
51. Dunleavy (1981); Cooney.
52. Dunleavy (1981), p. 54.
53. Dunleavy (1981), p. 54.
54. Dunleavy (1981), p. 99.
55. Fishman.
56. Fishman, p. 205.
57. Royal Institute of British Architects (1955).
58. Edwards, p. 83.
59. Wilson & Womersley, p. 11.
60. Smithson.

Chapter Eight

The Management of Council Housing

'All the assumptions of housing policy in the past have depended upon an image of grateful recipients who pay the rent but don't dream of making their own imprint on the fully-finished, fully-serviced (according to the standards of the day) housing.'

Colin Ward, *Talking Houses*, 1990

The Task of Council Housing Management

In contrast to all the effort that went into its design, little thought was given to what the management of council housing would involve. Like the construction of the dwellings, this was left to local authorities, and the fact that it was almost a completely new role for them was something that many, including the journal *Housing*, were nervous about. Central government guidance and control, however, were surprisingly small. Some discussion of problems, with recommendations, was offered by a special subcommittee of the Central Housing Advisory Committee (CHAC), which published two reports on the management of estates in 1938 and 1945, and a number more dealing with special aspects of management through the 1950s. But the management responsibilities of authorities were not regulated by central government, and in many cases it was years before they set up special departments of housing. Of fifty-seven consulted by CHAC in 1959, only twenty-seven had a separate housing department; eight had a housing manager without a department or section, and eleven still had no housing managers at all.[1] Even in the 1980s some small authorities still had no special department for housing.

The only precedents that might have been useful to the new local authority landlords were the model villages and philanthropic trusts, but there seems to have been little if any effort to consult these to see if their experience was relevant. There was however one obvious link, in the Octavia Hill school of management, which was already widely used in philanthropic housing. Although she had explicitly refrained from turning her method into anything as firm as a system, by the time of her death in 1912, Hill's style of management had been adopted by Manchester and the large Scottish cities, as well as widely in Europe. Her trained workers were later appointed to manage the munitions estates, and they were only now withdrawing from these, to make way for men returning from the war. It would, then, have been a natural progression for council housing to adopt her management method, and some inroads were in fact made with a report on housing management by the women's section of the GCTPA in 1920, and by a book on *House Property and its Management* by Edith Neville, which was circulated to local authorities. By 1921 a number of districts were employing women managers on Addison estates, and in the later 1920s Chesterfield and Rotherham appointed Hill trained workers. The 1938 CHAC report on management recommended the method (which it praised the city of Amsterdam for using) and by this time about half of all such managers were working for local authorities, although covering less than 5 per cent of their stock in total.

But a number of things militated against the wholesale adoption of the Hill style of management. The most obvious one was scale. The method was expressly designed to work on a small scale – the optimum size of estate for a manager was supposed to be not more than 300 units. Given that within a few years some estates grew to 2000 dwellings or more, it is easy to see why the Hill method would have been thought impossibly impractical, although ironically a much later study of housing management called for a return to local management on something very like the Hill scale.[2]

It was not only scale, however, but the institutional organization of management that ultimately ruled out the Hill approach. Local authorities already had departments that would naturally regard certain aspects of estate management as their own preserve, including treasurers', surveyors', borough engineers' and works departments. An obvious strategy was to parcel out responsibilities between them so that: 'the clerk commonly dealt with lettings and tenancy matters, the treasurer with rent collection, and the engineer or surveyor with maintenance.'[3] This left welfare of tenants out of the picture or, if in it, in an isolated position that would naturally be assigned to women. Women managers did in fact fight their corner, in spite of the engrained prejudice against women professionals at a time when, amongst others things, they were expected to give up their careers on marriage. An Association of Women House Property Managers had formed in 1916, with its own certificated training scheme. Eventually there emerged a Society of Women Housing Estate Managers (SWHEM) in 1932. Borrowing elements from the training of both sanitary inspectors and the Institute of Chartered Surveyors, they were able to take some pride in the breadth and rigour of their training. But the male-female divide bedevilled the slowly emerging profession of management. An Institute of Housing, which was predominantly though not exclusively male, had formed in 1931. Like SWHEM, it was asked to give evidence to CHAC's housing subcommittee when this was set up in 1935, and after some years of overlap of memberships there was an outright schism between the two bodies in 1936.

In fact, neither one was in a strong professional position at this time, and it was a further generation before a unified profession was established. The Institute grew during the 1940s, when there was a great demand for trained staff, and this made SWHEM consider whether or not to admit men to their society. This they eventually did in 1948, in the face of strong reservations on the part of some of their – mainly older – members. There was then slow progress towards full amalgamation, the principal impediment on the Institute's side being the continuing association of SWHEM with women's issues and welfare, while for its part SWHEM feared that a merger would lower their high standards and make it easy for men to jostle women aside. The merging of the two bodies was eventually achieved in 1965 – that is, long after the practices of council housing management were firmly set.

By this time the huge postwar expansion of council housing had enhanced the status of housing departments and management, and SWHEM's fears were more or less justified. The highest posts tended to be taken by men, while the position of women managers deteriorated. The 'hard' or technical functions were identified with male managers, as 'welfare' was with women; and the latter was regarded, not as central to the management and wellbeing of the whole sector, but rather an 'added on' function of management, to be used in special cases or crises. It had been the Institute's view in the 1930s that every estate should have a woman welfare worker, who would be able to teach such things as 'cleanliness' or give 'homely hints such as the making of curtains.'[4] CHAC also, though it grasped the essence of Hill's approach perfectly well, emphasized that welfare was naturally a women's function. In slum clearance, for example, it was women rather than men who had the skills 'to convert families to the right frame of mind for consenting to the cleansing of bedding and furniture and the destruction when necessary of vermin-infested articles.'[5] It was women again who could best get access to the housewife who was 'mainly concerned with ordering the household and who bears the brunt in times of sickness or adversity', while the husband had 'other preoccupations – his work, his hobbies, his weekend sport.'[6]

This male/female dichotomy was not the only sign of damaging weaknesses in the profession that affected the operation of council housing. Institutional fragmentation left housing managers with little responsibility and still less control over technical and financial matters. While they were usually responsible for the collection of rents, for example, they had no influence over rent levels, or the overall housing budget. They had no input into design, which as we have seen was driven by another momentum entirely. Neither the Dudley nor Parker Morris Report, dominated as they were by design prescriptions for how people should live, really discussed the management implications of their proposed designs, despite the range of management bodies amongst those they consulted. Repairs – which more than anything were at the interface of people and property – were almost always serviced from another department with more prestige and authority than management. There was an often uneasy relationship between housing managers and departments responsible for such things as lighting, cleansing and parks, which had a material impact on estates. Managers were left with a limited number of areas that no one else could or would want to poach. The most important of these were the selection and placing of tenants in the stock of dwellings available, coupled to the educative task of ensuring that people lived properly in their new homes.

As a lately developed profession, housing management lacked the prestige and status of the more technical, design and land-based professions and its own professional institute was much younger than theirs. A poor level of qualification was part of this picture. Initially there were hopes that management would be a graduate profession, but wartime staff shortages and rapid postwar expansion led to dilution with unqualified or underqualified staff and the training record remained poor. In 1979 there was still 'an appalling lack of training within housing departments': only just over half had any training budget and the average amount was £10 per head.[7] When in the 1970s a keen new head of management on a large London estate wanted to set up a fully integrated service, there were no training schemes available; most of his officers had only practical experience to guide them, and any efforts to improve were hampered by low job satisfaction and heavily bureaucratic but inefficient procedures. The high level of rent arrears on this estate, and the problems posed by a small number of 'difficult' families, seemed beyond managers' power to tackle, and were therefore avoided. An in-depth study of the estate made it clear that the situation would be little changed in the following years.[8]

Housing management, then, grew up *ad hoc*, to serve local authorities in their new landlord role. As it dealt with two low-status things – housekeeping and working-class affairs – it is not surprising that its importance and complexity were unrecognized. The local government reorganization of 1974 inflicted another 'devastating impact on the already weak and complex structures of housing management.'[9] By reducing the number of local authorities by more than three-quarters, at a stroke it increased their average holdings tenfold, from 1,400 to 14,000. In London the dismemberment of the GLC meant that its 360 flatted and 44 cottage estates (including the huge Addison estates) were distributed amongst the London Boroughs, giving them stocks of up to 40,000 units.

Scale, therefore, must be the first reason why management meant so much more to the operation of council housing than it ever did, for instance, to independent landlords or the model housing trusts. A further reason was that council housing was the property of the state, paid for by tax and rate payers. The presumed immensity of the benefit bestowed, with the feeling that people must be monitored to ensure that they did not abuse it, did a lot to determine the habitual style of management. Council housing was a scarce, bitterly fought for and contentious commodity, and strict equity had to be observed in sharing it out. Management was dominated by ideas of merit and need: who 'deserved' it (in a sense not so distant from the Victorian one) and who *needed* it the most. Managers could not avoid being involved with the conflicts and overlaps between these two categories. But while this provided them with an ethos – the protection of the property and the wellbeing of the people living in it – it did not follow that it also supplied an intellectual framework or philosophy enabling it to deal with the difficult or even unresolvable dilemmas that resulted.

Changing Times and Management Attitudes

In 1919, it was unclear to managers where, or indeed whether, there was any dividing line between those tenants able to look after themselves and others needing careful control. In principle, the Addison tenants, who were by definition respectable, should not have required much management at all. In practice, authorities showed mixed but cautious attitudes towards them: the first concern was that they should be able to pay the rents charged, and applications were scrutinized accordingly. At the same time, there was concern about the cultural gap between them and the new houses and estates. 'Some may never have known, some still have to learn anew, how to keep their house in order.'[10] This perhaps explains why the LCC's Addison estates had resident superintendents. But the real social challenge came when the constituency of applicants began to be widened by the Wheatley Act after 1924, and later with slum clearance. This, in particular, drew in people from outside the 'respectable' classes who would not previously have been entertained as tenants. The CHAC subcommittee report on management, to which as a member Raymond Unwin must have contributed, acknowledged that the task of local authorities was to be both trustee of public property and

'Moving Day' – Dogsthorpe Road, Peterborough 'scheme' of 14 houses – photograph published in *Housing*, 25 October, 1920.

tenants' counsellor and friend. It was to be sensitive to the complete upheaval in people's lives caused by being rehoused from the slums, and their consequent need for 'social education' to become 'housing minded'.[11] Like the Victorian reformers it saw a serious risk that a bad minority would bring with them, and perpetuate, a 'slum atmosphere' that would make life unendurable for the rest. This minority was admittedly very small – perhaps amounting to 5 per cent on one large scheme – but it included a still smaller number who were 'beyond reclamation', who would be 'a permanent charge upon the benevolence of the community and must be cared for', if only to ensure that their children would grow into better ways.[12] The report later conceded that the majority of tenants rightly resented interference in their private lives, although something more than a weekly doorstep rent collection was needed, even in their case, to ensure that they were not breaking regulations, for instance by taking in lodgers or living in houses that had become too large for their needs. Another advantage of the rent collector's call, often appreciated only after its discontinuance, was that it gave the best opportunity to report the need for repairs.

The general orientation of estate management, therefore, was towards regulation, education and control, while tenants were not expected to be in any way proactive in return. It was a paternalism that, though easily ridiculed by later generations, would not have seemed untoward at the time. Indeed, it was not uncommon for it to be fondly remembered by tenants in later years, when it contrasted unfavourably with the later and more impersonal style. The Honour Oak Local History Project, for instance, wanted in 1977 'to let the authorities know how much better the estate was managed and serviced in the past.'[13] Managers, rent collectors and, still more, caretakers were often resident on estates, and were themselves not socially far distant from those their job it was to oversee. One record of a manager appointed to the Becontree estate may be illuminating here:

I saw this advertisement by the London County Council's Valuation, Estates and Housing departments in the News Chronicle Newspaper. It was for Estate Clerks . . . The sub-committee of the Housing Committee interviewed me. They were rather helpful as I was a delegate to the London Trades Council and had got the secretary to stand as a referee. The other referee was my trade union organizer and as it was a Labour run council it went down fairly well. A letter then came to say I had been appointed as an Estate Clerk on the Becontree Estate for the princely sum of two pounds and ten shillings a week. It was December 1937 and I was just twenty-two years old.[14]

The problem was that management's paternalism became, so to speak, set in stone, and was carried through to an era when it was no longer appropriate for any section of tenants.

The management of property and the management of people could comfortably be regarded as one and the same, as long as tenants shared managers' (and designers') preconceptions; but the main preoccupation of managers was with those tenants whose living patterns did not meet the required standards.   Central government could recognize a crucial improvement in the main body of tenants. CHAC's second management report of 1945, for instance, was at pains to show there was a new management climate now that council housing was to serve the whole of society. Although this particular hope proved hollow, rising standards and expectations of the working classes called for a different management approach. As CHAC put it in 1959: 'Tenants as a whole are able to stand on their own feet and need less constant contact with the landlord.'[15] This applied even to slum clearance populations, who no longer exhibited the same huge difference in standards as formerly: they were more confident about moving from slums to new estates, where they would be able and prepared to adjust their budgets as needed, and only for some of the very poorest was rehousing still a 'major embarrassment'.[16]

One small but significant sign of the times related to disinfestation. It had been general practice to disinfest people's furniture and effects overnight with hydrogen cyanide, to prevent vermin being carried into the new houses; but while in some districts this was voluntary, and even welcomed by tenants because it covered their removal costs, in others it was compulsory and deeply resented. Sometimes, indeed, it was accompanied by a demeaning family medical inspection and delousing. Now bed bugs, the vermin mainly targeted, were dying out, and disinfestation was needed only occasionally. To apply it selectively, however, would be invidious but a way round the problem was to give out that it was done to eradicate woodworm, to which no particular stigma attached.[17]

At the face of estate management things appeared rather differently. The growing numbers of slum clearance tenants after 1955 meant that ordinary waiting list applicants were shouldered aside, their waiting time lengthened to unreasonable degrees – 7 years was given as normal for London, and some applicants waited for a quarter of a century.[18] At the same time the former slums were going through profound changes, not only because progressive clearance removed the oldest and worst of the stock, but because of the improvement and modernization encouraged by government grants for basic amenities, as well as countless independent installations of plumbing and heating, and the introduction of the same white goods and furnishings as were found in suburban homes. Much of this was done by occupants who now owned, rather than rented, their homes, and as a consequence there was no longer as much social stigma attached to living in areas formerly labelled as slums. During the 1960s and 1970s, the inner areas were for the most part re-defined as low-cost housing – humble and shunned by younger families, it is true, but filling a useful role for households who either did not want or could not afford suburban living. These included pensioners and others living alone, childless couples or single people, and various categories of 'transients' who did not expect to remain for long. In certain industrial districts the inner-city stock became the haven of immigrant populations, often living in extended families, who found in it their first and perhaps lasting foothold. Recent comers were normally ineligible for council housing. Although the postwar device of designing estates with a 'housing mix' was supposed to take care of a range of household types and sizes, accommodating those who did not fit managerial preconceptions and procedures was not so easily arranged.

In a subtler way, the voluntary or waiting list applicants corresponded to the old 'respectable' division of society, although the gulf that separated them from the latter-day 'roughs' was narrowing. The housing management profession was not well equipped, either institutionally or intellectually, to recognize and develop strategies to deal with the changes as they were happening. Its stock approach could be too paternalistic and controlling for the more affluent and self-sufficient tenants, while its strategy for the others was to keep trying to press them into a domestic cultural mould that was in any case becoming obsolete.

The Management of Domestic Lives

To the 1960s, at least, much of the energy of managers went into supporting, and directing, tenants in the use of their homes. Their expectations of tenants were on the whole modest: they wanted them to pay the rent regularly, take an interest in their homes, not allow unreasonable wear and tear, and 'to behave as a good neighbour and member of the community.'[19] It was a sacred management principle to uphold tenants' right to the peace and security of their homes – and in practice this usually meant protection from disorderly neighbours. Although it was always the male head of house who, as the legal tenant, was addressed, it was recognized that the condition of the house was due to the housewife – so much so, that at the end of the war the dilapidation of the stock was attributed to many wives having been absent from home because of war work. In the prewar years, the ultimate sanction for neglecting the house or the garden was eviction, and the main mechanism for encouraging the conventional and proper use of the home was the tenant handbook that authorities supplied and reissued down the years. Such handbooks constitute an archive that has never been given serious attention, although it affords many insights into management attitudes; and their very infrequent updates give them something of the quality of a folk literature. Always anonymous, they prompt curiosity as to their authorship. Their attention to detail suggests that it may have been women housing visitors, with their intimate knowledge both of dwellings and occupants. Tenants at Dagenham, for example, were exhorted (in a 64-page handbook) to

Be house proud. Keep your house clean and your gardens tidy. Make them the envy of your neighbours . . . Persevere in the formation of good garden paths. Many tenants have made splendid paths by simply rolling in the stones gathered from the soil during the cultivation of their gardens.[20]

The advice, possibly appropriate when it was first drafted, was repeated into the 1960s. 'Hints for Housewives' in the same handbook told people: 'When cleaning electric lamps, wipe with a damp cloth and do not place the lamps in water.' Tenants were also asked, 'Have you ever thought seriously about your front door and what it symbolises?' – and the question was followed by an instruction to polish it regularly all over.[21] Oxfordshire tenants around 1960 were reminded in no uncertain terms of their good fortune and consequent obligations:

It is a condition of your tenancy that you should look after your garden. With most tenants it is a matter of personal pride, and it is very true to say that the house inside can nearly always be judged by the garden outside . . . Is yours as good as it might be? . . . The County still has a large number of people on its waiting list urgently in need of homes of their own. Be thankful for what you've got, therefore, and make the best of it for the benefit of all – not least yourself.[22]

Many contemporary accounts suggest that early generations of tenants more than rose to the challenge of gardens, for many a new experience. In 1938 CHAC was 'pleased to note . . . the admirable way in which most of the gardens were kept by the tenants living on cottage estates. To some the garden was a new toy of which they were obviously proud.'[23] The same impression came from York: 'Go where you will in the different estates, everywhere carefully tended gardens meet the eye.'[24] The creation of a garden from what had only lately been a building site was no small feat, and the Becontree tenant handbook of 1933 was perhaps optimistic in estimating the cost of cultivating a garden as a few shillings a year; but people quickly learnt to take cuttings and scrounge necessary materials, spurred on by gardening clubs and the annual competitions and awards that were run on many estates.

Overseeing the gardens was an important management function. They were regarded as the responsibility of the husband, and the Becontree managers provided a chart showing how a bare plot could be laid out. Initially it was customary for councils to cut front lawns, hedges and creepers but later conditions of tenancy usually made lawns and hedges the tenant's responsibility. There were rules about hanging washing where it might be seen by the public and written permission had to be sought for any garden shed or structure, even down to such things as rabbit hutches, which must conform to strict rules as to position, size and type. There was no longer much emphasis on the worth of the garden for growing food. Rather, it was appearance that carried most weight. It was frequently pointed out how the odd unkempt garden could spoil the image of a whole street or estate, and offenders were issued with warnings, leading ultimately to an eviction notice if they did not come up to scratch.

Although 'digging for victory' was an important part of the war effort, the war of 1939–1945 was blamed for a decline in standards from which estate gardens (like public parks) never recovered. In any case, higher densities reduced the size of garden plots, so eliminating the orderly progression from the front garden's floral display to the back garden's lawn, flower borders and vegetable plot. People began to have other uses for garden space, such as tinkering with the family car, parking caravans or trade vans. Garden fences, which had already suffered from spending cuts, could reach the point of being damaged beyond repair and were never replaced. Gardens were then at the mercy of rampaging children and packs of dogs, which were now increasing alarmingly, to the despair of those who still took a pride in their gardens. The largely unexplored history of the domestic garden may have been strongly linked to changing patterns of child rearing in our society.

The burdens placed on tenants by rehousing, and particularly on those who had never had homes of their own before, was allowed for in various ways. The costs of removal were more than many could afford, and the 1936 Housing Act permitted councils to give clearance tenants grants towards it. As we have seen, if goods were removed for overnight disinfestation, this was at the council's expense. Some furniture was so verminous that it had to be destroyed, or so fragile that it fell to pieces when moved. In its new setting, something that had passed unremarked in the old home 'blushes for itself and soon its owner is blushing for it, too.'[25] The earliest tenants were often overwhelmed by the number of rooms in their new homes and to CHAC it was apparent that 'many people do not possess enough furniture to make their new house a home.'[26] Floors and windows posed the biggest problems, for as on new private estates, houses were handed over by their builders with bare boards and no curtain fittings. Amongst the really poor on Sheffield's Wybourn estate in the 1930s, newspaper hung from rods served as makeshift curtains.[27] A generation later, the primary need was felt to be lino, which was regarded as more important than carpet;[28] and some purchased their new floor coverings and also furniture months or years in advance, storing them in the shop until they could be put to use. Rehousing could also entail sacrifices like that of the old Oldham couple who give up their piano when they went to the new estate.[29]

It was hoped in the early, utopian phase of council housing that the interiors of people's homes would be as reformed, aesthetically, as the dwelling itself. The Honorary Secretary of the Women's Village Councils Federation in 1920 saw this as 'an unrivalled opportunity for raising the standard of decoration in the homes of the people'[30] and the same year a Design and Industries Association exhibition at Whitechapel Art Gallery showed 'how simple and beautiful the homes of the workers might become if they will only apply to the purchase of their commonplace domestic articles the test of "fitness for purpose", and to their furniture and decorative articles the tests of sincerity and cheerfulness of colour.' A suite of model rooms demonstrated 'ideas for changing the English parlour into a sweet and inviting sanctuary of rest and content.'[31]

Real life, unfortunately, did not live up to the hope, in spite of CHAC's proposal that since people had been 'left to determine their own standards' up to now, housing departments might collaborate with local schools of art in order to raise them.[32] It referred to a Council for Art and Industry exhibition that demonstrated how to furnish a two-bedroom house for as little as £50. One outstanding authority 'decided that they would be failing in their duty if, having provided good houses, they did no more to assist the tenants to achieve a higher standard of living'[33] – to which end they invited a consortium of local traders to tender for a list of basic items which could be bought in instalments paid with the rent. Churches and charities had second-hand furniture schemes, but for tenants these had the taint of charity, while authorities worried lest they harbour vermin. In practice, those councils that helped tenants furnish their

Six views of a completed furnished house on the estate illustrated on page 76 above. The date is 1920 and the interiors go far to explain why so many first-time council tenants described their new homes as 'little palaces'.

homes were probably not too particular about aesthetics. Under housing Acts of 1925 and 1936 they had powers to provide furniture 'in suitable cases', and these were confirmed in the 1949 Act, which also allowed them to offer hire purchase. Only a few authorities had furniture schemes before 1939, Leeds, Birmingham, Glasgow and London boroughs among them; and Leeds was one of the cities that opened furnished show houses and flats to the public. By 1939, there was already concern about tenants being persuaded by doorstep salesmen into purchases they could not afford. In the postwar boom in consumer goods hire purchase became such a serious social problem that legislation was passed to give purchasers some protection.

Technically, early council houses were able to function without any extra equipment from the tenant. Lighting was by gas or electricity, and nearly all but the earliest estates had the latter. Space heating was by an open coal grate, and cooking of a sort could be done on this. Food was stored in a ventilated larder. Laundry was done in a built-in, coal or gas-fired 'copper' or boiler, but estates of flats had common laundries. From the outset, and according to Tudor Walter recommendations, most of the cooking was expected to be done on a gas or electric cooker placed in the scullery, supplemented by the coal fire in the living room. Cookers could be rented either from the supply companies, an arrangement long since established in bye-law housing, or from local authorities, who added their rental to the house rent. The Dudley, and later the Parker Morris Report, assumed that tenants would provide their own cookers, although there were parts of the country – the Durham coalfield for one – where well into the postwar period, in the absence of gas, tenants were expected to cook on a range back-to-back with the living room open grate.

Tenants were required to clean windows weekly or fortnightly and to have chimneys swept once or more a year. Pictures were to be hung only from the picture rails provided, and with the specified type of hook. Some tenants needed written consent before fixing a large nail. The external decoration of the house was always the responsibility of the authority. So at first was internal redecoration, which was done in regular cycles of different lengths for different rooms. Wallpaper, paint or distemper were used, according to room, and tenants were usually given a very limited choice of colours and designs. People were peremptorily informed when the decorators were coming, and required to empty rooms completely. By 1939 some councils were making tenants responsible for interior decoration, with a small allowance towards its cost, and 20 years later this applied to the large majority of districts, to CHAC's satisfaction; for 'a council house becomes more of a home when it is decorated to the tenant's individual taste and not to a standard pattern, and far more care is taken of a house when the tenant has spent a good deal of time and trouble on it.'[34] This seemed amply confirmed by the many accounts of an orgy of decorating and general 'DIY' that took place on estates after the war, when husbands, in particular took up their paint brushes never to put them down again.[35] A Cardiff municipal tenants' handbook helpfully offered guidance on appropriate colourings for walls, pronouncing green 'restful', blue 'peaceful', brown 'concentrative', red 'stimulating', and yellow 'animating'.[36]

But although people were exhorted to 'treat your house as if it were your own – it is',[37] the tenancy conditions they signed up to made it difficult ever to forget that it was the property of the council. It was a particular deprivation for many on early LCC estates and doubtless elsewhere that no pets of any kind were allowed. Permission was required before taking in lodgers or boarders – a time-honoured expedient for households needing to supplement their incomes – and if given, a higher rent was charged. In certain periods some authorities extended the definition of lodger to adult earning children, and this became such an issue in Sheffield in 1967 that it actually unseated a Labour council. Other restrictions included the use of the home as a workplace, although many were tempted to keep illicit shops in back rooms – a much needed service when new estates were destitute of ordinary shops. Permission was needed to display a trade name plate (for instance of a midwife or corset-maker) and normally a charge was made. An early intention was for doctors and other professionals to take up residence on the estates where they practised, and special houses were built for them, for which a full economic rent was charged.

In regard to the dwelling itself, perhaps the greatest limitation was the number of bedrooms families were allowed to have. There was no possibility of opting for a bedroom more than was strictly needed and voluntarily paying more rent, for this would have flouted the principle of sharing out scarce resources by strictly defined health criteria. The only possibility of having a room above the prescribed level was perhaps in a 'miscellaneous property', which doubtless contributed to the popularity of this part of the stock. If with the passage of time people became 'overhoused' (that is, with a bedroom above standard), they risked being asked to move to a smaller property. Leeds after 1947 was one authority where overhoused tenants who refused to take a transfer had their rent raised.

When it came to changes tenants wished to make at their own expense, management attitudes were negative and restrictive rather than encouraging. Regulations always required reinstatement of anything that had been changed when a tenant moved on, and this made people go to ridiculous lengths to preserve obsolete fittings such as old fire grates that would never again be used. At the same time, when councils decided, usually very belatedly, to modernize estates, they would do so without reference to any of tenants' own improvements, which were swept away by the standardized improvement package. It is clear that the management system was simply not flexible enough to look at the housing stock as so many individual homes. Policies were determined by the 'worst case' scenario – that is, the harm that might be done by the uncultured or destructive, rather than the constructive use of the dwelling by those who were careful and discriminating.

The problem of substandard tenants who let their houses go to rack and ruin preoccupied official minds until well into postwar years.[38] Between the wars, tenants' housekeeping standards were regularly monitored and if they were found unsatisfactory warning letters were issued, the ultimate sanction being eviction. In Glasgow, with its old history of 'ticketing' and uncompromising attitudes towards slum dwellers, tenants' homes were regularly patrolled by a housing department factor assisted by the 'Green Ladies' or nurse inspectors introduced in 1927, and they were then graded good, fair, 'needs supervision', or 'unsuitable'. This was the period when the myth of the tenant who, if given a bath, would 'only keep coals in it' was given full rein. Perhaps occasionally, if ever, true of mining districts where pay was partly in large dumps of coal that had to be got off the street as quickly as possible, this was a myth that predated council housing and once was even raised in Parliament.[39] In 1947 the Labour government set up a national Institute of Houseworkers, an attempt to professionalize what it recognized as an important occupation. To some extent its role was that of a latterday 'lady bountiful' and one of its functions, it was suggested, might be to induct small groups of estate housewives into the use of new appliances and other arts of home making, such as making curtains.[40]

The ultimate unfreedom of tenants was in their inability in any real sense to choose their homes. It was a case of a benefit bestowed on but never chosen by the beneficiaries. Even those who escaped being steered to undesirable estates were not given a rational choice between two or more visible options: for instance, they were not allowed to put their names down for more than one estate and were led (or allowed) to believe that the refusal of an offer would bring penalties. It is true that all choices in housing must be constrained by what is available, but in the private housing sector constraints could still leave people feeling that they had exercised some autonomy, whereas in the public sector 'a council dwelling is not chosen, it is *allocated*'.[41]

From its central overview, CHAC in the 1950s recommended the relaxing of obsolete management practices and treating tenants as responsible agents.[42] Its report of 1969 reflected the wishes of its chairman, J.B.Cullingworth, that tenants should have more freedom of mobility and also choice in their own housing standards, although at the same time, and rather confusingly, it pleaded for 'more weight to be given to social need'.[43] The 1970s did see steps towards liberalization of housing management, as we shall see in the third part of this book, but it was opportunistically and over-optimistically linked to the centralization of management services. This involved less frequent rent collecting, and then the dropping of personal rent collecting altogether, and the ending of resident caretakers in favour of mobile squads that had no personal connection with estates at all. This withdrawal of personal contact and supervision was later agreed to be a major contributor to the social and physical decline of estates, affecting most of all those families with the highest degree of need.

Tenants and Rents

Probably the most important issue for tenants was the one most often ignored: the rent paid. The setting of rents was not a management function, but it was managers who collected them and applied any sanctions for non-payment. The ultimate penalty was eviction, which was routinely used before 1939, and what then faced the evicted was the old workhouse system or (from 1929) its derivative, the Public Assistance Committee, which was in turn replaced by the National Assistance Board in 1948. It is, then, curious that so much literature on estates – for example Willmott's study of Dagenham after 40 years, or Goetschius's study of community development on estates – is silent as to both rents and evictions.

Before 1914, the poorest were known to pay the highest proportions of their income in rent – a third being not uncommon. In eagerness to supply model housing for working people it seemed often forgotten that the original purpose of council housing had been to eradicate poverty. How far council housing did, or ever could have done this is closely related to the way it was funded and the resulting rents. Addison Act houses had rents some 50–100 per cent higher than rents of private landlords. After this, official expectation was that by 1927 council rents would bring an economic return on two-thirds of the capital outlay. Many authorities in fact set their rents below the recommended levels, to bring their new houses within reach of 'heroes' of war; but even so, rent arrears grew alarmingly, particularly on the former munitions estates. Disaffection extended even to the cream of tenants, and the protests of tenant associations became 'too numerous to chronicle'.[44] Birmingham and Glasgow were big centres of protest, and a rent strike organised by the leftwing National Union of Ex-Servicemen, though abortive, had some success in mobilising tenants' wives.

It could be argued that the level of rents was not critical for the mass of working-class people until council housing became their regular and, eventually, more or less their only choice of tenure. The many who began to be subject to slum clearance from the 1930s, were coerced (rather than persuaded, as Octavia Hill would have wished) into paying more for their homes. The succession of different acts, subsidies and dwelling types, with falling building costs after 1925, brought about a huge and confusing variety of rent levels which, apart from the Addison houses, were set by local authorities. The situation was further confused by the notional linking of rents to what landlords had charged in 1914. Wheatley rents were supposedly equivalent to average pre-1914 rents, but they were in reality about 25 per cent higher. Rates, not distinguished from rents by most tenants, added roughly another third.

Under the 1930 Act rents were supposed to be such as were 'ordinarily payable by persons of the working classes in the locality.'[45] In addition to their obligatory contribution, councils could further subsidize rents by a voluntary contribution from their general rate fund. A few began to introduce 'differential' schemes which in effect pooled all the different subsidies to create a unified scale where rents could be charged according to tenants' means; and the 1935 Housing Act enabled all authorities to do this. Differential rents, however, could be resented both by those who stood to benefit and those who stood to lose. For the former, the necessary means test of eligibility was uncomfortably close to the indignity of making an application for unemployment relief or dole, while the latter were faced with unwelcome rent rises. Some authorities explicitly hoped that differential rents would dislodge their more affluent tenants for good; and such people were now in the situation of having first been urged to take on the higher rent of a council house so as to release private accommodation for others poorer than themselves, only to be told now to make way for people from the slums. Announcements of differential rents, therefore, provoked a lot of resistance and rent strikes. In Leeds, a Labour council was unseated by a strike in 1934, but the largest was a successful one in Birmingham shortly before the outbreak of war. This was led by the Communist Party which saw tenant action as a field for social change, organizing a number of local tenants' associations city wide, where wives played a significant role.

In 1939 there were many kinds of differential or rebated rent schemes, some whose minimum level was zero rent, but most with a basic rent payable by all. Such schemes were often restricted to certain types of property, and not more than 10 per cent of authorities had them. During the 1930s council rents, with rates, absorbed about 15 per cent of an average manual worker's income.[46] While this was a substantial improvement on the pre-war situation, the very poor were still for the most part either excluded altogether, or stretched hard to pay their rent. Widespread publicity was given to a study of Stockton-on-Tees in the mid-1930s, where a rise in mortality on new estates was linked to malnutrition, because rents took too large a share of incomes,[47] and this was far from an isolated example.[48] Nor was the extra cost of estate life limited to rents. In addition to fares to work, higher shop prices, and other incidental costs of suburban life – where even the chimney sweepers charged more than in the old districts – there were the rates, which increased faster than the general cost of living over this period. While the class base of council housing was broader than in 1920, therefore, it was still weighted towards the upper end of the working classes. Its rents were some 20–25 per cent higher than controlled private rents (and only some 5 per cent lower than decontrolled ones), albeit for better accommodation. The whole rent structure, it was suggested, had been 'acquired as haphazardly as the British Empire', with 'no sort of consistent principles, economic, social or moral.'[49]

The first decade after the Second World War might be described as the peak period of council housing – certainly it was one in which many of the lasting public perceptions of it were formed. By 1955, rents were some 25–30 per cent lower in real terms than in 1939, taking little over 6 per cent of average manual earnings. Meanwhile those earnings, especially of the semi-skilled and unskilled, had risen relative to pre-war levels, and to middle-class salaries. This was the period of the newly secure and affluent manual worker with spare spending capacity, particularly when there were wage-earning adult children still at home. It was also the time when the middle classes felt their own living standards irrevocably falling and resented the workers for their careless enjoyment of what, up to now, had been middle-class prerogatives. The 'Jag' parked in front of the council house now joined the 'coals in the bath' image, expressing a sense of outrage that the working class should have access to such privilege. Yet there were still many tenants coming from slum houses with controlled rents, for whom council rents were a shock. In Lansbury in 1954, where the LCC applied a rough means test to applicants and excluded those deemed incapable of paying, 'the dominant topic of conversation . . . and the most serious object of complaint' was rent.[50]

Over the next 15 years, to 1970, council rents rose some 85–90 per cent in real terms, taking their share of average, post-tax earnings to over 10 per cent. Rent rises, which were imposed in large but irregular steps, outstripped any rise in earnings. It was in this period that rent pooling, or cross subsidy to newer from older estates with their now rapidly depreciating loans 'became the basic principle of local authority housing finance.'[51] Crucially, it helped to finance large building programmes and high borrowing rates. At the same time, even with raised rents, council housing was rapidly becoming the cheapest of any rented accommodation, especially in Scotland.

In 1969 only a third of authorities operated any rebate scheme, and most rent policies were still excluding low-income families.[52] By this time, however, there was a growing feeling, even within a Labour government, that resources should be targeted on the neediest through rent rebates, rather than giving low rents to everyone. This phase culminated in the short-lived 1972 Housing Finance Act of a Conservative government which aimed to put council housing finance on the same footing as the private sector, where 'Fair Rents' (at supposed market levels) had been introduced some years previously. The Act's intention was for the higher fair rent to subsidize rent rebates, and it obliged local authorities to set up rebate schemes based on a national model, so ending the freedom they had enjoyed since 1923 to set their own rents. This was an acutely political and therefore sensitive issue, and the resistance provoked ensured its summary ending under a new Labour government. Ironically, part of the funding structure remained intact, with the unintended consequence that more subsidy was put into housing, and tenants were more shielded than would otherwise have been the case.[53]

At this point the government put a temporary ban on rent rises. When councils were at last allowed to raise rents in 1975, some declined to do so and, overall, any increases were very small. By 1979, therefore, rents had again fallen in relation to general inflation. Meanwhile, there was an increasingly permissive attitude to those in arrears with their rent. The standard response was no longer eviction, now 'resorted to only in extreme cases',[54] but arrears were usually dealt with by series of letters of mounting urgency, a home visit and perhaps an office interview, where the various options open to the defaulter were reviewed, including a possible move to cheaper accommodation. Court action was used as a last resort, and was usually abandoned if there were any signs of the debt being paid off.

A fundamental reorganization of rents came in the 1980s, when a Conservative government was at last able to realize the policy that had aborted in 1972, and to switch subsidy from buildings to a means-tested 'housing benefit' for all who qualified. As part of the same policy, councils were coerced into significant rent rises. The government still expected that 'rents should generally not exceed levels within reach of people in low-paid employment, and in practice they will frequently be below market levels';[55] but as there was little if any comparable private housing to rent, this had little substance. For a brief period it was suggested that rents should relate to the valuations put on houses when sold to tenants under the 'right to buy', but this would have had the unfortunate result (from the government's point of view) of leading to rent reductions in certain districts, rather than rises – a reflection of the poor condition and status to which much council housing had now fallen. The strategy eventually adopted was a sliding scale of rises applied to different areas.

Notwithstanding these radical changes to housing finance, its complicated rent history left council housing at the end of the twentieth century still the cheapest family accommodation available. As a result of Conservative policies, privately rented housing was now more plentiful, but much of it was luxury accommodation beyond the reach of ordinary wage-earners. Housing associations, the successors to councils in provision of what was now called 'social housing', had a different funding structure which resulted in rents that were invariably higher than council rents. For those on full housing benefit this did not of course matter, while some of those paying the higher rents might feel they got value for money. The historical overview of council rents suggests that over the middle decades of the century they were comparatively cheap for the majority of tenants, but that for a minority they were always too high. That we do not know more about this minority – for instance their profile and distribution at different times and places – is due partly to the simplistic nature of the political debate and its effects on research. For as long as the debate was preoccupied with the relative merits of subsidy of buildings and subsidy of people (the old 'sanitary' approach[56]) the complex effects of subsidy structures in operation were not usually brought into the debate.

Rebates and housing benefit aside, the pooling of subsidies and rents meant that tenants got very unequal value for the rent paid. Those occupying older and in many cases inferior property paid rents that helped to subsidize newer and better property: in effect, the continuing expansion of council housing was partly financed by exploiting tenants living in the older stock. There could perhaps have been an argument for this if all applicants had been able to take their pick of properties available and choose the rent level to suit their means and preferences; but this was far from the case, as the next section of this chapter will show. Chronic shortage and constant high demand for homes combined with managers' selection procedures to privilege certain categories of tenant over others. As in owner occupation, but without its individual freedoms, the better off council tenants occupied the best property, and it was scarcely surprising that they jealously protected their rents and resisted anything that threatened the privileges they enjoyed, unless and until they were offered better ones.

This must go a good part of the way to explain why tenant militancy about rents was for the most part patchy and limited, to the disappointment of the Communist Party, which looked to the rent issue to mobilize the working class. Rent strikes took place when the rents of privileged tenants were threatened, as in Birmingham in 1939, or where housing stress was extreme, as in inner London boroughs in the 1950s and 1960s. They sometimes won concessions and they also helped to politicize those involved, although in the absence of a strong tenant movement the lessons learned could not be passed on; but the usual end was frustration and bitterness.[57] The big exception was the mobilization against the 1972 Housing Finance Act, which was strong enough to help change national policy and did more to induce tenant involvement in management than any previous campaigns. But until these developments, which will be further discussed in chapter 12 below, tenants' position *vis-à-vis* their managers was habitually a weak one, and only an extreme provocation could move them to break their contracts and put their own tenancies at risk.

The muddle and inequities of rents were not helped by the habitual hostility of the public at large who saw council housing as a burden on the taxpayer and ratepayer – a point of view that overlooked the fact that council tenants also paid taxes and rates. The issue that was never resolved, throughout all its history, was how far council housing was or should be an economically efficient enterprise, and how far a social service. One effect of this ambivalence was that, in the constant effort to keep rents down while at the same time expanding the stock, disrepair and dereliction increased, not only to the despair of the occupants but probably contributing more than anything else to the increasing notoriety of council housing from the 1970s onwards. One analysis lays most of the blame on poor management structures, in particular the fact that upkeep was seldom under the control of estate managers, but was managed remotely from other parts of authorities.[58] But underlying this was the inadequacy of the funds set aside for repairs and maintenance.[59] Authorities were not required to set aside any stated sums for maintenance, as was the case with housing associations receiving state grants; and although most authorities did keep a housing repairs account (and from 1958 to 1972 all were required to do so), either the funds set aside were insufficient, or they could be raided to keep rents down, or the necessary work was simply not done. A flurry of activity took place in the 1970s, when a repairs subsidy was briefly available; but for the most part rents were not set high enough to ensure the viability and continuation of much of the stock. Yet again, this demonstrates the damaging gap between the type of housing that society thought proper to provide and what some at least of its tenants were reasonably able to pay.

The Management of Estate Social Structures

The management function that made the single biggest contribution to the evolution of council housing was 'allocations', or the selection and placing of tenants. For most of its history council housing operated in conditions of acute shortage. It has been estimated that waiting lists contained some 5 to 10 per cent of the population, but this cannot be taken as a reliable measure because of the many who knew that it would be useless even to apply. It was not until towards 1970 that voids or unlettable property began to appear, and then only on 'problem' estates. For the most part council housing was a scarce commodity for which there was bitter competition, and access to it was through its 'gatekeepers', the housing managers. For the actual procedures used, central government only advised: discretion was left with local authorities and there were wide variations in their practices. In the early years – and for much longer in many smaller and rural authorities – it was common for the selection of tenants to be made by councillors, advised by their housing officers, and this was something widely regarded as invidious and prone to corruption. By 1949, it was usual in larger authorities for the whole task to be delegated to officers. Whoever performed it, it presented another problematic dimension of management, for it involved the observance of social equity, or the sharing out of available dwellings with as much fairness and attention to genuine housing need as possible. This was a moral balancing act that was in the last resort impossible, and it put local authorities in a position that no private landlord was in. It was closest, if anything, to the task of the model housing trusts, but with the vital difference that, as time went on, the stock became so large as to monopolize the whole rented sector – a stock that was paid for, moreover, with taxpayers' and ratepayers' money.

For would-be tenants, the hurdles were, firstly, admission to the waiting list, and then the award of some measure of priority, which might or might not be followed by the offer of a tenancy. There were significant numbers who were not normally admitted to the waiting list. Although it depended to some extent on period, these included single people, couples who were not married, married couples without children (except sometimes for newly-weds), tenants in arrears with their current tenancy, and perhaps exceptionally large families for whom councils had no accommodation of suitable size. Another almost universal condition was that applicants must have some sort of local connection. People were normally precluded from applying to a waiting list if they did not live or work in a district, or had not done so for a specified length of time. Most commonly this was one year, but it might be as long as five years, or a complicated equation of so many out of the last N years. It was this requirement, above all, that excluded recent immigrants, who were affected by other exclusions as well. For instance, they often initially lived as single men and women, or cohabited rather than married, while if their families were with them these were often too large for any houses available. Together with the fact that they were frequently ignorant of the rules and their own entitlements, this explains the great under-representation of ethnic minorities amongst council tenants through the 1950s and 1960s. In 1966, for instance, the proportion of immigrant populations housed by local authorities was only about a quarter of the that of native English populations.[60]

Residential qualifications were a matter of dispute between central and local government, which had different ideas about the purposes of council housing. Central policy-makers argued that they were prejudicial to returning servicemen and also inhibited general job mobility; but the objection was really a deeper one that concerned the size of constituency from which tenants were drawn. The central view was that this should be as wide as possible, to ensure that those in the greatest need were being catered for; but local politicians, with their own electorates in mind, were bound to take more note of 'the resentment with which people who have lived a long time in a district regard the letting of a house to somebody who they consider does not belong there.'[61] New developments from which local people were excluded risked being stigmatized from the outset.[62] The issue was highlighted in the 'sons and daughters' dispute that arose countless times on estates throughout the country. Here, the grounds of objection were that applicants who were strangers to an area were, on strict housing need criteria, given tenancies, while married sons and daughters born and bred on estates were forced to leave them because they themselves had no priority. It became a big issue in Dagenham after 1952, when an agreement of the borough council with the LCC, by which a certain quota of tenancies was reserved for sons and daughters, was revoked. A Housing Applicants' Association was formed, and for its Honorary Secretary, a Methodist minister, the battle was 'for a great ideal, a battle not only for the future community life of their township but one which could well have repercussions throughout the country. The key to England's future was in the housing estates; and by reason of priority in time and magnitude of its problem the key to the housing estates was in Dagenham.'[63] In its report of 1969, CHAC demonstrated from a nation-wide opinion survey that a majority of the public disagreed with local ties being given precedence in allocations. But when it came to the point, people felt and acted differently, and this not only for limited and selfish reasons, but for the principle long recognized by housing reformers, that some continuity of population down the generations was necessary if an estate was to develop any sense of community.

Once admitted to waiting lists, the chance of being offered a tenancy depended on an applicant's degree of priority, as well as what dwellings became available – and it was the interlocking of the two that enabled managers significantly to influence the social composition of estates. There were innumerable different schemes for placing applicants in priority order, in addition to any 'local' qualification. Weighting or 'points' were given for overcrowding and insanitary conditions, and for certain medical reasons – although in general, doctors' certificates alone were treated as 'quite useless' because so many people could produce them.[64] At times, ex-servicemen received priority, as did key workers. Frequently quotas were allotted to particular categories of need, which were then worked through in date order. Date order alone, or length of time spent on the waiting list, was sometimes the only criterion used. It had the benefit of simplicity and transparency, and an argument was put for it by CHAC in 1969, but most regarded it as too insensitive to real housing need. Some authorities used a 'merit' system where cases were decided individually on the discretion of housing officers, and from time to time simple balloting was used. Most selection schemes were mixes of complicated criteria and most authorities refused to divulge their details to the public until they were obliged to do so after 1980. However hard schemes tried to place applicants in some order of need or merit, any ranking order was likely to be invidious.

The case of people from slum clearance areas was different from that of ordinary applicants, for although the former eventually came to dominate in certain periods and locations, their legal entitlement was insecure and they were prey to lack of information, fears and rumours. Authorities' statutory obligations towards them were limited, in effect, to rehousing conventional families and other recognized groups such as pensioners. Those they could decline to rehouse included single people (who it was argued could find accommodation elsewhere), subtenants, tenants in furnished accommodation, lodgers (unless deemed to be part of a household), and anyone who had moved into an area after an official declaration of clearance had been made, whether or not they had been aware of it. Immigrants almost automatically fell into one or more of these categories. There were also anomalous cases like owner occupiers whose houses were not technically unfit but were included to facilitate a clearance scheme. Since in theory such people received full market compensation for their houses, they were charged a higher rent if given a tenancy – alternatively, if they paid the subsidized rent, their compensation was reduced. In practice, many in clearance areas rehoused themselves ahead of the bulldozer. The more fortunate bought a house elsewhere if they could, but many moved to even worse conditions as they were 'shunted on from one redevelopment area to the next.'[65]

After surmounting the hurdles of getting onto and rising to the top of the waiting list, the next was the choice of accommodation offered. Of all the tasks of management this was the most contentious, because of its direct impact on the social structure of estates. Quite soon, authorities found themselves owning a large range of property of differing qualities, locations and rents: a diverse stock into which a diverse population needed to be fitted as expeditiously as possible. It was here that the conflict between their landlord and their social service roles was most glaring. As landlords, their natural interest was to safeguard the property, which in practical terms meant putting the best rent payers and housekeepers into the best dwellings and estates, not only to ensure the upkeep of the property but for the maximum tenant contentment. To this end, 'undesirables' should be excluded outright, as they were for as long as authorities found it possible. Even so, there were many social grades to be accommodated and the preferred policy of managers was to place 'like with like' – a pragmatic way of dealing with latterday 'roughs' and 'respectables' where people of like standards were placed together, so broadly reinforcing the status quo. For households of seriously disruptive tenants there were two possible strategies, each with its advantages and disadvantages, One was to group them in enclaves, with the risk of these developing into ghettos within estates; the other was to scatter them piecemeal in the hope that they would not drag down their close neighbours, but rather be elevated by them. For this reason managers set great value on the 'ordinary' household with adequate but not too high standards, who would be tolerant towards an uncouth neighbour.

For the strategy to work, certain applicants needed to be steered or manipulated into the less good property, and this was not in fact difficult. In their ignorance of the overall picture some were easily convinced that their preferred destination was either unavailable, or too high-rent, or would involve too long a wait, to be an option for them. People's individual bargaining power depended on how desperate they were and how long they could afford to wait. Slum clearance people were in many ways most prone to manipulation, in spite of their legal entitlement to rehousing and the strength of numbers that might have given them power to resist or negotiate. In practice, they were often ignorant, confused and traumatized by the prospect of losing their homes and being kept in suspense about where they would be sent and how long they had to wait. There was a widespread belief that the council would give them, sequentially, 'two reasonable offers only'. Such restrictions – sometimes reduced to one offer – could legally be applied only to ordinary waiting list applicants, whose punishment for refusal was likely to be the loss of any accumulated priority points rather than outright removal from the list. But there is no doubt that officials traded on this misapprehension, as in the case of the elderly Sunderland widow and home owner in a clearance area, who received a letter from her town clerk informing her that she would be evicted if she did not accept the second offer made.[66] The implied threat in the phrase 'N reasonable offers only . . .' was that any subsequent one was likely to be even less desirable than the first, so creating a situation where confused or desperate applicants were panicked into accepting the first thing offered.

Unless they could be distributed in such casual vacancies as arose on existing estates, slum clearance populations were destined for purpose-built estates or estate extensions. A CHAC report cautioned against raising their hopes too high, since their new homes were 'more likely to be flats in the large towns, or if houses they will probably be built on the outskirts of a town and well away from the clearance areas.'[67] As long as new stock was being added, it was customary to offer longstanding, favoured tenants the pick of any new estates. Individually, requests for transfer carried little weight unless they fitted managers' own priorities, such as moving 'overhoused' tenants to make better use of the housing stock. Hence transfer requests could involve waiting times as long or longer than on the waiting list itself. One reason why authorities were so unaccommodating was the management costs involved, including the fact that disrepair came to light when houses were vacated, although this seems hardly adequate to explain councils' obstructive attitudes. In Leeds in the 1930s transfers were arbitrarily limited to four a week for the whole city, regardless of demand. Even mutual exchanges, a variety of transfer that gave maximum benefit to tenants at minimum cost to councils, were often forbidden or restricted by age or other considerations, including bans on certain property types or across district boundaries. Here again central government tried to encourage a more liberal approach that reflected its non-local orientation. For instance, it required the newly formed GLC to set up an exchange scheme that was open to anyone in the country, in contrast to an earlier LCC scheme restricted to its own tenants. By now it was becoming more common for authorities to operate exchange bureaux, and a voluntary National Mobility Scheme of local authorities came into force in 1981.

The selection practices that had such an overwhelming influence on the life and development of estates were based on an assumption that 'moral rectitude, social conformity, clean living and a "clean" rent book' were 'essential qualifications for eligibility – at least for new houses,'[68] All new applicants, including slum clearance people, required assessment, for which the device used was the home visit by a housing visitor. This had a number of purposes: to verify people's details and degree of housing need, and to give advice and information; but it was also used as a spying operation on people's domestic standards, allowing such things as the state of bedding and presence or absence of three-piece suites to be noted. In clearance areas, people were well aware of the procedure, and news of the housing visitor's approach was apt to be passed round, together with such useful items as packets of cleaning powder or small articles of furniture that would make a good impression. The grade awarded by the housing visitor, supposedly confidential, determined what sort of property an applicant was offered. In the worst cases the ominous phrase 'suitable only for . . .' was used.

A much debated question is how far managers were responsible for, or even engineered, the hierarchies of estates and social hierarchies within them, or how far they were simply reacting to social realities. Their pragmatic sorting and placing of applicants made them an easy target of leftwing critics, who were innately unsympathetic to suggestions that the working class was anything but unified and indivisible. In general, analysts of housing policy were quick to blame managers for the inequities of allocation and, as they saw it, the consequent stigmatization of estates. To one, the lettings process was a 'laborious and lethargic maze . . . solidifying sub-class divisions far more intensely than the old slums ever had, and creating communities at the bottom of everyone's aspirations, which inspired only a desire to escape.'[69] Most academics, including those on the left, had no personal experience of council estates and, like the social explorers of the haunts of the poor in the previous century, they were shocked at the way applicants and tenants were treated, and in particular the practice of 'grading'.[70]

Although the system was geared to the interests of the 'better' tenants, inevitably most effort was expended on those who presented problems. The relationship between managers and even the favoured tenants, however, was one of barely concealed power. It was not expected that tenants should be other than passive: 'as suppliants, they are expected to accept gladly whatever is offered';[71] and for long their ignorance was exploited: 'many tenants hesitate to make more than a few minor complaints to their landlord; they understand neither the selection process which supplied their home, nor how far they may complain without anatagonizing the department. Quite a few of our informants . . . believed they had obtained priority in getting a new house by virtue of being careful never to trouble the housing department for anything.'[72] It was not until tenants ceased to assent to the norms and values of their managers that they began to find the condition of tenant intolerably restrictive.

Through the stock as a whole (although not equally for all tenants) there was a continuous flow of movement. The 'churning' effect of transfers became increasingly significant, to the point where towards the end of the twentieth century they outnumbered newly created tenancies. More importantly, both ends of the sector were always open: at the top to home ownership, and at the bottom to other rented stock, although this was progressively harder to find, at least until housing associations started to augment it from the 1980s. By this time managers were having to carry out all their functions under much harder constraints, as will appear in chapter 12, and their careful mechanisms for social grading became redundant. Allocation policies had relied on the continuous expansion of council housing to keep the majority of residents tolerably happy and (though with more limited success) the sector as a whole abreast of social change. To say that managers showed social bias in their practices is not to say that they invented or even deliberately engineered the social hierarchies they had to work with. It was only when the expansion ended that their way of dealing with the inequities and unresolved dilemmas of council housing broke down. With its traditional ideological and institutional weaknesses, housing management was not then well placed to deal with the social and economic problems that, sadly, were concentrated in the public housing sector.

NOTES

1. CHAC (1959).
2. Power (1987*a*).
3. CHAC 1959, p. 6.
4. Brion & Tinker, 76.
5. CHAC (1938), p. 15.
6. CHAC (1938), p. 26.
7. Darke & Darke (1979), p. 132.
8. Andrews.
9. Power (1987*a*), p. 84.
10. *Housing*, II, p. 43.
11. CHAC (1938), p. 10
12. CHAC (1938), pp. 11, 24.
13. Honour Oak Neighbourhood Association, p. 2.
14. Rubinstein, p. 43.
15. CHAC (1959), p. 113.
16. CHAC (1956), p. 3.
17. CHAC (1956).
18. Allaun.
19. Ravetz (1974), p. 102.
20. Dagenham Borough Council (1956).
21. Dagenham Borough Council (1956).
22. Witney Rural District Council, pp. 22–23.
23. CHAC (1938), pp. 33–34.
24. Rowntree (1945), p. 20.
25. Bournville Village Trust, p. 99.
26. CHAC (1938), p. 21.
27. Hodges & Smith
28. National Council of Social Service (1960).
29. Ministry of Housing & Local Government (1970*b*).
30. *Housing*, I, 23 (24 May 1920), p. 310.
31. *Housing*, II, 35 (8 Nov.1920), p. 132.
32. CHAC (1938), p. 22.

33. CHAC (1938), p. 21.
34. CHAC (1959), p. 20. This was apparently not remarked by the early managers at Watling, who required tenants who had done their own decorations to strip and clean them off, or pay for this to be done, before the team of LCC decorators moved in (*Watling Resident*, September 1931).
35. Zweig.
36. City of Cardiff, 21.
37. Dagenham Borough Council (1949), (in bold type). This instruction was omitted from the next (1956) edition.
38. CHAC (1956).
39. Parliamentary Debates (1909), col.1534.
40. CHAC (1956).
41. Burke, p. 29.
42. CHAC (1959).
43. CHAC (1969), p. 151.
44. Englander, p. 297.
45. Holmans, p. 313.
46. Holmans.
47. McGonigle & Kirby.
48. Glass (ed); Jevons & Madge.
49. Bowley, p. 205.
50. Westergard & Glass, p. 43.
51. Holmans, p. 326.
52. CHAC (1969).
53. Holmans.
54. CHAC (1969), p. 113.
55. Malpass & Murie, p. 189.
56. Cf Bowley.
57. Hayes (1989).
58. Power (1987*a*).
59. Audit Commission (1986).
60. CHAC (1969).
61. CHAC (1949), p. 5.
62. Damer (1989); Cole *et al.*
63. Gill, Rev.Walter, pp. 3–4.
64. CHAC (1969), p. 37; see also Morris & Mogey.
65. Power (1987*a*), p. 93.
66. Dennis. See also Beckton, Docklands, where the Council 'do not usually make a second offer if the first is considered sufficient and the refusal reason thought to be inadequate' – Dunleavy (1977), p. 211.
67. CHAC (1956), p. 5.
68. CHAC (1969), p. 33.
69. Power (1987*a*), p. 91.
70. Damer (1974; 1989).
71. Morris & Mogey, p. 11.
72. Morris & Mogey, p. 4.

Chapter Nine

'Community' on Council Estates

'It is not enough merely to cover the ground with streets and houses. The site should be considered as the future location of a community mostly engaged in industrial pursuits having many needs in addition to that of house-room.

Tudor Walters Report, 1918

'There was little to do in Middleton, except live there.'

Keith Waterhouse, *City Lights: a Street Life*, 1994

Estates as Communities: the Physical Framework

Although preoccupied with relations between their tenants, managers were at some remove from the community life of estates: they wanted it to flourish, but this was another of the things for which they had no direct responsibility. The official expectation was that estates would become permanent and stable 'communities' with community associations and, ideally, an estate hall or centre. The National Council of Social Service (NCSS) founded in 1919 pressed central and local government to take some responsibility for community development on estates; and 10 years later, with two 'settlements', it set up the New Estates Community Committee (from 1945 the National Federation of Community Associations) to foster the growth of estate associations throughout the country. By 1939, over seventy such associations were affiliated, and around two hundred schemes for the building of community centres were in progress.

Between the wars the importance of health, motherhood and active citizenship was emphasized in progressive circles. Two pioneering ventures, in particular, had lasting influence: the Peckham Experiment, begun in 1926, whose member families subscribed to a Pioneer Health Centre providing sport, social life and regular health monitoring; and the four Cambridgeshire Village Colleges comprising schools, adult education, clinics and employment bureaux for their surrounding rural areas. War brought renewed emphasis on common purpose and the value to society of the national cultural heritage and constructive uses of leisure. To planners, with their core faith that better environments would bring about better societies, it seemed obvious that the necessary ingredients of community life could not flourish – indeed could not even exist – in slums or obsolescent working-class neighbourhoods. Even the new Lansbury scheme, with its ideal plan and a readymade population of local people, convinced the professionals that it could be successful in the long term 'only if this new neighbourhood is followed up by rapid, general development of London's working-class boroughs.'[1]

In planning theory, communities were not so much to be 'planned for' as produced by physical means. Architects in particular were convinced that 'the science of Social Studies provides the information needed to plan a community, whether a town, village or housing scheme.'[2] The device most favoured was the Radburn layout designed, as we have seen, to facilitate social encounters. A similar idea with a briefer vogue was the 'Reilly Green' proposed for the reconstruction of Birkenhead, which claimed to promote 'spontaneous co-operation' by setting 30-60 houses round a green. Three to five such greens would constitute a 'unit' of up to 1200 people, and larger ones would have a nursery or nursery school, while the whole complex would have an elementary school with swimming pool.[3] The premise common to both was that if people were arranged in certain approved ways on the ground they would develop an active cultural and community life. A necessary adjunct was the community or tenants' hall, as in settlements and model villages, for the absence of such meeting places on new estates without other public buildings was felt to be the main impediment to the emergence of community life. Sheffield's housing department, in anticipation of legislation, was the first to fund a community centre, on its Manor estate, in 1933. The 1936 Housing Act permitted local authorities to build centres that gave a 'beneficial service' to their tenants; but after this their provision fell within policy for physical training and recreation, and later for education. Under the 1944 Education Act, community centres came within further education, and as such were expected to serve wider populations. Sometimes the building of a centre was funded by a charitable foundation or a firm – Wythenshawe's Royal Oak centre, for example, was the gift of the shoe firm Timpsons' (and like many others at the time, it prohibited alcohol and politics). In default of any other suitable building, estate laundries sometimes became informal social centres for housewives, but this could last only as long as they were kept open – in the case of GLC estates, closures began as early as 1952.

Despite initially high, even grandiose, expectations, there was a lot of ambivalence in official attitudes towards estate centres. They were expected to provide 'such facilities for leisure pursuits that a network of interrelated social groups is created . . . In time the resultant co-operation and competition would establish local loyalties and integrate the residents into an organic social system. Such a system would not only satisfy many important needs, but ought also to act as an agency of social control, promoting interest in self-government and in schemes to improve the area and its residents.'[4]   There were, however, conflicting issues that were never resolved. One was the question whom was a centre to serve? Was it to be an amenity for the estate, or for the whole surrounding neighbourhood – or even, perhaps, the whole body of district ratepayers? This had implications for the source and scale of any funding, and whether a centre should be located inside or on the boundaries of an estate. The issue was apt to arouse strong feelings amongst tenants, who resented having to share with outsiders something they saw as provided for them alone.

Whether provision was through housing or education, a major dilemma was at what stage, and through whose efforts, a hall or centre should be built. Should it be there from the start, so that the absence of premises did not impede the emergence of community life? In that case, tenants might take it for granted and not be duly appreciative. Or should it depend upon their own efforts, so affording a valuable lesson in practical democracy? But then, the fundraising effort entailed would dominate their programmes for many years, to the detriment of more worthy cultural and educational pursuits. There was another dilemma when it came to control. In the interests of democracy and community development, a centre should be run by its members; but at the same time the authority needed to take responsibility for all important decisions, to retain financial control.

Campaigns for centres were often led by churches or by local Councils of Social Service, as well as residents themselves, often after long delays. At Watling, a residents' association had to operate away from the estate for a number of years, until it was able first to rent an estate house and then to gather funds for a building, opened by the Prince of Wales in 1933. At this point, the New Estates Committee funded a full-time secretary, and later there were protracted campaigns for a building extension. For estates of flats, however, authorities often recognized an obligation to provide tenant halls by way of compensation for high-density living. The Quarry Hill Flats were outstanding in their plans for an elaborate centre in the heart of the estate, including a theatre, tennis courts, bowling greens, gardens and a creche, for a population of some 4000 people. None of these ever in fact materialized, but residents' awareness of the plans dominated the history and internal politics of the estate through most of its short life.

Once a centre was built, there were further problems of furnishing, maintenance and running costs. The usual official expectation was that these should be borne by tenant associations, but in many cases the rents proposed, with other costs, were far beyond their means. The association at Quarry Hill resolutely refused to take on the running costs of the makeshift premises they were given in lieu of the promised centre. Eventually it was agreed that they should pay rent for their use, but this was on an indeterminate basis and the matter was never satisfactorily resolved. The confusion and conflicts over centres' running costs was of course a reflection of the priorities of council housing, in particular its emphasis on homes rather than the shared environment, and its constant obsession with economy. This meant that

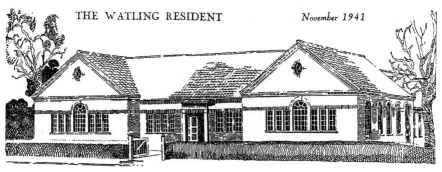

THE WATLING RESIDENT   *November 1941*

The Watling Community Centre. From July 1941 the monthly journal of the estate, *The Watling Resident*, was headed by this drawing and all subsequent issues were concerned with the nature, purpose and running of a community centre and association, and how far it was independent of the local authority.

centres, much as housing managers and architects argued for them, were frequently left hanging financially and, in a sense, ideologically.

In practice, then, tenants' halls brought as many problems as they solved, and there were innumerable histories of campaigns for new or extended buildings or the upgrading of temporary premises, with endless delays, hopes raised and dashed, misunderstandings between associations and authorities, and volunteer efforts defeated by official regulations and procrastination – not to mention conflicts between different cultural factions or different generations amongst the tenants themselves.

The war of 1939–45 affected in contradictory ways the centres established by that time. On one hand, the national mood was for co-operation, community spirit and cultural pursuits; but on the other, the blackout and general disruption of life made it difficult to run events. Many halls were requisitioned for military and civil defence, and some were destroyed or put out of action by air raids. After the war, the arguments and campaigns for centres proceeded as before, although social and cultural changes were starting to erode the taste for self-education and home-made local entertainment. Undoubtedly one of the chief causes of this was television, which dates its mass diffusion from the year of the Coronation in 1953. With the later additions of stereo, video recorder and personal computer, the home eventually became, in effect, a private theatre of media entertainment, compared to which tenants' fetes and carnivals were pallid affairs, appealing to an estate patriotism that was less and less meaningful for many residents. Tenant campaigns for community halls did not, however, die out; they continued to be a felt need, particularly by retired people and for children's play groups. In the 1960s and 1970s it was GLC policy to build and furnish simple premises for any tenant association that proved itself capable of running them. The city of Birmingham aimed to provide a hall for every 2000 tenants, and by 1969 had thirty-five of these. Halls continued to be built to the end of the century, albeit often after long campaigns by estate residents or even, in some cases, as the outcome of a riot, as was the case at Broadwater Farm.

The Culture of New Estates and its Leaders

At first it was taken for granted that community life was something the settlement movement would supply, as an extension of its sphere of interest from the slums to the new estates. In his preface to a 1938 report on *'New Housing Estates and their Social Problems'*, Ernest Barker referred to the new estate as a 'spiritual thing',[5] as it supported bodies like the British Legion and TocH and such activities as garden guilds, dressmaking, rambling, first aid, glee singing, morris dancing, film making, drama (written as well as acted by residents), metalworking, and the making of wireless sets. A canteen and other fundraising activities such as dances and whist drives ought not, in his view, to displace such improving activities.

At Becontree, pioneering work was done by Brigadier General Sir Wyndham Deedes, an ascetic social reformer who had previously operated in Bethnal Green. He founded the Pettit Farm centre in 1929, and its first annual report mentions a mock parliament, evening institute, and the Heathway Players. Deedes eventually became disillusioned and handed the centre over to the Dockland Settlement in 1937. On the contemporary estate of Watling, one of the most active and influential residents was 'Granny', formerly a member of a London settlement. Here Deedes again, with his helper Miss Murray, established a community centre, which however antagonized tenants, partly because they wanted to keep the name and identity of their existing association. His bait was a hall with fulltime secretary supported by the Carnegie Foundation and the local education authority (a 'first' for any such authority), and he got his way through the help of the Hendon and Middlesex education committees, as well as the New Estates Community Committee.

Becontree was the outstanding example of an estate that, as depicted, was all but swamped with 'settlement' culture. Its vicar opened a temporary church in 1922, which 'in its catholicity of activity was analogous to the work of a pre-Reformation monastery . . . It helped to educate the children, it helped to look after those who were sick or in distress, and it helped to start social organisations for all.'[6] The vicar's wife trained local women to staff a nursing and midwifery service, and the world famous Dagenham Girl Pipers (originally for children rather than as later for adolescents) were an inspiration of the Congregational Church. Terence Young, reporting for the Pilgrim Trust in 1934, listed fourteen churches or religious bodies and a Socialist Sunday school; two settlements; four working men's clubs; six tenant bodies; two ratepayers' associations; a Trades Council and Chamber of Commerce; associations of all political parties including Co-operative and Communist; branches of the YWCA and Workers' Educational Association; various friendly, choral, dramatic and other societies (including dogs and meccano) – all in addition to a commercial dog track, four cinemas and five estate pubs, with a further seven just beyond the boundaries.

Many centres owed their existence to settlement, social or community workers, who quite often lived on estates. At Bristol's deprived Filwood Park estate in 1935, the university settlement leased a house for use as a youth club, while the next door house was used as a hostel for social workers. In 1938 there followed a purpose-built social centre with dance hall, stage and gymnasium. After the war, the settlement opened a community house on 'Mossdene' estate, and with the Carnegie Trust supported a full-time resident warden. Like many such centres, this one was built with volunteer labour. At 'Tenement Town' in Lewisham, a community association was set up by social workers living in one of the flats and later developments, including a youth club, were initiated by a Pacifist Service Unit, which carried out a tenant survey demonstrating the need for a community centre. This pattern of intervention by professionals from within or outside estates always carried the risk of alienating residents who saw them as intrusive 'do-gooders'. At 'Mossdene', for example, the community house had been preceded by friction between the community association and a Community Advisory Council set up by non-resident professionals, and both became defunct before a new body could emerge and the necessary funds be found.[7]

Sheffield's Manor estate was a clear example of the cultural collisions that could come about when professionals were too high-handed. Its community association was founded by resident social workers and its centre had a full time warden. *The Manor and Woodthorpe Review*, its official and impressively produced monthly journal, appeared in 1934, price one penny. The keen and hopeful editor was the newly appointed warden, Mr H. Dawes BA, who after a 'brilliant career' at Cambridge followed by settlement work in Sheffield heralded 'a new age, both in life on the Estate and in journalism.' He saw the journal as 'an organ of propaganda for disseminating knowledge – not highbrow stuff, but the kind of thing about which every intelligent human wants to know – what his neighbours are doing at home and abroad . . . a useful tool helping the Association in its work of developing the cultural and educational life of the people.'[8] To that end it had book reviews – among others of works by J.B.Priestley and Hermann Goering – and also a regular feature called 'Philosophical Philanderings'. All the educational activities quickly flopped, however, and the editor made no secret of his disgust: 'Most of our members come only to take. It is absolutely impossible to run the Centre on these lines, and the only hope for the future lies in scrapping those who are not prepared to pull their weight and substituting others.' Accordingly, he removed the billiards and card tables and turned the recreation room into a reading and debating room, to provide 'the foundations of an intellectual and cultural self-contained community.'[9]

In spite of everything, membership continued to grow, and Warden Dawes considered making it conditional on participation in some serious activity. This was apparently supported by some members, but eventually his policy led to expulsions and divisions, and a centre that, although a 'social and cultural outpost in a wilderness of ignorance', was empty.[10] The *Review*, impressive as it was, did not outlast twelve issues.

Nearly half a century later, a similar rejection of an imposed 'elite' cultural strategy was noted on Oxford's 'Omega' estate.[11] But such an approach was not always at odds with estate culture. There were estates where more sober cultural pursuits appealed to some, at least, of the residents. Sometimes this owed a lot to wardens of centres or other leading citizens. A good example is Dagenham's own local historian, J.G. O'Leary, FSA, known as 'a bit of a wag', who was appointed to start a library service for Dagenham soon after it received urban district status in 1926.[12] A perhaps more subtle influence was a tenuous cultural identification with the landed estates on which some council estates were situated – examples were found in Edinburgh, Nottingham and Leicester.[13] Their rich parklands might afford a boating lake or other recreational opportunity, and if there was a mansion this could give scope for a museum or gallery. The outstanding example was Wythenshawe, whose mansion was gifted to Manchester in 1929 by the prominent Liberal politicians, Ernest and Shenagh (later Lord and Lady) Simon. With an echo of Port Sunlight's Lady Lever gallery, it became a branch art gallery, and Lady Simon was for many years a potent influence on the estate's development.

Some estates developed a rich growth of clubs and associations. Watling, for instance, had around seventy after 20 years, housewives being their

From February 1954 *The Watling Resident* was reduced in size and issued with the estate's Community Association programme which – presumably to foster local loyalty – depicted Watling as the proverbial idealised village.

Telephone: MILL HILL 2259   FEBRUARY, 1954

Watling Community Association

Watling Centre:
ORANGE HILL ROAD, WATLING, EDGWARE, Middx.

mainstay.[14]   This early cottage estate had at least two cultural identities. Although it was one of the LCC's 'select' estates, it was resented and feared by the nearby middle-class suburbans of Hendon and Mill Hill, who looked on it as 'Little Moscow' (while at the same time plundering it for domestic labour). The estate journal, *Watling Resident*, the monthly organ of a Residents' Association founded in 1927, worked hard to foster a sense of estate identity with such slogans as 'Watling for Watling' and 'We want Watling Garden City'. It carried series of articles on local history by a Mill Hill historian, and on 'citizens of Watling'.   There was also a serial about a pioneering tenant family which conveyed the clear moral that everyone should join in the community life of the estate.   At its peak, the journal was taken by over four-fifths of tenant households, but the circulation quickly declined.   Serious introspection about Watling and the role of its centre continued through the 1940s and 1950s, with literary, historical and musical contributions timed to coincide with the monthly events programme.

A similar role was played by the more commercial *Dagenham Digest Quarterly*, published from 1948 to 1965 and distributed free to schools, libraries and public houses.   Edited by O'Leary, the first issue declared itself 'proudly parochial in its outlook' and 'intended, principally, to interest you and your neighbours in municipal affairs.'[15]   Among its regular features were descriptions of the ancient monuments of Dagenham, reminiscences, a regular profile of the district called 'A Dagenham Day', and portraits of 'Dagenham characters' and leading citizens, including a series of 'ordinary housewives' who had served as Mayor.   A stream of periodicals issued from this estate, many starting as amateur but continuing as commercial publications.

The *Wythenshawe Recorder* begun in 1937 reappeared in 1946, later undergoing a number of name changes.   Although unlike most estate journals it was commercial from the start, it was militant for the estate, calling for self rule and making 'frequent comparisons with much smaller towns that had their own councils and often a Mayor.'[16] The adjacent and much more middle-class Northenden, with its listed buildings, grand houses and strong traditions of local history and amateur dramatics, obviously provided both a stimulus and a challenge to thrusting, council-owned Wythenshawe.   The latter was a good example of old cultural patterns being transferred to new habitats, alongside others that arose in the new environment.   The Anglican 'Whit Walks' or Whitsuntide processions of inner Manchester were brought to the estate in 1935, reaching their height in the 1940s and 1950s, by which time they were ecumenical.   There was the Rosemany Pageant, held in aid of a fund for children's holidays, and clothing and coals for the aged.   'Rosebuds' and 'Queens' were selected and crowned.   Civic Week, with a Miss Wythenshawe, was mooted in 1946 and instituted 2 years later – when the Lord Mayor refused to perform the opening ceremony, possibly because one of the participating community associations had paraded the Red Flag.   According to the *Recorder*, 'a Civic Week for Wythenshawe should have as its main role the instilling of civic pride in each of us to make us feel proud that we belong to Wythenshawe and Wythenshawe belongs to us and that it is our responsibility.'[17]   But the 'Week' was imperilled by vandalism and, with many of its supporting associations, it staggered to a close in 1964, while the Northenden Festival, at a much higher cultural level, continued.   Later, the estate's Civic Week was revived without official support as Impact 1970, developing into the Wythenshawe Festival in 1976.

From the many activities of the early years, there emerges the picture of estate culture lying somewhere between the 'settlement' legacy with its didacticism, and an autochthonous culture composed partly from what had been brought from the old neighbourhoods and partly from responses to life on estates.   To the settlements were owed a regular emphasis on drama and the inclusion of a stage in many community centres, however little demand for this there might be.   From the model village and garden-city traditions came the tennis courts and bowling greens that were such a ubiquitous feature of estate plans, even if they failed to materialize, while the galas and crowning of 'queens' derived from 'Merrie England' and Arts & Crafts.   How such elements were received by tenants depended on how far they identified with the tastes and values they represented.   Watling's estate carnivals were universally popular and its Drama Section nursed ambitions to open a People's Theatre – although this was probably owing to the strong presence of communists on this estate.

It was an unspoken assumption of those wanting to plant elite culture on estates that their inhabitants had no worthwhile culture or cultural leadership of their own.   Thus the NCSS in 1938 supposed that 'There is frequently a dearth of men and women who, through possessing some technical or professional qualification, can render special services to the new communities.' It suggested that 'Something could be done to meet this need if it were made more widely known among those residents of middle-class districts who have not yet realized the opportunity which is lying at their doors.   There are many people with a little leisure who can spare an evening two or three times a month to read a play with a group of would-be actors, to show the young how to box, perhaps to lend their skilled talents as lawyers or accountants to those who need such advice but cannot afford to pay for it professionally.   Only those who have had the experience can realize how warmly residents on New Estates welcome such neighbourly help, provided it is given in the spirit of friendly co-operation and on a basis of perfect equality on both sides.'[18]   The writer went on to extol the LCC's St Helier Estate with its League of Nations, Women's Citizenship Association and branches of all political parties, and Watling with its adult schools, Sunday evening lectures (on such subjects as youth hostels and town and country planning) and wireless listening groups, which were also found on the Manor estate at this time.

Not only was this proposed cultural colonization a forlorn hope, but it quite overlooked the existence of a working-class elite of experienced leaders, of political parties, trade unions, chapels, and a whole range of self-help organizations.   Not all of them took a leading role in estate activities, of course, but they must have had an impact, among other things contributing to the carry-over of organizational energy that could be seen after each world war. This was especially noticeable in women's organizations after 1919, when they turned from winning the vote to working for women's full participation in civil society. The Women's Co-operative Guild, in particular, was a significant presence on many estates. In the 1940s, *When We Build Again* counted on this talented working-class leadership to be 'the leaven that leaveneth the whole', trusting that it would draw in the passive majority and that out of ordinary everyday encounters between men and men, women and women, new tenant activities would naturally emerge.[19]

The activities chosen by tenants and their associations were not always, however, what middle-class professionals had hoped. Like the hapless warden of Manor and Woodthorpe, the latter deplored the dominance of frivolous social and recreational events – and they were particularly perplexed by the postwar rise of 'bingo', which remained a perennial favourite of tenant associations. Nor did the residents who enjoyed such activities get much sympathy from the Left. The Communist Party looked to tenants to create a militant working-class movement around rents, and researchers, who typically had a leftwing outlook, expected tenants to express their interests collectively. In practice, constitutions of associations invariably banned politics along with religion, and restricted lobbying to individual hardship cases. The exception to this was extraordinary provocations such as a local or national change in rent policy, or outright attacks on the very existence of council housing, as occurred in the 1980s. In normal, daily estate life, concern with rents or legislation ranked low in comparison with activities that 'fostered community spirit'. A comparatively late research study found that only 1 per cent of tenants mentioned them and there is no reason to doubt that it would have been much different in earlier years.[20]

It was natural for outside observers, not finding the kinds of cultural activity they thought valid, to conclude that estates had failed as communities. Research done for central government in 1974 found that twenty-three of its thirty case study estates 'appeared to have a divided community or to lack community spirit.'[21] But this made no allowance for the possibility that 'community' might manifest in other ways, such as the intense loyalty many residents expressed towards their estates, even when outsiders found them appalling. When viewed sympathetically there was seen to be a lot of vitality in estate culture. It would, for instance, have been difficult to find a poorer and more derelict estate than Sheffield's Manor in the late 1980s; but a painstaking six-part TV documentary on its life showed, amongst other things, pigeon fancying, boxing, weightlifting, pool, CB radio, a touring drama group, and the 'Manor Militaires' with band and resplendent uniforms – in addition to all the private pastimes of gardening, jogging, fishing and individual creative pursuits.[22]

Tenant Associations and their Leaders

It is difficult to theorize about tenant associations when their operations and activities were unformalized and their surviving records mere 'fragments of the thoughts and practices of thousands of people in a host of localities.'[23] They owed their origins, variously, to residents, professional workers in estates, housing and other departments of local authorities, or sometimes a combination of these. The attitude of authorities towards associations was ambivalent. The suggestion that they preferred community to tenant associations is broadly true, but that the former 'were deliberately organized to undermine tenant organizations'[24] credits authorities with more power than they had, as well as underestimating tenants' preference for social activities. The importance of either kind of association in fostering community spirit was recognized, but so was their potential for combined and subversive action, which their often expressed aim of providing a platform to 'air grievances' seemed to confirm. The italicized advice of CHAC, that *the wise course for the local authority is to treat associations as responsible bodies and seek to secure their confidence and co-operation*'[25] did not, therefore, carry much weight. On the inner London estate of 'Parkview' in the 1970s, part of the housing manager's brief was to encourage an association; but it became clear that what he had in mind was 'a single unified estate organization dealing with non controversial matters . . . Talk of a campaign against rent increases was deeply regretted . . . and put down to the influence of unrepresentative militants.'[26] The association here did in fact add its own clause to the model constitution it adopted, which emphasized social, moral and intellectual development. The added clause was 'to take up complaints on behalf of tenants when all other channels have failed.'[27]

Overall, the majority of associations seem to have sprung directly from tenants themselves. This was certainly the case in Quarry Hill Flats, which for 16 years had a remarkably active association, and also the early postwar Roehampton tower block Witley Point, whose tenants remembered bringing their own chairs out to meetings on the sixth floor landing.[28] Associations' greatest practical problem was finding and maintaining leadership. They were invariably hampered, if not by an outright dearth of leaders, by the difficulties of those who did come forward. Their numerous though fragmented records are littered with tales of factions, rivalries, betrayals, and leaders contending not only with their authorities but amongst themselves, and moreover doing it on behalf of uncaring and often carping tenant populations. One of the results was 'the small band of enthusiasts running the Centre, with a penumbra of less keen members' that was seen as a universal phenomenon by Mass Observation in 1943, when it examined the Becontree estate.[29] The same situation was reflected countless times in tenant journals so often launched with high hopes, only to go under within weeks or months. 'Time and again they appealed for others to join them, or at least for feedback on their journalistic efforts'; but there were no entries for the carefully compiled competitions, no letters to the editor, and no offers of help. 'The would-be journalists felt themselves to be a heroic minority flogging a needy but inert and uncaring tenant body.'[30]

Tenant leaders as well as housing managers and academic researchers were habitually critical of the low levels of support for associations on estates. It was universally agreed that participation rates were shamefully low, even though at times the evidence suggested otherwise – at Quarry Hill Flats, for instance, two-thirds of all households were at one time members of the tenants' association. Glasgow in the late 1960s had 34 active associations with memberships of between 80 and 2000,[31] and a south London estate of around 2000 people had 500 association members, with some 300 regularly turning up to events.[32] But the majority of estate residents seemed almost wilfully ignorant of programmes of events, and even of the very existence of an association, despite the time, energy and money spent on publicity. The main problem was one that (then as now) community activists seemed unable

Parade of Byker and St Peter's Juvenile Jazz Band, with banner showing Byker Wall, mid-1970s.

to grasp: that an overwhelming majority of people, by no means confined to council tenants, have neither time nor inclination to get actively involved in local issues. Large numbers would turn out in force for exceptional protest meetings on occasions when they felt their estate to be publicly vilified in an unfavourable newspaper, radio or TV item; but this did not lead to any lasting commitment to less dramatic but more regular forms of participation. It was also felt to be unfortunate that it tended to be the more 'respectable' households who dissociated themselves from estate affairs.[33]

This habitual passivity and apathy of the majority were so contrary to hopes and expectations that an identifiable reason was looked for. The first to hand was the high turnover of tenancies that occurred on some estates in their opening years, when the annual rate of removal could reach a quarter or even a third of all households. The underlying reasons, however, were likely to be specific to time and place. At 'Tenement Town', for instance, the cause was the almost instantly recognized and exceptionally bad estate design; but at Becontree early tenants who could not sustain the high rents and other costs were able in many cases to retreat to vacant accommodation in the districts they had come from. When by 1934 no clear sense of identity seemed to have emerged here, the estate's chronicler concluded that it was 'far more difficult for local authorities to inculcate local patriotism upon a transient population. Organizations of all kinds, particularly those unconnected with institutions, will have a membership which is more fluctuating and will be constantly in difficulties because of changes of officers.'[34] A study of Watling reached a similar conclusion, which hardened into a widely accepted dogma: 'the constant turnover of population is the greatest single handicap to its developing into a community.'[35]

It is true that mass clear-outs of tenant committees were not uncommon, although they were more to do with internal politics than anything else. Individually, office holders often survived such palace revolutions to remain in office for many years. As to the participation levels of tenants in general, this was far more likely to have deepseated cultural reasons than length of residence. Excessively high turnover cannot have helped the organization of community events but, once stabilized and throughout their middle years, council estates had some of the lowest mobility rates in the country, if only because of the management procedures previously described. Various researchers found no causal link between tenancy turnover and participation rates,[36] and from a study of 1975 it appeared that what were regarded as problem estates had exceptionally stable populations, with a lower than average turnover.[37] Yet managers continued to be alarmed at quite normal rates of movement such as an annual 5 per cent that would not have been in any way remarkable for owner occupiers, and to hold them responsible for the absence or weakness of community life. In fact, a 5 per cent turnover produced a mean length of tenancy of over 20 years, which in itself 'might appear to indicate a remarkable stability.'[38]

Tenant leaders, then, had to contend with the same levels of apathy that all community activists invariably encountered, albeit with the additional disadvantage of living in environments likely to be deprived and stigmatized. As in many other contexts, their leadership was often biased towards male rather than female office holders (although this may have been reversed towards the end of the century) and towards older rather than younger, and skilled rather than unskilled, individuals. Leaders suffered the typical handicaps of working-class people: lack of equipment such as telephones, typewriters, copiers; difficulties of attending meetings, especially if they worked shifts; and lack of time in general. There was also a dearth of information or knowledge of where to find it – for in prewar and early postwar Britain there was not the proliferation of rights and advice agencies that developed later. There was widespread ignorance of the skills of delegation, and little knowledge of constitutional and committee procedures – perhaps more importantly, the purpose of such procedures. Divisions arose between different generations, ethnicities, and even the different property types inhabited – there was an inbuilt animosity between flat and house dwellers, for example, especially when the former overlooked the private gardens enjoyed by the latter.

A deep personal insecurity, and the inability to see and discuss issues of passionate concern with objectivity, led to cliques, scapegoating, stormy relationships between committee members and unfruitfully aggressive attitudes towards authority. It did not help that the main body of tenants had no idea of the demands of organizational work and the skills it required, while professional community workers and officials were unable to respect or understand tenants' habitual styles of getting business done. The commonest cause of conflict and bad feeling was money and subscriptions, the collection of which made ordinary members feel that they were being 'done down' by honorary office holders bent on lining their own pockets. The sums involved might be very small, but to people on low wages and hard pressed in their personal lives they could seem unreasonable and suspicious. Bad feeling was particularly common when such things as children's treats excluded those whose families had not paid their subscriptions.

Successive generations of tenant leaders, therefore, were apt to feel unsupported and unappreciated, their labours rewarded with charges of feathering their own nests. A 'tireless helper' from Watling concluded: 'It's not worth it. Why destroy your health for those who do not appreciate the work you do?'[39] This was a repeated pattern in the history of associations. Old regimes retired exhausted or were swept away, often by a group that was younger or of the opposite sex. At Quarry Hill Flats, the committee was dominated by men until 1960, when a new committee referred to, not quite accurately, as 'the women' briefly took control. The London estate of 'Parkview' in a period of two and a half years had seven committees with 'breaks marked by a coup, election or mass resignation. This is followed by the formation or reformation of a new committee and the expression of high hopes regarding potential achievements. These are dashed by the appearance of factions and splits within the committee and the pattern then repeats itself.'[40] Leadership crises were often reflected in estate journals, which as much as anything were a tool for rallying fellow tenants. The *Watling Resident* was reborn several times. Given a new format in 1952, it referred the following year to the extreme difficulty of selling copies. It was relaunched with fewer pages in 1954, and again in 1960, only to fade out in 1961. After a brief reappearance in typescipt, it was suspended around 1970, but resumed to mark 'a new chapter' in 1973. Now with only four pages, it had low standards of literacy and production, as well as a rather sketchy knowledge of the estate's history. There was another false start in 1975; but in the absence of any outside contributions, the editor finally put out a last edition a few months later.

Tenant Action in the 1970s

By around 1970, there was a strong feeling in management circles that estates had failed as communities, and that this was due in large measure to the shortcomings or absence of tenant support for their own associations. Yet the impetus for these did not cease and they continued, reborn or newly created, into the last 20 years of the century, when fundamental changes in the relationship of management to tenants gave them an entirely new importance (see chapter 12, below). Of a number of authorities surveyed around 1990, more than two-thirds had at least one active association and nearly a third had over five. Forty per cent of the associations were up to 6 years old and 37 per cent twenty or more years old.[41]

The struggles around the Housing Finance Act of 1972 had an important though difficult to quantify effect on tenant activism. As we have seen, rent issues did not in general loom large in tenant associations, perhaps because the majority of tenants were satisfied that their housing was a reasonable bargain; and the rent strikes that had been such a feature of private rented housing before 1914 were not carried over into the public sector, other than sporadically and locally. There was a rash of council rent strikes in East London, Birmingham and other cities shortly before the outbreak of war in 1939, in which the Communist Party played a prominent role; and in 1948 the communist-inspired National Association of Tenants and Residents was formed, with several hundred estate associations affiliated. The first large postwar rent strike was in St Pancras in 1959-61, when a federation waged a strong and at times violent campaign against private landlords following the deregulation of rents and the strikers revived the old Glasgow slogan of 1915, 'Not a penny on the rent'. There followed a turbulent period when the 'fair rents' established for private accommodation in 1965 were anticipated for council housing. In London, where an Association of London Housing Estates (ALHE) had re-formed in 1966, the election of a Conservative GLC provoked 'a massive explosion of tenants' activity'[42] in which some hundreds of thousands were involved. In Sheffield, numerous tenant associations sprang up 'almost literally overnight'[43] in response to a Labour proposal for a new rebate scheme with higher rents. Tenants were antagonized not only by the rises but by the 'lodger tax' previously mentioned. A federation of tenant associations was formed, and the protest cost Labour control of the District Council.

In recasting housing subsidy, the Housing Finance Act of 1972 called the whole basis of public housing into question, and the storm of protest it evoked was to do with a political philosophy as well as rent rises – amongst other things it was concerned with the extent to which local authorities should be able to act independently of central government. Throughout the country eighty or more rent strikes took place, in some cases lasting for months and involving large majorities of tenants. A number of strikers were sent to prison and occasionally small reductions in the proposed rises were won. The ALHE took a leading role in trying to persuade boroughs not to implement the Act, while its more militant rent committee called for strikes. Overall, the campaign was judged a failure as, with only a tiny handful of exceptions, authorities fell into line and began, however reluctantly, to put it into operation. The protest campaign had been a complex one, with much factionalism and bitterness between tenant organizations, the Labour Party and the trade union movement, which never gave the hoped-for support. It is suggested that the failure to defeat the Act caused the collapse of the tenant movement,[44] or at least made sure that henceforth rents were 'largely stripped from its agenda';[45] but the whole episode did perhaps achieve more than appeared in its immediate aftermath. A ceiling on rent increases had already been imposed in 1969, and although (to the disgust of militants) some of its parts were retained, the Act itself was quickly repealed by the incoming Labour government.

Nor did the tenant movement die out, and locally some of the effects of the protest were long lasting. In Sheffield the shock inflicted on the Labour Party (which had regained control of the council in 1969) caused it to make a number of promises, including more estate halls and a housing advisory committee. The structures set up went through various changes with mixed success, but in 1978 a new federation of twenty-seven associations was formed, with a full-time organizer funded by the council and representation on a number of the city council's standing committees. It was possible to regard this as a defusion of any real tenant militancy – in one view 'an historic compromise',[46] as rents were no longer an issue. On the other hand the whole episode left its mark on wider strategies in the city, such as its Family and Community Services Committee, which employed estate community workers, and a number of non-housing issues where tenant bodies supported council policies.

Next to rent, design and building standards would seem to be natural campaigning issues for tenants. In the opening years of council housing, as we have seen, there was no formal involvement by prospective tenants in design; but they as much as anyone would have endorsed the garden-city model adopted. Repairs as an issue were constantly raised at estate or sub-estate level, sometimes explicitly linked to rents by those who 'felt deeply and bitterly about the conditions in which they had to live and for which they were now being asked to pay more and more each half year.'[47] But mass action only came about when certain types of building became intolerable to live in, and this above all related to high-rise buildings. Through the 1970s and throughout the country there was protest about the inadequacy of lifts, the cost of heating by electricity (with consequent disconnections), vermin, damp and mould, and the presence of lethal asbestos in buildings.[48] Activists from Liverpool's Netherley estate deposited refuse and vermin at the town hall and kidnapped a rent officer. Protest was sometimes linked with anti-clearance campaigns and the replacement housing people were offered. After the collapse of Ronan Point, for instance, local people announced 'We will flatly refuse to leave our present slums to enter modern slums . . . You claim you're bettering us but you're not' – to which their town clerk replied: 'Whether the blocks become slums or not will depend on the people who live in them.'[49]

The managerial response to these protests was at first invariably dismissive. Dampness in particular was blamed on tenants' lifestyles, and they were instructed to keep their windows open with heating turned up night and day. They were also cautioned against boiling kettles, and even in some cases indulging in heavy breathing. When they could, therefore, tenants turned to independent consultants willing to be expert witnesses on their behalf. During the 1980s they developed regional or national protest bodies, some of them directed towards the problems of certain patented building 'systems', such as Bison and 'YDG'. The latter was used in four cities by the Yorkshire Development Group consortium of local authorities and tenants of Leeds's YDG estate compiled their own report, *DAMP – Hunslet Grange: an Experiment and its Victims*, before contributing to the action guide, *High and Dry*, for all the cities involved. In Newham, a tower blocks campaign started in 1981 after the suicide of a young mother whose child had fallen from the block to his death (there had been earlier instances of such fatalities leading to similar campaigns in Liverpool and at Hulme) and this led to the National Tower Blocks Network which published a directory in 1987 and a bulletin, *The View*, for tenants nationwide. From a 1985 conference on 'the Deck Access Disaster' in Hulme there came the National Systems-built and Tower Block Project Ltd, its company structure 'a unique departure in the history of the tenants' movement, ensuring both its independence but also by formally linking local authorities into a body *controlled* by the tenants.'[50] It expected to give rise to a network of tenant organizations.

The Significance of Tenant Action

Whether there really was a tenant movement with a conscious identity and purpose, and if so what its achievements amounted to, is a perplexing question. Those writing on the subject (who do not include tenants or their organizations) either screened out those activities they did not consider valid, or denigrated them for not meeting their own expectations. Possibly this accounts for the notion that the tenant movement collapsed after the failure to prevent the 1972 Act, whereas it is clear that tenant activity continued and there are even signs of organizational growth. In 1977, there were thirty federations of tenants or residents throughout the country,[51] their revival owed partly to a National Consumer Council conference that prompted the formation of new federations, as well as the revival of old ones. In London by this time the number of bodies affiliated to the ALHE had increased to over 260, and its journal *London Tenant* first appeared in 1976. Rent strikes were apparently a thing of the past, aside from occasional, localized instances, but the perennial social and welfare activities continued as before: the management of tenant halls, luncheon clubs and bingo for the elderly, children's treats, perhaps a summer gala, the chasing of individual complaints and production of a newsletter.

For those who had expected something more of tenants this represented a 'decline into a monotonous round of social events.'[52] It showed that tenants had failed to recognize their collective interests, and consequently were not strengthening their position. The underlying assumption of the view was that, as a section of the working class, they should be a militant force challenging the state and the class system, in a similar way to trade unions. Manuel Castells went some of the way to justify their apparent lack of political edge by classifying them, with community action of various kinds, as an 'urban social movement'. As such they were a 'latent social base' with the potential to engage in the class struggle and ultimately bring about social transformation.[53] One problem with the argument was the increasing separation between social class and tenure, as more and more tenants became home owners; but the greater problem was that it tried to cram into a certain mould long years of activities and actions that were diverse, sporadic and incomplete, with a fluctuating sense of common identity and purpose. 'What has been termed the "tenants' movement" in Britain has been typically limited, localized, occasional and defensive,'[54] operating 'on the periphery of the formal party system.'[55] In spite of their obvious differences of view in what the purpose of tenant action should be, there was an important common ground between the class-oriented Marxists and those who may be termed 'romantics': that is, the early settlement and community development workers on estates, the architects and housing managers, who believed that tenants should band together to form 'communities'. The assumption common to both sides was that tenants were, and should recognize they were, a collectivity. Both, consequently, were disappointed; and it was a disappointment shared by tenant leaders themselves, who had to learn 'the most painful lesson . . . that there was no organised tenants' movement, although tenants in a number of different localities reacted as though they were part of one . . . members were out of touch with the true intention of the tenants they represented.'[56]

The reason why the looked-for militancy did not materialize was, at bottom, the social divisiveness of the housing system, of which council housing was part. As we have seen, it recognized and catered for social divisions, and if anything the way it was financed, allocated and managed, 'de-collectivized' tenants rather than the reverse. In addition, it had an ever open exit to home ownership, and from the earliest years tenancies were used as a stepping stone to this superior status. By the 'romantics' who wanted estates to become 'communities', this was seen in the light of a betrayal;[57] but there was of course no compelling reason why people should remain loyal to a tenure that did not in itself provide a satisfying collective identity.

By setting their sights on ulterior aims for tenant organizations, both the Marxist and the 'romantic' critiques underestimated what tenant bodies did in fact achieve for their estates over the years. As well as failures there were countless victories in matters of repairs, improvements, better utilities and public services, with occasional rent and rates victories.[58] Sometimes this brought tenants onto professional and political arenas: Woodberry Down tenants, whose association was the first tenant body to address the Institute of Housing on 'the tenants' point of view', were 'well known at County Hall as determined and hard bargainers for their estate.'[59] But even those activities dismissed as 'social', and therefore trivial, were valid for estate populations who were unprivileged and disempowered – not least by council housing itself. Understandably, they gave priority to things where there was most consensus, in particular the interests of the very young and the elderly. By intent, there was no sharp intellectual or political cutting edge, which would only have bred conflict and division. Consequently it was not often that tenant bodies took strategic action on policy. Alliances between council and private tenants seem to have been rare and possibly confined to London, where their interests were most likely to coincide (for instance, in the problems posed by gentrification). There was no organized national movement against the right to buy given in 1980,[60] for the obvious reason that many tenants benefited from it. It was resisted in Labour strongholds like Sheffield and in Scotland, but in the nature of things resistance and acceptance were individual decisions. The worst fears of housing managers about Communist subversion, therefore, were never fulfilled; and much as the Communist Party tried to mobilize tenants, it did not apparently have any lasting influence, and most probably alienated more than it politicized.

In general, estate associations, like the working-class culture they were rooted in, were essentially benign, though limited and conservative (for instance, in their hostility towards black minorities). Exceptionally, when national policy changes unambiguously threatened the homes and security of all, there was a fair degree of nationwide organization. This happened in the run-up to the 1972 Housing Finance Act, and would happen again, as we shall later see, after 1988. But this was the exceptional situation: the normal one was the low level 'social and welfare' activities that outsiders found insignificant. Their arena was the estate for, rather than tenure, it was this that provided a collective identity or felt community of interest, even if not quite the 'community' that had been hoped for.

The point is of considerably more than academic interest because in the last 20 years of the twentieth century tenants were increasingly looked to by governments to take on the rescue and regeneration of their estates – once again on an unspoken assumption that they had the will and capacity to act collectively. How far they did so, and how far it was realistic to appeal to their loyalty and solidarity, are questions the final part of this book will return to. They would be crucial to the success or failure of a range of official measures for dealing with the crisis in council housing as what was brought forward from earlier years, however ambiguous and perplexing, would determine the fate of many estates in the century to come.

NOTES

1. Westergaard & Glass, p. 51.
2. Journal of the Royal Institute of British Architects, p. 126.
3. Kuper; Glendinning & Muthesius.
4. Morris, R.N., p. 297.
5. National Council of Social Service (1938), preface.
6. Young, T, p. 42.
7. Jennings, Hilda.
8. *Manor & Woodthorpe Review*, Vol. 1, no. 1, p. 1.
9. *Manor & Woodthorpe Review*, Vol. 1, no. 4.
10. *Manor & Woodthorpe Review*, Vol. 1, no. 5, p. 3.
11. Reynolds.
12. Bernard T. Dodge 'MS of 1977' Dagenham: a personal retrospect 1928-1963, and official opening of John Gerard O'Leary Room, Valence House, 1987. O'Leary wrote *The Book of Dagenham*,1937 (2nd ed. 1949, 3rd ed. 1964). He also published a withering review of Peter Willmott's study of Dagenham after 40 years, *The Evolution of a Community* (1963), in particular attacking the theory of 'matrilocality'.
13. Gale.
14. PEP (1947).
15. *Dagenham Digest*, November, 1948, p. 3.
16. Deakin, D, p. 155.
17. Deakin, D, 129.
18. National Council of Social Service, 1938, p. 19.
19. Bournville Village Trust, p. 98.
20. Cairncross *et al.*
21. Burbidge *et al*, Vol. 1, p. 9.
22. Channel 4.
23. Hague, p. 245.
24. Grayson, 36.
25. CHAC (1959), 26, para.116.
26. Andrews, p. 197.
27. Andrews, p. 163.
28. Witley Point Tenants' Association.
29. Mass Observation, p. 212.
30. Ravetz (1990), p. 137.
31. Goetschius.
32. Mitchell & Lupton.
33. Goetschius; PEP (1947; 1948).
34. Young, T., p. 241.
35. Durant, 119.
36. Morris, R.N; Andrews.
37. Baldwin.
38. Morris & Mogey, p, 165.
39. *Watling Resident*, March, 1963.
40. Andrews, p. 254.
41. Cairncross *et al.*
42. Lowe (1986), p. 89.
43. Lowe (1977), p. 124.
44. See Grayson.
45. Lowe (1986), p. 93.
46. Lowe (1986), p. 110.
47. Sklair, p. 270.
48. Grayson.
49. Dunleavy (1977), p. 206.
50. Lowe & Hawtin, p. 22.
51. Hayes (1989).
52. Lowe (1986),102. See also the pages of Community Action around this time.
53. Castells (1977; 1983) and rebuttals by Lowe (1986), Cole & Furbey.
54. Cole & Furbey, p. 153.
55. Lowe (1986), p. 84.
56. Hayes (1989), p. 66 (of AHLE).
57. e.g. Power (1987*a*).
58. See among many instances: Benwell C.D.P (of Newcastle's Pendower Estate in 1924); University of Liverpool; Witley Point TA; Grayson.
59. Woodberry Down Memories Group, p. 63.
60. Grayson.

Chapter Ten

Patterns of Working-Class Life

'It became clear to me that the move to a new council home was a major life experience for Glasgow's working class'.
Sean Damer, *From Moorepark to Wine Alley*, 1989

'When she got this house, with a bathroom and a back garden we could play in and our own front door, she thought she was in heaven'.
Anna Rubinstein, Age Exchange, *Just Like the Country*, 1991

The Results of a Social Experiment

As a bold social experiment, it would be natural to ask what steps were taken to evaluate the social success – or otherwise – of council housing. This may be a legitimate question, but it is also a simplistic one. The mechanisms for monitoring major social innovations are seldom in place: indeed the more ambitious the experiment, the less likely it is to receive serious assessment, for this could only be arrived at after extensive periods of time, during which the original purposes are forgotten or changed. The century of council housing was one of immense social and economic transformation, and it can never be certain how far housing was an active agent in this, or how far simply a reflection of it. As always, the search for answers lies not only in its actual impact on a class or classes that were subject to many other influences, but the particular stance from which our knowledge of it was created: from whose perspective and in whose language.

It may be said at once that there was no concerted working-class voice to provide an evaluation of council housing. This could be taken partly as a tribute to its mainly satisfactory operation, at least in its early and middle years; but it is also partly owed to the fact that domestic issues seemed less important than trade union affairs or party politics. The labour movement was in general as culpable as any complacent housing chairman or manager in assuming that council housing, at least in its ideal form, was an unquestioned benefit for the working class, and that the only thing needed was more generous provision. This meant that untold numbers of tenants and their families endured years of mounting problems and were powerless to make themselves heard until the problems became so evident that they erupted, so to speak, into public awareness. The one solitary voice that warned of the potentially disabling centralism of council housing was that of Colin Ward, writing from an anarchist perspective.[1]

At a governmental level some evaluations were undertaken, but they started late and were for the most part within strict limits. The CHAC advisory reports, as we have seen, were sensitive to the impacts and changing trends of council housing, but they were couched in general, prescriptive terms. The research section of the Ministry of Housing and Local Government (later Department of the Environment) began to publish a series of Design Bulletins in 1962. At first concerned with narrowly technical matters, these increasingly dealt with design and the reactions of occupants to different house types and layouts. A set of three of 1970-71 were exceptional in looking at people's experience of clearance and rehousing from a slum in Oldham.[2] This broader approach was carried still further in the mid-1970s, in an inner London study (made during a year of residence) where the minutiae of estate life were looked at in relation to housing management and aspects of 'community'.[3] A later set of reports on problem estates also took cognisance of the historical and cultural dimensions of estates, though of necessity very briefly.[4] The main source of knowledge about the impacts of council housing, however, is the considerable body of research from universities, institutes and, in some cases, settlements or trusts. A collection of some two dozen monographs, books and papers on the then relatively new estates began in 1934 with Terence Young's study of Becontree and Dagenham, written from a 'settlement' perspective, but the main body of work ran from the mid-1950s to around 1970, based in the tradition of Booth and Rowntree, and relying on social survey techniques with some participant observation. Described then as urban sociology, it would today be considered ethnography with its main focus, taken from anthropology, on the role of 'kinship' in working-class populations.

However perceptive such work was (and some of the studies were of outstanding quality) there remains a virtually uncrossable barrier between the observer and the observed. For anything closer to the actual subjective experience of living in council housing, we can only have recourse to a growing number of historical and autobiographical reminiscences. Occasional records of adult education tutors and writers in residence on estates also provide insights from a middle-class experience of estates, even if, like Vernon Scannell's experience of Berinsfield, they are sometimes excruciating reminders of the great cultural divide between the classes.[5] Undoubtedly the classic of the sociological or ethnographic genre is Young's and Willmott's *Family and Kinship in East London* (1957), which seemed to see the neighbourhood in question, Bethnal Green in London's East End, as an exotic and distant place, far removed from the old perception of working-class slum, although this was, of course, the one which planners and housing officials still held. The book refers surprisingly little to homes or housing standards. Any interest it shows is mainly confined to the common pattern of young couples starting married life with in-laws, and 'Mums' finding tenancies for their married children. Pledged to examine 'the effect of one of the newest upon one of the oldest of our social institutions'[6] – that is, the family – the main focus of the study is on the extended family patterns of Bethnal Green people and the effects on them of removal to the outlying estate of 'Greenleigh' (Debden) in Essex.

Bethnal Green was not at this time a clearance area, and the impression given is that there was a large degree of choice in whether or not to move out to the new estate. The attraction, for those who did opt to do so, was a new house and the prospect of a healthier life for the children, even at the cost of leaving behind the grandparents. Moving to the new estate was in effect to move from 'a people-centred to a house-centred existence'[7] where husbands and wives developed common interests and family life was concentrated in the home. Outside the home, there were less friendliness and fewer meetings with people, with more formality, snobbery, acquisitiveness and competition.

Two studies of the same time reached similar conclusions. That by John Mogey of 1956 compared St Ebbe's in central Oxford and the Barton estate, begun in 1937 but built mainly after 1945, which was a reception area for people 'cleared' from St Ebbe's. This old district, with its 'parlour' houses, fifty-six shops and thirty-nine industries and services, was still to external appearances a Victorian world that set store on a 'good funeral', where children played in the street, and scoured doorsteps, polished front doors, knockers and even keyholes gave out their particular messages.[8] The new estate at Barton, on the other hand, had a conflict-ridden community centre whose officers resigned over various bungled projects, and where the warden appointed to run it was resented as an outsider who attempted to introduce alien and unwanted activities such as discussion groups, music and drama. Repeated delays and bad relations with the council succeeded in dissipating the willingness of some two hundred volunteers to build a new community hall.

In the two districts the accepted indicators of respectability had diverged. In St Ebbe's, it was still 'respectable' for wives to take paid work and not respectable to have only one or no children. In Barton, it was less acceptable for wives to have jobs; it was 'respectable' to have only one child, and to furnish the home with such things as matching suites and framed certificates. As at 'Greenleigh', the emphasis here was on the nuclear family, whose members sat down to meals and went for walks together. For the first time, family holidays were taken, and children's play was confined to the boundaries of the home.

In general, the shift was summed up as one from a neighbourhood-centred to a family-centred society. St Ebbe's provided the 'cultural equipment' that enabled a majority of its people 'to live happy and well-adjusted lives under conditions of work and housing that would daunt many people'[9] – and the key was the solidarity of the extended family with strong local loyalties. In Barton, people had more contact with their immediate neighbours, at least at first, and they had four times as much formal involvement in local associations and affairs as at St Ebbe's. With perhaps more than a tinge of wishful thinking, the author concluded that the estate residents had 'lost their ties to a neighbourhood and gained in return citizenship in the wider and freer atmosphere of the varied associational life of a city.'[10]

Hilda Jennings' study of the redevelopment of Barton Hill in East Bristol conveyed a closely similar picture. This was a district of homogeneous and 'respectable' parlour houses, although the great majority lacked electricity, bathrooms and indoor WCs. Home ownership was as much as 30 per cent in some parts, and there was a strong local identity. Slum clearance which was hotly opposed by home owners, tenants, shopkeepers and led by the vicar, cut some streets in half, one even in quarters, and while houses stood empty the Council used them for problem families. Removal to a large new estate split up families and generations. The move separated more than half the new tenants from their parents or married children, and grandparents, though often staying behind from choice, were no longer able to help with child care. Some of the old who did undertake the move were said to have lost the will to live because of it. Less than half the estate tenants still had the same neighbours, and although neighbouring patterns were to some extent rebuilt, wives suffered from loneliness as their husbands worked overtime to offset some of the higher living costs. The old district was eventually rebuilt with tower blocks and maisonettes, but few of its original residents took the option to move back to it. Eventually, however, a network of extended families was re-established here, and more than half of the sample had parents, married children or other relatives living nearby, half in the same block. The carefully picked tenants of these new flats, in fact, reproduced some of their old patterns of socializing: 'popping in and out' on one another, now vertically rather than horizontally, was 'as easy as going in next door.'[11]

The same social and cultural transition was repeatedly reported in other estate studies of the time: for instance a study of Clydesiders rehoused from tenements to a new estate revealed a transition from 'a closed network of relationships, where all friends and kin are mutually known to each other, because they live in the same area, to an open network, where the circle of friends and contacts of a particular family are not interconnected.'[12] But the point must be made that the old neighbourhoods examined, though appearing stable and perhaps enjoying something of an Indian summer, were already in a process of transition. In the district of 'Crown Street' in central Liverpool around 1960, nearly two-thirds of those interviewed wanted to remain; but although three-quarters of the wives had been born there and had extensive networks of relatives living close by, people were aware of the decline of the old 'ordered and respectable living.'[13] Among others looked on as 'intruders' were those who had been bombed out of the docks area just down the hill, who now tenanted some interwar Corporation flats. Many other districts were experiencing a spontaneous draining of population, quite independently of slum clearance and rehousing. The population of Bethnal Green, for instance, had almost halved between 1931 and 1951, and that of a ward in the Gorbals lost a fifth of its population in the same period.

Another process to be taken into account is the spontaneous *embourgeoisement* of the higher working classes which, as we saw in chapter 2, was active from the later nineteenth century. This was associated with higher nutritional and child care standards, the cult of the parlour, and the taking up of gardening by husbands, catered for by the early twentieth-century allotments movement. Both in the home and at school, men and boys were encouraged to become more domesticated, while the full-time housewife was able through her labour to enhance the economic status of the family, and through this to establish a 'power-base' in the home.[14] These trends must first have taken root in the pre-1914 housing stock, helping to account for its gradual modernization and improvement. The quest for 'privatism', with smaller families and more conjoint marriages, led some of the more ambitious to buy into the semi-detached market, or to converted apartments in superior districts.[15] Council estates when they first became available also attracted those who had 'already assumed certain middle-class values in their domestic conduct' and were 'capable of adapting their behaviour to new forms of provision.'[16] In the early 1950s in Liverpool it was possible to show how far the living patterns of council tenants were converging with those of people living in larger and superior bye-law houses or new semi-detached houses. Council tenants were beginning to have their dinner in the evening rather than at midday, if only because of their greater distance from work. They were taking Sunday afternoon tea, giving hospitality and holding meetings in their homes, even hanging the same things on their walls and putting the same flowers in vases as their counterparts in other house types. Three-quarters of them were as content with their surroundings and had as little desire to move as the home owners of new 'semis'.[17]

Pictures of Working-Class Life

The post-1945 estate studies imparted a very different picture of working-class life from those of Victorians and Edwardians concerned with 'the poor'. It seems that, as a category, 'the poor' were no longer part of the debate. This is of course understandable, considering that it was now, not poverty, but rather affluence which was most striking about the lives of the workers – and it was supposed that council housing was making a large contribution to this. What is perhaps more puzzling is that what the Victorians and Edwardians had seen as 'the working classes' were now increasingly subsumed under the label of a single and by implication homogeneous 'working class'. Even when its differences were acknowledged, it seemed that these were less important than the question of how far it was converging with the middle class. In their later book on the predominantly middle-class suburb of Woodford, Willmott and Young admitted that they had at first seen Bethnal Green as 'a "classless" or rather one-class community.'[18] They now admitted that both working and middle classes had many strata (the middle more so than the working class) and they saw the latter, crudely defined as manual workers, as splintered by its adoption of middle-class habits and values. Thus while housing policy-makers and managers were still dealing with 'slum people' in time-honoured way, it was this convergence that most impressed middle-class sociologists, even those who through education and war service had themselves risen from working-class origins to professional positions. Fascinated with what he saw as the cultural challenges of 'emerging classlessness', Richard Hoggart felt that 'the great majority of us are being merged into one class. We are becoming culturally classless.'[19]

This was, of course, a view that soon seemed outdated and was then continuously revised; but it had a strong and lasting influence on the literature of council housing, largely because the 'Bethnal Green' view of working-class life supported the comfortable conventional wisdom that there was a unitary working class with a cohesive 'community'. It followed, therefore, that nothing ought to divide it. In its conclusions, *Family and Kinship* questioned the wisdom of breaking up the tight 'community' of Bethnal Green, even for the sake of better housing; and while there was much to be said for this as a suggestion to planners, it took no cognisance of the inherent and longstanding urge for mobility, both social and spatial, amongst working-class people. The feeling that such mobility was somehow invalid was a barrier to understanding, not just of the pressure for transfers among council tenants, but about the way their estates actually functioned.

The 'Bethnal Green' view of working-class urban neighbourhoods presents what has been aptly called a 'retrospective community',[20] with the more unpalatable elements removed and the more cosy and harmonious ones emphasized. None of these was faked; on the contrary, they have been confirmed countless times in histories, reminiscences and sociological studies. It is more a question of over-generalization and over-simplification, with the harsher elements of violence, intra-class divisions and the scapegoating of minorities omitted. It also tends to be a static picture that ignores the dynamics of working-class neighbourhoods over time. Across a century or more, and of course starting at different times in different places, the urban industrial neighbourhood emerged, evolved and declined. Its turbulent earlier stages, with successive immigrations of new industrial workers, have been given the label of 'heroic'.[21] In this stage, according to a seminal study of Preston in the mid-1880s, people got their main support from networks of kin or the extended family.[22] Later, many neighbourhoods settled into a 'classic' phase, which again occurred at different times and was of different lengths in different places. 'Once families could live for more than a few years, and then for more than one generation within the same area of streets and "turnings" . . . "neighbourhood" became a web of assumptions and associations that Anderson's Preston immigrants had only begun to weave.'[23]

Conventionally, the First World War marked the terminus of this period with its 'classic slum' (as Robert Roberts termed 1900-1925 Salford[24]). From then on, such neighbourhoods, stripped of their grosser elements, may have enjoyed lingering Indian summers, as perhaps did Bethnal Green; or they may, like St Ebbe's and Barton Hill, have been the standing shells of a social order that was virtually defunct. The typical working-class neighbourhood of the future was to be the council estate; and around 1960 it seemed that this was going to accommodate a new working-class affluence. Full employment, social security, free health care and universal secondary education were rapidly removing the more blatant stigmata of working-class existence. Another enormous influence was the 'new consumerism', already well on its way by 1939, where 'gradually, it seems, workers in the high-wage sectors of the economy came to regard themselves as consumers rather than as producers.'[25] One of the arguments for clearance was that letting people remain in substandard houses hindered consumption, both in the building industry and in the domestic retail market – and for this very reason, rehousing was resisted by the traditionally minded, as in the case of the old fashioned Essex villager who complained that 'people are all competing now . . . what one has, the others have to have.'[26]

One researcher into this new affluence saw a progression from the late 1940s, when the British worker was still in 'the cocoon of his traditional mode of living . . . customs, habits and values of a closely knit community life,' to a time when he was 'well on the way to becoming a property-owning class.'[27] For the time being, any property owned was mainly in the form of household goods and cars, and many remained content with the status of tenant; but home ownership would shortly become a key factor. Even before this stage, however, setting up home in a council house was observed to bring about 'a considerable social change in husband-wife relationships in the working classes' with 'a bearing on the world of man's values.' Thus in place of the domineering or absentee father, a 'new image of a benevolent, friendly and brotherly father is emerging.' In particular, his enthusiastic 'DIY' efforts in the home made his weekends 'the most trying and exacting period of the whole week.'[28]

The 'affluent worker' hypothesis was soon challenged as over-simplistic, and in Richard Titmuss's *Income and Social Change* (1962) the ground was prepared for the 'rediscovery' of working-class poverty. By the mid-1960s it was possible to show from revised data that a sixth of the British population was still living in poverty,[29] although its typical location was perhaps the declining late Victorian neighbourhood rather than the council estate. At least, this was the setting of *Poverty the Forgotten Englishman* (1970), based on St Ann's in Nottingham, which shared the low material standards of St Ebbe's or Barton Hill, but which unlike them had been stripped of its local institutions and networks, and had a hostility to outsiders that verged on the pathological.[30]

A further stage of the 'affluence' debate was how far it remained valid to talk about working-class experience and working-class identity. It was possible to argue that in spite of the many changes and improvements under way, working-class life was still recognizable because it 'offers the same kind of *experience.*'[31] For a relentless critic of consumerism, the much vaunted higher material standards were merely another kind of exploitation that 'lay in ambush' to people in their own homes.[32] The question of how far a working-class identity survived through all the changes was eventually dealt with in a more searching way, by allusion to the fact that it had never at any time been stable and homogeneous but, rather, involved 'a variety or repertoire of strategies, resistances, subordinations and solutions' which were continuously remade and transformed amidst material change.[33] At the same time it was suggested, somewhat ominously, that the core of a continuing working-class identity was the solidarity gained from productive and skilled work. Those with no experience of such work – namely adolescents and perhaps to some extent ethnic minorities – were less likely to share the identity.

The picture of working-class life before its transfer to council estates and the postwar transition to 'affluence', is composed from innumerable histories and personal accounts that were of necessity filtered through the literate tradition, and to that extent tinged with middle-class perceptions and prejudices. What emerges is a picture of a society conditioned by poverty, insecurity, low housing standards, and much overcrowding. In these circumstances, mutual aid was not so much chosen as imperative for survival – and it was the voluntary involvement of some in tenant activities on estates that most forcibly struck those looking for signs of change in these locations. In the old districts, people in crises or difficulties had to rely on extended families if they had them, or on neighbours. The role of neighbour was a crucial but delicate one, requiring a sense of how to give help when needed without causing embarrassment, and of when tactfully to withdraw. The ideal neighbour was one who did not trade on favours given, and there was strong disapproval of gossiping or habitual scrounging. Above all, when poverty or strained relationships between husbands and wives might be painfully apparent, neighbours were expected not to intrude in the home, or to be 'nosy parkers'.[34]

Such a life engendered its own group and personal psychologies. Our understanding of these is likely to be coloured by the bias of much social research and writing towards London's East End, but doubtless much of these have a wider validity. Hardship and low status generated an 'underdog' mentality that was sceptical, fatalistic, mistrustful of authority and deeply conservative. On the positive side, there was a rueful humour and will to 'battle through' in adversity. The working-class neighbourhood was a culturally and physically bounded environment, and within it the area that people personally identified with was often very small – no more than a few streets or, in Scotland, as little as a close or stair. Strangers were easily spotted, and viewed with hostility. People were acutely aware of their own territory and the visible or invisible boundaries that hemmed them in. For within what to an outsider seemed like a single space, there could be many layers of a complex social hierarchy. At one pole were the undesirables or 'roughs', and at the other those who were 'posh', 'stuck-up', or 'think they own the place'. The level that most felt comfortable with was the 'ordinary', or 'decent working-class folk like us', and one of the uses of an elaborate social geography was that it never failed to provide inferiors to oneself, at however small a spatial or psychological distance. It also justified the rejection of outsiders such as immigrants, or any who deviated from the norm in their beliefs and behaviour.[35]

At its richest, the 'classic' neighbourhood was a lively place with everything necessary for life: a range of employment, pawnbrokers for loans, corner shops for goods and credit, churches and charities for assistance, and a range of bodies for religious, musical, literary, co-operative, political and sporting activities. Much of the neighbourhood's life took place on the streets. Although many of their ancient uses had been banned or died out, streets were still, in the more traditional and 'rougher' districts, a place for men to meet and talk, lounge, gamble, fight and drink.[36] Streets were used by women for 'gossiping' – an activity that in spite of its general disparagement was the channel for neighbourhood lore and wisdom, and a mechanism for enforcing mores.[37] They were also used by children for a rich repertoire of games (whereas an important goal of housing reformers was to provide families with private gardens to avoid children being 'forced' onto the streets to play). The street was also the arena where a common understanding of local life, and life in general, was constructed. Here neighbourhood events were recounted and embellished, in the way of non- or semi-literate cultures, enabling people to come to terms with their lives through endless repetitions of episodes and events, rather than intellectual analysis. In this manner a verbal tradition with its own characters, plots and rituals was perpetuated, or created.[38]

Many skills were involved in accessing all the resources offered by a lively neighbourhood, and this was something to raise self-esteem, as well as the respect of one's peers. Possibly it was the confidence generated by such skills that fostered the middle-class perception of traditional neighbourhoods as tight and cohesive 'communities'. But for many of its inhabitants the heart of the neighbourhood was the home, and for those who wished to dissociate from street life this became a place of defensive withdrawal, of that 'keeping ourselves to ourselves' on which the respectable classes had so long prided themselves. For others, 'home' offered an ever-open door, an opportunity to watch the passing life of the neighbourhood, give and receive favours, hear and speak confidences, with minimal demands in terms of dress, hospitality, or advanced social skills. The fulcrum of the home was 'Mum', a quasi-mythic figure who, as we have seen, historically determined the family's place in the social hierarchy, the educational and employment aspirations of its children. 'Mum's' work was not finished with her childbearing years – rather, she came into her own then, as the fount of experience and mentor of grandchildren.

In housing, mothers were credited with subtle manipulation of local opportunities, by spotting vacancies and lobbying landlords on their children's behalf. One result was a considerable degree of 'matrilocality', or the grouping of married offspring (more often daughters than sons) around the parental home. In the course of time, intricate settlement patterns of extended families grew up: a ripe example is provided by a study of central Liverpool, where in one short street of twenty-two houses, eight were occupied by members of one family: mother, daughter, father-in-law, sister-in-law, uncle, and three cousins.[39]

Extended families did not, however, normally share houses, apart from newly-married sharing a parent's home, which was usually a strictly temporary arrangement arising from necessity rather than choice.

Richard Hoggart, who provided the classic picture of working-class life in Leeds between the wars, stressed the hold that the neighbourhood had on its people. Its grip was such that after the age of twenty-five or so it was difficult for them to move to another district, even one of a similar kind. 'Most react instinctively against consciously planned group activities; they are used to a group life, but one which has started from the home and worked outwards in response to the common needs and amusements of a densely packed neighbourhood.'[40] In a sense, the neighbourhood with its tie to 'Mum' kept people infantile, unwilling or unable to face new situations.[41] Residents often fought stoutly to remain in their home neighbourhoods when these were threatened with clearance, although this could be for valid practical as well as psychological reasons. Those threatened with removal from central Liverpool found the prospect of being sent out to Speke 'worse than Siberia',[42] and the campaign against the clearance of Hulme in the 1930s delayed the redevelopment of this part of Manchester for a generation. Although some housing reformers recognized this reluctance it was their self-appointed mission – endorsed by the more adventurous inhabitants – to educate, persuade or, failing these, force people to leave their home territories.[43]

Perhaps a more fruitful concept to apply to traditional working-class life than the ambiguous one of 'community' would be 'localism'. It was the immediate locality that supplied the economy, the shared culture and the frameworks of personal development. At the same time, localism in no way implied autonomy. It existed, at best, in periods of favourable economic circumstances, when a demand for local labour kept income flowing in. In its purest form, the 'classic' neighbourhood, sometimes even a whole town, grew up around one industry such as shipyards, railways, sugar refining. This gave the protection for a neighbourhood culture to flourish, but the downside was that the collapse of the staple industry could bring down the whole area. Even where there were more mixed economies, there were other trends threatening neighbourhood stability: as well as the age-old process of invasion by another and usually lower class, these included the closure of local institutions and services, and the death by attrition of local shops, industries and businesses. The contributions of housing policy were also immense. New council housing, as we have seen, was not normally fitted into existing neighbourhoods, although when it was, it was popular and successful. Above all, it was mass slum clearance that first blighted and then physically excised older neighbourhoods; or when they were left standing, combined with other processes to leave them denuded of their once rich society and culture.

The Transfer of Working-Class Culture to Estates

How far working-class life was well catered for on council estates must be answered by reference to a number of things: rent levels and management policies on one hand, localities and the social strata tenants came from on another. By 1939 it was clear that there was much poverty on council estates, shown amongst other things by the key pointer of infant mortality.[44] While this was a perverse sign of the success of Wheatley and Greenwood policies in reaching down to the poor, it also showed the failure of council housing to eradicate – perhaps its ability even to generate – poverty. For though selection policies meant that tenants' earnings were above average for their areas, their households were poorer than average because of their high numbers of dependent children. In Bristol, about half the estate families were in outright poverty or with insufficient income, and this was roughly half as many again as in the city as a whole.[45] Another contributing factor was unemployment, which was high on some estates: in Bristol in the 1950s-1960s, the level was 15 per cent, compared to 9 per cent for the city as whole. Things that contributed to this were the distance of new estates from any likely employment, and even such details as a poor postal service to estates, which cost some people job offers.[46] Juvenile earnings were eroded by the high cost of fares, and wives' chances of picking up part time or casual work were much reduced. Overall, it was 'harder for those living on a Corporation estate to earn their livelihood by casual work or to secure a permanent job. Casual workers who could gain a living doing odd jobs in the centre of the city, such as hawking for furniture removal, certainly found such a means of livelihood impossible when living on the outskirts.'[47]

For some, moving to an estate meant not so much absolute poverty as a switch in spending priorities that could have warmed the heart of Octavia Hill. Thus the East-enders who moved to 'Greenleigh' gave up drinking and going out at night because rent, food and television used up all their income. They made a virtue of the last, however, as the family watched it together and 'None of us ever have to go out now'[48] – although the original motive for acquiring it had been to keep the children off the streets. Strong in its domestic sphere, the estate was strikingly deficient in its public one. There was much green space, but nothing much could be done on or with it. The interwar estates of Bristol had one public house per 12,000 inhabitants and, as we have seen, some authorities excluded pubs altogether. There were few shops and post offices compared to older neighbourhoods. The only public buildings were schools, which sometimes took years to be built, and the churches and community centres which depended on voluntary initiative. Concentration on the home and the general demands of suburban living, with the weakness of the public realm on estates, were disincentives to engage in union or political activity, as indeed the early council housing crusaders had intended.

At the same time, there is much evidence that people knowingly moved to estates, when they had choice, for the sake of their children. Bethnal Greeners left their wider kin (sometimes with relief) because 'Greenleigh' was 'better for the kiddies'; they were still acting for the family, but in a different sense, 'on behalf of the younger rather than the older generation.'[49] Those who made the move to Kirkby in the 1950s-1960s felt that 'It is a new way of life when we come here: we don't benefit but our children will.'[50] The bias to two-generation families led to huge child populations on estates: 48 per cent of Kirkby's population, for instance, were under fifteen, compared to the national proportion of 27 per cent. This had an incalculable effect on the life and history of estates: 'The seething young life on a housing estate, especially on a new one, gives a special character to the whole atmosphere. Children are the conspicuous members of the estates and the pivot of daily life.'[51]

In some ways, moving to new estates suited the interests of women, although the overall change in their position is hard to assess. The priority given to the home was compatible with 'respectable', home-oriented working-class culture and the longstanding desire of many women to be efficient housewives, with the accommodation and equipment to do the best for their families.[52] The mere fact of having enough bedrooms to separate children of different sexes spoke for itself – although it must be said that initially people accustomed to sharing rooms, if not indeed beds, found it difficult to sleep alone.[53] As we have seen, husbands and wives took a common interest in the house and garden, and the move was often a turning point for men in ways that benefited the rest of the family. But there were respects in which women's position deteriorated: it was more difficult for them to earn money of their own, and having a public landlord removed their informal mechanism of 'bespeaking' accommodation for their about-to-be-married children: yet another reminder of the importance to tenants of the 'sons and daughters' issue.

The street's last inhabitant. Burley Lodge clearance area, Leeds, early 1970s.

Rehousing impacted on the wider family, in particular grandparents, for whom there was at first no accommodation. It was sometimes suggested that if they wished to stay with their families they could become subtenants to their own children – a neat reversal of the traditional pattern where couples began their married life as lodgers of one or other set of in-laws. Whether or not they stayed behind from choice – and the impression is given that they often did – the lives of the old could no longer be so integrated with the younger generations. Daily contact with children and grandchildren was brought to an end by distance, and also cost – in which connection it is worth remembering that the domestic telephone was effectively restricted to middle-class households until the 1960s or later. Grandparents were no longer able to 'mind' grandchildren in dinner hours or after school, and the patterns of 'popping in' that had informally sustained the links between the generations (among other things allowing a watchful eye to be kept on the fragile elderly) had to be replaced by arranged and inevitably less frequent visits. So time spent with relatives diminished measurably: in Bristol, for instance, rehousing parted over half those who had parents or married children in the city, and the same thing was found in Birmingham and Liverpool.[54]

Yet in spite of all the apparent obstacles, the extended family did re-establish itself to a surprising extent on many estates. In the case of 'Greenleigh', relatives voluntarily followed one another's example and applied for tenancies. In Kirkby, within 20 years nearly two-thirds of tenants came to have parents or children nearby, and about half had brothers or sisters.[55] Similar patterns were found on postwar Blackbird Leys, where high rates of turnover may have made it easier for applicants to get a tenancy. On some of the early estates an important contributing factor was the high rate of intermarriages, which owed a lot to weekly dances in the tenants' halls.

The neighbour role continued to be important on new estates, and some authorities even arranged for former neighbours from clearance areas to be placed together, although there were others that expressly vetoed this. Poverty and hardship amongst tenants meant there was a continuing need for neighbourly support, although at the same time there was 'an almost equal emphasis on withdrawal';[56] but it is possible that the process of moving made neighbouring a more conscious act than it had traditionally been. The fine nuances of the situation were neatly captured in Tom Ismay's memory of the day in the 1930s when he cycled over to take possession of his house on Sheffield's Manor estate. Popping her head over the hedge, the next door tenant enquired cheerily: 'Do you neighbour?' Taken aback for a moment, but with something of the tone of declining an extra pint of milk, he replied: 'No; no thank you.'[57] Each knew what was implied in the exchange and it is likely that no offence was given on either side.

One of the most important questions about estate life was the degree to which it accommodated, perhaps even created anew, the old social hierarchies. Rooted as they were in dilemmas about the 'respectable' and 'undeserving' poor of Victorian and Edwardian times, the housing Acts and subsidies, as we have seen, were designed with such stratification in mind. They were also a continuing reality for tenants. In postwar Coventry, for instance, tenants made distinctions between 'problem', 'ordinary' and 'superior' or snobbish people, with still finer gradations between.[58] The term 'respectable' was still in use at Blackbird Leys in the 1980s.[59] The presence, real or imagined, of these social gradings posed a problem for researchers steeped in belief in a homogeneous 'working-class community', especially when they found, as was invariably the case, that people never willingly identified themselves or their immediate neighbours as the 'not respectable'. 'Roughs' were always located at a distance, even if this was no further than the end of the road[60] – so much so, in fact, that it led to the absurd situation where 'If you had a pair of researchers at opposite ends of an estate asking where the bad part was the chances are that, at the same moment, there would be two tenants out on their doorstep pointing with cold incontrovertibility towards each other, like a couple of distant duellists.'[61]

These intra-class divisions were apparent to Sean Damer in his classic 'Wine Alley' study, which revealed a working class 'characterised by an apparently contradictory mixture of levels of class and gender solidarity, on the one hand, and a complex mosaic of close-based groups which live in mutual ignorance and suspicion on the other.'[62] But he was unable to explain the rough/respectable dichotomy as anything other than a mischievous capitalist device to fragment a unitary working class, in the same way (he suggested) as it created the conventional division between the skilled and unskilled. The continuing working-class awareness of a 'rough' culture is too strong to ignore, however, especially given that it is rooted in a historical reality that predated council housing by many years.[63] Its reality in people's lives as late as the 1970s is seen in a despairing tenant's application for transfer from a Merseyside estate: 'When I first moved down to this area 6 yrs ago I was quite happy with the district and my neighbours but for the last 2 yrs things have gone from bad to worse . . . The class of people who have come here in the past 2 yrs have made it impossible to bring my children up decently no matter how hard I try . . . I still have 6 girls to bring up respectable which I cannot do in this district.'[64]

How housing managers tried to deal with this social stratification has already been discussed. However much they are to be criticized for the results, they were confronting a real situation of populations who in their older neighbourhoods might have had mechanisms for creating social distances, by physical and non-physical means. The management of council housing only to a limited degree, and perhaps mainly for its own benefit, respected working-class territoriality. It accepted certain natural boundaries and directions of movement, such as east-west or north-south of a river, but its estates and patterns of allocation were usually on a far larger scale than traditional working-class perceptions or patterns of movement. And in the last resort, estate populations had no defence against being invaded by those seen as aliens, like the car workers brought from opposite ends of the country to Dagenham in the 1930s, or to Blackbird Leys a generation later. Even the hapless 'Wine Alley', contrary to the conclusions passed into general circulation, was not in the first place stigmatized through outsiders' prejudice or its own intrinsic defects, but rather because the natives of Govan, where it was situated, had hoped and believed that it was intended for themselves and were outraged to find it allotted to people from the Glasgow slums. The relative success (or at least lack of failure) of ordinary but normally functioning estates can be attributed, at least in part, to their having escaped such invasions.[65]

At the same time, council estates could actually generate social divisions, as at Pollok in Glasgow which within 6–8 years developed distinct social areas, each with its own reputation and standing, the worst as bad as anywhere in Govan, where the tenants had come from.[66]   One unexpected and little recognized phenomenon is the 'pioneer' effect, also found in new towns or any deliberately 'planted' settlement where a body of people suddenly find themselves all in the same boat together. Pioneers give each other moral and social support, for the very fact that 'they have all made this big step from the city has tended to bind them together.'[67] Even when they had not known one another previously, people on new estates hailed others from their home area with relief.[68] The sinister side of this was that it seemed cliquey and exclusive to subsequent arrivals, a phenomenon that the fully preserved tenancy records of Quarry Hill Flats made possible to trace in great detail. The pioneers here were so well established that a core of them stayed longer than any subsequent group; and several later intakes that were larger than average made their presence similarly felt. But it also caused a faster turnover amongst those who followed – presumably because they felt cold-shouldered and excluded.[69] It is of course a possibility that the same phenomenon occurred in pre-1914 neighbourhoods when these were newly built; but they were not normally 'planted' in the manner of council estates and this, with their more gradual evolution, must have made it easier for incomers to slot themselves into their established codes and patterns of behaviour.

The Effects of Council Housing on Working-Class Life

From the middle of the twentieth century the council estate replaced the pre-1914 neighbourhood as the locus of working-class life. But this life (or lives) were changing, and the question is how far estates merely accommodated and how far they contributed to the change. The rehousing of working-class people represented, potentially, a massive cultural dislocation from the traditional neighbourhood, although this might have had only a short history and be facing an uncertain future. A good few of its features were, at first, replicated on the new estates. These included extensive networks of kin (though the role of grandparent was much damaged), patterns of neighbouring, and group activities that could be re-creations of the old or conscious attempts to express a new way of life. While many of the social layers of working-class populations were accommodated, this was through bureaucratic mechanisms committed to serving much wider constituencies than they commonly recognized. The one thing that tenants were precluded from doing was to 'self sort' – something that had often by chance been possible in pre-1914 neighbourhoods. The ability of women to manipulate the local housing market was taken away, or at best it was reshaped within the constraints of tenant selection; and so was the autonomy of tenants in general, because of the blocks on transfers and the 'sons and daughters' issue. To this extent, working-class populations that could once manipulate their neighbourhood resources to their own advantage now experienced a loss of power.

Council housing, historically, had two goals: the cure of poverty and the replacement of a working-class culture deemed undesirable by a new and 'ideal' one. In regard to the first, it was clear that, whatever later faults appeared, their new homes did at first lift people from substandard housing and degrading slums, enabling them to live dignified and modern lives on something like a par with the middle classes. This was rewarded by the consistently high levels of satisfaction with the home that were recorded in the official Design Bulletins and countless other surveys of tenant opinion. Even after 60 years, the offer of a council tenancy even of a flat or maisonette was capable of working a transformation in people's lives and relationships.[70] However, council housing could also induce as well as remove poverty, as already appeared in the 1930s. After 1945, rising incomes and still quite exclusive tenant selection policies seemed to put an end to this; but the resumption of mass slum clearance in the 1950s, and in particular the obligation from 1977 to house homeless families, began to change the situation.

The external estate environment was always more problematic than the home. In tenant opinion surveys it regularly gave less satisfaction than dwellings – and the implications of this will be further explored in the following chapter. Failures in performance were not only to do with buildings, but how estates were used by all their residents, or in other words with their cultural patterns. The official hope that tenants and their families would form 'communities' was simply an abstract one. Only a minority of tenants supported it, and still less were able to breathe life into it. In spite of the concessions won by their many actions over the years, they did not create an ideal and distinctive estate culture.

This then raises the question whether traditional working-class culture was actually emasculated by the housing policy intended to help and elevate it. The answer is in the last resort unknowable, because it is impossible to know how that culture would have developed if it had been left *in situ*. The evidence used above suggests that pre-1914 working-class neighbourhoods were already in decline independently of housing and especially through industrial change. It seems beyond dispute, however, that in spite of some promising early signs, the transportation of working-class families to new estates ruled out any constructive future development of such neighbourhoods. The single strongest influence on tenant culture was the availability of affordable home ownership, which was an ever open door for the more able and ambitious. As home owners they could, if they wished, join the mainstream pattern of living where affiliations and loyalties were national or even (eventually) global, rather than local. Home was, if anything, of increasing importance, but where it was located was of diminishing importance. This is not to say that home ownership drained off all tenant households with talent and initiative, but that those who remained were left in a setting and way of life that was increasingly by-passed by the mainstream.

Estates continued, however, to generate strong loyalty and attachment – often beyond the credence of middle-class observers, who saw only their worst points. Outsiders saw Quarry Hill Flats, for instance, as a grim fortress that people could not wait to get out of, whereas the record is of the strong attachment of many of the older residents, and their desolation when the estate was demolished.[71] The enduring loyalty that attached even to the worst estates is found too often to be ignored.[72] Typically, residents explained away any problems by saying 'There's good and bad all over' – in effect an acknowledgement that stigmatization was a crude caricature of a living environment that was in many ways satisfactory. Even the dreadful label 'sink estate' could conceal 'the stability, warmth, enthusiasm, skills and energies, which, in practice, exist within local communities, even if realization of these strengths is difficult and even if confidence has drained from individuals and communities.'[73]

As an attempt by one class to provide an improved environment and culture for another class, council housing at best accommodated existing working-class culture: it did not renew it. As long as the main tenant body consisted of those with a self-confident working-class identity and domestic aspirations close to those of their housing providers, it resulted in stable and more or less contented, if inert, populations. The serious problems, always latent, emerged with the rise of populations now far removed, in experience and values, from what is described above as stable and traditional working-class life. For such people, not only were the design and management styles of council housing unsuitable, but the very fact that they were coralled into these high profile enclaves, rather than distributed throughout the 'normal' environment, made them more visible and their difficulties more extreme.

NOTES

1. Ward (1974; 1976).
2. Ministry of Housing and Local Government (1970a, 1970b, 1971).
3. Andrews.
4. Burbidge et al.
5. Scannell. The poet was Writer in Residence here for 9 months in 1975.
6. Young & Willmott, p. 11.
7. Young & Willmott, p. 154.
8. Mogey.
9. Mogey, p. 152.
10. Mogey, p. 156.
11. Jennings, Hilda, p. 198.
12. Hole, p. 171.
13. Vereker et al., p. 46.
14. Bourke (1994b), p. 197.
15. Franklin.
16. Hole, p. 173.
17. Chapman.
18. Young & Willmott, p. 113.
19. Hoggart, pp. 342–343.
20. Bourke (1994a), p. 137.

21. Meacham (1977).
22. Anderson.
23. Meacham (1977), p. 47.
24. Roberts.
25. Benson, p. 147.
26. Strathern, p. 96.
27. Zweig (1976), pp, 15, 22.
28. Zweig (1961), pp. 32, 23, 100.
29. Abel Smith (1965).
30. Coates & Silburn.
31. Jackson, Brian, p. 166.
32. Blackwell & Seabrook, p. 28.
33. Clarke, p. 253.
34. Cf. Bracey; Kuper; Allaun; Hole; Ravetz (1974). See also Harrington (of old Edinburgh tenements): 'We had good neighbours . . . but we never went in and out of each other's houses'.
35. Thompson, F.M.L.; Roberts; Hoggart; see also, for race, Bourke (1994a).
36. According to B.S. Rowntree (1941), the use of the street for drinking had died out by 1940.
37. Tebbutt.
38. Joyce.
39. Vereker *et al.*
40. Hoggart, p. 69.
41. Kerr.
42. Vereker *et al.*, p. 102.
43. Simon, E.D; the Rev. Charles Jenkinson, housing reformer in Leeds, berated any of his parishioners who were content to remain in their slums (Ravetz 1974).
44. Glass (ed).
45. Jevons & Madge.
46. Rubinstein.
47. Jevons & Madge, pp. 33-34.
48. Young & Willmott, p. 143.
49. Young & Willmott, p. 128.
50. Pickett & Boulton, p. 73.
51. Jevons & Madge, p. 27
52. Bourke (1994a, 1994b).
53. Hole & Attenburrow.
54. Jennings, Hilda; Norris; Meegan.
55. Meegan.
56. Hole, p. 167.
57. Channel 4.
58. Kuper. Pickett & Boulton show the same hierarchies in the 1970s.
59. Reynolds.
60. Mogey; Hole.
61. Tucker, p. 76.
62. Damer (1989), p. 139.
63. Mogey; Kuper; Hodges & Smith; Hole.
64. Gill, Owen, pp. 30-31.
65. See for instance Parker.
66. Brennan.
67. Allaun, p. 138.
68. Allaun.
69. Ravetz (1974).
70. Parker.
71. Information gathered on site visit during demolition.
72. Baldwin (1974).
73. Stewart & Taylor, p. 65.

Chapter Eleven

Estate Histories

'The stranger is conscious at once of being in a planned environment.'
Planning PEP, *Watling Revisited*, 1947

'These flats used to be lovely.'
Jeremy Seabrook, *What Went Wrong?* 1978

The 'Normal' Estate

When council housing was first mooted there was no apparent need to think
or plan for the future of estates. It was tacitly assumed that they would
develop into stable and permanent settlements, and that they might develop
otherwise only began to be apparent with their emerging social and technical
problems. Ultimately, the decline or even breakdown of whole categories of
estate came to dominate public awareness and specialist research to such an
extent that they crowded out those estates that were, presumably, maturing
normally. Yet in 1980 only some 5 per cent of the total were recognized as
'problem estates',[1] and it must be assumed that throughout most of its history
the bulk of council housing functioned as the housing managers would have
it, to give tenants 'the quiet enjoyment of their own homes.' The impression
conveyed by the cottage estates and even many flatted ones, over the middle
years of the last century, was of environments that were peaceful to the point
of stagnation, where tenancy rules and management styles militated against
any changes instigated by tenants, either collectively or individually.

No one can say what is the natural span of a residential district; but a
period of stability lasting 40 or more years is perhaps not all that uncommon.
Suburbs had an inbuilt instability, as their higher classes moved outwards and
lower classes or different uses invaded, and this could occur within one
generation. What was distinctive about both council and owner-occupied
estates from the 1920s onwards was the degree of protection from non-
residential uses each enjoyed: the former because of subsidy constraints and

tenancy rules, and the latter because of the protection given by town and country planning. But in other respects there were significant differences between the two. In an estate of home owners, the original settlers either moved on, having sold their houses to another generation of family builders, or they remained into old age. In its class composition it could remain stable or decline in the social scale; but overall, the way it evolved was the sum of countless individual decisions. The obvious difference of the council estate was that its management precluded incremental change produced by individual choices and actions. This throws further light on the recurring 'sons and daughters' issue, which at first sight looks unreasonable and illogical. For the married offspring of home owners had no automatic right to settle on the same estate as their parents – in any case, the dictates of social mobility would encourage them to move on, to 'better' themselves. But in council housing tenants' feeling that married children should be given tenancies could be seen as an attempt to claim hegemony over the territory where they found themselves 'put', in many cases involuntarily. Not only did their offspring have no automatic right to follow on, but unless they acquired the necessary 'points' they had no right of access to council housing at all.

When a picture is dominated by the 'abnormal' case, it is next to impossible to deduce what would be a 'normal' pattern of development. Some inferences for council estates may perhaps be drawn from those tenants who opted to buy their homes. From the 1920s councils had discretion to sell at a discount to sitting tenants, and some did so in large numbers in the 1960s and 1970s. A study of 416 households in Birmingham and London (including Becontree) who had bought their homes between 1968 and 1973, showed that over half in each city were still occupying the same houses up to 20 years later.[2] It seems that these people liked their homes and estates well enough to want to stay, and their change of tenure did not lead to immediate social change.

The 'right to buy' given to all in 1980 resulted in a much larger transfer of ownership. Councils were now obliged to offer all their stock for sale to tenants who had held public sector tenancies for 3 (later 2) years, with discounts that rose as high as 70 per cent for flats, and other financial inducements. There was a virtual stampede to buy in certain places, notably good suburban estates of houses, although flats sold very little in comparison. Within 10 years over a million dwellings were converted to owner occupation, depleting the council-owned stock by a quarter. By 1995 it was again clear that most of the purchasers had not rushed to resell at a profit. Indeed some found their homes, especially if these were flats, impossible to sell, and others, unable to keep up their loan repayments, had their homes repossessed. Overall, 14 per cent of the houses were being resold annually and their purchasers were described as latter-day versions of early, 'respectable' council tenants: that is, youthful and financially secure family builders. Selling prices were, overall, some 10 per cent below prices of comparable properties not on council estates.[3] It might be argued, therefore, that the take-up of 'right to buy' did not demonstrate a huge desire of tenants to escape, nor was likely very quickly to change the social composition of estates.

Yet council estates did not, to all appearances, develop into 'normal neighbourhoods' like the old bye-law districts or newer owner-occupied suburbs. There were huge numbers of stories of decline, but few or no examples of estates spontaneously improving,[4] other than the programmed regeneration schemes. Virtually everywhere, older tenants speak of a golden age when their estate 'used to be lovely'. The remark is applied to all kinds and conditions of estate, including flats as well as houses and notorious estates like 'Wine Alley', Sunderland's Ridges estate (later as 'Meadowell' known for its riots), and countless others.[5] 'Golden age' memories are easily put down to nostalgia for a past that never existed, but they are often borne out by examination. Personal, if paternalistic, management style, strict enforcement of tenancy rules, weekly house-to-house rent collection, resident caretakers and residents who valued better housing standards, all contributed to well-kept environments. Above all, high child densities were more tolerable because of the number of authority figures keeping children under control, officials as well as parents, while young adolescents were either at school or at work. When, in addition, many of the tenants came from the same districts and enjoyed community events together, estate life was something to be fondly remembered.

In the nature of things the 'golden age' would seem to pertain to pre- rather than postwar estates – for, apart from the time factor, once slum clearance ended tenants were less likely to share the same origins or to find their new homes much better than those they came from. But the phenomenon is in fact found on postwar estates, and sometimes unexpected ones. It was present, for instance, at Oxford's Blackbird Leys and Hull's Orchard Park, both regarded as problem estates, and at the inner London estate of 'Beechwood' which had the familiar history of being 'a close-knit local community' spoilt by invasions of new people, including homeless people, one-parent families, and others with no connection to the locality.[6]

Council Estates as Places

There can be few British people unable to recognize what is or is not a council estate. What they are reacting to, subliminally as much as consciously, helps to account for patterns of estate history and in particular the fatal divergence between architectural intention and lived experience. Council estates added vast new built-up areas to towns and cities, and significant additions even to villages, yet they remained surprisingly unintegrated in their surroundings – unlike public housing in other parts of Europe, apparently, which developed into 'normal neighbourhoods'.[7] Greenfield sites for estates were normally bought by agreement, but if necessary they were purchased compulsorily, and a rare example of opposition was in Lancaster, where property owners held up such a purchase because of the higher rates that would result from building 'charity houses for the select few.'[8] Slum clearance areas were, of course, automatically owned by councils, and under the planning system council housing was one of the statutory functions 'deemed' to have planning consent. It did not, therefore, go to public enquiry if there were objections – a useful reminder that estates were built without public consultation as to their location, size, or even need.

The British council estate was a dormitory area brought into being by fiat and lacking a dynamic of its own. Driven by economies of scale, outlying estates very easily reached the size of small towns. Becontree and Dagenham were intended to have 29,000 houses with a population of over 100,000. Bristol's Knowle and Bedminster, begun at the same time, had over 6000 units for a population of 28,000, and the city had three other estates approaching 2000 units. In the postwar period sizes in excess of 3000 units were common. Easterhouse on the outskirts of Glasgow (predominantly high flats) and Kirkby in Lancashire each had around 50,000 population. In inner clearance areas it was possible for contiguous estates to create one enormous townscape, and in some of the London boroughs where large numbers of bye-law houses had been acquired in advance of clearance there was a virtual monopoly of local authority ownership.

Larger estates were in general less popular than smaller ones, especially when the latter were located near existing centres used by a range of social classes. Even old tenement blocks were sought after when they were centrally located; but most popular of all were the 'miscellaneous properties' acquired piecemeal, and also the postwar 'prefabs' typically clustered on small blitzed sites. Apart from their own intrinsic qualities, it is easy to account for the popularity of houses that were part of the ordinary street scene, or small infillings that blended into their surroundings. 'People liked living in an ordinary house on an ordinary street.'[9]

Another feature of council estates was their geographical isolation, not only on the forgotten periphery but in central locations also. Leeds's Quarry Hill Flats was a classic example of an 'island' estate, circled by main roads, one of which became in time almost a motorway, and with perimeter walls of flats that fed a local myth that the estate was gated and outsiders excluded. Deck access design almost automatically created estate 'fortresses' like Broadwater Farm in Tottenham, whose gleaming white walls made it an alien intrusion into the standard London bye-law streets. Another example, not normally recognized as a council estate, was the City of London's Barbican, built for high-rent business and residential uses, with a cultural centre that outsiders were unable to find until a yellow line was painted to guide them in. In other instances estates were almost wilfully cut off from their surroundings. Because of a locked railway footbridge, the 'Tenement Town's' children had to trail round a mile to reach a school only 200 yards away from their homes (a tenants' campaign resulted in the gates being unlocked for two 20-minute periods each day). But probably the commonest situation of all was the placing of estates where no one would ever choose to live – like the 'Beechwood' estate of slab blocks 'located in an inner urban area on a triangular site between railways and engineering works.'[10]

Sometimes the isolation went as far as the walling in of estates. The most notorious example was the Cutteslowe Walls in North Oxford, erected in 1934 by a developer anxious to protect the value of the new properties he was building for rent. The high brick walls topped with iron spikes survived protests, and even one demolition, for a quarter of a century.[11] More often such walls were built by home owners to seal themselves and their property from contamination by the poor and uncouth.[12] In a more subtle manner, council estates are 'cut off' by being, in effect, off the map. It is often impossible to find them in street atlases under the names they are known by, and the absence of conventional streets in Radburn and deck-access layouts makes them impenetrable to the uninitiated, and sometimes even their own residents, in spite of signs pointing to runs of 'odds' and 'evens'.

In other respects also names are significant. The street or row names betray their official origins, often suggesting what first came to the minds of local councillors. A child growing up on a Leeds estate in the 1930s, remembered 'all the streets and crescents and the drives wide enough to herd cattle down were named after Lake District beauty spots . . . with the aim, no doubt, of persuading us that we were somewhere else.'[13] Certain names such as 'garth' and 'dene' seem generic to council estates, but 'street' is rarely found (presumably because it is associated with bye-law neighbourhoods) while terms like 'The Avenue', 'The Mount', 'The Drive', which often grace private estates, are absent. Some names were chosen to impress residents with the local history, as in the deck-access 'Citadel' of Killingworth in Northumberland which was divided into Old and New Garth with streets called East and West Bailey. At the same time accidental and unplanned open spaces or natural features were left unnamed and, unless nicknamed by residents, remained anonymous – a barrier to their recognition and hence utilization as part of the estate environment.

Because estates so often carried a social stigma, residents were ashamed of their addresses and identified themselves when possible with an adjacent district that was more acceptable. Insulting names were attached to stigmatized estates: 'Colditz', 'Alcatraz', 'The Piggeries'. The surrounding and protecting wall of flats at Byker inevitably attracted the term 'Berlin Wall', although it was in fact lovingly designed to provide its residents with a private, sheltered and sunny outlook. But it is not the function of labels to be discriminating and, once bestowed, they are hard to efface. From time to time authorities tried to redeem a problem estate by an official change of name. Bristol's notorious Knowle West was re-named Filwood Park in 1938, and 50 years later Merseyside's Cantril Farm was, with tenure changes, given a new identity as Stockbridge Village. A rare, perhaps unique, example where residents chose to keep their original name when they had the opportunity to pick another was a small scheme of tenant-designed houses attached to the huge, problem-ridden Blackbird Leys estate.

Council estates did not, unlike flourishing private suburbs between the wars, develop their own commercial centres and industries. The provision of shops (either lock-up or residential) was strictly under council control and usually limited to the four or five basic foods and a tobacconist-newsagent – with the addition on well provided estates of a general co-operative store and fish and chip shop. The 'cart before horse' nature of council estate development is illustrated by a publicity leaflet of the LCC for Becontree advising that 'Sites for Factories are available', then adding as if in afterthought: 'houses, churches, schools, shopping centres, cinemas, etc. have been provided.'[14]

As planted environments, estates had few legacies of past evolutionary processes. Even clearance areas were denuded of most of their commercial and public buildings and often the only things left standing were a public house and a disused church. Estates could not experience the piecemeal and cumulative change seen in ordinary neighbourhoods. Not only were they designed and built at one time, or in a series of programmed stages, but any programmes of improvement were similarly phased. One of the things that made Byker outstanding when it was designed for a huge site cleared in the 1970s was the architects' insistence on retaining a church ruin and bath house, relics of the old working-class neighbourhood that had been condemned before they arrived on the scene. Features of their design were deliberately open-ended and flexible, to accommodate a future evolution that might go in various different ways. Open spaces were designed to be suitable for a number of uses and could be changed to suit residents' patterns of living, and a number of scattered 'corner shops' evocative of the past were intended to add life and identity. Even the 'wall' of flats that helped to stigmatize the estate was designed in the first place to buffer it from a planned motorway.

If they were not naturally evolving places, what sorts of place were council estates? The early cottage estates set out to be working-class suburbs or even garden-city settlements; but their tight management control, with the poverty of many of their tenants, made it difficult for them to function like the suburbs of the middle classes. These themselves were undergoing a subtle transformation after 1945, as society in general became less localized and family-oriented. By the time the working-class exodus to suburban estates gathered its full momentum, the main trend was towards more physically and culturally mobile lifestyles, greatly assisted, of course, by car ownership. Eventually, many council tenants could also afford a car, many of them in due course becoming natural beneficiaries of the right to buy; but there were those – and towards the end of the century they increased in numbers – whose lives remained constricted by insecurity, poverty and dependence on welfare. They were then, in effect, either stranded on estates that were abortive suburbs, or concentrated in high flats and maisonettes that all too easily became social ghettos. The proper functioning of such estates required high standards of maintenance and management, as well as a certain level of discipline and sophistication from their users. The challenges of the 1980s and 1990s were how to cope with the concentrations of poverty found on both inner and outer estates, and in particular how to enable them to have some sort of natural evolutionary development.

Council Estates as Architecture

One of the things making the Byker estate unique for its time was not only its design but that its designers, Ralph Erskine and his team, entered into a continuing dialogue with the people enduring the trauma of clearance and also persuaded the city to adopt practices to make it more bearable.[15] The normal way of commissioning and designing estates with no consultation with future tenants was as much due to bureaucracy in environmental health and housing as to architects. The latter, as we have seen, took the architectural status of council housing seriously. Council houses were proudly exhibited at the Ideal Homes Exhibition in the early 1920s, and again in the 1940s. Best examples were given serious appraisal in works on modern architecture, along with housing in new towns.[16] The new estate of Lansbury (named after the old socialist hero) was chosen to be the 'living architecture' exhibit of the 1951 Festival of Britain. Designed as a 'town within a town' to cater for people bombed out of this part of Poplar, it had nearly 500 houses, maisonettes and flats in blocks of varying heights, a shopping centre and open-air market, with pubs, schools, churches, a communal laundry and, for the Festival, various pieces of whimsy like the 'Rosie Lee' tea room and 'Gremlin Grange', a life-size mock-up of a jerry-built speculative house.

But there was never to be another such public celebration of the architecture of council housing. Many so-called 'show' estates were such only in name, although some were destinations for repeated foreign delegations, not altogether welcomed by their residents.[17] The Quarry Hill Flats were the target of countless such delegations and were endlessly cited in housing and planning sources, but Leeds people were ashamed rather than proud of them, and certainly never ventured into them for interest or pleasure. Much the same was true of Sheffield's Park Hill estate, the postwar analogue of Quarry Hill. Also in a central location and of roughly the same size and population density, this was built to replace once notorious slums, using innovative techniques (which included the Garchey waste disposal system) and with yet more generous social provision, including forty-two shops, four pubs, several playgrounds and a community hall. The estate was similarly modelled on Continental example, in this case Le Corbusier's lately opened Unité d'Habitation in Marseilles, but although its designers, the city architect and his team, could not have been unaware of the Leeds estate nearby, they drew no lessons from it, presumably because they were so sure they could improve upon it.

Park Hill went one further than its Leeds predecessor by having a resident sociologist to assess its first year of operation. She reported back to the city council that the estate was an outstanding success, with such 'an exceptionally vigorous residents' association' that any appearance here of social apathy was a 'remote possibility.'[18] The design achieved the ideal combination of friendliness and privacy, and the 3-metre wide decks were said to function as sociable meeting places with people gossiping in doorways and small children running around in complete safety. To an eminent architectural critic Park Hill was 'one of the most heartening architectural prospects in England;'[19] but even as the plaudits flowed, serious flaws were coming to light. The buildings were hugely expensive to maintain; the Garchey system frequently backed up and flooded; and the estate had what was claimed to be the country's largest concentration of young people under eighteen. Like Quarry Hill, its central location saved it from being hard to let, but its architectural distinction did not exempt it from the familiar range of estate problems, or from being publicly stigmatized.

Nowhere is the gulf between architects and people clearer than in the listing or proposed listing of certain estates by English Heritage, to protect them from inappropriate change or destruction. The criteria for listing are technical and design innovation, cultural and historical significance, including uniqueness, and there is no reason why council estate architecture should not be as eligible as any other category of building. The early LCC estates of Boundary Street and Millbank were already listed while others, like Liverpool's 'Bull Ring' in St Andrews Gardens, had been spot-listed when threatened with demolition, when in 1998 a fresh batch of council housing was considered for listing. To the consternation if not disbelief of its residents, Park Hill was one of those included and the potential listing of Byker is, at the time of writing, finely balanced against its demolition as a failed estate. Should demolition be the option chosen, this would be an outstanding example of the failure of design and management innovations to counteract reputation and other adverse factors.

The improvements made to houses by those tenants who bought them demonstrate what was to them important by way of design. Typically, the changes they made were cosmetic rather than structural: new front doors with 'carriage' lamps, plastic window frames with leaded lights, fancy wall cladding – all such things as personalized their homes and made them stand out from their still rent-paying neighbours. Their choices were in fact removing the stigmata of council housing. Much the same could be said of the choices made by members of housing co-operatives and tenant design schemes who were in a position to work with an architect on dwelling and estate designs. Though availing themselves of Parker Morris standards, none elected 'modern' looking dwellings. All opted for 'cottagey' houses, brick built with pitched roofs and relatively small windows, often set in culs-de-sac, with lavish landscaping and planting.[20]

Diagnoses of 'Problem Estates'

By the later 1960s it was no longer possible to ignore the fact that estates could go seriously wrong, and the terms that began to come into circulation were 'difficult to let', 'difficult', 'problem', or 'sink' estate, and later the apparently more neutral 'peripheral estate'. The phenomena these described were hardly new – there had been early warning signs at least since the 1930s – but up to now they were mainly of concern to housing managers and policy-makers, whose preoccupation was with the 'problem tenant' rather than the 'problem estate' – which serves to confirm how long the general perception of council housing was of something stable and not outstandingly problematic.

There was apparently no foolproof way of preventing descent into the problem category. As we have seen, the so-called 'show' estate was not exempt. The massively high public profiles of Quarry Hill and Park Hill did not save them from disparagement and decline, and the GLC's Brandon estate (immortalized as Tony Parker's *Providence*) was another that was regarded simultaneously as a showpiece and 'in some senses a problem estate'.[21]   If architectural status had some influence, it was likely to be on management rather than social development.   Managers picked their tenants with extra care – in the case of Quarry Hill they were particularly mindful of the estate's politically contentious origins and believed that its innovations, especially the passenger lifts, required select tenants.   In the event, life behind the estate's curtain walls was remarkably peaceful; but this was not enough to quell its reputation or prevent wild rumours circulating about its roughness and general undesirability.

Underlying attempts to explain what turned an estate into a problem estate was the question that for so long vexed Victorian reformers: how far was failure due to the inherent defects of the dwellings, and how far to the defects of their inhabitants?   That the question still needed to be asked at all perhaps showed how low the early idealism of council housing had fallen.   The belief that slum people were a race apart had now all but receded into history, but, with underpinning from psychology, it was replaced by the notion of a small minority of 'problem tenants'.   A study of the 1950s of two Bristol estates defined as 'difficult': 'those estates which have acquired or threaten to acquire a public reputation for "difficulty" because enough of their residents outrage the sense of conventional respectability which authority expects.'[22]   Dividing residents into the three categories of 'Solids', 'Brittles' and 'Difficults', the author found that the two high-risk periods for estates were at their inception, when their 'anonymity' and 'wide-open emotional spaces' deprived the vulnerable 'brittles' of their traditional neighbourhood supports; and any time when new populations were introduced, bringing with them 'the aggression or clamant squalor of disintegrative personalities.'[23]   The majority of 'solid' residents coped well with the strains of moving to their new homes, but the disruptive if tiny minority made 'difficult' housing estates 'a potentially permanent feature of the social landscape.'[24]

Other studies took a similar line.   On Edinburgh's 'Newkirk' estate, for instance, moving was found to have disturbed people's self-image and sense of identity because 'the old groups, of which they are a part, have broken up.'[25] On the Deneside estate in Oldham, there was a residuum of deprived 'dissociates', and it was suggested that they belonged to a subculture that was to be found in most urban areas.[26]   A study done for a housing authority consortium of pre- and postwar estates of houses, flats and maisonettes, found that they contained anti-social families who liked to 'gravitate' to certain estates 'because, being of a like mind to others in the area, they find their behaviour accepted and even condoned.'[27]   Although they amounted to less than 1 per cent in total, they were irredeemable, and it was suggested that this unpalatable truth should be faced and housing standards lowered to cater for such people, even at the risk of creating a ghetto.

A slight shift of perspective arose from criminology, with a focus on delinquent youth, and a 1977 study of part of a Merseyside estate labelled 'the worst street in Crossley' anatomized the 'creation' of a delinquent area which had been built less than 10 years earlier. The so-called delinquents were youths whose unruly behaviour expressed their territorial needs; but it was suggested that the 'moral panic' of the authorities, in particular the confrontational reaction of the police, inflated the problem, which was then sensationalized by the media and the public generally.[28] A similar situation viewed in a similar way was seen in the study of Blackbird Leys, represented as the 'final solution' to all of Oxford's housing needs when it was built in the 1950s. With around 3000 houses and flats, many of them with public lawns lapping right up to their private windows, it had a 'bizarre and skewed age distribution' where a quarter of the population were under five and another quarter of school age. Within a very few years the estate had a reputation for being rough and criminal, its problems stemming from the 1 per cent of delinquent youths who, among other things, kept the estate shopkeepers under siege. But the 'real' problem was identified as the magnification of these difficulties by authority, and especially by intolerant 'respectable' tenants, and the author concluded that its labelling as a problem estate 'really meant an area that caused problems for the authorities in the amount of work and resources it demanded.'[29]

This was the perspective taken into the conventional wisdom of most academic housing studies and housing campaigns. Its exoneration of the much maligned 'problem tenants' and unruly youth meant that it was the 'problem' label itself that needed investigation; and if it was not justified by resident behaviour it must, by default, be attributed to management. This was the line taken by Sean Damer in his hugely influential study of Moorepark, or 'Wine Alley', in Govan. This was a 'rehousing' (and therefore bottom standard) scheme of 516 walk-up flats, built in 1934 at the then very high density of 158 persons to the acre. In nine months residence on the estate, Damer was unable to track down the alleged anti-social or criminal minority, finding only the 'complex mosaic' that has been mentioned above (p. 170). His conclusion that the estate was unfairly stigmatized, set in his wider belief that all council housing was something wrested by a militant working class from a reluctant state, remained largely unchallenged, although his later in-depth publication of the Wine Alley research permits a more careful analysis of the roots of the problem. The nickname was bestowed, in the first place, by disgruntled Govanites, natives of a proud and once independent township, who resented the introduction of people from the slums of Glasgow, a minority of whom were alcoholics or 'winos'. Yet in spite of this, and the estate's low technical specifications, it was not seen by its early inhabitants as the 'punishment park' that Damer claimed, but rather – in the words of tenants – a 'paradise' or 'oasis'.[30]

Few researchers followed Damer's example and actually went to live on the estates they studied, if only for short periods; but the Wine Alley hypothesis that estates were branded through sheer prejudice was salient in the academic debate for a generation or more. This created an awkward paradox, namely that leftwing protagonists for council housing were constantly calling for more of it, while at the same time they consistently disparaged the way it functioned in reality. As the passionately argued *Whatever Happened to Council Housing* (product of one of the Community Development Projects mentioned in chapter 12, below) confessed in 1976, 'the council housing programmes of the local authorities described in this report reveal a uniformly depressing picture of lost ideals and penny-pinching inadequacy'; at the same time they were 'part of the ongoing political struggle of the working class to establish the right to decent housing at a reasonable cost for all who need it', and more should be provided.[31] That the way council housing operated, with all its imperfections, was perhaps due to strong historical or cultural imperatives was evidently too disturbing to contemplate.

In the event, it was careful though less dramatic analysis of the nature of 'problem estates' that began to influence policy in a practical way. An 'exploratory study' of 1978 looked for variables that distinguished problem from non-problem estates and found them in populations that were weighted towards the unskilled, wives not in paid employment, large families yielding high child densities, and rates of tenancy turnover as high as 20 per cent annually.[32] It agreed that the periods of most risk were when estates were new and when they were 'invaded' by different populations; for among other things this could renew the high child densities of the opening years, so preventing the natural ageing process of the original population. Evidently this was what happened at Blackbird Leys, with an importation of car workers from Coventry. Another reason for 'invasion' was a change in status of the owning authority: when Meadowell's district became 'metropolitan', for instance, this immediately changed it from an estate with a social cross-section to one used for the homeless, as the worst stock of a much larger housing authority. Yet even with such problems, estates continued to satisfy a majority of their residents who, helped by better housing to make a fresh start in life, were 'well able to take care of their own affairs.'[33]

A broad profile of so-called problem estates was provided by a survey and fieldwork of the mid-1970s, published by the Department of Environment in 1980. The estates looked at were of many sizes, from less than 200 to upwards of 2000, and contained all dwelling types, from semi-detached houses to walk-up and deck access flats and maisonettes. They included five pre-war and ten post-war estates, none of them strictly speaking unlettable. All were fully occupied, but they could only be kept so by admitting people on low incomes or with social problems, and they all had higher than average rates of tenancy termination and applications for transfer. Of the postwar estates, built between 1956 and 1971, the majority had 'presented problems from the time they opened,'[34] and for some the option of demolition was already being considered. Other remedies were being applied but they were piecemeal and unco-ordinated.

The category of peripheral estate became salient in the 1980s when comparisons began to be made with the inner-city areas that had always received much policy attention. Four cities (Glasgow, Hull, Knowsley and Middlesbrough) came together in 1984 to form RIPE (Radical Improvements for Peripheral Estates) which amongst other things commissioned a research report that recognized their increasing social and physical isolation, as one-class areas of 'entrenched material poverty'.[35] Liverpool's outer estates were planned with industrial expansion in mind, but when this failed to materialize their populations were stranded, without either skills or jobs. One of them was Cantril Farm (later renamed Stockbridge Village), built in the 1950s-1960s 8 miles from the city centre, and having one of the highest child densities in the country. But in many ways the most extreme case was Glasgow's Easterhouse, built in the 1950s 5 miles from the city centre, with a population of 50,000 accommodated in a forest of tower blocks.

Failed Estates

There were no estates that failed to work as housing of some sort, at least for a time. The Department of Environment's studies made it clear that, in their terms, 'difficult to let' did not mean strictly unlettable, but simply that it became progressively harder to fill any voids with acceptable tenants. But though all estates functioned up to a point, this point was sometimes reached after a distressingly short time. The United Kingdom's most blatant example was Belfast's Divis flats on the war-stricken Falls Road, finished in 1972 and declared the 'youngest slum in Europe' the following year – although nine of its twelve blocks were still standing in 1986. There were more than a few estates that were alleged to 'fail' from their very beginning – 'Wine Alley', as we have seen, placed rather unfairly among them. A more convincing example was the Noble Street estate in Newcastle, consisting of 5-storey blocks of flats and maisonettes built in 1956-58 near the city centre. 'From its inception the most notorious street in Newcastle', it generated its own informal lettings category of 'only fit for Noble Street.'[36] Nevertheless it did service for a quarter of a century before being demolished. Another candidate for instant failure was the vast system-built, deck-access Aylesbury estate, which 'was called a slum on the day of its official opening ceremony'[37] and was regarded as the equivalent, for vandalism, of the American Pruitt Igoe flats to be mentioned below.

In the main, however, there were few outright failures, even of estates that were notorious. Broadwater Farm provides an example. Constructed 1967-70, by 1973 it was classed as hard-to-let. Its beginning had been both physically and socially inauspicious: the buildings had to be put on stilts because the site easily flooded, and they incorporated three miles of decks or walkways, which gave unlimited scope for criminal behaviour. By the time it was finished, the borough's slum clearance programme was winding down, leaving the estate short of tenants from the locality, and half its units were allocated to the homeless and other urgent cases. It was plagued by inter-generational and inter-racial conflicts, and in 1979 was deemed too bad even for 'Priority Estate' status. Yet after (and to an extent because of) a particularly dreadful riot in 1985, involving a death and a murder, there opened a further and more hopeful chapter (p. 221, below).

The new Gorbals, Glasgow: redeveloped with high- and medium-rise flats in the 1960s, much of it lay abandoned and awaiting demolition by the mid-1970s.

It was usually only when an estate proved no longer habitable – whether because its structure was deemed dangerous and too expensive to rectify, because no one was willing to live in it, or because those who did so could no longer be controlled – that the final solution of demolition was reached. In 1974, when the much publicized demolition of the estate of Pruitt Igoe in St Louis, Missouri, took place, it seemed that no such thing could ever occur in Britain. Quarry Hill Flats, however, was already condemned by that time, although this was an exceptional case which had not failed technically or socially, but where previously rectified building defects were used as an argument for demolition (so clearing a strategic and potentially valuable site).[38] The first credited tower block demolition in Britain was not far off: in 1979 Birkenhead blew up three deck-access, 10-storey blocks, which observers from other local authorities were invited to witness. This had a certain historic symmetry, for Victorian Birkenhead had been the first authority in the country to build working-class tenements. Constructed some 20 years before, the demolished blocks had been empty for 5 years. The same length of useful life, sometimes shorter, applied to blocks demolished in the 1980s and 1990s. They included the deck access estates of Hunslet Grange and Netherley in Liverpool, the latter after a 5-year campaign for demolition by the tenants, and also Liverpool's Everton Heights, better known as 'The Piggeries', which consisted of three 15-storey blocks built in 1966 and completely wrecked by 1978, when they were offered for sale to any taker on 99-year lease. In spite of rumours of being sold off for ten new pence, they waited until 1981 before being sold (and within 3 years the council was seeking to repossess them).

The 'solution' of demolition was most often applied to flats – in 2000 Birmingham announced plans to demolish 300 of its tower blocks, for instance – but prefabricated houses were also quite often demolished as they came to the end of their technical life. In this as in other respects council estates differed from the estates built for owner occupiers, which seldom if ever made use of experimental building systems. They only rarely included flats, and these normally no higher than two or three storeys, and were not intended for families with children. As private developers refrained from building until there was judged to be a market, the demolition of unwanted or 'failed' speculative estates was a thing not heard of. On the comparatively rare occasions when they were unable to shift newly completed schemes, developers would make deals with local authorities, who incorporated them into their own stock.

If simplistic explanations are laid aside, any speculation as to what makes an estate fail must take account of a possible range of 'causes' or contributing factors that could work together to bring about either a faster or a slower decline. It is clear that fatal combinations are not confined to any one dwelling type, date, location, design, or size of estate. But equally, some types are more prone to failure than others: flats rather than houses, peripheral rather than central locations, and prefabricated rather than traditional construction. The most failure-prone layouts were those of the Radburn type, with their unfamiliar geometries, unclear distinctions between public and private space, and networks of public footpaths that encroached on domestic privacy. But the highest risk of all attached to deck access estates, which combined similar drawbacks to Radburn with their own peculiar horrors of interlocked dwellings, public walkways over domestic ceilings, and ground levels given to stores and parking space that were rapidly abandoned to wreckers.

Even in these cases, however, there were distinctions to be made. A case in point is provided by the YDG deck-access system used in Sheffield, Leeds, Hull and Nottingham. All but one of the schemes, among which Hunslet Grange was included, were demolished in the 1970s or 1980s. The sole survivor, a block on Hull's Thornton estate, made an interesting contrast with a YDG complex on the city's huge peripheral estate of Bransholme. On the extreme edge of the city, with an electrical heating system costing more to run than the rent, and the disheartening experience of overlooking houses with their own private gardens, this complex was immediately hard to let, and its eventual demolition was regretted by none. The Thornton estate, on the other hand, enjoyed a central location and its tenants opposed clearance to such effect that most of it was reprieved. In the event, and mainly for reasons of cost, only one block was ever improved, and the rest were demolished. In close consultation with the residents, the improved block was given a pitched slate roof, timber framed windows in place of the original ribbon glazing, decks that were glazed, carpeted and heated, and a resident caretaker. With external landscaping and other features, the apartments here were then much sought after by local people.

The social factors in estate failure can be divided into failures of provision and management, and inappropriate behavioural patterns of residents, with a significant additional contribution supplied by local reputation, often grossly inflated by the local press. Failures of provision included the inadequate supply of shops, services, play space, and generally poor upkeep. Damaged fences and railings, and broken or abandoned play equipment were ubiquitous, and no subsidy was available for the upkeep of playgrounds, landscaping, community halls and other public facilities. The centralization of management and caretaking, in particular the ending of door-to-door rent collection, also contributed to the degeneration of estates. Allocation policies and differences of architectural style, standards and quality within estates could, as we have seen, generate jealousy and conflict between different groups of tenants, especially when ethnic minorities or non-local people were involved. Towards the end of the century, when allocations had to be increasingly weighted towards families dependent on benefits, many estates developed a damaging split between them and the shrinking body of older, traditional tenants. The enormously high child and youth densities on estates like Blackbird Leys, especially when combined with layouts and dwelling types unsuitable for children, could generate levels of vandalism and disturbance that were offensive or terrifying to older residents. At this point it was easy for adult supervision and control to break down completely, as young people found increasingly violent and criminal ways of amusing themselves, especially when they were caught up in the spreading culture of drugs.

The responses that these trends called forth will be the concern of the last part of this book. Partly paving the way to their blend of social and design measures was a further development of theory, which was to do with the ways design could influence tenant behaviour. The impetus came from Oscar Newman's study of high-rise public estates in New York in the 1970s, which put forward the concept of 'defensible space'.[39] His hypothesis was that particular types of building and layout could induce either social or anti-social behaviour, and that the latter resulted when design precluded any sense of personal ownership, control or surveillance over the immediate surroundings of the home. The idea was essentially a liberal one, its intention to give people more power to personalize and so exercise control over their living places; but it was also used to pursue a deterministic explanation of tenant behaviour. A large-scale study of high-rise and deck-access estates in London ostensibly supported his theory, by demonstrating that size and other features induced not only such things as vandalism and littering, but general 'social malaise' – which included such things as child abuse, unemployment and 'social decline'.[40] The detail and scale of the study persuaded the Prime Minister Margaret Thatcher, to divert housing funds to 'DICE', a special programme for rectifying the 'design disadvantagement' of seven chosen estates. This among other things involved the demolition of bridges linking deck access blocks, a strategy already in use by some authorities. In the event no conclusive results emerged from the experiment.[41]

What the theory behind DICE ruled out was any possible reciprocal relationship between the social and physical dimensions of estates, and its choice of Blackbird Leys to demonstrate that suburban, low-rise estates were in all circumstances superior to high-rise ones proved unfortunate, for some years later this estate fell victim to some spectacular rioting. Other and more discriminating studies led to the more considered conclusion that the social and environmental contributions to difficult-to-let and problem estates were usually inextricably mixed, while major policy changes, as in legislation for homelessness, could also play a crucial part. Such studies suggested that estates identified as 'problem', with 'concentrations of poverty, apathy and vandalism, were often the consequences of policies, practices and processes that affect all council housing, not just a minority, although not everywhere in such concentrated form.'[42] It followed that no single blueprint for remedial action existed: design and management measures as well as deeper policy changes were all involved. At the same time, all the more comprehensive studies agreed that tenants must be actively engaged if estates were to be changed in a positive way.

Life Histories of Council Estates

With the exception of the small minority that met their end by demolition, council estates have not yet run their course as part of the built environment, and of the housing and social systems. Their histories have been strongly constrained by the legislative and bureaucratic frameworks, and these have stood in the way of their spontaneous and gradual evolution. The commonest estate biography is a hopeful beginning, which provides a long remembered 'Golden Age', followed by gradual or occasionally sharp decline. The delayed manifestation of design or building defects may be a large contributing factor to this pattern, but the causes are at least as likely to be social: in particular, the introduction of newcomers who are, or are considered to be, of inferior status. Social considerations such as group antagonisms or social stigma may be as or more important than layout, dwelling type or building technology, and this makes possible the not uncommon occurrence where well designed and sound houses and estates that, under other ownership or with other residents, would be desirable, become neglected, vandalized, and even written off.

How far this pattern was exclusive to council housing is a question that should be asked. A similar pattern may have occurred before 1914 in some urban neighbourhoods, which only maintained their standards for as long as they were inhabited by the groups for whom they were intended, and for as long as these groups had the means to look after them. Decline set in when their residents were driven out by influxes of newcomers who were poorer and of lower social status. In particular, the Great War of 1914–1918 caused catastrophic social disruption, in neighbourhoods as in other areas of life.[43] Although it was not anticipated and would certainly have appalled the idealistic initiators of council housing, it appears that it too, like the bye-law stock preceding it, was doomed to go through a downward spiral, often to the point 'where run down and outwardly neglected council estates take the place of the cleared slums.'[44] Whether, as was so often alleged, the fault lay in governments lowering standards, or whether in wider social and economic trends, it was a tragic end to the bold ideal of reforming people's lives by reforming their living conditions.

Once wholesale slum clearance was abandoned, there was no longer any agenda for branding a whole sector of housing and replacing it with a different type and tenure, as 60 years earlier, and any such suggestion for council housing would have alienated much public opinion as well as tenants. A change of tenure did, however, take place with increasing momentum under Conservative policies of 1979–97, and its results will be a concern of the following chapter. The termination of Parker Morris standards in the same period was abandonment of an ideal, and it finally brought to a close the historic claim of council housing to set trends in design. Design and technical changes, with changes of tenure, would perhaps in future make council estates more like owner-occupied ones, especially in districts where housing demand was strong enough to overcome prejudice against locations and identities that had long been stigmatized. But 20 years after the start of 'right to buy', apart from select parts of London, former council houses were still marketed as 'ex-local authority', and their prices discounted accordingly. Whatever the future

Byker estate, Newcastle upon Tyne, 2001. Thirty years on, residents still sun themselves on this lavishly landscaped and planted estate, which was explicitly designed to encourage people to make full use of their gardens and to socialize out of doors.

of estates, it could hardly fail to be coloured by their previous life patterns. Two features, in particular, would be salient: the degree to which they met or failed to meet the needs and demands of children and young people, and the contrast between the habitual passivity of most tenants and their dogged defence of homes and territories when these were in any way threatened. Both would be crucial for the success of policies for either terminating or radically transforming council housing around the year 2000.

NOTES

1. Burbidge *et al.*, Vols. 1-3.
2. Forrest & Murie.
3. Forrest *et al.*
4. Pickett & Boulton; Kirby.
5. Gill, Owen; Niner; Hulme Estate Manchester (see chapter 12); Lower Grange Estate, Bradford.
6. Burbidge *et al.*, Vol. 2, p. 3.
7. Power (1997), p. 140.
8. Jennings, J.H., p. 134.
9. Holloway Tenant Co-operative, 51.
10. Burbidge *et al.*, Vol. 2, p. 3.
11. Collison
12. Allaun; Grayson; Rubinstein.
13. Waterhouse, p. 92.
14. Rubinstein, p. 56.
15. Ravetz (1976).
16. Gale; Cleeve Barr.
17. Woodberry Down Memories Group.
18. Womersley, p. 148; City of Sheffield Housing Department (covering letter of housing manager).
19. Darke & Darke (1972), p. 560.
20. Co-operative Development Services. See also (in Sheffield) United Kingdom Housing Trust.
21. McIntosh, p. 16.
22. Wilson, Roger, pp. 21–22.
23. Wilson, Roger, p. 21.
24. Wilson, Roger, p. 41.
25. Harrington, p. 136.
26. Shenton.
27. Northern Consortium, p. 5.
28. Gill, Owen, p. 166.
29. Reynolds, p. 56.
30. Damer (1989), p. 54; (1974), pp. 234-235.
31. Community Development Project (1976), p. 11.
32. Attenburrow *et al.*
33. Attenburrow *et al.*, p. 11.
34. Burbidge *et al.*, Vol. 2, p. 2.
35. Holmes, p. 3.
36. Burbidge *et al.*, Vol. 3, p. 40.
37. McIntosh, p. 22.
38. Ravetz (1974).
39. Newman.
40. Coleman, pp. 170, 180.
41. Hill, Stephen (1997).
42. Burbidge *et al.*, Vol. 1, p. 35.
43. Stowell.
44. Burbidge *et al.*, Vol. 2, p. 4.

Chapter Twelve

Turning Points: The Parameters at the Turn of the Century

'What once evoked the dignity and clamour of a powerful social constituency, part of the body politic . . . now described only the edge of a class and the end of the city.'
Beatrix Campbell, *Goliath: Britain's Dangerous Places*, 1993

'The estate as an entity hopefully disappears and becomes a neighbourhood.'
Waltham Forest Seminar, London Housing Research Group, 25 May, 1995

Council Housing in a Changing Society

By the end of the twentieth century council housing was having to function in a society very unlike the one for which it had been devised. Had its utopian expectations been fulfilled, its estates would presumably have been self-regenerating by now; but instead they were increasingly identified with poverty and social breakdown. There was no longer any question of adopting the remedy of summarily removing their inhabitants to better environments, for the problem now was not just how to deal with the poor, but how to deal with the environments created to eliminate their poverty. Even in the parts of council housing that were apparently functioning quite well, the future was already compromised by a huge backlog of repairs and renovations.

By 1980 the social effects of long-term economic change were increasingly obvious. The decline of manufacturing industry, long masked by wars and postwar reconstructions, left some regions with levels of unemployment not seen since the 1930s. There was a growing divide between a skilled (though not necessarily secure) elite and unemployed, casual or poorly paid labour living in a poverty 'not simply on a scale that had not been seen for more than 40 years but which was also of a kind that simply *had never* been seen here at all.'[1] Working-class identity and culture no longer centred round common occupations. Much of the 'working class' was in fact workless, and the convenient term 'underclass' was found for those dependent for their support on the state. But unemployment as a way of life could no longer, as once, be buttressed by a fierce solidarity. The prevailing, and perhaps for many the only, culture was that of consumerism with values disseminated by the popular media. To be poor was to be excluded from but not therefore independent of mainstream fashions and desires. Poverty was no longer a public health problem, for it could reasonably be assumed that everyone lived in sanitary conditions and even those on state benefits managed somehow to have fashion clothing and such 'luxuries' as TV and stereos (which could, of course, be given or stolen as well as bought). It was more a question of how – and whether – people in this condition could participate in the wider society – and here again, a useful term made its appearance: the 'social exclusion' given currency by New Labour when it came to power in 1997.

Thus the social stereotype for which council housing was devised, the two-generation family with father in full time work and mother (ideally) at home with the children, no longer held true; and the public housing sector was called on to accommodate the very thing it had been designed to avoid: idle populations dependent on welfare, with high concentrations of unsupervised youths and children. In the last third of the century the number of children living in one-parent families trebled, and while this was no more than 6 per cent for the population at large, it was 50 per cent in the black minority population. Marital violence and child abuse were everyday problems in some estate populations. No class, of course, was immune to unemployment, changing patterns of marriage and parenting, or the use of illegal drugs; but such things impacted hardest on the 'new poor'. Traditional father-to-son transmission of skills and jobs was broken; school leavers could not expect to find regular work, and for many thieving seemed a viable occupation. The spreading drugs habit was largely supported by a trade in stolen or illicitly imported goods.

Social change was not of course always for the worse, and one positive and constantly recurring theme in estate regeneration was the power of mothers as catalysts for protest and action.[2] But the breakdown of former economic and family frameworks had a particular impact on children and adolescents. Most of society's traditional authority figures had disappeared, not only from the family but from schools, churches and public services, where such people as caretakers, park keepers and bus conductors had been sacrificed to economy. With the loss of adult supervision there arose new means of defiance and assertion centring round the ultimate cult object, the car. 'Twoccing' (taking away without consent), joy riding, hand brake turns and giving stolen cars a 'burn' were opportunities to demonstrate skills and gain peer respect. So in its own way was shoplifting, especially in Asian-run estate shops that were regarded as fair targets.[3] In heightened circumstances, and with ill judged police interventions, minor incidents could develop into full-blown riots. The first of a long series took place in inner Liverpool's Toxteth in 1972 and within 10 years there followed riots in Bristol, Brixton and many other places. That at Broadwater Farm occurred in 1985. In 1991-95, twenty-eight 'disturbances' were counted, and the council estates affected were for the most part neither high-rise nor in the worst physical condition. What they had in common was that they had been built for slum clearance and had high concentrations of young people. Almost without exception the rioters were young white males, and their rioting usually achieved not so much reprisals as additional attention and resources for their estates.[4]

Fundamental social change is accompanied by a radical revision of political and social philosophies, not only within the political parties but in public attitudes in general. The welfare state was based on an inter-party consensus between 'wet' Toryism and middle-of-the-road Labour, both using Keynesian economics, where differences were often as much about style or degree as intrinsic content. The New Right government coming to power in 1979 repudiated this consensus, and blamed the Welfare State with its 'culture of dependency' for economic underachievement and virtually all social problems. Its aim was to substitute an 'enterprise culture', where business success and wealth creation would be properly valued and all citizens would take responsibility for their own lives, with minimal intervention by the state. Therefore the poor were no longer seen as victims of an economic system – let alone former contributors to society with an entitlement to its protection – but, in quasi-Victorian terms, authors of their own misfortunes, who would only be further pauperized by state assistance. Policy was reshaped to market principles and among its favourite instruments were the 'task force' that brought business acumen to bear on particularly difficult problems and areas; the leverage of private investment through short, sharp injections of state money; and competition for limited funds among deprived areas and constituencies that were required to 'bid' against one another. Programmes were delivered through 'partnerships' between private and public sectors with, as third partner, the 'community' (however this might be defined).

Such partnerships – which were also impressed on local authorities under 'Agenda 21' of the Earth Summit in 1992 – were in theory opportunities for power sharing with local people. At the same time the new policy climate clearly had no place for, or even comprehension of, the deeply rooted if flawed utopianism expressed in council housing and town and country planning. Although the programme for new towns was fairly abruptly closed in the early 1980s, planning as a regulatory function was not discarded – for if nothing else it gave vital protection to certain sectoral interests. The size and role in the housing system of council housing put the closure of this out of the question; but as an indiscriminate subsidy to the 'undeserving' and a monopolistic service of local government, it was seen at best as expensive and inefficient, and at worst a spectacular disaster. Yet it was assumed that it could be efficient, even profitable, if run by profit-making companies or independent agencies such as housing associations. As it was an electoral base for its local authority landlords – particularly the 'new urban left' metropolitan councils that were now openly defying central government on various issues within their control – amending (or ending) it presented the opportunity to drive a wedge between them and their electorates. An even more direct approach was to abolish the troublesome metropolitan tier of government, beginning with the GLC in 1986, whose enormous stocks of housing were distributed amongst the London boroughs.

In its 18 years of power, the New Right successfully established a new social – virtually a new moral – order in place of the discredited Welfare State. Its New Labour successor did not repudiate, but rather built on, this edifice. It defined poverty or 'social exclusion' as lack of freedom to engage in the market – so in effect making it into an individual rather than a social or class condition, and consequently one to be addressed by individual effort rather than combined action. The partnership approach with its dependence on a third or 'community' partner was retained. Policy moved forward, therefore, with an odd tension between increasing individuation on one side, and on the other reliance on a collective 'community'. This then was added to the range of existing policies for an 'urban' problem (in reality a complex of social and economic problems) that was still apparently growing, in spite of 30 years of definition, research and remedial action. It was as if 'community' was invoked when all else had failed, and the poor were – as the phrase went – required to manage their own poverty when everyone else failed to do so.

But it seems there was something more than crude 'last resort' remedies at work. The ferment of the 1960s and 1970s with their plethora of experiments in co-operatives, squatting, self-building, community arts, landscaping, and community protest in general, had produced a whole generation of seasoned activists and professionals, resulting amongst other things in the foundation of pressure groups, some of which, like Shelter and Child Poverty Action Group, became political forces in their own right. Another outcome was the growth of new opportunities for professional practice, either independently or in central and local government. New ideas, priorities and principles like minority rights and equal opportunities were passed into general currency. Among them was the idea that local people should be consulted about policies impacting on them, if only for the reason that such policies would otherwise be undermined. Even an extreme right government was influenced by this, and a stated commitment to 'community' consultation and partnership became a condition of all central funding, not excluding the distribution of lottery funds. The principle was crucial to the latest phase in the history of council housing, for it meant that a body of people, the tenants, throughout their entire history cast in a passive role, were suddenly expected to respond actively to the many opportunities to join in 'partnerships'.

Council Housing and Urban Regeneration

It was not for some 20 years from the end of the Second World War that urban regeneration rose to prominence on the policy agenda, and still longer before it became specifically attached to council estates. In 1945, the planning lobby could still hope that social and economic reconstruction would be achieved through town and country planning, if only this were applied strenuously enough. In the event it proved quite inadequate for the task, for a string of new towns and such decentralization of industry as was obtained could not have obviated industrial and urban decline or removed poverty – indeed, the way planning operated seemed often to exacerbate them. So little was the public now concerned with utopian prescriptions, however, that planning's failure to live up to expectations went largely unheeded. The crying need for people, and consequently for politicians, was enough decent housing; and for the time being it seemed that slum clearance coupled to council building programmes would deliver this. The first major re-direction of policy was the introduction of the General Improvement Area or GIA in 1969, which grant-aided the repair and modernization of houses provided their owners paid a specified proportion of the costs. In effect an early form of urban renewal for pre-1914 neighbourhoods, the GIA was also widely used by local authorities to renovate some of their own older estates.

The shaping of urban policy was strongly influenced by the example of the United States, where inner areas of northern cities flooded by southern black migrants were subject to race riots, mass property abandonments, arson and other ills. Britain's major industrial cities also had immigrant reception areas that were eventually dominated by ethnic minorities as their indigenous populations aged or moved away. Nationwide, the British black population reached no more than 6 per cent, but it was unevenly distributed, with heavy concentrations in inner London boroughs and major conurbations. Early urban regeneration measures, therefore, were in the hands of the Home Office, who chose to see the problems as transitory. There was what seems, in retrospect, an astonishing confidence in the power of research to define both problems and solutions. The Community Development Projects (CDPs) were set up in 1974 in chosen deprived areas throughout the country, for 5-year 'action research' programmes by multi-disciplinary teams that included a wide range of professionals from community artists to social scientists. Council estates sometimes fell within their boundaries, in which case issues like rents and repairs would be addressed.

Not surprisingly, the CDPs proved an embarrassment to the Home Office when, seeking the structural reasons for economic and social decline, they armed local people with information and drew them into direct confrontations with the *status quo*. Two of the projects and a central co-ordinating and advisory unit were closed down prematurely, but the CDP research reports continued to be issued for several years, their findings in many ways anticipating those of later council estate studies, and especially the Priority Estates Project of the 1980s. By this later date, however, increased recognition of the seriousness of the situation, with 10 or more years of agitation between, made tenant grievances more credible, and there was more willingness to discuss any possible solutions than had been the case with the CDPs.

Legislation following the more professional and less inflammatory Inner Areas Studies set up in 1973 was directed to bringing industry and employment back to the inner city – thus marking a reversal of historic planning principles derived from the Garden City – and high priority was now given to voluntary and 'community' schemes that would help improve local conditions and make neighbourhoods more self-reliant.   The Urban Programme, with greatly increased funding, was moved from the Home Office to Environment (DoE), and a number of towns and cities were selected for 'Partnership' or 'Programme' status: an apparatus still in force when Margaret Thatcher's government came to power in 1979.   The course of policy for urban renewal after 1945, therefore, was from the largely inoperative utopian blueprint inherited from the Garden City, through successive and often abortive attempts to apply multi-disciplinary approaches to urban problems, to the 'partnerships' that increased in scope towards the end of the century. While the policy perspective had broadened, its location within the DoE helped to ensure that strategies for regeneration were framed in a spatial perspective, although the problems to be dealt with were 'primarily not spatial in character.'[5]   It is also worth noting that they were strongly urban, even metropolitan, in their orientation, reflecting the bias of their authors at a time when the economic and social problems of rural areas did not loom large in public perception.   It fell to the Thatcher government to act on a long-standing suggestion that the energy and resources channelled into new towns should be diverted to the more deserving inner cities.   The first of ten Urban Development Corporations was set up in 1981 on Merseyside in the wake of the Toxteth riots.   For limited periods these bodies took planning control out of the hands of their local authorities and vested it in boards of government appointees, including prominent business leaders, as well as local councillors.

The strategy of making areas of greatest need 'bid' against each other, first used in council housing in the Estate Action initiative described below, was extended in the 1990s to City Challenge and the Single Regeneration Budget. After 1997, New Labour continued the strategy, and in 1998 its Social Exclusion Unit announced the 'New Deal for Communities', to 'turn round' selected neighbourhoods with 'severe joined-up problems'.   They were to consist of around 3000 dwellings, not only on council estates but in any locations and not excluding owner occupied districts, and their programmes included not only housing but all dimensions of regeneration.   Seventeen 'pathfinder' areas were announced, with further batches to follow.   In announcing them, the Unit paid tribute to the earlier efforts of the Urban Programme, Urban Development Corporations and Task Forces, all of which had had 'some successes', although none had succeeded in setting in motion a 'virtuous circle' of regeneration, with improvements in jobs, crime, education, health and housing all reinforcing one another.[6]   Interestingly, the new policy with its insistence that pathfinder projects should be led by residents rather than by officers or appointed bodies, again owed much to housing initiatives such as the Priority Estates Project described below.   Council estates were bracketed with other areas of deprivation for purposes of the policy, and peripheral estates were also included although they were not in targeted inner-city areas.

How successful the 'New Deal' would be was still unclear at the start of the new century. Its stated aims raised many questions. What was meant by a 'sustainable community' and did, or could, such a thing exist? Could the considerable demands the policy would make on community partners be met, when by definition they were likely to be drawn from the 'socially excluded'? And would the unpaid community leaders vital for success emerge in sufficient numbers, and be equal to the tasks laid on them? The questions were still being framed, but not answered, at the time of writing.

The End of Council Housing:
Privatizations and Liquidations

The operation of council housing had been changed for good by the passing of the Housing (Homeless Persons) Act in 1977, the culmination of many years of agitation for the homeless, whose right to permanent homes of their own was only slowly conceded by the rest of society. In the early postwar years families not qualifying for a place in the expanding council sector came under the jurisdiction of social services, who had emergency accommodation in the form of the infamous 'Part III' hostels that were, in many cases, revamped workhouse wards. The help given was a latter-day version of 'indoor' poor relief, where mothers and children were placed in overcrowded and even insanitary conditions, while husbands were often left to fend for themselves. After a stay of months or sometimes years, they could, on satisfactory reports from their social workers, be promoted to 'halfway' accommodation, and thence to a council tenancy.

The increasing notoriety of the Part III hostels, with the realization that homelessness was growing rather than the reverse, led to mounting agitation from the late 1960s onwards. The significance of the 1977 Act was that for the first time it made councils responsible for housing those of the homeless who fell into priority groups, provided they had not made themselves homeless 'intentionally'. The groups included families with or expecting children, and any who were vulnerable for age or other reasons. The Act did not, of course, increase the supply of housing, and authorities applied it with differing degrees of enthusiasm. Its great weakness was the vagueness of the concept of 'intentional homelessness', which was subject to widely different interpretations and abuses. In areas of housing stress like London, in order to meet their statutory obligations, councils made use of the notorious bed and breakfast 'hotels' that were in effect modern versions of the Victorian 'common lodging house', and sometimes in desperation they 'exported' their homeless to vacant tourist accommodation in out-of-season resorts.

None of this would necessarily have disturbed the tenor of council housing had it gone on expanding as before, for the placing of homeless priority cases would have been neither more nor less destabilizing than the batches of slum clearance people planted on estates in earlier years. But as new building starts fell dramatically after 1979 and the take-up of right to buy began to decimate councils' portfolios, the priority homeless came to usurp ordinary waiting list applicants, who could only qualify for housing by becoming homeless themselves. Together, the two measures accelerated the 'residualization' of council housing, where a less desirable stock housed the least desired tenants. As well as poorer, tenant populations were becoming progressively younger, so that by 1997 well over two-thirds of new tenants were in the 16–29 age group.[7]

To the extreme right Conservative government of the 1980s, council housing represented all that was profligate in public spending, an egregious intervention in the market, and a featherbedding of the undeserving. A new criticism was that it contributed to unemployment by preventing tenants from moving in search of work: an interesting reversal of the old belief that estate populations should be as static as possible. To this government, it was axiomatic that the status of council tenant was a sort of serfdom, and its aim was to end council housing as soon as possible, by stopping any further expansion and transferring existing stock to other owners and tenures. This created a strange overlap between the rightwing approach and the radicals, who had for years campaigned for tenants' liberation from their bureaucratic and overbearing landlords. Crucially, council housing lacked the protection of that broad band of middle classes who effectively championed the health service and state education, services that they used themselves.[8]

This was the point at which council housing was superseded by 'social housing', previously known as the 'voluntary housing' run by non-profit housing associations. Regulated by the Housing Corporation (a 'quango' founded in 1964 and reorganized in 1974), registered associations received grants for accommodating those not normally housed by councils, or for whom councils had little property, such as the elderly, single working people, and people with special needs. Most of the old philanthropic housing trusts chose to register with the Housing Corporation in order to qualify for grants. Altogether, 'voluntary' sector holdings at this time were around a tenth of the local authorities' stock, and no more than 2 or 3 per cent of the total national stock of dwellings. A small minority of housing associations were large bodies operating nationwide; but the majority were local and small-scale, typically working in close relationship with their councils who provided them with development sites and lists of nominees or approved applicants. From 1974 their housing association grant, or 'HAG', was generous enough to build, to Parker Morris standards, well designed and typically small-scale estates and to charge 'fair rents' that, though considerably higher than council rents, were far below what would have been charged for comparable property on the private market. In any case the rent was normally covered in full by housing benefit, so that for a period housing association tenants enjoyed superior accommodation at moderate or even nil cost to themselves.

Once they were converted into 'social landlords', however, this favourable treatment of associations changed. In 1988, HAG covering the full costs of building was ended, and rapidly expanding development programmes had to be financed by borrowing specified proportions of costs from lending institutions. Parker Morris standards were by now abolished and, like councils, associations were expected to 'build down' to the standards of private developers. Another consequence of the new financial regime was that, like private landlords, they now gave 'assured' rather than 'secure' tenancies, entailing higher rents and a reduction of tenant rights. None of this was lost on council tenants, whose many stands against being transferred to housing associations seem to have taken the makers of central policy by surprise.

An essential part of the new framework was housing benefit, introduced in 1982, which finally achieved what the Housing Finance Act of 1972 had failed to do and transferred housing subsidy from property to the neediest tenants. The benefit – in effect a subsidy to landlords – was a whole or partial contribution towards the rent charged, dependent on an assessment of a tenant's income. Although it came from the social security and not the housing budget, it was administered by local housing departments – a move that deflected blame for cuts and maladministration, as well as the inevitable means testing formula, onto local rather than central government. By merely shifting rather than cutting the overall level of housing subsidy, the new arrangement was shown to be 'a major failure in public expenditure policy.'[9] It was always, of course, dwarfed by the hidden but rising subsidy to home owners, through various tax reliefs; but the growing numbers of unemployed and low paid who were entitled to the benefit made it increasingly costly to government, who introduced progressive exclusions. In its first 4 years, the rules for eligibility were changed seven times, removing a million people from benefit, and the benefit itself was reduced in an Act of 1986.[10] Further savings were made by other cuts, including abolition of grants for 'urgent needs' (such as purchase of essential furnishings) and their conversion into loans to be repaid out of even the tiniest incomes – something that impacted badly on first-time tenants, particularly those who had previously been homeless.

Another part of the Conservative housing finance reform was to drive up council rents, kept low for so long as we have seen. The device used was to lower central government support to local authorities in proportion to expected rent rises, which in fact were so steep in the early 1980s that they took some three-quarters of English and Welsh authorities out of housing subsidy altogether. The formula was then recast to make rents rise sharply once more. At the same time, in 1989, councils' housing revenue accounts were 'ringfenced' to disallow any transfers of either surpluses or deficits between their housing and general accounts – a measure particularly aimed at London's Labour borough councils, which had habitually subsidised their rents from general funds. By a complicated logic, the new financial regime calculated the housing benefit paid to council tenants in such a way that it could be claimed that, collectively, it was borne by those still paying full rents – an imposition that happened in no other housing tenure.

The administration of housing benefit proved complex, costly, and open to levels of fraud that could not apparently be brought under control. It was criticized for creating divisions between those who did and did not receive it; but possibly its greatest defect was that it acted as a disincentive to the unemployed to seek jobs, because of the 'poverty trap' or sharp taper by which the benefit (along with many other welfare supports) was withdrawn in respect of earnings. This applied even to short, temporary periods of employment, when the difficulty of getting withdrawn benefit reinstated could cause havoc in personal and domestic lives.

The new financial regime of housing was irrational in so many ways that it is best explained as an assault on local government autonomy for ideological, as much as financial, reasons.[11] Because of a general taboo on public spending, councils were allowed to spend only a fraction of their fast mounting receipts from the right to buy and other disposals. By 1985 this was lowered to a fifth, most of which had to go towards debt redemption, while none could be used to limit rent increases. Authorities were not therefore able to use their enormous reserves of housing capital to repair deteriorating stock; yet, while not in full control of their property portfolios like other landlords, they were blamed for not being good ones. Accused of inefficiency, they were denied the autonomy necessary to operate efficiently.

Housing associations were now being actively encouraged, and funded, to take over the role of local authority landlords. This forced them into a much larger scale operation than ever before, yet there were still huge stocks of council-owned housing whose only salvation was seen by the government to lie in diversification of tenure. In practice this meant transfer to other ownership, or the introduction of new tenures to estates, as through 'shared ownership' or part purchase-part rental of dwellings. By far the largest and most significant change of tenure was brought through the 'right to buy' instituted in 1980, which was binding on all councils and applied to all who had been tenants in the public sector (which included new towns and Ministry of Defence Property) for at least 3, and later 2, years. Properties were valued and sold at a starting discount of 32 per cent, which was increased with every further year of tenancy, until the ceiling of 60 per cent for houses and 70 per cent for flats was reached. Some authorities were slow to apply the measure, and there were even some who tried, unsuccessfully, to resist it altogether.[12] But the government was evidently right to assume a pent-up demand for home ownership amongst council tenants, and the policy was an instant success, so persuading the Labour Party to incorporate it into their own housing policy in 1985. The peak year for sales was 1982, with a total of over 215,000, or roughly the same as the amount built in the expansionist years of council housing. Even then, central government tried further to stimulate sales by various means, including the progressive raising of discount ceilings and an experimental 'rent to mortgage scheme' of 1989 to tempt poorer tenants into home ownership.

By 1996, the right to buy had removed over two million dwellings from a stock that at its height had contained some six millions, and it could claim to be the most successful of all the New Right's many privatizations of public assets. Whereas the earlier sales of homes to sitting tenants did not promise any fast social change on estates, a somewhat different picture was now emerging. There were marked regional variations in the take-up of right to buy and it was conspicuously slow in cities like Sheffield, and in Scotland, where council housing had always had wide support. There were also strong local differences within districts, where sales were higher in houses than flats, and on suburban rather than inner estates. Those purchasing their homes combined the 'ability to pay with occupancy of an attractive property.'[13] In the main, therefore, they were of middle age, in skilled or white collar occupations, and often in households with more than one earner. When they eventually sold their homes, it was likely to be to first-time buyers who were younger and at an earlier stage of their family and housing cycles. While in many ways resembling the carefully selected tenants of the earliest council estates, such people tended to treat this purchase as merely a stage in their housing careers, meaning to move on before long. The overall effect of the right to buy was not simply to reduce the size of the council sector but to convert it into one 'with a different stock than in the past.'[14] In effect it removed the mechanism by which, however controversially, managers had accommodated a fairly broad social cross-section, leaving it with a 'residualized' stock and populations analogous to the poorest and most immobile slum clearance tenants of former years. At certain places and times, less fortunate right-to-buyers found themselves unable to re-sell their houses at any price and sometimes, having been tempted into home ownership beyond their means, they were repossessed and made homeless – at which point it was debateable whether they were 'intentionally' or unintentionally so.

Although the same Act that gave the right to buy in 1980 had measures for disposing of council housing *en bloc*, it was not for some years that this was actively pursued. In 1986 councils were empowered to empty estates for disposal to firms for refurbishing or rebuilding, either for existing tenants or for the open market. Certain of the major housing developers were interested in entering what looked like a profitable opening, sometimes buying estates that they had themselves constructed for local authorities a generation before. Barratt, Regalian and other leading housebuilders set up 'urban regeneration' subsidiaries and their particular interest was in centrally located, interwar flats which could be made to appeal to young, childless professionals, or 'yuppies'. It was usual for developers to spend more than the purchase price over again on refurbishment, and their improvements showed what was required to make them into desirable dwellings: lifts, central heating, full security systems, warm and inviting entrance foyers, perhaps a porter's lodge, efficient caretaking, landscaping, perhaps a pool or fitness centre – above all, a name change to give a new identity. So St John's Estate became Battersea Village; Liverpool's Minster Court was transmogrified into Myrtle Gardens; and the Wirral's Woodchurch or 'smack city' transformed into Arrowebrook Park, a 'triumph of government privatisation policies.'[15]

The councils most eager to dispose of their stock to private developers were the smaller, Conservative and often rural ones whose high quality housing fetched a good price. The big urban authorities were unwilling as yet to relinquish their holdings – other considerations apart, they did not wish to alienate their electorates. It seemed that the government had overestimated developer interest, and though eventually some hundreds of schemes were involved, this had little impact on council housing overall. In many cases, estates were so run-down that they had only a negative value, and far from yielding money to repair and improve other stock, special dowries had to be given to those taking them on. The only entitlement of dispossessed tenants was another tenancy elsewhere, with a 'home loss payment' towards removal costs. This aroused considerable tenant protest – apart from anything else it abrogated their recently given right to security of tenure – and two Teesside tenants who successfully challenged their evictions were allowed to stay in their homes, though surrounded by home owners on what was now a Barrett estate.

This lack of success doubtless influenced the next measures for block disposals under the 1988 Housing Act: 'Tenants' Choice', popularly known as 'Pick a Landlord', and the Housing Action Trust or HAT. So far as they were used at all, both were subverted by tenants for their own ends. As conceived, Tenants' Choice was a way for private landlords to take over estates, in whole or in part, with tenants having only the power of veto – a device that resulted in an extraordinary balloting system where abstentions counted as votes in favour of transfer. It was vehemently opposed by tenants nationwide, and in the event the Housing Corporation was given the role of scrutineer of would-be landlords and adviser to tenant groups who thought of choosing a new landlord or even becoming their own landlord. Most tenant interest was in London, on estates formerly belonging to the GLC, where there was a lot of dissatisfaction with their new borough landlords; but the failure rate of initial proposals was high. The first and also the most outstanding example of Tenants' Choice was Walterton and Elgin Community Homes, the creation of a tenant action group that had already spent some years fighting the disposal, at bargain prices, of borough assets by an extremely rightwing Westminster Council. The council was now starting to operate a policy of sealing up homes as they became vacant (despite hundreds of homeless and waiting list applicants) and charging the cost of this and a new home sales centre to tenants' rents. These and other dubious practices eventually brought to court the council leader, Dame Shirley Porter, on charges of gerrymandering. Meanwhile the tenants of Walterton and Elgin, a mixture of tower blocks and pre-1914 houses, asked the borough for a 'dowry' of at least £30 millions to help redeem years of neglect.

The companion measure, the HAT, was devised for those estates deemed too bad to attract any private landlord. Offering injections of public money averaging £5000 per property over 3 years, it took its cue from the short-term programmes and summary powers of the Urban Development Corporations. On completion of its work, the HAT tenants were to have a choice of landlord, including a return to their own councils. Prospective HATs were announced without any prior tenant consultation – presumably in the belief that the estates in question were so bad that their residents would welcome the money about to rain down on them. The first HATs proposed, however, were all outvoted by tenants (who owed their right to ballot to a belated House of

Lords amendment), or they were quietly dropped because of tenant opposition. This could be very strong: on a Sunderland estate, 77 per cent of tenants turned out to vote, and of these 80 per cent opposed the HAT proposal. In Manchester's Hulme, already sensitized by several generations of development and redevelopment (as will appear below), the mere possibility of being given HAT status was pre-empted by tenants, so setting in train its eventual regeneration under a different mechanism. What the government of the day had not reckoned with was the extent to which tenants were suspicious of its motives and tenacious of their existing homes and landlords. They feared losing their rights, including the right to buy, and stuck to their belief that a council was more accountable than any other landlord, even a housing association, could ever be.

The eventual total of HATs was only six, including a tenant-run one at Waltham Forest consisting of four estates already subjected to a 'community architecture' exercise, and gaining from governmental desperation to get at least one scheme launched. None of the actual HATs fitted original expectations. Hull North had the strong support of its council, who used it to bargain for concessions benefiting the rest of their stock; and in contradiction of the original guidelines, the Liverpool HAT comprised 35 clusters of a total of 67 tower blocks, a score of which were due for demolition. Other HAT estates were far from being the worst of their kind, and the programme as a whole scarcely confirmed that tenants longed to be liberated from their council landlords.

It was the intention of the Conservatives, had they stayed in power, to enforce the 'voluntary transfer' of the remaining council stock to housing associations or other registered social landlords, and associations had in fact taken over more than a quarter of a million dwellings by 1998. Yet another initiative, the Estate Renewal Challenge Fund begun in 1996–97, targeted on the very worst estates, made possible the development of 'local housing companies' to be voted for by tenants and given dowries to cover costs of repairs and improvements when private loans were not forthcoming. Even now, after shedding a third of its stock through various privatizations, Britain still had the largest public housing sector in the capitalist world outside Eastern Europe. Its condition was not promising: in many areas there was falling demand, and over 80,000 units were empty, while the cost of essential repairs and renovation had for many years been estimated as between £18 and £20 billions. There was a brief, illusory flash of utopianism in 1997, as a new Deputy Prime Minister mused publicly on a solar-heated 'council house of the future' and estates designed for public transport and energy efficiency;[16] but those who had anticipated an instant release of money from the huge banked receipts from right-to-buy sales were disappointed. Anxious to demonstrate their prudence in government, New Labour maintained the same taboo on public spending as their predecessors, continuing to preserve the convention by which local authority spending on housing was counted as public expenditure, while private money put into housing, including borrowing by housing associations, was not embargoed in this way. The way forward, then, was to be the wholesale transfer of stock to social landlords, either newly formed or old housing associations. The transfer of 200,000 units a year, it was suggested, would fund a 10-year programme of the necessary 'repairs revolution' for the stock remaining in councils' ownership.[17]

At this point the idea of 'market lettings' was being mooted in various quarters, to replace the old allocation systems based on comparative degrees of housing need. Vacancies would be advertised as in the private market, and selection of tenants would be made with the needs of estates as much in mind as the needs of applicants. Rents were no longer to be held to artificial levels but set with a 'logic in the price paid',[18] to reflect the size, quality and location of a property, as in the private market. As for the neediest, 'We do not believe that social housing should only be allocated to the poorest and most vulnerable.'[19] In the last months of the Conservative government, changes had been made to the treatment of the homeless: the priority criteria remained, but under the 1996 Housing Act councils no longer had a duty to provide them with homes for more than a 2-year period.[20] From its original ideal of permanent communities, council housing had declined to a temporary resort of the homeless. 'Residualized' both physically and socially, its future was doubtful, and prospective tenants were warned, 'The days of council homes for life are over'[21] – a revolution indeed.

Despairing at last of ever having the funds to rescue their declining estates, even the larger urban authorities were now prepared to discard what could only ever be an unending liability. The future lay in the operation of the former public housing sector as a 'quasi market',[22] where their best chance of keeping any role in housing was by influencing the other social landlords. By the end of 1996, one Scottish and 49 English housing authorities had transferred their entire stock, in all but one case to housing associations created for the purpose. Up to now, the 'large scale voluntary transfer' or LSVT was permitted only where the value of the stock transferred exceeded any outstanding debt; but later this promised to change, with an additional subsidy to cover the debt. For a transfer to take place a ballot of tenants was required, and the majority voted in favour, even though this entailed losing the right to buy and 'secure' tenancy status. Instead there were rent guarantees, but only for limited periods. By 2000, the largest ever number of estate transfers was in hand, amounting to roughly a tenth of the stock still owned by councils, and there were predictions that they would become compulsory under any future government. The housing Green Paper of that year added another option, the Arms Length Company which would manage housing still owned by councils, or both manage and own, with councillors, tenants and other 'partners' equally represented. The Green Paper, which proposed to harmonize rents and tenancy conditions in all social housing, made it clear that rents would rise, whichever option was chosen. Although there remained the possibility of a much reduced but improved stock still in council ownership, it was forecast that council housing would in effect disappear within 10 years – possibly first in what had always been its greatest stronghold, Scotland.[23]

The Changing Culture of Council Housing

With all these many attempts at disposals to other owners, there were changes in the aims and style of management, the main thrust of which was to encourage tenant autonomy. Central government, as we have seen, had always taken an interest in how councils managed their tenants, partly because it could afford to take a more detached and liberal stand than local bodies closely scrutinized by their electors; but the extent to which the New Right of the 1980s-90s devolved power to tenants, collectively, does seem to call for special explanation. Much of the motivation, doubtless, was to reduce the power of local authorities and it is suggested that tenant management was promoted 'in an almost casual fashion, as a by-product of registering a wider – but little fulfilled – ambition to diversify ownership away from councils.'[24] In a deeper sense it suited a political philosophy that claimed to value 'freedom, choice, self actualisation and achievement',[25] and though slow to start, participation in housing soon went 'further than in any other area of local government.'[26]

The tenants' charter of 1980 had obvious appeal for a Conservative government committed to liberating tenants, although it was not in fact their own creation. Calls for such a charter had been made throughout the 1970s by tenant organizations and others. The National Consumer Council and Association of London Housing Estates each drafted charters, the latter, in 1977, arguing that an organized and articulate tenant movement had for years made a positive contribution to the housing debate, so making management less inefficient than it would otherwise have been. A charter conferring security of tenure, access to allocation schemes, with some influence in selecting tenants and the ending of petty restrictions, was advanced in a Labour Green Paper of 1977, while some local authorities produced their own charters or tenant agreements in these years.

Up to this point, council tenants had no enforceable rights and legally speaking were less protected than tenants of private landlords. Managers were not accountable to them in any way, and while their regime, as we have seen, was mainly benign, tenancy regulations were often arbitrary and served the interests of managers rather than residents. The Charter of 1980, though less radical than the Labour Bill preceding it, codified a number of 'rights' hitherto conferred, if at all, by custom and favour. They included security of tenure, the right to be given information and be consulted, rights to exchange tenancies, take lodgers, sublet, pass on tenancies to close relatives or household members, and to carry out improvements. It was argued, however, that the charter made little practical difference since, among other things, it omitted rents and repairs, so 'has not fundamentally altered the position of the council tenant and remedied problems of "serfdom" associated with the tenure.'[27] The rights given were on an individual rather than collective basis and, in a sense, they were all eclipsed by the additional right to buy, which was in effect 'the right to cease to be a tenant.'[28]

It was the firm conviction of the New Right that housing associations, the new 'social landlords', were vastly better ones than councils, if only because they operated outside party politics. The reality was, of course, that associations were neither elected by nor accountable to their tenants, nor indeed to anyone other than the Housing Corporation which agreed their grant money.[29] The assumption that local authorities were inherently less efficient landlords was put in question by a 1989 report to the DoE, which found high levels of satisfaction on both sides, so suggesting 'something less than a crisis in social housing management.'[30] In general, associations spent nearly half as much again as councils on management and, for money spent, best value was given by councils, whose failing was not so much inefficiency as underspending on management. Around the same time the Audit Commission, though curious to know why some housing departments were far less cost effective than others, affirmed that management alone was not able to salvage the worst estates – by implication, therefore, it was not only management that caused their problems.[31]

These points were reinforced when associations began to take over large estates with the typical range of difficulties. They had always taken some, sometimes all, of their tenants from council nominee lists, but they did not commonly provide family accommodation, and this, with their usual small scale of operation, meant they had avoided some of the trickiest management problems. Once responsible for former council estates on a large scale, they began to meet with challenges unknown to them before. By 1996-97, four-fifths of their tenant households had young children or lacked any working adult, and one in seven were in rent arrears. On a third of estates examined new housing association properties were proving difficult to let, and the pressure to keep rents low was causing financial problems.[32] A new initiative, 'Housing Plus', piloted in five London associations in 1995, was to involve associations in general neighbourhood regeneration; but as it received no special funding it could be disparaged as a 'usefully nebulous' concept.[33]

After 1985, with policies to boost private rented housing (and the suggestion of a 'right to rent'), the government took steps to increase tenants' collective rights – as if in tacit recognition of the large amounts of housing still in council control. Acts of the later 1980s obliged councils to consult their tenants about variations in their security of tenure, and to provide them with annual reports. The device of compulsory competitive tendering (CCT) for council services was already affecting housing operations through direct labour and service organizations, which had to tender against private contractors for maintenance and repairs. From 1988, CCT was extended to other estate services such as grounds maintenance, and from 1996 it was gradually applied to housing management itself. Vast amounts of officer time and resources were put into preparing tenders – in some areas to no practical purpose, as no private bids were received. Though in many respects wasteful, the exercise did oblige authorities to consult their tenants, and in doing so they were forced to scrutinize themselves.[34] CCT for management never became fully operative, as the succeeding government replaced it by 'Best Value' in 2000. This carried with it a Tenant Participation Compact, which extended   tenants'   involvement   beyond   the   immediate   estate   to neighbourhoods and 'local problems or issues affecting the quality of life.'[35]

A further extension of its commitment to liberate tenants was the Conservative government's promise to give them rights to run their own estates by tenant management co-operatives, to ask other bodies to manage their estates or, individually, to transfer their homes to any social landlord. The 'Right to Manage', embodied in an Act of 1993,[36] was eventually lost from sight amidst the hard practicalities of estate regeneration; but the tenant management co-op or TMC was already in existence, having been promoted by a Labour government in the radical 1970s, when local housing departments were given discretion to devolve management to such bodies without loss of subsidy. The first TMCs were pioneered by Shelter and other agencies in London and Liverpool, and by 1981 the Borough of Islington had established thirteen, with one in seven tenants serving on their management committees. They covered around 2000 households on old and new council estates, as well as municipalized pre-1914 stock. The borough established a Cooperative Development Section and extended an invitation to all tenant associations to form TMCs; but eventually concluding that these were 'slow, labour-intensive, unpredictable and extremely local and small-scale',[37] it took the route of decentralization instead. Outside London and the Home Counties, the biggest concentration of TMCs was in Glasgow, which by the late 1980s had some 6000 units under their management.

With all-party support and further encouragement in the 1986 Housing and Planning Act, it looked as though the TMC was about to undergo a big expansion.[38] But it made particularly heavy demands on its members, and the joint tenant-council estate management board or EMB was regarded as a more realistic option, lying as it did part way between full tenant responsibility and full local authority control. Although preceding it, the EMB was put into general circulation by the Priority Estates Project (PEP), begun by the DoE on a handful of estates with severe problems in 1979, 'an era of turmoil and anxiety.'[39] From 1984, the PEP was extended, in partnership with local authorities, to the whole of England and Wales and later became an independent limited company. The essence of its approach was locally based and small-scale projects (between 500 and 1500 units), with full-time estate-based management controlling an estate budget. The co-operation of both councils and residents was required, and the preferred management instrument, the EMB with a tenant majority, increased tenfold in the next few years.[40]

EMBs as well as TMCs multiplied further under Estate Action, which began as the Urban Housing Renewal Unit in 1985, originally with the object of expediting the emptying of estates for sale to developers. At first operating only in relatively small areas in England, the programme was considerably enlarged and local authorities were invited to put in 'bids' with the usual criteria of 'partnerships', tenant participation and devolvement of management. Though at first antagonistic, local authorities made extensive use of it to upgrade their estates, although there was an argument that it was used to fund schemes already decided, and brought no more tenant

Regeneration through Estate Action, Gipton estate, Leeds. Revamped houses and provision for parking, with just a hint in the closed-up house that physical improvement alone does not guarantee the social regeneration of an estate.

involvement than would have happened in any case.[41] By 1992 the DoE was able to identify 117 tenant management organizations plus 54 local authorities that had taken steps towards setting them up.[42] To many, a more acceptable route was the Estate Agreement pioneered by the London Borough of Camden in 1990, when it recognized that 'the majority of tenants did not wish to manage their own estate.'[43] The agreement was a negotiated document setting out management's commitments and subject to periodic reviews.

Perhaps in response to the complexity of the problems found on estates, the scope of Estate Action was broadened to include all dimensions of regeneration: physical, social and economic, so going beyond a simple 'market' approach. Together with PEP and the various, sometimes conflicting, tenant 'rights', the initiative had that strange conjunction of libertarianism and market principles, idealism and opportunism, that so confusingly characterized housing policy in the last 20 years of the century. Perhaps after all it was the outmoded polarities such as Left/Right, libertarian/authoritarian, that did not do justice to a dynamic and developing situation.

Changing Local Authority Practices

As so many of the changes were instituted by central government, it is difficult to know how far local authorities would have changed their style of management had they been left to their own devices. One view is that they only made common cause with tenants to score against central government, or when they had difficult-to-let stock, rather than out of genuine commitment to tenant empowerment. It appears, however, that their antagonism towards central interference (as in the CDPs), and towards participation in general, started to change in the mid-1970s. In 1977 it was reported that 'the idea of tenant participation in council housing has come a long way in a short time

. . . today it is accepted as established professional practice in many local authorities.'[44] Labour councils in particular 'began to overcome their traditional distrust of autonomous tenants' organisations'[45] and helped them by providing liaison officers, information services, news sheets and incomes derived from small levies on rents. Some authorities allowed tenant control over area budgets. Between 1977 and 1987 there were significant increases in occasional or regular meetings with tenants, joint advisory committees and tenant representation on housing committees or subcommittees.[46] At the later date four-fifths of councils had some sort of formal scheme for participation, although there were large variations in what it comprised.[47]

It seems that even before the emergence of central programmes some local authorities used their own resources to support community development, job creation and training on estates. Their physical improvements included selective demolition, lopping and converting maisonette blocks to houses, and the conversion of high blocks to uses such as sheltered housing schemes. There were countless unrecorded conversions of store rooms and other unused spaces to utility or recreation rooms for tenants' use. On occasion councils allowed tenants to re-design demolished estates and houses, for themselves or future occupants. Such tenant design projects in London included estates of walk-up flats in Hackney, one of them an inspired 'community architecture' revamp of Lea View House, built in the 1930s,[48] and there were several Southwark schemes, including Cherry Gardens by the Thames, the old stamping ground of Dr Alfred Salter, whose extant garden-city type houses influenced the design of the new scheme. Examples from other parts of the country included the previously mentioned Thornton estate in Hull and parts of Sheffield's Wincobank and Manor estates. A group of Blackbird Leys tenants in Oxford were invited to design an estate extension. The highly innovative scheme of Lewisham self-build, mentioned below, was initiated by the borough architect. What tenants themselves invariably chose to replace flats, deck access blocks or flat-roofed, prefabricated houses were conventional brick houses typically set in 'mews' or culs-de-sac, with securely fenced front and back gardens.

Sometimes authorities combined social and physical renewal, using whatever policies were to hand. A surprising early example was the once notorious 'Tenement Town', where a GIA was used to carry out selective demolition and 'lavish' provision of lifts and internal improvements costing £14,000 per dwelling. The GLC decided to 'flood the area with resources', including an advice and information centre that gave rise to youth and pensioner clubs, discussion, chess and local history groups, the latter producing a history of the estate. In spite of unintended effects that divided the estate into three camps, it was reported that 'gradually tenants . . . are beginning to control and organize their own activities', although staff were still needed to fill the 'cultural gap' that arose from the absence of neighbours and close family.[49]

It seems, therefore, that a good many local authorities were spontaneously changing their practices and management styles, although examples were disparate and did not cohere into a national policy.[50] Central measures were inevitably more co-ordinated and systematic, and so able to achieve more. One local innovation in management, which to some heralded a new and accountable form of socialism,[51] was decentralization. The earliest and most celebrated example was the Labour-held council of Walsall, which in 1981 replaced its central housing department with 31 neighbourhood offices where housing was integrated with social work, with other services to follow. The costs of the reorganization (which provoked a strike at head office) were decribed as astronomical, and the experiment was never completed. Islington and a small number of other authorities also implemented decentralization, but as this, typically, was 'hatched by a coterie of senior officers and members and then "delivered" to other staff and tenants,'[52] it could not claim to increase tenant involvement in management. The more general trend was towards localization rather than decentralization, and by the later 1980s about a third of authorities had area offices and 12 per cent had neighbourhood offices below area level,[53] while all PEP estates were of course implementing estate-based management.

In the nature of things, local authorities could not be expected to innovate in housing tenure, although some did make a contribution through homesteading, practised in inner London and other areas of housing stress like Glasgow, where derelict or unwanted properties were sold to home buyers at knock-down prices, with loans for their renovation within a given time-scale. Another innovation was the Segal self-building scheme adopted (by a narrow margin) by Lewisham Borough Council in 1976, where tenants and waiting list applicants were invited to build a small cluster of prefabricated houses and bungalows that were converted into shared ownership on completion. Another possible opening, though one not normally supported by councils, was the common ownership or 'par-value' housing co-operative whose members collectively owned, and sometimes designed and developed, their own estates. There were some isolated cases, including Sheffield and Middlesbrough, where councils promoted such co-ops, but Glasgow's hoped-for 'community ownership co-ops', a device to raise private mortgages to pay for repairs, were blocked by the Scottish Office. The city later promoted several par value co-ops through the usual channels, among them Calvay, a particularly problem-ridden part of the vast Easterhouse estate.

In general, co-operative housing was the road not taken in the British housing system, even though one form of it, the co-partnership society, had played an important part in garden-city development. A similar form, the co-ownership housing co-operative, received a stimulus in 1964, when grants were made available through the Housing Corporation; but after 10 years this body ceased to promote it and existing schemes dissolved when their members were offered the right to buy. Co-ownership was displaced in favour by the par-value co-op, which in 1974 was put on the same terms as housing associations for receiving HAG for the rehabilitation of old, or the building of new property. A supportive Labour government set up the short-lived Co-operative Housing Agency in 1976 to promote it, and about sixty English new build co-ops were started in the 1980s, more than half of them on Merseyside. In the majority of cases their impetus came from housing associations or secondary co-ops, either acting on their own initiative or pressed by tenant groups.

It was the Liverpool housing co-ops, founded by council tenants from prewar flats and others in flight from private landlords, that highlighted the fundamental differences between local authority and co-operatively owned housing. Co-ops were small in size (usually no more than forty units) and their implementation took several years, during which places were of course earmarked for their own members. Typically, these were self-selected groups of friends and neighbours, whose strict housing entitlement might be less than other applicants on the waiting list, and certainly less than the homeless. Thus they breached the principle of impartial allocation according to housing need. Another fault of co-ops, in the eyes of the Left, was that their inevitable preoccupation with their own scheme precluded their involvement in wider tenant campaigns.[54] An early batch of seven new-build co-ops in Liverpool 8, begun as part of the council's housing programme, was municipalized by the Labour Militant Tendency that came to power in 1983. Later schemes, therefore, had to be on land under the control of the sympathetic Merseyside Development Corporation, or owned by the more tolerant Knowsley Borough Council. It was in this politically charged situation that the largest and most outstanding co-operative project emerged, initiated by tenants of the inter-war Eldon Street council flats. Obstructed by the city, they successfully appealed to the 'Task Force' minister for Merseyside and so obtained Housing Corporation backing. Eventually they developed into the Eldonian Community, with an ambitious vision, not just for their own residential 'village', but for the re-creation of an entire neighbourhood with shops, businesses, health and leisure initiatives.[55] Coin Street on London's South Bank was likewise opportunistic in exploiting a rift between central and local government (here the about-to-be abolished GLC) and it was similarly idealistic in its plans to recreate a neighbourhood – in this case one threatened with devastation by high-value property development.[56]

The day-to-day management of the still large council-owned stock was meanwhile going through some radical changes, as it became less and less possible to operate council housing as a closed system. In the last 20 years of the century, in a stock less than four-fifths of its previous size, net turnover was up by 10 per cent and there was more movement in and out of different tenures – in particular, movement in from owner occupation now exceeded movement out to it. There was more movement within estates, and more exchanges, especially between council and private tenants. The average length of tenancy was falling, and it was even suggested that the right to buy might in the long run make estates into 'transitional neighbourhoods' because of the short time people were prepared to stay.[57] While this would put an end to any historic claims of council housing to create stable and permanent settlements, a more optimistic view would be that it could help to turn estates into something more like the 'ordinary neighbourhoods' that their residents had long wanted them to be.

The tenant profile, overall, was poorer, and during this time acceptance of homeless priority cases rose by 28 per cent. Although there were immense regional variations, overall there were higher and still growing proportions of unemployed, one-parent families, teenage parents, and people coming from institutions under the 'Care in the Community' programme of the 1980s. Further contributions were made by students filling hard-to-let accommodation, and asylum seekers. The proportion of tenants who were 'disruptive' was judged to amount to 3 per cent, which represented a six-fold increase over the previous 30 years.[58] These trends coincided with, and made their own contribution to, a rising public panic about crime and anti-social behaviour, although how far this was actual, imagined, or whipped up by media exaggeration, is difficult to tell. The British Crime Survey of the years 1981-95 was not conclusive either way, showing only some falls in both actual and perceived crime in the mid-1990s. There were, however, new forms of crime and higher profiling of such things as racial harassment, neighbour nuisance and 'incivilities' within estates and public places. These mainly concerned young people's comportment on the street, increasingly monitored by CCTV, and it included 'teenagers standing about', which many perceived as threatening.

Such things were now lumped together in a new category of 'anti-social behaviour' that was felt to 'result in a degree of damage to the fabric of communities and the quality of life of other people.'[59] Local authorities had for some time had powers to deal with things like noise nuisance (invariably a main source of complaints) and packs of stray dogs; but new powers now given to them made their management more 'legalistic and punitive'[60] than their previous permissive if paternalistic style. Part V of the 1996 Housing Act made 'conduct causing a nuisance' a ground for repossession, and it extended to any member of a tenant's household, including visitors. It permitted 'introductory' (that is probationary) tenancies that could be terminated without legal process, and allowed powers of arrest to be attached to injunctions, so in effect short-circuiting the normal procedures of establishing guilt or innocence in court. Offending tenants, unlike people in any other tenure, could thus be punished by losing their homes as well as any penalty for their offence. Also dating from this time were temporary or permanent exclusions, or embargoes on those considered undesirable, while the 1998 Crime and Disorder Act criminalized behaviour causing 'alarm, harassment and distress'. It enabled authorities and other social landlords to operate child curfew schemes and established Parenting and Child Safety Orders that were targeted on truanting.

In practice, councils and other social landlords did not rush to implement these powers since they were aware that their use tended only to transfer problems to other locations. They recognized that the creators of nuisance were often vulnerable people with special problems, mental illness high among them. At the close of the century, less than a third of local authorities were using probationary tenancies and only around half had formal exclusion policies. Eviction notices, however, more than doubled between 1996 and 1998.[61] Some authorities were experimenting with constructive measures to combat deviant behaviour, such as Newport's patrols of rangers, financed by a 15p surcharge on rents, or Dundee's award-winning Family Project, a unit of three family flats monitored three times daily.

How to deal with the poorest and most uncouth of society was, as we have seen, a preoccupation of housing managers from the 1930s or earlier; but in so far as they were accepted as tenants at all, the allocation system was trusted to sort them out, while families and neighbours were relied on to socialize their own young. The residualization of the stock from 1980 onwards meant that dubious and potentially disruptive households could no longer be contained in pockets but were more randomly distributed. The focus, now, was on individual problem cases rather than estates or segments of estates – a reversal of the earlier pattern where the home itself was the instrument to civilize the uncouth, with inspection and regulation used to screen people for their suitability for the home. In one way, stricter regulation of deviant tenants seemed to answer the longstanding wish for council housing to operate like any other housing sector, so that it and its occupants would no longer be stigmatized; but the dropping of standards meant the final abandonment of the ideal of using housing to elevate all to higher material and cultural standards. It was scarcely relevant to ask where those not admitted as tenants, or excluded because of offences committed, were to go – for it was made clear that no special arrangements would be made, and certainly there were no promises of new supplies of cheap rented housing being made at this time. The increase of 'affordable housing' (which did not promise to be cheap) would in future depend on local planning authorities negotiating deals with private housing developers who, if they did not wish to include it on their estates might pay cash sums instead.

Tenants in Partnership

By the end of the century there were more opportunities and precedents than ever before for tenant involvement in the improvement and running of estates, and it was conventional wisdom that 'partnership is the way forward.'[62] The parameters and purposes of partnership, however, were not entirely clear. Was it to be for the rescue of particular estates, or the benefit of all oppressed tenants? Was it to bring the isolated and deprived up to modern standards, or to pioneer a new participatory democracy? What were the costs, how met and for how long, and what continuing support might be needed? What exactly was the role of the tenant 'partners', how would they be made to understand it, and could replacements for them be found when necessary? Were there one or many models to follow, or perhaps none at all?

The role of estate residents in regeneration extended the long history of tenant activism which was, if anything, heightened rather than subdued by the privatization and shrinkage of the council-owned stock. Nearly a third of tenants, by 1990, were reported to belong to an association, although most associations were less than a hundred strong.[63] But as before, in the absence of a coherent and sustained national movement, there was no way of passing on experience and most groups had 'a fairly precarious existence [making] it difficult to secure the financial and material resources or the time and effort of members which they require to sustain their activities.'[64] Yet involved tenants were seen as fundamental for regeneration. PEP, for example, found that as well as paid community professionals, they were essential to override the habitual apathy of the majority, and most of its estates already had, or soon developed, strong and active tenant associations.[65]

In being asked to become 'partners', tenants were in effect expected to step out of their habitually reactive mode. It is scarcely surprising that they found it 'harder than they expected to move from campaigning and mutual support activities to managing their own services,'[66] and official expectation typically overestimated what, realistically, they could do. It was difficult for officers and professionals with a vested interest in partnership projects to understand that people did not share their priorities, and the levels of apathy in long ignored tenant populations were a constant source of surprised regret. Even when an initiative seemed to meet with a positive response, it was often not sustained. PEP found 'a level of hostility or apathy on all the estates that made it impossible to use existing channels in order to get constructive feed-back from anything like a representative sample of residents', and found it 'difficult to overcome the sense of defeat and cynicism that affected both the residents and the council.'[67] It was only towards the close of the century that authorities seemed more able to face the fact that tenants had no strong wish for self-management, although 'there was a general need for greater consultation with tenants generally about housing management decisions at an estate level.'[68] An official leaflet for the Tenants' Compact lurched rather unsteadily between this realization and the old notion that it was everyone's duty to participate: 'You don't have to get involved at all if that's what you prefer – but it is important that you take this decision on the basis of full and clear information from your council, knowing the range of opportunities that are available and why your views matter to your council. You will need to discuss and agree a way forward together with your council and be realistic about both your own time commitments and how quickly arrangements can be up and running.'[69] Unhappily, those able to make such finely tuned choices were not, on the whole, those that the authority most needed to engage.

There was an important though usually overlooked distinction to be made between two kinds of non-participant. One consisted of those who were cynical and obstructive, often out of personal or collective deprivation and grudges for past disappointments with authority. The other consisted of those disinclined to involve themselves in estate affairs because other things took precedence in their lives: 'the fact is that the majority will continue to prefer to lead a full family life and cultivate their gardens.'[70] On York's Bell Farm estate, a fairly typical response to its regeneration programme was: 'No, all I'm bothered about is my own place. After that I'm not bothered.'[71] Special efforts were needed to involve people from ethnic minorities; but it was a recurring pattern that an estate mother or group of mothers provided the catalyst to 'turn round' a problem ridden estate.[72]

Though now given more official encouragement than ever before, tenant involvement was still beset by the old tensions of all tenant associations. There was the familiar problem that 'a few longstanding leaders carried a disproportionate burden';[73] and this was now heightened by the scale of the new responsibilities.   Tenants involved in the Drumchapel Initiative mentioned below had 'swiftly to come to terms with the planning of a major joint local authority initiative'; they attended over 300 meetings in one year, but even then 'were unable to influence how the Initiative developed and there is little sign that they played a role in setting priorities.'[74]   Pembroke Street Estate Action in Devonport, with only 160 flats, held at least three committee meetings a week and its honorary secretary worked more or less full time.   Its admittedly outstanding estate management board wrote their own design brief, employed their own advisers, raised their own money and were one of only two in the country to employ their own staff.   New applicants for the estate were required to attend training sessions leading to a certificate.   Yet while admired by fellow tenants, the board members were also regarded as a self-serving and exclusive clique.[75]

Stamina was needed not just for the load of work but because of the long time scales involved.   It took almost 7 years to get the Devonport Estate Action up and running, in 1994, and the original impetus for self-management went back a further 2 years.   Five years was considered the minimum needed to get a project off the ground and 'for groups of tenants to develop into a fully fledged financial and legal entity with sufficient stability, knowledge and security to gain independence.   The drain on the most active and able tenants through many hours of voluntary work can be divisive as a majority sit back and enjoy the fruits of their efforts.'[76] Entirely new skills were called for, in administration, negotiation and coalition building, and not only for the estate but on the vastly bigger context of national policy and finance.   There was a quantity of technical, legal and financial information to be mastered, in the unfamiliar language of officialdom and the professions.   Lay partners had to learn that officers in different departments did not, as might be expected, communicate with one another, and that often they knew less than themselves about a project.[77] Much of the energy of tenant partners, therefore, went into fathoming inter-departmental and inter-agency politics and discerning the different interests and power games of the authority figures they dealt with. On their side, the many 'official' partners habitually underestimated the 'resources and time required to build up a successful and credible partnership with the community,'[78] so failing to see any need to change their own practices.

The psychological burdens imposed by voluntary work at this level were considerable.   It was a case of 'responsibility without power' from which, unlike civil servants and local government officers, unpaid community partners could never walk away.   With no career development pathway or recognized criteria of performance, their experience had to be internalized, making 'burn-out inevitable.'[79] Ultimately the thing being created was a new level of 'governance' that brought tenants into an entirely new relationship with their authorities,[80] a new circuit of power spanning 'the barriers between the structures and professions of government on the one hand and the socially excluded and often disgruntled local populations on the other'[81] – a new but unmarked-out territory that new policies were increasingly invoking.

Tenants realized that they needed training for this new and difficult role, and it was obtained from a variety of sources. Besides PEP, it was supplied by some local authorities, including the GLC and Association of Municipal Authorities, and by a variety of independent and semi-official agencies. Among these were TPAS (Tenant Participation Advisory Services): independent, non-profit agencies serving tenants, councillors and housing associations, that originated in Scotland and had their English base in Salford. Another was ACTAC (Association of Community Technical Aid Centres), launched in 1982 with backing from both tiers of government and the Cadbury and Rowntree foundations. Based in Liverpool and Manchester, it was a loose federation originally set up 'to provide service of a more politically committed nature' than offered by RIBA.[82] Housing associations and secondary housing co-ops also provided training, as did Comtechsa, a co-operative of some hundreds of Merseyside groups founded in 1979. Other significant bodies were the Neighbourhood Initiatives Foundation (NIF) whose 'Planning for Real' exercise was widely used for involving people in estate and neighbourhood regeneration; the Newcastle Arts Workshop; Free Form Arts Trust; and CLAWS (Community Land and Workspace). Tenants could also be advised or trained by local Councils for Voluntary Service, Community Law Centres, Citizens' Advice Bureaux and the Church of England Urban Fund. The environmental professions made their own contributions: the RIBA had Community Projects and Community Aid Funds, which matched government money to run Architecture Workshops; and the RTPI had national and regional planning aid units.

Under the 1986 Housing and Planning Act (Section 16) tenant training became a profession in its own right and there were many independent consultants in community development and community architecture, the latter including Hunt Thompson who carried out the Lea View House restoration and advised many tenant groups, often using 'Planning for Real'. There were also, as we have seen, tenant groups who wished to disseminate their own experience, as in the tower blocks campaign. In Glasgow, a Technical Service Agency set up by a group of seasoned activists had over 160 tenant and community organizations affiliated to it, becoming 'a recognised and much needed catalytic force' in the city.[83] In 1995, a residential National Tenant Resource Centre near Chester (following a Danish precedent) provided a base for tenants nationwide to exchange ideas and develop youth opportunities and models of good practice.[84]

Training was rooted in two opposing philosophies, that were reconciled only with some difficulty. One came from the community architecture and community technical aid movements of the 1970s, when 'bare-foot professionals' put their expertise at the service of local people rather than serving their own internal and elitist dictates. Their aim was to enable people to 'own' their environments on the principle that 'a community that has been involved in and understands the process behind the product will be more likely to take responsibility for it.'[85] The other approach was a formal one attached to the Training and Vocational Initiative, where the aim was to develop an economically competitive workforce: 'hard-working, self-reliant, non-dependent, optimistic, innovative, risk-taking and generally "enterprising".'[86] In 1992 a National Certificate in Tenant Participation based in colleges and universities was launched by the Chartered Institute of Housing, in close consultation with the DoE. This formal approach to training was criticized for working to a government rather than a tenant agenda, to produce a standardized, 'professional tenant'.[87] The emphasis of Section 16 on 'competence to manage' led, it was suggested, to pre-determined goals and off-the-peg solutions, without reference to the deeper causes of estate decline.

In practice, however, it was not always easy to see the dividing line between the two approaches. The very notion that tenants could be trained for partnership breached the old barriers between officers and clients (Kirklees was one authority that opened its internal training sessions for housing staff to tenants) and for some tenants a training course, particularly when concurrent with practical experience, was nothing short of revelatory. For those with no previous experience of adult education at any level, the formulation of problems and exchange of ideas was comparable to a degree course in respect of the new worlds it opened: '. . . one woman said she had used training to: "evaluate my life . . . Before I came on this I'd never thought of going to college or university. I am now! I think it's come out of all this. It's made me realize there's a lot more out there for people".'[88]

Much of what was described as training took the form of personal counselling and psychological preparation for re-entry (or in some cases first entry) to the formal world of work. It helped to bridge the long gap since school which had, for many, stopped at elementary level if not below and, for many, it needed to start at basic levels of thinking and the ability to develop arguments without getting carried away by emotion. This confirmed the still immense cultural gap that existed between policy-makers, providers and managers, on one hand, and their subject populations on the other.[89]

Creating Estate Futures

At the time of writing, it is too early to say how much difference tenants' participation in management, or in regeneration initiatives generally, would make to the future of estates. There was a growing literature of case studies, but it was largely exhortatory and highlighted what were perhaps exceptional cases. There were estimated to be some 2000 estates in immediate need of regeneration, with about a quarter of that number actually subject to schemes.[90] By implication, therefore, the remainder did not need attention, and many of them must by now have large amounts of home ownership, or a mixture of tenures supplied by new social landlords. There was no means of knowing whether the 500 estates undergoing treatment of one kind or another were reducing the total of 2000 or, if not, whether this was static or growing. It might be remembered that Estate Action was a bidding exercise where awards to winners reduced the funds available for losers and non-bidders. By any reckoning, therefore, there were throughout the country estates that were forced to continue in an unimproved state, whose tenants were as powerless as ever to get any improvements done – indeed, this was the main motive for the swing towards 'large scale voluntary transfer' around the turn of the century.

PEP, though not on the scale of Estate Action, had the more articulated theoretical base. Its selected estates, which were of all periods and building types, were for the most part problematic in a 'typical' way – that is, they were not, in the main, high-profile cases in the media spotlight, but had a full range of the social and technical problems. PEP's aim was, through estate-based management, to 'turn round' estates to more 'normal' conditions.[91] What was meant by 'normal' appears to have been not overly ambitious, but simply adequate management without the grosser signs of neglect, voids and crime. PEP was influenced by official studies of the 1970s and 1980s,[92] but above all paid homage to the spirit of Octavia Hill: not of course her Victorian paternalism, but her emphasis on localism, small scale, and the inter-connectedness of the buildings and people. It was the object 'to enhance the formal role of residents in the running of their estates' since, following the precepts of community architecture, 'only where the community is at the forefront of changes do improvements succeed in inspiring its support.'[93] The approval and co-operation of residents were therefore essential to the success of the programme.

The essence of PEP lay in landlord/tenant relations and its main instrument was local management, with a full-time estate office whose manager controlled the estate budget and had power to co-ordinate repairs and all necessary services. As far as possible, those servicing estates should be resident: flats in particular should always have resident caretakers, and ideally cleaning, gardening and repairs staff should live on the premises. The damaging divide between white and blue collar workers should be ended. PEP practices were a mixture of what was already, or was becoming, 'best practice' in management, including performance monitoring and tenant consultation, with ongoing training for staff and residents, and the re-apportioning of the estates' open spaces. Some of its practices, however, were a radical departure from conventional ones, such as allowing 'overhousing' or the occupancy of houses larger than strictly needed, advertising campaigns and 'promotions' for new tenants, and allowing managers discretion over internal transfers.

A survey of 3 years progress on nine of the first PEP estates noted impressive improvements in repairs, cleaning, arrears and voids, at a cost that was only slightly higher per unit than conventional management (£422 compared to £412 per annum), with other balancing savings.[94] A Home Office study of just two estates gave a more mixed picture, where the hostility of managers towards PEP compromised its operation, and design improvements that improved things for old-established tenants inadvertently brought in young homeless people who 'attracted crime to themselves, both as perpetrators and victims.' This then polarized the population, for 'the reality of life on high crime estates is that the "community" is socially fragmented . . . the most able and stable families from which PEP draws its core of activists, tended to keep themselves apart from the other, more vulnerable residents . . . Indeed, their concern was to have these groups removed from the estate.'[95] The PEP approach was not, then, powerful enough to stem large-scale social trends, although there were numerous PEP and other examples showing how, in a controlled situation like Lea View House, design measures hammered out with residents could turn disaster estates into highly desirable ones.[96]

PEP itself was guarded about what made its method work. Though resident participation was clearly essential, 'it was not quite clear what actually brought the project estates into some kind of social order from disorder, but a transition did take place.'[97] Much of the academic critique centred round how far regeneration initiatives were 'top down' or 'bottom up': that is, how far they were imposed by authority of one kind or another, or how far they sprang from local people. There was a prevalent belief that 'bottom up' was by far the better approach, as it meant that tenants were 'in control'; but a general review of a hundred estates in the 1990s came to the conclusion that 'although there is still bottom-up pressure for participation, the primary impetus is top-down, focused on management systems and geared to the individual rather than collective involvement.'[98] Another study showed that the influence of the tenant partners was mainly confined to the early stages.[99] PEP itself adopted a pragmatic approach, finding in the high levels of resident loyalty, even on estates seen by others as deplorable, 'a positive thread in the life of all the estates which could be unravelled and built upon when a rescue was attempted.'[100]

This was borne out by two estates that conspicuously 'refused to die' when all with any inside knowledge of them would have given them up for lost. Broadwater Farm and Meadowell, post- and prewar estates of flats respectively, both had disastrous locations and were socially stigmatized from their opening days. Both reached a point where housing managers were barely in control; and both were riddled with crime and had periods of virtual severance from civil society. Meadowell's (more strictly, South Meadowell's) criminality took the form of ram-raiding, organized with quasi-military precision by a fraternity who took pride in outwitting the police. At Broadwater Farm it was blatant drug dealing that provoked heavy-handed policing, which in turn inflamed a population of disaffected black youths. Each estate eventually suffered a serious riot that was all the more tragic for following on a phase of hope and improvement;[101] and on each estate the vital catalyst for renewal was provided by women. At Broadwater Farm it was a long-time black resident and mother of six, who set about founding a Youth Association to harness the energy of young people. At South Meadowell a small group of women inspired a credit union, food co-op, estate centres and clubs, and made themselves responsible for running a children's playground (until they were alienated by the appointment of a professional playworker, made without consulting them).

Tenant activism on Meadowell went back to its life as 'The Ridges' in the 1930s; but estate women were politicized by a CDP operating there in the 1970s, and when this closed down they staged a 'sit-in' to ensure the continuance of its advice centre, which remained in business to 1990. Meadowell women were the force behind a campaign to defeat a threatened HAT, and participated in national demonstrations against the poll tax. Among other things, their enthusiasm inspired visits to other estate initiatives, a skills survey of tenants, the conversion of empty houses to an enterprise and training centre, a housing management course (under Section 16), and a TMC. All this was a good grounding for the Meadowell Project of the NIF, whose 'Planning for Real' exercise eventually led to an officially endorsed report, *New Heart for Meadowell*, and a Community Development Trust working to a 5-year plan which in turn became the basis of a City Challenge bid.

In spite of so much promise, other tensions were building up. Vandalism and intimidation by children and teenagers escalated to the point where the women were literally besieged in their meetings, and there was a state of juvenile anarchy. Everything came to a head in the riot of 1991 which followed on the accidental deaths of two young 'twoccers' being pursued by the police – an event blown up to mythic proportions in estate lore. Like a

Broadwater Farm estate: elderly residents leave the Luncheon Club run by the estate's Youth Association.

battle zone after the riot, Meadowell would have been in a state of famine had it not been for haphazardly looted foods and what the credit union was able to bring in. Even at this point, however, there were new ideas for a positive future for Meadowell, including a Community Village that would rise from the ashes of the old, torched centre. The experience here showed how 'the process of small initiatives by small numbers of residents, leading to gradually wider participation and the involvement of professional facilitators can be successful in getting the authorities and residents to agree a common, practical vision'; but it also showed 'that progress on reaching this common accord can be too slow to stop frustrations from building up.'[102] Rather similarly at Broadwater Farm, after its very marked improvement as a PEP, the story went through many further twists and turns, with growing tensions between police and black youths culminating in a riot, in the course of which a constable was killed after the accidental death of an elderly woman during a police raid on her home. Even then, in the face of public demands for complete demolition, a legal inquiry found surprisingly positive attitudes to the estate amongst its residents,[103] and there were many further initiatives, including the establishment of an estate management agreement.

These two outstanding examples of tenants' tenacity and capacity for innovation show how much they owed to outside support, for practical and other reasons, and on each estate professional and voluntary intervention played an important part. At Meadowell it was supplied by a church resource centre and, at a later stage, the NIF; at Broadwater Farm, by several religious groups operating on the estate, including a community of nuns who were 'welcomed by residents, as they offered background, quiet support and advice.'[104] The same inter-dependence was seen at Pembroke Street, whose indefatigable tenants owed much to an Information and Resource Centre that promoted tenant associations in the area, and to the Devon Co-operative Development Agency and a keen new project architect who devoted his own time to the design consultation. The authority here was willing to learn and appointed an officer to develop 'a new perspective and fresh ideas, someone not involved in existing practices who could turn around the attitude, working practices and culture of officers and give them a new direction.'[105]

It appeared, then, that there was a crucial but complex interaction between official and 'community' partners, outsiders and insiders, that made it fruitless to seek too rigid a distinction between 'top down' and 'bottom up'. By the end of the century the feasibility of 'turning round' an estate through better management, revised design and less alienated tenants was (given the necessary resources) established beyond doubt; but it was also clear that 'each estate is unique and regeneration strategies need to start from a careful assessment of the nature and history of a particular estate, the factors which shape it, and the resources available to it.'[106] Estate politics were, and were likely to remain, complex, both between tenants and authorities and within tenant populations; and this, aside from anything else, precluded a simple formula for regeneration to fit all cases. In effect, tenant partnership opened lines of communication between various levels of authority and subject populations characterized, at different points in history, as poor, deprived, feckless, criminal, excluded, but always problematic. Unlike the situation in Victorian times, when people were plucked from environments of poverty and put into new ones designed by a cultural elite, it was now a question of somehow renewing these replacement environments in consultation with their inhabitants.

The catch was that many of those most able to engage in such consultation had exited to home ownership, leaving a shrinking population of the conforming, law-abiding and decently respectable – who in any case were not the problem: the problem was those most distant from authority and its cultural values, the disorderly in high levels of stress through poverty and its many associated personal and social handicaps. It would appear, then, that partnership in regeneration depended on a rare sort of tenant, not only able and willing to make the great sacrifices of time and energy required, but still loyal and committed to the tenure, and with sufficient talents, self-confidence and courage to embark on working out meaningful strategies with degrees of self-management. Such people, where they existed, would be of the same breed that was being called for, around 2000, to bring about neighbourhood renewal over much wider areas than council estates, in a more participative local democracy. It is not surprising that extraordinary efforts and resources were needed to engage council tenants at this level, and that, even when it appeared to be reached, there was a question how far it could be sustained into the future.

Reintegrating Council Estates with Society

It would of course take more than a reform of housing management to re-connect some of the worst estates to mainstream society. One very obvious need was for estate populations to have an economic *raison d'être*, to bring not only income but self-respect, and respect from outsiders. There was an average of 57 per cent unemployment on some PEP estates, and on Merseyside, Tyneside and Greater Manchester estates it often passed 70 per cent. Meadowell around 1990 was reported to have 85 per cent of its households with no breadwinner. While official policy for unemployment was based on an assumption that its cause was lack of skills and motivation, the more systemic reason was a changing economy, where growth was in professional and managerial positions, part-time work, and in towns and areas outside the conurbations. In the 15 years following 1981 the latter lost nearly a quarter of their full-time male occupations, many of them the semi-skilled and unskilled work that would once have been done by those living on estates.[107] Such people were in no position to move with employment trends, and could make little use of part-time opportunities because of the loss of benefits they entailed.

From the 1970s onwards, central government policies, and all its urban policies, addressed the problems of training and unemployment, particularly for young people. There were rising levels of activity through the 1980s and

1990s, when training and employment initiatives were linked to regeneration in a wide range of partnerships and 'task forces'. There were independently constituted bodies such as Bootstraps and Community Economy Ltd that provided research, feasibility studies and action research for local authorities. Virtually all housing initiatives made some provision for employment, including PEP, Estate Action, Local Housing Companies and Housing Plus. The Waltham Forest HAT, comprising 2500 households, was one example of what could be achieved. Its community and economic develoment programme, begun in 1993, ensured that all its construction projects had local employment targets. It had contracts with several different bodies to manage training in construction, business skills and careers advice, with mechanisms for advice and support for self-employment and new enterprises. Among its many activities were English language classes, childminding, play provision and childcare skills.

The possibility of estates themselves generating employment was clear to many. The Action for Homes and Jobs campaign launched in 1987 (with Sheffield playing a leading role) was a reaction against the contraction of council housing and also of direct labour through CCT, and its argument was simple: people needed homes and unemployed builders needed jobs, so the case for more council house building was made. Although this campaign did not achieve its aims, there was a perennial need on estates for caretaking, cleaning, decorating, repairs, gardening and security, as well as white-collar jobs in management, which not only made work opportunities for residents but met the requirement for in-house services. They could also, potentially, develop into income generating businesses if contracted out to other estates and other enterprises could be located on estates provided they were well managed and had some stability. The establishment of a comprehensive local management office at Broadwater Farm in 1983, for instance, made possible the development of over a hundred estate-based jobs for residents, some three-quarters of them in a large co-operative company, while enterprise workshops were planned for the derelict spaces under the decks. With well organized community groups with imaginative ideas for improving the estate, this was associated with a halving of crime rates between 1983 and 1985.

'Community business', much of it based on estates, had its most impressive growth in Scotland from the late 1970s, when it was stimulated by the Highland and Islands Development Board; and there were estimated to be 140 established enterprises by 1990.[108] An example of initiatives on large peripheral estates was Drumchapel Opportunities, which emerged from the Drumchapel Initiative established in 1985 as a three-way partnership between Glasgow, Strathclyde Region and the residents of this slum clearance estate of some 19,000 people. With a community council that provided training and many welfare and advice services, as well as a theatre, it became a significant local employer, with a board of local directors and a turnover of over £1m. Enterprise was often accompanied by credit unions, which enabled the financially disempowered to have access to loans, and LETS, whose currency was tradable skills rather than coinage. Other common activities were creches and toy libraries, 'one stop' advice shops and projects for improving health and diet – as in the Health Project of Hartcliffe estate in Bristol, which in 1990 produced a report, *We live there, we should know.* Such things were not of course exclusive to council estates, but estates provided a natural context – as we have seen, its credit union was a lifeline for Meadowell after its riot.

Though tending to exist from year to year because of the stops and starts in their funding, such services were less fragile than attempts to start new, profit-making businesses, which were commonly shortlived. Their vulnerability seems to have stemmed from two causes: one was the attitudes of school leavers and others habituated to unemployment, which might be either over-optimistic about what they could achieve, or lacking in the self-discipline needed for regular work. The other was a chronic lack of business experience and guidance, particularly in the area of financial accounting and forecasting. This was due, not only to the inexperience of the would-be entrepreneurs, but what was very often an amazing laxness on the part of grant givers and bodies who should have exerted control. It was not, therefore, surprising to find that 'the field is littered with failed enterprises and a growing disillusion with the concept.'[109]

The considerable detail with which the Manor Employment Project (MEP) in Sheffield was documented and analysed illustrates the pitfalls waiting for idealistic schemes for community enterprise and work generation, as well as the surprising reactions that sometimes occurred when very different cultures collided. After the virtual collapse of the Sheffield steel industry in the 1970s, The Manor fell into the category of 'worst deprivation' by the council's own definition. MEP was the inspiration of a group of professionals living on the privileged side of the city. With the backing of the City Planner and with Urban Programme and other funding, it operated for 6 years from 1981, using a redundant works site leased by the city. Probably there was never sufficient clarity on its objectives, in particular how far it was to meet business targets of efficiency and profitability, and how far its function was community or even personal development. Thus it went through various conflicts of leadership and ideas, in cycles where 'long slides into depression, due to blockages, difficulties and general draining of energy are followed by dramatic steps forward, often accompanied by high hopes and over-inflated expectations.'[110] It reached its high point in 1983, after a shedding of personnel and a reassessment that made it possible to announce: 'We are now "in business" and not some community project!'[111] Altogether eight businesses providing fifty jobs were set up, including co-ops for sewing, cleaning and carpentry; car valeting, haulage, a weighbridge, wooden fencing project and an estate nursery. There were constant problems rising from unsuitable premises, lack of business expertise – particularly financial control – and a bad relationship with the city's Employment Department. After a critical review in 1985 the project drew to an orderly close, leaving as its legacy Matrec, a training and advice service (still functioning at the time of writing), as well as four firms, the estate newspaper, a wildlife project and the nursery – plus incalculable gains for some of the individuals involved. With a presumably unintentional irony, the site was eventually used for a profitable park-and-ride scheme for the city centre.

With hindsight it is possible to see how the splits in MEP were along the naturally existing fault lines: most obviously, the different attitudes to work of men and women, where men typically followed union lines geared to productivity and the traditional separation of home and work. Women who up to now had seen themselves as home-makers in a male oriented society, were headily politicized during the brief spell on the project of an articulate, communist and feminist development worker. There were other fault lines, in such oppositions as cosmopolitan and local; external 'do-gooders' and resident activists; winners and 'lame ducks'; competitors and co-operators; profits and personal development. In the end it was the women's approach that won through, for MEP had 'a determination to place women, their work and concerns, at the centre'[112] and the 'orgies' they held during the early phase belittled and undermined male supremacy. To outsiders, MEP understandably seemed 'naive, chaotic and woolly-headed'; but to those involved it was 'exciting, stimulating, hopeful', with 'a joy of life about it whilst it lived, and it lived long enough to make a difference in the lives of individuals and also in the wider community.'[113] It may not be an irrelevancy that these heights of experience evoked the communitarian fervour of an earlier age.

The same sense of liberation, especially for women, came from the use of the creative arts for estate regeneration, and there was the additional advantage that they could be classified as work schemes – an oral history project in Middlesbrough, for instance, was funded by central government. An international conference on 'The Art of Regeneration' in 1996 argued the case for the arts as a 'creative economy', a 'social capital' whose use would be a cost effective way to open up communication and develop imaginative solutions.[114] The arts were in fact an acid test of how far estates were, or could be, integrated with mainstream culture. As we have seen, they did at one time develop their own homely culture, with carnivals and 'queens', tenant news sheets, treats for children and the elderly, bingo and other community centre activities; but previous attempts to plant them with 'elite' culture were few and on the whole unsuccessful, as in the early case of Secretary Dawes' management of the Manor community centre, or Vernon Scannell's later disastrous spell as writer in residence on the Berinsfield estate.[115] A generation further on, it was easier for a community artist to bridge the two cultures, as when the artist in residence on The Manor in 1985 exhibited her views of the estate at the Graves Art Gallery in Sheffield. By now, there was an established profession of 'community arts', which functioned alongside community development. At Meadowell writing groups led by a writer in residence and member of a film collective produced a volume of life story writings and a feature film, *Dream On*, which was shown on Channel 4 in 1992. Described as 'sinister, witty, surprising', it concerned three estate women and their problems, revealing what they had to put up with from men, and how they could find strength to change their lives.[116] In this context, 'high' culture was not so alien, as appeared when the

Birmingham Ladywood estate performed *Macbeth* for BBC2, and changed the life of at least one of the players: 'Before I got involved with Shakespeare On the Estate . . . I was an unemployed lorry driver and my life was just a case of getting through every day and knowing nobody was going to give me a chance. Now I have ambition.'[117]

Video and photography were particularly accessible tools for campaigning and self-affirmation. Women of the Halton Moor estate in Leeds, for instance, used them to resist a proposed HAT, and their exhibition (which was shown at the civic hall) was designed to show the minister concerned 'why we like where we live . . . We aren't totally satisfied with the council but we do have a say.'[118] It drew attention to all the positive aspects of living on Halton Moor, and demonstrated how misleading stereotypes could be, by placing side by side pictures of council estate gardens that were resplendent and owner-occupied ones that were ugly and neglected. In Manchester, the Hulme Play written and performed by members of Hulme Tenants' Alliance recounted the story of the Hulme Study mentioned below. Getting the audience to savour 'some of the ludicrous things that have happened in and to our community from the powers that be, we have also hopefully convinced people of the point of joining with us and others, to demand a say from now on . . . It was hard work, but a welcome change from only working together in meetings and demonstrations . . . we now know who can sing, play an instrument, run up a quick costume, ad lib a stream of jokes . . . We have added to our potential for being a better informed and better resourced community.'[119]

Cultural projects, then, had the dual function of interpreting and validating estate life to outsiders, and reinforcing residents' solidarity and identification with where they lived. There remained the question whether they could convert estates into 'normal' environments, or whether they simply reinforced their difference. It was not, of course, uncommon for small districts and neighbourhoods to publicly defend and celebrate themselves on special occasions; but in the case of estates it was less an expression of their normality than their abnormality. Community arts, however sensitively applied, could not entirely escape the taint of cultural evangelism, and to locals their practitioners were often seen as a 'bunch of weirdos'. At the same time they could make many valuable contributions and at their best draw out the unarticulated experience and creativity of local people, as was very much the case at Hulme.

The Re-attachment of Hulme to Manchester

The inner-city estate of Hulme in Manchester provides the most convincing demonstration to date that it might be possible for a large and deprived council estate to be re-absorbed into the physical and social fabrics of its city. In some ways a typical inner-city estate, it was in other ways untypical, and its regeneration story was unique in its scope both of time and place. This made it not 'just another inner city estate making short-terms gains from a soon-to-be forgotten government scheme', but potentially a 'metaphor for regeneration.'[120]

Old Hulme, before becoming a target of public health and planning, could aptly be described as the 'classic slum'.[121]   It contained unnumbered workplaces, including feeder factories supplying well known national companies, and a renowned high street, the Stretford Road, whose shops and places of worship and entertainment were known throughout Manchester. It was first put in an ambitious slum clearance programme in 1933 but huge local resistance, not only by property owners but also by tenants alarmed at the thought of banishment to Wythenshawe, was so obstructive that the intended crescents of flats were not begun when war broke out in 1939. The old Hulme was still very much alive in the year of the Coronation (1953), when a city handbook stressed the strength of its community life and 'sense of belonging' – to which later oral history projects abundantly testified.[122]

The first postwar flats were built in 1946, but slum clearance proper did not begin for another 10 years, when some 15 per cent of all the unfit housing in England and Wales was attributed to Manchester. Hulme was then replanned as a Comprehensive Redevelopment Area of 350 acres, in five phases of flats and maisonettes where 'Hulme V' formed nearly a quarter of the whole. This segment comprised the award-winning but almost instantly notorious 'Crescents': four roughly parallel, five-storey, deck access blocks containing nearly a thousand dwellings, designed by same architect as Sheffield's Park Hill. Because of Ronan Point, their intended gas central heating was replaced by an electric hot air system described as 'the most effective and expensive way to thermal discomfort ever invented, [which] was to prove the downfall of the Crescents.'[123]   The district as a whole was bisected by the Princess Parkway, a new and partly sunken dual carriageway, while its main artery, the Stretford Road, was severed and demoted to the status of footpath. Shops and services were mainly concentrated in a purpose-built district centre shared with the deprived district of Moss Side. All the new housing consisted of maisonettes and flats in towers or slabs, linked by high walkways and islanded in seas of open space generously planted with trees. The rebuilding of Hulme was said to be on a scale surpassed only in Rotterdam, Warsaw or Hiroshima, and the city's planning department boasted that it was 'the first major comprehensive project to be conceived within the framework of an overall town design' and 'deliberately planned to allow . . . as many people as possible to live near and have direct access to the Centres of community life, the shops, clubs, libraries, public houses etc', so as to 'encourage social contact and contribute to a sense of community.'[124] The more sober reality was that its new layout severed Hulme from the rest of the city at least as effectively as its earlier slums had done. It was a further irony – though later an unforeseen saving grace – that it lay only a short stroll from two expanding universities that for all practical purposes might have been on a different planet.

Hulme's subsequent history made it 'hard to know whether it was the physical or social fabric that started to fail first.'[125] The defects of the hastily thrown-up Crescents were manifest within months of their opening in 1971. The rise in price of electricity after 1973 made heating bills of up to £500 a quarter not uncommon in Hulme V, with consequent disconnections; and in

1975 a tenants' campaign was able to show that 96 per cent of those canvassed wanted to be moved. On a rare foray into the estate in 1973, the city's director of works was driven to almost literary heights in describing his encounters with the 'resident dog', the 'phantom piddler' of the lifts, and the vacant garage turned into a cannabis den, with an 'atmosphere of abandonment that pervaded the whole of Hulme.'[126] But tenants and interested outsiders were now mobilizing to some effect. A flat in the Crescents was taken over for a People's Rights Centre, and skilful manipulation of the media (which was to be a hallmark of Hulme campaigns) goaded the council into making improvements to the decks, although they were not well received by residents. A commitment to remove all children from the Crescents was largely fulfilled by 1980; but this then made them available to students, artists, travellers, squatters and drug addicts, among others, and flats were illicitly knocked together to form studios, workshops and shebeens. Unsolicitied works of sculpture appeared overnight on walkways and public spaces, and murdered bodies were dumped on an estate that 'seemed to exist without connection or reference to the outside world . . . even natives began to half seriously refer to it as "Planet Hulme".'[127] This state of near anarchy was exploited by an extreme Left fringe, so confirming the worst fears of those who deplored the 'loony left' policies of Manchester's 'New Urban Left' council.

All of Hulme deteriorated further through the 1980s, and the city's rescue attempts were quite inadequate for its problems. At one point tenants mounted a 7-week occupation of its Hulme Project office, and in general relations between council, tenants, and also trade unions, were so stormy that 'there must have been times when simply abandoning Hulme to the forces of nature would have seemed the easier option.'[128] Towards the end of the decade rumours of Hulme being given a prototype HAT were calculated to drive tenants back into the council's arms, and their well orchestrated resistance (sympathetically listened to by the Conservative housing minister of the time) led to the surprising outcome of the 'Hulme Study', in which the tenants placed an almost touching confidence. It was a unique 'government-funded exercise into the structure, future and essentially the viability of a community,'[129] with a full-time development worker and an impressive array of consultants; but when its long awaited first – and in the event only – report finally appeared, it could hardly have been other than disappointing to the activists, although in the long term it perhaps helped them to feel more self-confident and more at home in the worlds of consultancy and policy-making. The abandoned study soon gave way to a bid for City Challenge, made over heads of tenants. They were therefore deeply sceptical, although for the time being they managed to save face by pressing their own document – *Hulme City Challenge: a response from the community* – on the Secretary of State for Environment while in flight between London and Manchester. It was 'the first of many "alternative" responses that tenants would present over the next few years.'[130] By now, all parties were so deeply implicated in a future for Hulme that no policy chosen could be allowed to fail.

The City Challenge project was managed by Hulme Regeneration Ltd (HRL), a joint company of the council's Hulme Subcommittee and the multi-national development company AMEC. The Subcommittee had three subsections: one each for social and economic issues, and Hulme Community Homes, which in turn was a three-way partnership of the city's housing department, the housing associations operating in Hulme, and tenants. In addition there was the Hulme Tenant Participation Project (HTPP), an autonomous and unique body composed of local people and generously funded by City Challenge and the Housing Corporation. After a shaky start – and in contrast to Hulme Community Homes which was conflict ridden and negative – this developed into 'an immensely valuable resource in promoting communication between the disparate players in the redevelopment.'[131] The strategy of HRL was to demolish Hulme's 2900 deck access dwellings and to replace them with over 1000 rented housing association units and 1500 for sale to owner occupiers, while the remaining 600 council dwellings were to be improved. The occupants of the Crescents, however, were now strongly opposing their demolition and determined 'to hold onto what we have . . . through fear of being dispersed again' – this 'recurrent theme throughout the regeneration process'[132] was now deeply engraved in the Hulme psyche.

In the regeneration structure tenants had, in fact, less formal representation than before. They experienced the familiar difficulties of all tenant activists: the tensions amongst themselves, and the resentment of an apathetic majority (who were so unobservant of the whole process that in the end they credited everything to 'the Council'), with the additional factor of an ever diminishing constituency, as those rehoused lost interest, and with a dwindling number of tenant associations in the Tenant Alliance. With women, as always, playing a crucial role, the tenant partners went to 'exhaustive and exhausting' lengths to prove their claim to be representative, taking particular pains to trace former residents who for a limited period had a 'right of return'. To some extent the sharing of information and power by the HTPP helped prevent the emergence of a 'tenant expert' elite, but that they were only partially successful is not surprising, given 'the history of conflict and disempowerment, the background of change and disruption and the growing realization of the demands faced by residents prepared to put themselves forward.'[133] The concessions won included the right of current tenants to a tenancy in Hulme, and as many of the squatters as possible were given the 'right to stay' and converted into regular tenants. Besides the 'right of return' there was 'advance allocation' of tenancies, one of the management innovations of the Byker redevelopment, which enabled tenants to prepare for their new homes before they were built, to specify certain design details, and to opt to stay next to their existing neighbours. A campaign for affordable rents was successful to the extent that the levels of housing association rents were mitigated by the nil value given to land. A demand for 'one move only' for any household as redevelopment progressed, though it worked for some, was not achieved for all.

All partners, not only the tenants, found the regeneration process difficult and unfamiliar. For the company building houses for sale it took a leap of faith to invest in an area so long stigmatized, and they found themselves reaching out to unfamiliar constituencies – for instance by advertising in the gay press. The city's housing department was forced to abandon long established design and management principles, and had to learn that while tenants wanted better management, they did not necessarily want to undertake it themselves. 'Tenant involvement is no longer seen as a ladder with full tenant management on the pinnacle. Indeed, such solutions could rather be interpreted as a failure on the part of those whose job it is to manage housing.'[134] The eight housing associations involved in Hulme (a number described as 'partnership and diversity gone mad'[135]) were forced into working collaboratively in ways entirely new to them. They included two large national associations and two completely new 'community' ones, of which the tenant-led People First began injudiciously when it launched £1 shares that were thought by some purchasers to entitle them to a home. It was saved only by being taken under the wings of a series of other associations; but eventually, by buying some of their stock, it ended as the largest, and a key player in the regeneration. In the end all the associations were more or less obliged to adopt unfamiliar practices such as uniformity of rents, advance allocations, and even their policy towards pets – for many Hulmans owned 'large numbers of very large pets indeed.'[136] Eventually the housing associations (through Housing Plus) and the private housing developer made significant contributions to the new Hulme. They included a household insurance scheme, ten corner shops, a community building, a surgery, and support for disabled, youth and enterprise schemes, including a credit union and furniture project with community cafe. Among their contributions to the local economy was a requirement that at least 20 per cent of contractors' labour should be local.

The most unexpected achievement of all was Homes for Change, a housing co-operative that emerged from the 'alternative urban culture' of the infamous Crescents, which at Housing Corporation insistence was put under the wing of the large and venerable Guinness Housing Trust, which could never before have encountered 'such an unlikely collection of articulate and informed residents in a deprived urban area.'[137] The co-operative, housed in 'the greenest building in Europe', was designed to reproduce the best features, not of the cosy 'classic slum', but the close community that had developed on the Crescents, with its 'tolerance of different lifestyles and the rich mixture of living, working and playing which characterised [them] at their best.'[138] It also accommodated two small sister co-operatives, Build for Change and Work for Change, which had workspace, a small theatre, and a lengthy 'ethical code'. In its entirety the complex formed 'a privileged enclave for young, white, middle-class, ex-students that sits uneasily in the traditional working-class Hulme community', forming 'one of the most extraordinary British housing developments of the decade.'[139]

Perhaps the most remarkable thing in the Hulme regeneration was its lasting influence on planning policy for the rest of the city. The city's own planning strategy for Hulme had already aroused tenants' suspicions, partly because of the experience of a nearby deck-access estate that was replaced by the culs-de-sac of houses then in fashion, a school of design that emphasized the 'island' quality of estates and the mentality that produced them. A new design code commissioned by AMEC was based on a grid plan reminiscent of the Victorian town and, following the debate this provoked, HRL appointed two of the leading community activists, from HTPP and Homes for Change respectively, to amend this and make it more flexible. Meanwhile, amongst other things through a visit to Byker, Hulme tenants had become 'remarkably knowledgeable in a short space of time about design matters.'[140] With encouragement, particularly from a Planning for Real exercise, longstanding local residents articulated their 'fond memories of the terraced streets and the corner shops and pubs . . . without necessarily knowing it, they already had a knowledge of the language of urban design principles.'[141] This was worked into a design code, with the help of a new concept of 'permeability' (which favoured linkages and accessibility over the seclusion of culs-de-sac) which promoted high-density (rather than high-rise) environments where streets were lined with terraced houses with small forecourts, gates and railings. There was limited parking provision and a 20 mph speed limit in residential streets, and there were more evocations of Victorian towns in a recreated 'mini high street' (later supplemented with a supermarket), some small, informal parks serving the housing clusters, and a large new city park on the edge of Hulme.

This was not accepted without considerable difficulty by the various bodies operating in Hulme, as it contravened the principles of residential planning that had evolved since the abandonment of the unpopular 'Radburn' school of design. The current fashion for culs-de-sac, however, also gave priority to the separation of pedestrians and cars, while it was also supposed to deter break-ins. When many of its principles, aspirations and language were adopted into a new City Development Guide, therefore, it met with fixed opposition from planners and highway engineers. The debate around road safety and accidents was 'one of the most emotive and rancorous that the Council Chambers had seen for some time';[142] planning officers, in particular, felt they were being told to 'ignore national legislation, breaching good faith, be deceitful and invent council policy that does not exist.'[143] The price to the city was the resignation of its chief officers of engineering, planning, and land and property; but in Hulme the housing associations coerced into this strange new school of design were won over and, surprisingly, so too were the police.

Estate Regeneration: Sustainability and Replicability

Hulme City Challenge ended in March 1997, when HRL gave way to the Moss Side and Hulme Partnership, which took over many of the HRL team. It could not of course be known how far the work of HRL would guarantee a sustainable future for Hulme, or how far it would be capable of replication elsewhere. To those most closely involved, 'it must have felt like one long round of intense activity that was, by turns, exciting, energy-sapping, challenging and bewildering.'[144] In this it resembled many other regeneration projects including Manor Employment Project, the Waltham Forest HAT, the valiant rescue programmes of Meadowell and Broadwater Farm, and the countless projects where tenants became responsible for the design or management of their own estates. There was, however, a special intensity about Hulme, because of its long, and long remembered, history of clearance, failed redevelopment and struggle. Those who stayed through it all emerged from a ravaged area on the very fringe of society, through years of uncertainty, demolition and reconstruction, to a new-found dignity and security in homes they regarded as 'superior to most of the private housing that has been built.'[145]

Some 70 per cent of Hulmans elected to stay on, some of them second or even third generation council tenants, with returners from the 1960s diaspora. Their understandable fears of being swamped by the home owners proved unfounded – indeed, some of the latter even joined tenant campaigns as they were concerned with the low standards of their own houses, and there were signs of multi-landlord residents' associations emerging. Travellers and others who had used Hulme as an 'urban crash-pad' were shed; but members of the 'alternative urban culture' who first came as students or squatters were now becoming settled, family-oriented citizens. By the same token, some of the erstwhile protest groups were transforming into established service and care providers. One result of the Hulme regeneration was the inclusion of people with special needs, mental or physical, and 5 per cent of the new housing was designed for wheelchair use. Flexibility in design allowed dwelling types not previously possible, such as one-bedroom houses and even new types of maisonette, while flexible allocation created a mixed population where, for instance, single people lived beside couples and families. Hulme's still unusual population profile, among other things, sheltered it from high child densities.

Although it was too soon to see if the new Hulme would develop into a real 'neighbourhood', early signs were auspicious. For the first time in generations it was possible to get milk and papers delivered, and children and cats were seen on the streets, rather than packs of feral dogs. It was of course clear that a mere simulacrum of the old, mixed-use environment did not automatically bring it back to life, and there was an argument that as social housing remained dominant, 'large chunks of Hulme will still find it hard to throw off the "estate" image and to be taken seriously as a neighbourhood or quarter, a problem with no easy solution.'[146] But Hulme would almost certainly be helped by its location so close to a vibrant city centre, while the fact that housing association tenants no longer had the right to buy blocked any immediate gentrification. It remained to be seen if its past reputation would continue to dog Hulme – for, as was now recognized, 'an estate's reputation does not automatically improve as the estate improves.'[147] There had been conscious efforts made to court a change in Hulme's public image, as in the careful organization of the Planning For Real weekend by HTPP and Hunt Thompson, and the opening of the symbolic Hulme Arch on the Stretford Road, which was done with great eclat by the light of a giant burning phoenix.

There were so many unique and, as it were, larger than life features of the Hulme regeneration that it was hard to see in it a pattern that estates throughout the country could follow. Hulme mattered to its authority, partly from a sense of compensation owed for past planning policies, and partly because Manchester was trying to modernize and redeem its own image as a city at this time. No culture mix like Hulme's was likely to be found anywhere else, unless perhaps parts of central London. One of its components came from a dogged working-class population with a long memory, to whom the skills of partnership did not come naturally, but who had an impressive capacity for self improvement. The tenant representatives

Hulme Regeneration: the Hulme Arch, 2001. The Arch, which straddles the Princess Parkway which is in direct line of descent from Barry Parker's pioneering 'Parkway' route to Wythenshawe is, with Hulme Park to the left of the upper picture, the crowning symbol of the regeneration carried out under City Challenge in the 1990s. At the entrance to the park are several lines of paving slabs depicting Hulme's history from prehistoric times and celebrating the 'struggles, celebrations and everyday stories' of its people.

on Hulme Community Homes, for instance, ran a shadow board to improve their effectiveness, with a code of conduct that prohibited 'swearing, aggressive pointing with the finger or six foot microphones, abuse of chair.'[148] Another component was the 'new urban culture' of students, artists, squatters and other colonists of the Crescents, whose 'Madchester' exploits doubtless alarmed and alienated many of the native Hulmans. Their crucial difference from other professional community artists and development workers, however, was that they lived on and identified with the estate, rather than treating it as a target for cultural evangelism. As well as artistic talents they had the confidence to take on leadership roles, in ways that did not come easily to the working-class inhabitants of Hulme.

This rich mix of traditional tenants' cheek and outrageous creativity, with much imaginative support from the housing associations and the Rowntree Foundation, brought a flowering of public and community arts in Hulme. The environment itself was celebrated, as in a 'Signs of Life' trail of symbols and signs, and the incorporation of people's hand and foot prints in the wall of the new community centre. Building starts and openings were made into festive occasions. Even demolition was turned into 'stunning, though temporary, works of art'[149] when local youths sprayed empty blocks under the guidance of graffiti artists, and when the 'Dogs of Heaven' mounted a 'spectacular' for the final end of the Crescents, where flaming vehicles were pushed over the parapet. History too played an important role: a Centenary Project commemorated the trades of Hulme in 1895, and a 'Hulme Sweet Hulme' living history exhibition linked present and past, while two volumes of the *Hulme Views* project gave voice to the memories and hopes of all who wanted to contribute.[150] An estate newspaper, *Hulme PIG*, was also produced in these years.

But the reconnection of Hulme to Manchester, with its promise of becoming an integral part of the twenty-first century city, was no guarantee of estates throughout the country having an equal success. The neglected inner-city or small town estate, and in particular the isolated peripheral estate, did not have Hulme's special advantages but would have to rely on the sheaf of policies in force for the remedy of poverty and its manifestations in social housing. Housing policies now in force included, as we have seen, an increasing diversity of tenure on estates, increased investment in their repair and modernization, stricter management, and a firm forecast of rising rents. There was already increased movement of households within estates, and signs that, for many, they were only a first or intermediate step in their housing careers. More generally, there were in place policies and funding for areas of deprivation, including economic initiatives for jobs and training, and these would, in the long term, impact on difficult estates; but the old idea of using the estate and the dwelling themselves as tools to eradicate poverty was now gone for good. It remains to be seen if any policy will eventually shrink poverty to its vanishing point. Society's 'poor' are now a small minority – incalculably fewer than the masses so labelled a century before; they remain a stubborn problem nevertheless, and one typically located on certain council estates. But until such time as it is eliminated, poverty must make its home somewhere. In the words of one observer, 'if the Meadowell had not existed, somewhere else would have fulfilled the same function.'[151] To this one estate might be added the hundreds or thousands of others that, like it, still bear some physical traces of a forgotten dream.

Epilogue: A Failed Experiment?

One of the incidental entertainments offered by history is to observe how dilemmas and problems persist through different generations, under different terminologies. Language apart, there was much about the housing situation in the year 2000 that would not have phased Octavia Hill. The shift in the physical benchmarks of poverty might well have surprised her, but not the conflicts and animosities between incompatible tenants, the stress on estates with too many children, or the apparently unbridgeable gap between the cost of decent housing and the means of the poorest. After a century of state intervention, it remains 'not so much a question of dealing with the houses alone, as of dealing with the houses in connection with their influence on the characters and habits of the people who inhabit them.'[152] Admittedly, the general perspective has broadened – for the poorest are no longer outside the body politic but are encouraged to engage with mainstream society – but it is tempting to draw parallels between the populations of twentieth-century 'sink' estates and that 'submerged tenth' that around 1900 was judged to be beyond the reach of policy altogether.

Historical games aside, the lasting legacies of council housing appear something as follows. It made a significant contribution, though one hard to quantify, to public health, by giving access to large numbers of the poor and even not so poor to homes whose quality was the admiration of overseas observers down to the 1950s or beyond. It was a quality owed, in origin, to the espousal of the garden-city school of design, whose utopian driving force reasserted itself in 1945, and later, with a different end product, in the decade of high-rise flats. Its underpinning was belief in the possibility of effecting social and cultural improvement through raised material standards. This was coupled to superficial and usually shortlived attempts to establish the sort of community and cultural life favoured by the followers of the garden-city and arts-and-crafts movements, with further borrowings from the tradition of nineteenth-century philanthropy; but council housing was in fact at its weakest in the attention paid to human relations, and it was particularly careless of the importance of housing management for the functioning of estates.

There were nevertheless numbers of tenants and their families who tried to establish community life on their estates, organizing events to bring people together, or seeking to remedy the defects of their environments. That their efforts did not grow into a continuous and concerted movement is explained very largely by the absence of organizational structures to encourage it; but more profoundly, it reflected the social and cultural divisions of working-class populations, who came to estates already stratified and divided. In its expansionist years of 1920–70, the management of council housing accommodated such differences, though not without strain. After this time, it was obliged to accept people that it would previously have excluded and, with a shrinking and deteriorating stock, it was forced into a role it had never been intended for, as 'housing for the poor'. Meanwhile, the client-like status of tenants allowed full scope to architectural fantasies and enthusiasms, leading to a series of uncongenial dwelling forms and designs.

The eventual and virtual monopoly of council housing in rented family housing (again something not originally intended) had a major and disabling impact on working-class lives. The continuing housing shortage, coupled to an unending search for economies, placed tenants and would-be tenants in competition with one another for a public 'benefit' that was seen by many as undeserved. The sense of difference (particularly when 'outsiders' from different social strata or different regions were planted on estates), with the perpetuation of the Victorian quest for 'respectability', explains much in the history of estates, in particular the 'it used to be lovely' phenomenon. Residents and managers conspired, so to speak, to accommodate social differences with the least discomfort to themselves, although this flouted the assumption of politicians, academics and community workers, among others, that there existed a tenant 'community' with common interests. The whole edifice, of course, broke down in the stresses of the last part of the twentieth century when, as a result of economic change and draconian rightwing 'reforms', estates became inevitable repositories of social marginalization and failure.

The ascendancy of council housing was co-terminous with the rise to dominance of home ownership, which attracted precisely those 'respectable' families (or their latterday counterparts) for whom the earliest council housing was intended. Not so long after its inception, therefore, it was not only seen as catering for the socially inferior, but in itself constituted a 'housing class' that stigmatized the inhabitants, regardless of their domestic standards or the types and qualities of the homes they rented. Something begun as a measure of equality and opportunity, therefore, turned into a mechanism for accentuating social inequalities.

Does the story, then, conclude as a failed experiment, in spite of its public health achievements and the many series of tenant campaigns on behalf of their own estates? This was not, as it transpires, the end of the story, for the problems and stresses of the last quarter of the century gave rise to efforts to generate brave and imaginative solutions, even while the very existence of council housing was under attack. It is far from clear from what quarter or quarters the inspiration mainly came. It owed much to a strong academic critique of design and management practices; but perhaps as much as anything it sprang from a new generation of community professionals of one kind or another, schooled in that critique, or bringing new artistic skills to bear on problem estates, and bent on avoiding paternalism, cultural elitism and entrenched bureaucracy. But there were also the estate populations themselves to take into account. What made Hulme significant and quite possibly unique was the coming together of community professionals, housing associations as 'social landlords', and a particularly dogged tenant experience with a long tradition of resistance and protest, which had not up to now realized its potential. Even here, the going was tough and outcomes by no means guaranteed. There is also the paradox that the end looked to was not a new and utopian social order, but simply the possibility of converting this much disabled environment to one that is 'normal' enough to blend in with the norm.

But neither is this quite the end of the story; for the experimental regeneration of estates by means of one policy measure or another, begun in the 1980s, became a model for the regeneration of other distressed urban neighbourhoods – virtually a metaphor for the regeneration of cities in general. New perceptions of the nature of poverty and how it manifests in the environment, with new ideas for neighbourhood governance and culture, begun in a quest for solutions for problem estates, were exported into the wider practice of 'urban regeneration'. Council housing, then, had contributions to make to the devolution of power and resources, new ways of ordering society, perhaps even new cultural forms and experiences. As with many good stories, the end becomes another set of questions and possibilities – perhaps even a new beginning.

NOTES

1. Davies, p. 32.
2. Cole & Furbey; Campbell. Cp Power (1987a), p. 223: 'a strong tenants' leader, invariably a woman, would sometimes emerge, with a clear belief that "enough is enough", we've got to stop it.'
3. Campbell.
4. Power & Tunstall.
5. Cullingworth (1985), p. 288.
6. Social Exclusion Unit, p. 9.
7. Findings (1997).
8. Cole & Furbey.
9. Malpass & Murie, p. 106.
10. Cole & Furbey.
11. Malpass & Murie; Cole & Furbey.
12. Malpass & Murie.
13. Malpass & Murie, p. 278.
14. Findings (1998), p. 2.
15. Owens, p. 16.
16. Bevins, p. 7.
17. Dwelly, p. 18.
18. Dwelly, p. 21.
19. Dwelly, p. 21.
20. Housing Act 1996. In certain circumstances extensions could be given. The 2000 Green Paper also proposed to widen priority categories and restore their right to permanent housing.
21. Dwelly, p. 19.
22. Goodlad, p. 32.
23. Mullins.
24. Lusk, p. 78; see also Hague, p. 250.
25. Cole & Furbey, p. 193.
26. Goodlad, p. 43.
27. Malpass & Murie, p. 117.
28. Hughes, p. 29.
29. Tenants of housing associations had a Tenant Guarantee instead of charter and their right to buy ran for a shorter period.
30. McLennan Report, para 7.76.
31. Audit Commission.
32. Findings (1996b).
33. SEARCH, p. 9.
34. Leeds City Council.
35. DETR, p. 2.
36. Leasehold Reform, Housing & Urban Development Act, 1993;

Housing Regulations (Right to Manage) 1994.
37. Power (1988), p. 14.
38. Birchall.
39. Anne Power: Shelter Conference, Hulme, Manchester, July 1988.
40. Power (1984). There was at least one independent EMB, in Leeds, set up in 1985.
41. Pinto.
42. Lowe (1997).
43. Findings (1995), p. 2.
44. Richardson, p. 1. See also Burbidge *et al.*, Vol. 2, p. 2.
45. Hague.
46. Goodlad.
47. Furbey *et al.*
48. Thompson, John.
49. Burbidge *et al.*, Vol. 3, p. 19.
50. RIPE, mentioned in chapter 11, was a rare example of a joint strategic approach of local government.
51. Seabrook. Deakin, N, claimed that it also appealed to the political right.
52. Cole, p. 162.
53. Malpass & Murie, quoting Audit Commission.
54. Grayson.
55. Cowan *et al.*
56. Community Action (1990).
57. Findings (1998), p. 3.
58. Power (1987a).
59. Brown, Peter, p. 80.
60. Papps, p. 653.
61. Findings (2000b).
62. Stewart & Taylor, p. 62.
63. Findings (1990).
64. Findings (1990), p. 3.
65. Power (1987B); Findings (1995).
66. Joseph Rowntree Foundation (1995), p. 3.
67. Power (1987b), p. 18.
68. Findings (1995), p. 2.
69. DETR, p. 7.
70. Deakin, N., p. 24.
71. Cole & Smith, p. 73.
72. Women's input was crucial on the Meadowell, Broadwater Farm and Plymouth Street (Devonport) estates discussed below.
73. Power (1988), 36.

74. Hastings & McArthur, p. 182.
75. Watson.
76. Stewart & Taylor, p. 30.
77. Smith, p. 25.
78. Stewart & Taylor, p. 57.
79. Findings (2000b), p. 2.
80. Stewart & Taylor, p. 62.
81. Findings (2000a), p. 2.
82. Community Action, 1985.
83. ACTAC (1986), p. 8.
84. Wishart & Furbey.
85. ACTAC (n.d.), p. 11. The passage continues: 'involvement in the design exercise builds skills within the community that can be reinvested in other activities, from community business to the management of housing'.
86. Furbey *et al.*, p. 258.
87. Furbey *et al.*, p. 265.
88. Wishart & Furbey, p. 205.
89. Holmes.
90. Power (1987b) I; Power (1997).
91. Power (1987a, b).
92. Burbidge *et al.*; Andrews.
93. Power (1987a), p. 243.
94. Power (1987b) II.
95. Foster & Hope, p. 91.
96. Thompson, John. Other examples were the provision of concierges and receptionists for blocks of flats, as at Gloucester House on the South Kilburn Estate, in the 1980s, through the intervention of the Brent Community Law Centre.
97. Power (1987a), p. 222.
98. Stewart & Taylor, p. 8. Rowntree Action on Estates Programme, f.1992, looked at 100 estates in 33 projects.
99. Findings (1996a).
100. Power (1997), p. 293.
101. Campbell.
102. Gibson, p. 2.
103. Power (1997).
104. Power (1997), p. 210.
105. Watson, p. 61.
106. Joseph Rowntree Foundation (1995), p. 2.
107. Findings (1999).
108. McArthur, p. 108.
109. McArthur, p. 222.

110. Pedler *et al.*, p. 26.
111. Pedler *et al.*, p. 27.
112. Pedler *et al.*, p. 186.
113. Pedler *et al.*, p. 206.
114. Joseph Rowntree Foundation (1996).
115. Scannell.
116. Campbell.
117. Turner.
118. T.H.A.T.s Action Women exhibition, Leeds Civic Hall, March 1990.
119. Community Links, p. 51.
120. Ramwell & Saltburn, p. v.
121. Roberts.
122. Hulme Comunity Council.
123. Ramwell & Saltburn, p. 5
124. City of Manchester (n.d.), p. 7.
125. Ramwell & Saltburn, p. 6.
126. City of Manchester (1973), p. 1.
127. Ramwell & Saltburn, p. 9.
128. *Ibid*, p. 10.
129. *Ibid*, p. 11.
130. *Ibid*, p. 15.
131. *Ibid*, p. 29.
132. *Ibid*, p. 11.
133. *Ibid*, p. 33.
134. *Ibid*, p. 105.
135. *Ibid*, p. 27.
136. *Ibid*, p. 97.
137. *Ibid*, p. 59.
138. *Ibid*, p. 59.
139. *Ibid*, p. 59.
140. *Ibid*, p. 55.
141. *Ibid*, p. 75.
142. *Ibid*, p. 81.
143. *Ibid*, p. 82.
144. *Ibid*, p. 106.
145. *Ibid*, p. 83.
146. *Ibid*, p. 39.
147. *Findings* (2000*c*), p. 1.
148. Ramwell & Saltburn, p. 25.
149. Ramwell & Saltburn, p. 66.
150. Hulme Views (1990, 1991).
151. Byrne, p. 70.
152. Hill, Octavia, p. 102.

Bibliography

Abel-Smith, Brian (1965) *The Poor and the Poorest: a new analysis of the Ministry of Labour's 'Family Expenditure Surveys' of 1953 and 1960.* London: Bell.

ACTAC (The Association of Technical Aid Centres) (1986) *First Report.* Liverpool: ACTAC.

ACTAC (nd) *Reclaiming Estates: a new approach to estate improvements.*

Allaun, Frank (1972) *No Place Like Home: Britain's housing tragedy (from the victims' view) and how to overcome it.* London: Deutsch.

Anderson, Michael (1971) *Family Structure in Nineteenth Century Lancashire.* Cambridge: The University Press.

Andrews, C. Lesley (1979) *Tenants and Town Hall. DoE Social Research Division, Housing Development Directorate.* London: HMSO.

Armytage, W.H.G. (1961) *Heavens Below. Utopian Experiments in England 1560-1960.* London: RKP.

Ashworth, William (1954) *The Genesis of Modern British Town Planning: a study in economic and social history of the nineteenth and twentieth centuries.* London: RKP.

Attenburrow, J.J., Murphy, A.R. & Simms, A.G. (1978) *The Problems of Some Large Local Authority Estates – an exploratory study.* C/P 18/78. Building Research Establishment. London: HMSO.

Attfield, Judy & Kirkham, Pat (eds.) (1989) *A View from the Interior: Feminism, Women and Design.* London: The Women's Press.

Audit Commission (1986) *Managing the Crisis in Council Housing.* London: HMSO.

Baldwin, John (1974) Problem housing estates – perceptions of tenants, city officials and criminologists. *Social and Economic Administration*, Vol. 8, no. 2.

Baldwin, John (1975) Urban criminality and the 'problem' estate. *Local Government Studies*, Vol. I, no. 4, October.

Barnett, the Rev. and Barnett, Mrs S.A. (1888) *Practicable Socialism. Essays on social reform.* London: Longmans & Co.

Baylis, Darrin (2001) Revisiting the cottage council estates: England, 1919–1939. *Planning Perspectives*, Vol. 16.

Beevers, Robert (1988) *The Garden City Utopia. A critical biography of Ebenezer Howard.* London: Macmillan.

Benson, John (1989) *The Working Class in Britian 1850–1939.* London: Longman.

Benwell C.D.P. (1977) *Pendower. Whatever Happened to the Homes for the Heroes.*

Joint Report of Benwell C.D.P. & Newcastle Housing Department. May. Newcastle:Tyneside Free Press.

Bevins, Anthony (1997) Sunny outlook for New Labour's model council house of the future. *Independent,* 14 July.

Birchall, Johnston (1988) *Building Communities the Co-operative Way.* London: RKP.

Blackwell, Trevor & Seabrook, Jeremy (1985) *A World Still to Win: the reconstruction of the post-war working class.* London: Faber & Faber.

Blatchford, Robert (1895) *Merrie England.* London: Clarion Newspaper Co.

Blavatsky, H.P. (1987) *The Key to Theosophy* (reprint of 1889). London: Theosophical Publishing House.

Booth, Charles (1902) Life and Labour of the People in London. Vol.III pt.1: Model dwellings blocks. London: Macmillan.

Booth, Charles (1903) *Life and Labour of the People in London.* 3rd series, Final Volume: *Notes on Social Influences and Conclusion.* London: Macmillan.

Bourke, Joanna (1994*a*) *Working-class Cultures in Britain 1890–1960. Gender, class and ethnicity.* London: Routledge.

Bourke, Joanna (1994*b*) Housewifery in working-class England 1860–1914. *Past and Present,* No.143.

Bournville Village Trust (1941) *When We Build Again. A study based on research into conditions of living and working in Birmingham.* London: Allen & Unwin.

Bowley, Marion (1944) *Housing and the State.* London: Allen & Unwin.

Bracey, H.E. (1964) *Neighbours on New Estates and Subdivisions.* London: RKP.

Brennan, Tom (1959) *Reshaping a City.* Glasgow: House of Grant.

Brion, Marion, & Tinker, Anthea (1980) *Women in Housing: Access and Influence.* Cambridge: Heffers.

Brockway, Fenner (1995) *Bermondsey Story. The life of Alfred Salter.* London: Humphrey.

Brown, Kenneth D. (1977) *John Burns.* London: Royal Historical Society.

Brown, Peter (1999) Redefining acceptable conduct: using social landlords to control behaviour. *Local Government Studies,* Vol. 25, no. 1.

Buder, Stanley (1990) *Visionaries and Planners. The Garden City Movement and the Modern Community.* New York & Oxford: Oxford University Press.

Burbidge, Michael, Wilson, Sheena & Kirby, Keith (1980) *An Investigation into Difficult to Let Housing.* Vol. 1. *General findings.* Vol. 2. *Case studies of post-war estates.* Vol. 3. *Case studies of pre-war estates.* Housing Development Directorate Occasional Papers 3, 4, 5/80. Department of the Environment. London: HMSO.

Burke, Gill (1981) *Housing and Social Justice. The role of policy in British housing.* London: Longman.

Burnett, John (1978) *A Social History of Housing 1815–1970.* Newton Abbot: David & Charles.

Byrne, David (1993) Review of Barke, M. & Turnbull, G. '*Meadowell, the Biography of an 'Estate with Problems'.* Housing Studies, Vol. 8, no. 1.

Cairncross, Liz, Clapham, David & Goodlad, Robina (1992) The Origins and Activities of Tenants' Associations in Britain. *Urban Studies,* Vol. 29, no. 5.

Campbell, Beatrix (1993) *Goliath: Britain's Dangerous Places*. London: Methuen.

Carey, John (1992) *The Intellectuals and the Masses: pride and prejudice among the literary intelligentsia 1880-1939*. London: Faber.

Carpenter, Edward (1916) *My Days and Dreams, being autobiographical notes*. London: Allen & Unwin.

Castells, Manuel (1977) *The Urban Question: a Marxist Approach*. London: Arnold.

Castells, Manuel (1983) *The City and the Grassroots*. London: Arnold.

Census (1935) *Census of England and Wales 1931. Housing Report*. London: HMSO.

CES Ltd. (1984) *Outer Estates in Britain*. Interim Report. Paper 23. London: CES Ltd.

CHAC (Central Housing Advisory Committee) (1938) *The Management of Municipal Housing Estates*. First Report. London: HMSO.

CHAC (1944) *Design of Dwellings (Dudley Report) including Report of a Study Group of the Ministry of Town & Country Planning on Site Planning and Layout in relation to housing*. London: HMSO.

CHAC (1949) *Selection of Tenants, Transfers and Exchanges*. Third Report. London: HMSO.

CHAC (1955) *Unsatisfactory Tenants*. Sixth Report. London: HMSO.

CHAC (1956) *Moving from the Slums*. Seventh Report. London: HMSO.

CHAC (1959) *Councils and their Houses*. Eighth Report. London: HMSO.

CHAC (1969) *Council Housing Purposes, Procedures and Priorities*. Ninth (Cullingworth) Report. London: HMSO.

Chamberlayne, Prue (1978) The Politics of Participation: an enquiry into four London boroughs, 1968–74. *London Journal*, Vol. 4, no. 2.

Channel 4 (1988) On the Manor.

Chapman, Dennis (1955) *The Home and Social Status*. London: RKP.

Cherry, Gordon E. (1972) *Urban Change and Planning: a History of Urban Development in Britain since 1750*. Henley-on-Thames: Foulis.

Cherry, Gordon E. (1974) *The Evolution of British Town Planning*. Leighton Buzzard. Leonard Hill.

City of Cardiff (nd) *Municipal Tenants' Handbook*. Issued with the Compliments of the Estates Committee for the Use of Tenants of Municipal Houses and Flats. (*c*.1950). Gloucester: British Publishing Co.

City of Leeds (1943) *Postwar Housing Report*. Leeds: Housing Committee, April.

City of Liverpool (1937) *Housing*. Liverpool: Housing Department.

City of Manchester (1973) *Report on Operation Clean-up – Hulme and Other Areas*. Private and confidential report of Direct Works Department to joint Subcommittee of Housing and Direct Works Committees. Manchester.

City of Manchester (nd) *A New Community: the Redevelopment of Hulme*. Manchester: City Planning Department.

City of Sheffield Housing Department (1962) Park Hill Survey, September (typescript).

Clarke, John (1979) Capital and Culture: the post-war working class revisited, in: Clarke, Crichter & Johnson (eds.).

Clarke, John, Crichter, Charles & Johnson, Richard (eds.) (1979) *Working-Class culture. Studies in history and theory*. London: Hutchinson.

Cleeve Barr, A.W. (1958) *Public Authority Housing.* London: Batsford.

Coates, Ken & Silburn, Richard (1970) *Poverty, the Forgotten Englishman.* Harmondsworth: Penguin.

Cole, Ian (1993) The decentralisation of housing services, in Malpass & Means (eds).

Cole, Ian & Furbey, Robert (1994) *The Eclipse of Council Housing.* London & New York: Routledge.

Cole, Ian, Gidley, Glen, Ritchie, Charles, Simpson, Don & Wishart, Benita (nd) *Creating Communities or Welfare Housing? A study of new housing association developments in Yorkshire/Humberside.* Report for Chartered Institute of Housing and Joseph Rowntree Foundation. Coventry: John Rowntree Foundation.

Cole, Ian & Smith, Yvonne (1996) *From Estate Action to Estate Agreement. Regeneration and change on the Bell Farm estate.* Bristol: Policy Press.

Coleman, Alice (1985) *Utopia on Trial. Vision and Reality in Planned Housing.* London: Shipman.

Collison, Peter (1963) *The Cutteslowe Walls: a study in social class.* London: Faber & Faber.

Community Action (1985) ACTAC, No. 7, July.

Community Action (1990) Coin Street community plan in action. No. 83, Spring.

Community Development Project (1976) *Whatever Happened to Council Housing?* A report prepared by National Community Development Project workers. London: CDP Information and Intelligence Unit.

Community Links (1989) *Ideas Annual.* Sheffield: Community Links.

Cooke, Philip (ed.) (1989) *Localities. The changing face of urban Britain.* London: Unwin Hyman.

Cooney, E.W. (1974) High Flats in Local Authority Housing in England and Wales since 1945, in Sutcliffe (ed).

Cooper, Charlie & Hawtin, Murray (eds.) (1997) *Housing, Community and Conflict: understanding resident involvement.* Bodmin: Arena.

Co-operative Development Services (1987) *Building Democracy: Housing Co-ops on Merseyside.* Revised edition. Liverpool. CDS.

Cowan, Robert, Hannay, Patrick & Owens, Ruth (1988) Community-led regeneration by the Eldonians. *Architects' Journal.* 23 March.

Creese, Walter (1966) *The Search for Environment. The Garden City: Before and After.* Newhaven & London: Yale University Press.

Cullingworth, J.B. (1966) *Housing and Local Government.* London: Allen & Unwin.

Cullingworth, J.B. (1985) *Town and Country Planning in Britain,* 9th ed. London: Allen & Unwin.

Dagenham Borough Council (1949) *Municipal Tenants' Handbook. A compendium of useful information for Tenants of the housing estates of the Borough of Dagenham.* Dagenham: Borough Council.

Dagenham Borough Council (1956) *Tenants' Handbook. Municipal housing estates.* Dagenham: Borough Council.

Dagenham Digest (1948–1965) Quarterly Journal of the Borough of Dagenham.

Damer, Sean (1974) Wine Alley. The sociology of a dreadful enclosure. *Sociological Review,* Vol. 22.

Damer, Sean (1989) *From Moorepark to 'Wine Alley'. The rise and fall of a Glasgow housing scheme.* Edinburgh: The University Press.

Darke, Jane & Darke, Roy (1972) Sheffield revisited. *Built Environment.* November.

Darke, Jane & Darke, Roy (1979) *Who Needs Housing?* London: Macmillan.

Darke, Roy & Walker, Ray (eds.) (1977) *Local Government and the Public.* London: Leonard Hill.

Darley, Gillian (1990) *Octavia Hill.* London: Constable.

Daunton, M.J. (1987) *A Property Owning Democracy? Housing in Britain.* London: Faber & Faber.

Davey, Peter (1980) *Arts and Crafts Architecture: the search for earthly paradise.* London: Architectural Press.

Davidoff, Leonore & Hall, Catherine (1987) *Family Fortunes: men and women of the English middle class 1790–1850.* London: Routledge.

Davies, Nick (1998) The New Statesman essay: There is nothing natural about poverty. *New Statesman,* 6 November.

Day, Michael G. (1981) The contribuition of Sir Raymond Unwin (1863-1940) and R. Barry Parker (1867–1947) to the development of site planning theory and practice c.1890-1918, in Sutcliffe (ed).

Deakin, Derick (ed.) (1989) *Wythenshawe: the Story of a Garden City.* Chichester: Phillimore & Co.

Deakin, Nicholas (1984) Two cheers for decentralisation, in Wright, Stewart & Deakin.

Denford, Steven (1996) Luxury living for the lower classes. *Camden History Review,* no. 20.

Dennis, Norman (1970) *People and Planning: the sociology of housing in Sunderland.* London: Faber & Faber.

DETR (Department of Environment Transport and the Regions) (nd) *Tenant Participation Compacts – a guide for tenants (1999/2000).* London: DETR.

DoE (Department of the Environment) (1991) *New Life for Estates.* London: DoE.

DoE (1994) High Expectations: a guide to the development of concierge schemes and controlled access in high rise. *Social Housing.* August.

Diacon, Diane (1991) *Deterioration of the Public Sector Housing Stock.* Aldershot: Avebury.

Dunleavy, Patrick (1977) Protest and quiescence in urban politics: a critique of some pluralist and structuralist myths. *International Journal of Urban & Regional Research,* 1

Dunleavy, Patrick (1981) *The Politics of Mass Housing in Britain 1945–1975. A study of corporate power and professional influence in the Welfare State.* Oxford. Clarendon Press.

Durant, Ruth (1939) *Watling: a survey of social life on a new housing estate.* London: P.S. King.

Durman, Michael & Harrison, Michael (1995) *Bournville 1895–1914: the model village and its cottages.* Birmingham: The Article Press.

Dwelly, Tim (2000) ROOF's guide to the housing green paper and interview with housing minister Nick Raynsford. *ROOF,* May–June.

Dyhouse, Carol (1989) *Feminism and the Family in England 1880–1939.* Oxford: Blackwell.

Edwards, Brian (1995) *Basil Spence 1907–1976.* Edinburgh: The Rutland Press.

Englander, David (1949) *Landlord and Tenant in Urban Britain 1838–1918*. Oxford. Clarendon Press.

Findings (1990) Tenant Participation in Council Housing. Housing Research Findings 8, January.

Findings (1995) The Effectiveness of Estate Agreements. Housing Research 160. November.

Findings (1996*a*) Community Involvement in Estate Regeneration Partnerships. Housing Research 167. February.

Findings (1996*b*) Housing Association Investment on Local Authority Estates. Housing Research 199. November.

Findings (1997) The Changing Population in Social Housing in England. Housing Research 202. February.

Findings (1998) Reviewing the Right to Buy. December,

Findings (1999) The jobs gap in Britain's Cities. May.

Findings (2000*a*) Strengthening Community Leaders in Area Regeneration. July.

Findings (2000*b*) Social Landlords' use of legal remedies to deal with neighbour nuisance. July.

Findings (2000*c*) Challenging Images: housing estates, stigma and regeneration. October.

All Findings published York. Joseph Rowntree Foundation.

Fishman, Robert (1982) *Urban Utopias in the Twentieth Century. Ebenezer Howard, Frank Lloyd Wright and Le Corbusier*. Cambridge, Mass. MIT Press.

Foot, Michael (1973) *Aneurin Bevan: a biography*. Vol.2. *1945–1960*. London: Davis-Poynter.

Forrest, Ray & Murie, Alan (1990) *Moving the Housing Market: council estates, social change and privatization*. Aldershot. Avebury.

Forrest, Ray, Murie, Alan & Gordon, Dave (1995) *The Resale of Former Council Homes*. Housing Research Report. DoE. London: HMSO.

Foster, Janet & Hope, Timothy (1993) *Housing, Community and Crime: the impact of the Priority Estates Project*. Home Office Research & Planning Unit Report. Home Office Research Study 131. London: HMSO.

Franklin, A. (1989) Working-class privatism: an historical case study of Bedminster, Bristol. *Environment & Planning D: Society and Space*, Vol. 7.

Furbey, Robert, Wishart, Benita & Grayson, John (1996) Training for tenants: 'Citizens' and the enterprise culture. *Housing Studies*, Vol. 11, no. 2.

Fyrth, Jim (ed.) (1995) *Labour's Promised Land? Culture and society in Labour Britain 1945–51*. London: Lawrence & Wishart.

Gale, Stanley (1949) *Modern Housing Estates. A practical guide to their planning, design and development, &c*. London: Batsford.

Gaskell, S. Martin (1981) The 'Suburb Salubrious': town planning in practice, in Sutcliffe (ed).

Gibson, Tony (1993) *Estate Regeneration at Meadowell*. Findings. Housing Research Findings 97. October. York. Joseph Rowntree Foundation.

Gill, Owen (1977) *Luke Street: housing policy, conflict and the creation of the delinquent area*. London: Macmillan.

Gill, Rev. Walter (nd) The Fight for Permanent Community Life. Kept at Valence House, Dagenham. [1956].

Glass, Ruth (ed.) (1948) *The Social Background of a Plan. A study of Middlesbrough.* London: RKP.

Glendinning, Miles & Muthesius, Stefan (1994) *Tower Block: modern public housing in England, Scotland, Wales and Northern Ireland.* Newhaven: Yale University Press.

Goetschius, George (1969) *Working with Community Groups: using community development as a method of social work.* London: RKP.

Goodlad, Robina (1997) Local Authorities and the New Governance of Housing, in Malpass (ed.).

Grant, Carol (1992) *Built to Last? Reflections on British housing policy.* London: ROOF Magazine.

Grayson, John (1997) Campaigning tenants: a pre-history of tenant involvement to 1979, in Cooper & Hawtin (eds.).

Greenslade, Roy (1976) *Goodbye to the Working Class.* London: Marion Boyars.

Hague, Cliff (1990) The development and politics of tenant participation in British council housing. *Housing Studies*, Vol. 5, no. 4.

Hambleton, Robin & Thomas, Huw (eds.) (1995) *Urban Policy Evaluation: Challenge and Change.* London: Chapman.

Hannay, Patrick (1988) View from the top (Building Feature). *Architects' Journal*, 19 October.

Hardy, Dennis (1979) *Alternative Communities in Nineteenth Century England.* London & New York. Longman.

Harrington, Molly (1965) Resettlement and self-image. *Human Relations*, Vol. 18.

Harrison, Michael (1981) Housing and town planning in Manchester before 1914, in Sutcliffe (ed.).

Hastings, Annette & McArthur, Andrew (1995) A comparative assessment of government approaches to partnership with the local community, in Hambleton & Thomas (eds.).

Hayes, John (1988) The Development of the Association of London Housing Estates, 1957–77. *The London Journal*, Vol. 13, no. 2.

Hayes, John (1989) The Association of London Housing Estates and the 'Fair Rent' issue. *The London Journal*, Vol. 14, no. 2.

Hill, Octavia (1869) Four Years' Management of a London Court. *Macmillans Magazine*, July, in Whelan (ed.).

Hill, Stephen (1997) A Roll of the dice. *ROOF*, July/August.

Himmelfarb, Gertrude (1991) *Poverty and Compassion: the moral imagination of the late Victorians.* New York: Alfred A. Knopf.

Hodges, Mark W. & Smith, Cyril S. (1954) The Sheffield Estate, in University of Liverpool (ed.).

Hoggart, Richard (1957) *The Uses of Literacy. Aspects of working-class life with special reference to publications and entertainments.* London: Chatto & Windus. (1958). Penguin Books.

Hole, Vere (1960) Social effects of planned rehousing. *Town Planning Review*, Vol. 30.

Hole, W.V. & Attenburrow, J.J. (1966) *Houses and People: a review of user studies at the Building Research Station.* London: HMSO.

Holmans, A.E. (1987) *Housing Policy in Britain*. London: Croom Helm.

Holmes, Ann (1972) *Limbering Up. Community empowerment on peripheral estates*. Middlesbrough: RIPE.

Honour Oak Neighbourhood Association (1977) *'A Street Door of Our Own'. A short history of life on an LCC estate by local people from the Honour Oak Estate*. London: Honour Oak Neighbourhood Association.

Horsey, Miles (1990) *Tenements and Towers. Glasgow working-class housing 1890-1990*. Edinburgh: Royal Commission on Historical Monuments Scotland.

Housing (1919-1921) Vols. I-II. Issued by the Ministry of Health Housing Department.

Housing (Additional Powers) Act 1919. c.99.

Howard, Ebenezer (1965 ed.) *Garden Cities of To-morrow*. Edited with Preface by F.J. Osborn. London: Faber & Faber.

Hughes, David (1991) Tenants' rights, in Lowe & Hughes (eds.).

Hulme Community Council (1953) *Official Handbook*, Coronation Year. Manchester: Hulme County Council.

Hulme Views (1990) *Self Portraits*. Hulme, Manchester: The Hulme Project.

Hulme Views (1991) *Views from The Crescents*. Hulme, Manchester: The Hulme Study.

Jackson, Brian (1968) *Working Class Community. Some general notions raised by a series of studies in northern England*. London: RKP.

Jackson, Frank (1985) *Sir Raymond Unwin: Architect, planner and visionary*. London: Zwemmer.

Jennings, Hilda (1962) *Societies in the Making. A study of development and redevelopment within a county borough*. London: RKP.

Jennings, John H. (1971) Geographical implications of the municipal housing programme in England and Wales 1919–1939. *Urban Studies*, Vol. 8.

Jevons, Rosamond & Madge, John (1946) *Housing Estates. A study of Bristol Corporation policy and practice between the wars*. University of Bristol. Bristol: Arrowsmith.

Joseph Rowntree Foundation (1994) Lessons from Hulme. Housing Summary 5. September.

Joseph Rowntree Foundation (1995) Unleashing the Potential: bringing residents to the centre of regeneration. Housing Summary 12. December.

Joseph Rowntree Foundation (1996) The art of regeneration: urban renewal through cultural activity. Supplement to Social Policy Summary 8. June.

Joseph Rowntree Village Trust (1954) *One Man's Vision. The story of the Joseph Rowntree Village Trust*. London: Allen & Unwin.

Journal of the Royal Institute of British Architects (1946) Human Needs in Planning – conference at the RIBA. February.

Joyce, Patrick (1980) *Work, Society and Politics: the culture of the factory in late Victorian England*. London: Harvester Press.

Kerr, Madeline (1958) *The People of Ship Street*. London: RKP.

Kirby, D.A. (1971) The inter war council dwelling. *Town Planning Review*, Vol. 4, no. 2.

Kumar, Krishan (1987) *Utopia and Anti-Utopia in Modern Times*. Oxford: Blackwell.

Kuper, Leo (ed.) (1953) *Living in Towns*. London: Cresset Press.

Leeds City Council (nd) *CCT and You – Your Chance to tell us what you expect.* Leeds. Tenant Involvement Office.

Lowe, Stuart (1977) Community groups and local politics, in Darke & Walker (eds.).

Lowe, Stuart (1986) *Urban Social Movements: the city after Castells.* London: Macmillan.

Lowe, Stuart (1997) Tenant participation in a legal context, in Cooper & Hawtin (eds.).

Lowe, Stuart & Hawtin, Murray (1986) Systems built housing and tenants' associations. *Housing and Planning Review*, Vol. 41, no. 1, February.

Lowe, Stuart & Hughes, D. (eds.) (1991) *A New Century of Social Housing.* Leicester: University Press.

Lusk, Paul (1997) Tenants' Choice and tenant management. Who owns and who controls social housing? in Cooper & Hawtin (eds.).

McArthur, A. (1993) An exploration of community business failure. *Policy and Politics*, Vol. 21, no. 3.

McGonigle, G.C.M. & Kirby, J. (1936) *Poverty and Public Health.* London: Gollancz.

McIntosh, Neil (1975) *Housing for the Poor. Council housing in Southwark.* London: Southwark CDP.

McKenna, Madeline (1991) The suburbanization of the working-class population of Liverpool between the wars. *Social History*, Vol. 16, no. 2.

McLennan, Duncan (1989) *The Nature and Effectiveness of Housing Management in England. A Report to the Department of Environment by the Centre for Housing Research.* Glasgow: University Press.

Malpass, Peter (1992) Rents within reach, in Grant (ed.).

Malpass, Peter (ed.) (1997) *Ownership, Control and Accountability: the New Governance of Housing.* London: Chartered Institute of Housing.

Malpass, Peter & Means, Robin (eds.) (1993) *Implementing Housing Policy.* Oxford: University Press.

Malpass, Peter & Murie, Alan (1982) *Housing Policy and Practice* (3rd ed. 1990). London: Macmillan.

Manor & Woodthorpe Review (1934-35) The Official Organ of the Manor Community Association (monthly). Vol. 1, April-March. Housed at Sheffield Central Reference Library.

Mass Observation (1943) *An Enquiry into People's Homes.* London: Murray.

Meacham, Standish (1977) *A Life Apart: the English working class 1890–1914.* London: Thames & Hudson.

Meacham, Standish (1994) Raymond Unwin, in Pederson & Mandler (eds.).

Mearns, Rev. Andrew (1883) *The Bitter Cry of Outcast London. An inquiry into the condition of the abject poor.* Facsimile edition 1969 ed. Cedric Chivers. Bath: Portway.

Meegan, Richard. (1989) Paradise Postponed: the growth and decline of Merseyside's outer estates, in Cooke (ed.).

Miller, Mervyn (1989) *Letchworth the First Garden City.* Chichester: Phillimore.

Ministry of Housing and Local Government (MHLG) (1961) *Homes for Today and Tomorrow* (Parker Morris Report). London: HMSO.

MHLG (1970*a*) *Living in a Slum: a study of St Mary's, Oldham.* Design Bulletin 19. London: HMSO.

MHLG (1970*b*) *Moving out of a Slum: a study of people moving from St Mary's, Oldham.* Design Bulletin 19. London: HMSO.

MHLG (1971) *New Housing in a Cleared Area: a study of St Mary's, Oldham.* Design Bulletin 22. London: HMSO.

Mitchell, G. Duncan & Lupton, Thomas (1954) Neighbourhood and community: the Liverpool Estate. in University of Liverpool (ed.).

Mogey, J.M. (1956) *Family and Neighbourhood. Two studies in Oxford.* Oxford: University Press.

Morris, R.N. (1963) The Berinsfield Community Centre. *Sociological Review*, Vol. 10.

Morris, R.N. & Mogey, John (1965) *The Sociology of Housing. Studies at Berinsfield.* London: RKP.

Morris, William (1882) *Hopes and Fears for Art.*

Mowat, Charles Loch (1961) *The Charity Organisation Society 1869–1913.* London: Methuen.

Mullins, David (2000) Stock taking. ROOF, March–April.

Municipal Journal (1960) RDC builds a £500,000 village. 12 August.

Muthesius, Stefan (1982) *The English Terraced House.* New Haven: Yale University Press.

National Council of Social Service (1938) *New Housing Estates and their Social Problems.* Community Centres and Associations Committee. Preface by Ernest Barker. London: NCSS.

National Council of Social Service (1960) *Setting up House. Furnishing problems on New Housing Estates: a survey by the Manchester and Salford Council of Social Service.* London: NCSS.

Newman, Oscar (1972) *Defensible Space. People and design in the violent city.* New York: Macmillan.

Nicholas, R. Rowland (1945) *City of Manchester Plan.* Norwich: Jarrold.

Niner, Pat (1999) *Insights into Low Demand for Housing.* York: Joseph Rowntree Foundation, July.

Northern Consortium of Housing Authorities (1981) *Difficult to Let Estates.* Report of a Study Group.

Norris, June (1960) *Human Aspects of Redevelopment.* Studies in Housing and Industrial Location No. 2. London: The Midlands New Towns Society.

Orbach, Laurence F. (1977) *Homes for Heroes: a study of the evolution of British public housing 1915-1921.* London: Seeley.

Owens, Ruth (1987) Born again. *Architects' Journal*, 18 March.

Papps, Pauline (1998) Anti-Social Behaviour Strategies – individualistic or holistic? *Housing Studies*, Vol. 13, no. 5.

Parker, Tony (1983) *The People of Providence. A housing estate and some of its inhabitants.* London: Hutchinson.

Parliamentary Debates (Hansard) (1909) Vol. VI.

Parliamentary Debates (Hansard) (1923) 5th Series Vol. 163.

Parliamentary Debates (Hansard) (1962) 5th Series Vol. 656, 20 March.

Pearson, Lynn F. (1988) *The Architectural and Social History of Cooperative Living.* Basingstoke & London: Macmillan.

Pederson, Susan & Mandler, Peter (eds.) (1994) *After the Victorians: private conscience and public duty in modern Britain.* London and New York. Routledge.

Pedler, Mike, Banfield, Paul, Boraston, Ian, Gill, John & Shipton, John (1990) *The Community Development Initiative – a story of the Manor Employment Project in Sheffield.* Aldershot: Avebury.

Pelling, Henry (1965) *The Origins of the Labour Party 1880–1900.* Oxford: Clarendon Press.

PEP (Planning) (1947) Watling revisited. Vol. XIV, no. 270.

PEP (Planning) (1948) Councils and their tenants. Vol. XIV, no. 282.

Pickett, Kathleen G & Boulton, David K. (1974) *Migration and Social Adjustment: Kirkby and Maghull.* Liverpool: University Press.

Picture Post (1941) A Plan for Britain. 4 January. (Great Newspapers Reprinted Special No. 7, 1974).

Pinto, Ricardo R. (1993) *The Estate Action Initiative.* Aldershot: Avebury.

Power, Anne (1977) *Five Years On. Holloway Tenant Cooperative and North Islington Housing Rights Project.* London: Expression Printers.

Power, Anne (1984) *Local Housing Management.* London: Department of the Environment.

Power, Anne (1987a) *Property Before People. The management of twentieth-century council housing.* London: Allen & Unwin.

Power, Anne (1987b) *The PEP Guide to Local Housing Management.* 1. The PEP Model. 2. The PEP Experience. 3. Guidelines for Setting up New Projects. The Priority Estates Project, Estate Action. London: DoE, Welsh Office.

Power, Anne (1988) Under new management. The experience of thirteen Islington Tenant Management Cooperatives. *PEP,* November.

Power, Anne (1997) *Estates on the Edge. The social consequences of mass housing in Northern Europe.* London: Macmillan.

Power, Anne & Tunstall, Rebecca (1997) *Dangerous Disorder. Riots and violent disturbnaces in thirteen areas of Britain 1991–92.* York: Joseph Rowntree Foundation.

Priestley, J.B. (1934) *English Journey.* London: Heinemann.

Purdom, C.B. (1913) *The Garden City: a study in the development of a modern town.* London: Dent.

Ramwell, Rob & Saltburn, Hilary (1998) *Trick or Treat? City Challenge and the Regeneration of Hulme.* York: North British Housing Association and Guinness Trust.

Ravetz, Alison (1974) *Model Estate: planned housing at Quarry Hill, Leeds.* London: Croom Helm.

Ravetz, Alison (1976) Housing at Byker, Newcastle upon Tyne: appraisal. *Architects' Journal,* 14 April.

Ravetz, Alison (1989) A View from the interior, in Attfield & Kirkham (eds.).

Ravetz, Alison (1990) Estate journalism: part of the cultural history of council estates. Housing Review, Vol. 39, no.6.

Ravetz, Alison (1995a) (with R. Turkington). *The Place of Home. English domestic environments 1914-2000.* London: Spon.

Ravetz, Alison (1995*b*) Housing the people, in Fyrth (ed.).

Reiss, R.L. (ed.) (1945) *Rebuilding Britain Series No.13.* London: Faber & Faber.

Reynolds, Francis (1986) *The Problem Housing Estate. An account of Omega and its people.* Aldershot: Gower.

Richardson, Ann (1977) *Tenant Participation in Council Housing Management.* DoE Housing Development Directorate Occasional Paper 2/77. London: HMSO.

Roberts, Robert (1971) *The Classic Slum. Salford life in the first quarter of the century.* Manchester: University Press.

Rowntree, B. Seebohm (1941) *Poverty and Progress. A second social survey of York.* London: Longmans.

Rowntree, B. Seebohm (1945) Portrait of a city's housing, in Reiss (ed.).

Royal Commission (1884-45) On the Housing of the Working Classes. C. 4402 Vol. xxx.

Royal Commission (1917) On the Housing of the Industrial Population of Scotland, Rural and Urban. Cd. 8731.

Royal Institute of British Architects (1955) *High Flats.* Report of a Symposium held on 15 February. London: RIBA.

Rubinstein, Antonia (ed.) (1991) *Just Like the Country. Memories of London families who settled the new cottage estates 1919-1939.* London: Age Exchange.

Scannell, Vernon (1977) *A Proper Gentleman.* London: Robson Books.

Seabrook, Jeremy (1997) *The Idea of Neighbourhood.* London: Pluto.

SEARCH (1997) Added extra. No. 28. Autumn.

Sheffield Handbook of Workmen's Dwellings (1905) October. Sheffield Reference Library.

Shenton, Neil (1976) Deneside – a Council Estate. Papers in Community Studies, Department of Social Administration and Social Work. University of York.

Shock, Maurice (1971) Christopher Addison 1869–1951. *Dictionary of National Biography.*

Simey, Margaret B. (1951) *Charitable Effort in Liverpool in the Nineteenth Century.* Liverpool: University Press.

Simon, Alfred P. (1936) *Manchester Made Over.* London: King & Son.

Simon, E.D. (1933) *The Anti-Slum Campaign.* London: Longmans Green & Co.

Sklair, Leslie (1975) The Struggle against the Housing Finance Act. *The Socialist Register.*

Smith, Jerry (1992) *Community Development and Tenant Action.* London: National Coalition for Neighbourhoods and Community Development Foundation.

Smithson, Alison & Peter (1967) *Urban Structuring.* London: Studio Vista.

Social Exclusion Unit (1998) *Bringing Britain Together: a national strategy for neighbourhood renewal. September.* London: HMSO.

Steeley, Geoffrey (1998) The Path to Real Reform in: Special Supplement: One Hundred Years of To-morrow. *Town and Country Planning,* October.

Stewart, Murray & Taylor, Marilyn (1995) *Estate Empowerment and Estate Regeneration: a critical review.* Bristol: The Policy Press.

Stowell, Gordon (1929) *The History of Button Hill.* London: Gollancz.

Strathern, Marilyn (1981) *Kinship at the Core. An anthropology of Elmdon, a village in north-west Essex in the nineteen-sixties.* Cambridge: University Press.

Sutcliffe, Anthony (1981) *Towards the Planned City – Germany, Britain, the United States and France, 1780–1914.* Oxford: Blackwell.

Sutcliffe, Anthony (ed.) (1974) *Multi-Storey Living: the British Working-Class Experience.* London: Croom Helm.

Sutcliffe, Anthony (ed.) (1981) *British Town Planning: the formative years.* Leicester: University Press.

Swenarton, Mark (1981) *Homes Fit for Heroes. The politics and architecture of early state housing in Britain.* London: Heinemann.

Swenarton, Mark (1989) *Artisans and Architects. The Ruskinian tradition in architectural thought.* Basingstoke & London: Macmillan.

Tarn, J.N. (1971) *Working-Class Housing in 19th-Century Britain.* Architectural Association Paper No. 7. London: Lund Humphreys.

Tarn, J.N. (1973) *Five per cent Philanthropy. An account of housing in urban areas between 1840 and 1914.* Cambridge: University Press.

Tebbutt, Melanie (1995) *Women's Talk? A Social History of 'Gossip' in Working-Class Neighbourhoods, 1880–1960.* Aldershot: Scolar Press.

Thomas, Ray (1998) Howardian Economics and the Future of London in: Special Supplement: One Hundred Years of To-morrow. *Town & Country Planning*, October.

Thompson, F.M.L. (1988*) The Rise of Respectable Society: a social history of Victorian Britain, 1830–1900.* London: Fontana.

Thompson, John (1985) *Community Architecture: the Story of Lea View House, Hackney.* RIBA Community Architecture Group. London: RIBA.

Tucker, James (1966) *Honourable Estates.* London: Gollancz.

Tudor Walters Committee (1918) Report of the Committee . . . to consider questions of building construction in connection with the Provision of Dwellings for the Working Classes . . . &c. Cd. 9191.

Turner, Jill (1997) Pulp Shakespeare. *The Guardian*, 5 April.

United Kingdom Housing Trust (nd) *UKHT and Sheffield: a Partnership for Housing (1986/7).* London: UKHT Ltd.

University of Liverpool (ed.) (1954) *Neighbourhood and Community: an enquiry into social relationships on housing estates in Liverpool and Sheffield.* Liverpool: University Press.

Unwin, Raymond (1902) Cottage Plans and Common Sense. Fabian Society Tract 109.

Unwin, Raymond (with Barry Parker) (1901) *The Art of Building a Home.* A collection of lectures and illustrations.

Vereker, Charles, Mays, John Barron, Gittins, Elizabeth & Broady, Maurice (1961) *Urban Redevelopment and Social Change. A study of social conditions in central Liverpool 1955–6.* Liverpool: University Press.

Vicinus, Martha (1985) *Independent Women. Work and community for single women 1850–1920.* London: Virago.

Ward, Colin (1974) *Tenants Take Over.* London: The Architectural Press.

Ward, Colin (1976) *Housing: an anarchist approach.* London: Freedom Press.

Ward, Colin (1990) *Talking Houses.* London: Freedom Press.

Waterhouse, Keith (1994) *City Lights. A street life.* London: Hodder & Stoughton.

Watling Resident (1927– Monthly) Vol. 4, no. 5. Housed at Hendon Central Library.

Watson, Dick (1994) *Putting Back the Pride: case study of a power-sharing approach to tenant participation.* Liverpool: ACTAC.

Webb, Beatrice (1982) *Diary I 1875–1892*, ed. Norman and Jeanne MacKenzie. London: Virago.

Westergaard, John & Glass, Ruth (1954) A Profile of Lansbury. *Town Planning Review*, Vol. 25, no. 1, April.

Whelan, Robert (ed.) (1998) *Octavia Hill and the Social Housing Debate. Essays and Letters.* 'Rediscovered Riches' No.3. London: IEA Health & Welfare Unit.

White, Jerry (1949) *Rothschild Buildings: life in an East End tenement block 1887-1920.* London: RKP.

White, L.E. (1946) *Tenement Town.* London: Jason Press.

Wilding, Paul (1973) The Housing and Town Planning Act 1919: a study in the making of social policy. *Journal of Social Policy*, Vol. 2, no. 4.

Wilson, Hugh & Womersley, Lewis (1965) *Hulme 5 Redevelopment.* Report on Design to the City of Manchester.

Wilson, Roger (1963) *Difficult Housing Estates.* Tavistock Pamphlet No. 5. London: Tavistock Publications.

Wilson, S. & Burbidge, M. (1978) *An Investigation of Difficult to let Housing.* Social Research Divison. Department of the Environment. London: HMSO.

Winter, J.M. (1985) *The Great War and the British People.* London: Macmillan.

Wishart, Benita & Furbey, Rob (1997) Training for tenants, in Cooper & Hawtin (eds.).

Witley Point Tenants' Association (1989) *Rising Above It.* London: Witley Point Tenants' Association

Witney Rural District Council (nd) *Tenants' Handbook.* (c.1960). Witney: The Rural District Council.

Wohl, A.S. (1977) *The Eternal Slum: housing and social policy in Victorian London.* London: Edward Arnold.

Womersley, J.L. (1964) Housing at Park Hill, Sheffield. *Architects' Journal*, 16 January.

Woodberry Down Memories Group (1989) *Woodberry Down Memories: the History of an LCC Housing Estate.* London: ILEA Education Resource Unit for Older People.

Wright, Anthony, Stewart, John & Deakin, Nicholas (1984) Socialism and Decentralisation. Fabian Tract 496.

Young, Michael & Willmott, Peter (1957) *Family and Kinship in East London.* London: RKP (Revised edition Pelican Books 1962).

Young, Terence (1934) *Becontree and Dagenham: a report made for the Pilgrim Trust.* Becontree Social Survey Committee. London: Sidders.

Zweig, Ferdynand (1961) *The Worker in an Affluent Society: family life and industry.* London: Heinemann.

Zweig, Ferdynand (1976) *The New Acquisitive Society.* Chichester. Barry Rose.

Index

National Federation of Community
 Associations 137
National Housing Reform Council 69
National Institute of Houseworkers 93, 124
National Tenant Resource Centre 218
Neighbourhood Initiatives Foundation
 (NIF) 218, 222, 223
 'Planning for Real' 218, 222, 233, 236
neighbourhoods: 102, 160, 172, 177,
 190–191, 235; see also Radburn
 'classic' and 'heroic' 162, 165
 neighbourhood unit 102
 traditional working-class 159, 162–166,
 172–173
neighbours 109, 118, 132, 164, 169
Nettlefold, J.S. 69, 70
New Earswick (York) 35, 41, 57, 60
New Labour 194, 196, 198, 205
 Housing Green Paper 2000 206
 New Deal for Communities 198–199
New Lanark 33–34, 42–43
New Right 195, 207
new towns 5, 56, 67, 81, 82, 83–84, 101,
 102, 103, 195, 197, 198, 202
Newcastle upon Tyne, city of
 Byker estate 179, 180, 182, 191
 Noble Street estate 186
Newman, Oscar 189
Nottingham, city of 143
 St Anne's 163

old people 96–97, 155, 160; see also
 family: extended families, grandparents
Oldham (Lancs)
 Deneside estate 183
Osborn, Frederick 64, 81, 82
Owen, Robert 34, 42–44, 64
 Owenism 42
 Owenite communities 48
owner occupation see home ownership
Oxford, city of
 Barton estate 159–160
 Blackbird Leys ('Omega') estate 142,
 169, 170, 177, 184, 185, 189, 190
 Cutteslowe Walls 178
 St Ebbe's 159–160, 163
Oxfordshire
 Berinsfield estate 158

Parker and Unwin architectural practice
 56–57, 59–61, 65
Parker, Barry 57, 99, 103
Parker Morris Committee and Report 97,
 113, 122, 191
parlour (in houses) 10, 27, 60, 63, 90, 93,
 96, 159, 161; see also Ministry of
 Health, Women's Housing
 Subcommittee

'parlour houses' 85, 91–93
partnerships
 tenants in 215–219, 223–224 see also
 Manchester, Hulme
Peckham Experiment 137
philanthropic housing trusts 23, 29, 31, 32
poor, poverty 11–18, 28, 32, 54, 93, 117,
 120, 161, 164, 172, 180, 186, 193–194,
 195, 196, 215, 224, 226, 237, 238,
 239; see also Hill, Octavia; slums
 Poor Law and New Poor Law 12–13, 27
 Royal Commission 1909 Royal
 Commission 18
 Stockton-on-Tees estate 126
 workhouse 12–13, 26–27
Port Sunlight 35, 53, 143
'prefabs' 178
Preston (Lancs) 162
Priestley, J.B. 44, 142
Priority Estates Project (PEP) 197, 198,
 209, 216, 218, 220–221, 223
privatization of council estates en bloc
 203–206
'problem' estates 130, 182–186, 219–220;
 see also Priority Estates Project
 'difficult to let' 182
 labelling 179
 'sink' estates 173, 182
Pruitt Igoe flats, U.S.A. 186, 187
Pugin, Augustus (the Younger) 46
Purdom, C.B. 54, 64, 79, 81, 82

Queen Anne Style 58

Radburn, Radburn planning 102–103,
 138, 179, 188, 234; see also
 neighbourhoods, neighbourhood unit
rate compounding 28, 72
Reilly Green 138
rents; see also housing benefit
 arrears 114, 208
 collection 124, 177
 ontrol 72, 86, 88, 96;
 council 78, 87, 88, 90, 113, 115, 118,
 124–129, 146, 147, 149, 201, 204, 206
 housing associations 208
 Housing Finance Act 1972 152
 Letchworth Garden City 64
 pooling 83, 89
 Scotland 71
 strikes 28, 33, 71, 76, 125–126, 129,
 151–152, 154
 tenements 32
residualization of council housing 200,
 206, 215
'respectable', respectability 26–27, 43,
 115–116, 118, 149, 159, 160, 165, 169,
 170, 184, 238